UP THE STEEP AND STONY ROAD

Society of Biblical Literature

Academia Biblica

Steven L. McKenzie,
Hebrew Bible/Old Testament Editor

Sharon H. Ringe,
New Testament Editor

Number 25

UP THE STEEP AND STONY ROAD
The Book of Zechariah in
Social Location Trajectory Analysis

UP THE STEEP AND STONY ROAD
The Book of Zechariah in Social Location Trajectory Analysis

Byron G. Curtis

Society of Biblical Literature
Atlanta

UP THE STEEP AND STONY ROAD
The Book of Zechariah in
Social Location Trajectory Analysis

Copyright © 2006 by the Society of Biblical Literature

All rights reserved. No part of this work may be reproduced or transmitted in any form or by any means, electronic or mechanical, including photocopying and recording, or by means of any information storage or retrieval system, except as may be expressly permitted by the 1976 Copyright Act or in writing from the publisher. Requests for permission should be addressed in writing to the Rights and Permissions Office, Society of Biblical Literature, 825 Houston Mill Road, Atlanta, GA 30329, USA.

Library of Congress Cataloging-in-Publication Data

Curtis, Byron G.
    Up the steep and stony road : the book of Zechariah in social location trajectory analysis / by Byron G. Curtis.
        p. cm—(Society of Biblical Literature Academia Biblica ; no. 25)
    Includes bibliographical references and index.
    ISBN-13: 978-1-58983-238-1 (paper binding : alk. paper)
    ISBN-10: 1-58983-238-8 (paper binding : alk. paper)
    1. Bible. O.T. Zechariah—Criticism, interpretation, etc. 2. Bible. O. T. Zechariah—Authorship. I. Title.

BS1665.52.C87   2006b
224'.98066—dc22

2006028595

Printed in the United States of America
on acid-free paper

Dedicated to my beloved wife,
Sue Ann,
and to our amazing children,
Nathan and Naomi

מַיִם רַבִּים לֹא יוּכְלוּ לְכַבּוֹת אֶת־הָאַהֲבָה

Song of Songs 8:7

TABLE OF CONTENTS

Acknowledgements	viii
Abbreviations	ix
Charts	xii
Introduction: The Matrix and a Steep and Stony Road	1
Chapter 1: The Sociological Study of the Prophets: Prophecy, Charisma, and Social Location in the Weberian Tradition	7
Chapter 2: Social Location Trajectories of Prophets and Prophetic Movements: A Socioethnographic Model	25
Chapter 3: Five Case Studies in Social Location Trajectories of Prophets and Prophetic Movements	43
Chapter 4: Haggai and Zechariah: Two Prophets and Two Books?	81
Chapter 5: History, Literature, and Social Location: Part One: Zechariah 1-8	115
Chapter 6: History, Literature, and Social Location: Part Two, Unit One: Zechariah 9-11, the First מַשָּׂא	155
Chapter 7: History, Literature, and Social Location Part Two, Unit Two: Zechariah 12-14, the Second מַשָּׂא	207
Chapter 8: The Unity of Zechariah	231
Chapter 9: Conclusions: Up the Steep and Stony Road	277
Works Cited	281
Ancient and Medieval Sources	305
Modern Authors	314
Subject Index	320

Acknowledgments

In presenting this book, I gratefully acknowledge the kind assistance I have received from many. Only some of them can be named here.

My wife, Sue Ann, and our children, Nathan and Naomi, who sacrificed much to make it possible for me to have the time and energy to engage in this research. This book is dedicated to you. I love you all.

My father and mother, Robert E. and Jean G. Curtis, who raised me to be curious, and who gladly provided financial support over many of the long years of study to feed that curiosity.

Dr. Peter E. Enns and Professor Michael B. Kelly of Westminster Seminary, Philadelphia, who gave enthusiastic encouragement again and again.

Dr. Mark Boda of McMaster's University, for his careful and judicious review of the original dissertation manuscript upon which this book is based.

Dr. Eric M. Meyers of Duke University, under whose tutelage I first undertook to study the book of Zechariah.

Dr. Edward Tiryakian of Duke University, who introduced me to the sociological study of the African prophets reviewed in this work.

Dr. Orval Wintermute of Duke, and Dr. Lloyd Bailey, formerly of Duke, who read early drafts of the first chapters and gave critical review.

Dr. Willem A. VanGemeren, now of Trinity International University, under whose tutelage I began the study of Hebrew in 1974.

Dr. John H. White, President Emeritus of Geneva College, without whose timely help this work may not have been completed; Dr. Dean R. Smith, Chairman of the Department of Biblical Studies at Geneva College, whose support counted for so much; and Dr. David Guthrie and Dr. Kenneth Carson, for the Geneva Faculty Development grant that helped me transform a dissertation into a book.

Dr. Howard Mattsson-Boze, Dr. Don Opitz, and Dr. Jonathan Watt of Geneva College, who commented helpfully upon the sociological work.

Dr. Helen Brown of Oaktree Software, for the kind permission to use Accordance software's fonts for Hebrew (Yehudit) and Greek (Helena).

My research assistants, Heather M. Gideon, who prepared the works cited and abbreviations pages, and Thomas Parkinson, who gave substantial help with the indices.

The congregation of Peace Presbyterian Church, Cary, North Carolina, for support, spiritual nurture, prayer, and love, and for the grant that made some of the early research and writing possible; and the congregation of Chapel Presbyterian Church, Beaver, Pennsylvania, who also gave love and support.

Not all the scholars named here would concur with what I have written; my mentioning them indicates my enduring gratitude for their contributions to my life and scholarship. Any mistakes and errors of judgment that may appear in this work are, of course, entirely my own responsibility.

ABBREVIATIONS

AB	Anchor Bible
AIC	African Indigenous Church
AJSL	*American Journal of Semitic Languages and Literatures*
ANET	*Ancient Near Eastern Texts Relating to the Old Testament.* Edited by James B. Pritchard. 3d ed. Princeton, 1969
AOS	American Oriental Series
ASR	*American Sociological Review*
ATD	Das Alte Testament Deutsch
AUSS	*Andrews University Seminary Studies*
B11	The Book of the Twelve, *minus* Zechariah
B12	The Book of the Twelve
BA	*Biblical Archaeologist*
BBR	*Bulletin for Biblical Research*
BDB	Brown, Francis, S. R. Driver, and Charles Augustus Briggs. *A Hebrew and English Lexicon of the Old Testament.* Oxford, 1907
BHS	*Biblia Hebraica Stuttgartensia.* Edited by K. Elliger and W. Rudolph. Stuttgart, 1983
BM	British Museum
BZAW	Beihefte zur Zeitschrift für die alttestamentliche Wissenschaft
CAT	Commentaire de l'Ancien Testament
CBET	Contributions to Biblical Exegesis and Theology
CBQ	*Catholic Biblical Quarterly*
DB	Darius's Behistun Inscription (in Kent 1953, 116-135)
DPT	Density per thousand words (lexical density)
ET	English Translation
FOTL	The Forms of the Old Testament Literature
GBS	Guides to Biblical Scholarship
GKC	*Gesenius's Hebrew Grammar.* Edited by E. Kautzsch. Translated by A. E. Cowley. 2d ed. Oxford, 1910.
HAR	*Hebrew Annual Review*
HUCA	*Hebrew Union College Annual*
ICC	International Critical Commentary
IEJ	*Israel Exploration Journal*
ICAME	*International Computer Archive of Modern and Medieval English Journal*
IRT	Issues in Religion and Theology
JAAR	*Journal of the American Academy of Religion*
JAOS	*Journal of the American Oriental Society*

JBL	*Journal of Biblical Literature*
JETS	*Journal of the Evangelical Theological Society*
JJS	*Journal of Jewish Studies*
JNES	*Journal of Near Eastern Studies*
JSOT	*Journal for the Study of the Old Testament*
JSOTSup	Journal for the Study of the Old Testament, Supplement Series
JSSR	*Journal for the Scientific Study of Religion*
JTSA	*Journal of Theology for Southern Africa*
K	ketiv
KAT	Kommentar zum Alten Testament
KJV	The King James Version
L	The Leningrad Codex
LBH	Late Biblical Hebrew
LP	The Latter Prophets
LXX	Septuagint
MT	Masoretic Text
NAB	The New American Bible
NAC	New American Commentary
NEB	New English Bible
NICOT	New International Commentary on the Old Testament
NIV	New International Version
NJPS	*Tanakh: The Holy Scriptures: The New JPS Translation*
NRSV	New Revised Standard Version
OIP	Oriental Institute Publications
OTL	Old Testament Library
OTS	Old Testament Studies
PN	personal name
PPC	Prose Particle Count
PPD	Prose Particle Density
Ptcs.	participles
Q	qere
r.	ruled
RB	*Revue Biblique*
RelSRev	*Religious Studies Review*
RevExp	*Review and Expositor*
RSV	Revised Standard Version
SBL	Society of Biblical Literature
SBLDS	Society of Biblical Literature Dissertation Series
SBLSP	*Society of Biblical Literature Seminar Papers*
SBLWAW	Society of Biblical Literature Writings from the Ancient World
TOTC	Tyndale Old Testament Commentary

Abbreviations

VT	*Vetus Testamentum*
VTSup	Supplements to Vetus Testamentum
Vulg.	Vulgate
WBC	Word Biblical Commentary
ZAW	*Zeitschrift für die alttestamentliche Wissenschaft*
ZRGG	*Zeitschrift für Religions- und Geistesgeschichte*

QUMRAN SCROLLS
1QS	*Serek Hayyahad*, or *The Rule of the Community*

RABBINIC LITERATURE
'Avot	*Pirqe 'Avot*, or *The Sayings of the Fathers*

CLASSICAL LITERATURE
A.J.	Josephus, *Antiquitates judaicae*
Hist.	Herodotus, *Histories*

CHARTS

Chart 4.1	Date Formula in Haggai–Zechariah	93
Chart 4.2	Locations of the Date Formulae in Jeremiah	96
Chart 4.3	The Date Formula in the Babylonian Chronicle	104
Chart 4.4	Date Formulae and Events in the Babylonian Chronicle	106
Chart 4.5	The Babylonian Chronicle: Dated Events regarding Shrines	107
Chart 5.1	The Structure of Zechariah	127
Chart 5.2	Chisholm's Chiasm	150
Chart 5.3	Butterworth's Chiasm	150
Chart 6.1	The Structure of Zechariah 9–14	163
Chart 6.2	Prose Particle Density by Chapter in Zech 9–14	184
Chart 6.3	Prose Particle Density by Unit in Zech 11	185
Chart 6.4	Prose Particle Density by Unit in Zech 9	185
Chart 6.5	Prose Particle Density by Unit in Zech 2:1–17	185
Chart 6.6	Prose Particle Density by Unit in Zech 11	196
Chart 6.7	Governors of Yehud, 538 B.C.–433 B.C.	203
Chart 7.1	The Structure of Zech 12–14	208
Chart 7.2	Prose Particle Density by Unit in Zech 12–14	208
Chart 7.3	Prose Particle Density in Zech 14	222
Chart 8.1	Distribution of Participles (DPT) in the MT	237
Chart 8.2	Distribution of Participles (DPT) in the Latter Prophets	238
Chart 8.3		

Charts

Distribution of Participles (DPT) in the Book of the Twelve	238
Chart 8.4 Summary of Lexical Densities	248
Chart 8.5 Summary of Unusual Terms in Zechariah Compared to MT, Latter Prophets, and the Twelve	249

INTRODUCTION:
THE MATRIX AND A STEEP AND STONY ROAD

What was the social matrix that gave birth to the strange fourteen-chaptered form of the book of Zechariah? This is a question that has been little pursued of late. Standard multivolume commentaries such as those by David L. Petersen (1984, 1995) and Carol L. Meyers and Eric M. Meyers (1987, 1993), despite much excellent analysis of the text, ignore the question. Michael H. Floyd notes, "It is odd that no recent commentaries have attempted to grasp either the ideational concept or the sociohistorical context forming the matrix of the book [of Zechariah] as a whole" (1999, 262). This dissertation is an attempt to answer that question by making it possible to ask once again whether the book of Zechariah may, after all, have but one principal author, the eponymous prophet whose name is borne by all fourteen chapters of this strange book. Minimally, I shall argue that a single tradent group in a single generation of time is responsible for all fourteen chapters. Maximally, I shall attempt to establish grounds that make the unitary authorship of the book once again a tenable hypothesis. I shall not attempt so much to disprove multiple authorship as to make single authorship a plausible, perhaps probable, conclusion.

The ideas that led to this dissertation originated in a gut-level reaction to a statement in Paul D. Hanson's *Dawn of Apocalyptic* about "the ignominious path upon which the prophetic office was sent by Haggai and Zechariah" (1979, 247). According to Hanson, Haggai and Zechariah "placed prophecy in the uncritical service of a specific political system" and gave up "the revolutionary element which was always an essential ingredient in genuine prophecy" (1979, 247). I felt that this approach erred. Instead of an "ignominious path," I saw a steep and stony, yet serviceable road, strategically important for the social consolidation and survival of a particular people, and with them, their faith.

Severing Proto-Zechariah from Deutero-Zechariah makes Hanson's political-crony reading more sustainable. But a unified Zech 1–14 can hardly be attributed to a pack of yes-men, and Zech 1–8 alone contains more social criticism than Hanson recognized. These postexilic texts were not produced by cronies sold out to cutthroat politicos. This stony but serviceable road was capable of supporting social criticism—even scathing social criticism. This dissertation explores that steep and stony road. It attempts to portray the social matrix of the book of Zechariah as a whole.

Hanson's negative assessment of late prophecy is the intellectual grandchild of Julius Wellhausen. Wellhausen wrote: "Prophecy dies when its precepts attained to the force of laws; the prophetic ideas lost their purity when they became practical" (1983 [1883], 488); "That externalisation towards which the prophetical movement, in order to become practical, had already been tending in Deuteronomy finally achieved its acme in the legislation of Ezra; a new artificial Israel was the result; but, after all, the old would have pleased an Amos better" (497). For Wellhausen, Jeremiah was "the last of the prophets; those who came after him were prophets only in name" (404). Thus the activity of exilic and restoration prophecy is relegated to service of that "immense retrogression" (422), the emerging theocratic state. Yet even for Wellhausen this "retrogression" is not entirely without praise, though the praise is faint indeed:

> At the same time it must be remembered that the kernel needed a shell. It was a necessity that Judaism should incrust itself in this manner; without those hard and ossified forms the preservation of its essential elements would have proved impossible.... [They] thereby preserved for themselves, and at the same time for the whole world, an eternal good. (497–98)

In my estimation, Wellhausen's assessment, and with it, Hanson's, is unnecessarily pejorative. Can a positive alternative be erected? The challenge proved inviting.

A second influence came by way of Rex Mason's interaction with Gerhard von Rad. Von Rad proposed that it was Levitical preaching that formed the milieu of the Chronicler's "sermons" (1966 [1934], 267–80). Mason counterproposed, "It could be argued that in the work of the Chronicler the 'sermons' belong, if anything, more to the prophetic tradition" (1985, 226). He then proceeded to show how certain elements in Zech 1–8 matched the characteristics of the Chronicler's sermons described by von Rad. If, as Mason suggested, the oracles of Zech 1–8 represented temple preaching, what of the larger unit, Zech 1–14? And what of the still larger literary unit comprised of Haggai–Zech 1–8, Zech 9–14, and Malachi? What justifies its present interconnectedness as a literary unit concluding the Book of the Twelve Prophets? Could such connectedness serve as evidence of a continuity of tradition and approach that marks the work of a tradent group? The hypothesis of a single prophetic tradent group arose in my mind as suitable for extended testing and analysis: Is a single such group responsible for the temple preaching and other material that concludes the Book of the Twelve, the present books of Haggai, Zechariah, and Malachi? Confines of space restrict the present study to Zech 1–14, but future work could press the model to encompass the whole concluding trilogy.

A third impetus came from the reassessment of Max Weber (1864–1920), a founding father of modern sociology, and his work on prophecy. Much sociological discussion of prophecy represents a stereotyped approach, equating prophets with charismatic authority, and seeing their principal social role as undermining political authority, and leading counter-cultural movements legitimated by peripheral groups disenchanted with established institutions. This analysis also depended much on Wellhausen, whose perspective on Israel's prophets Weber largely assumed uncritically into his own (so Zeitlin 1984, *passim*). This approach is surely present in Weber's sociology, but it is not the only paradigm implicit in Weber's work. Theodore E. Long's reassessment of Weber on prophecy (1986, 1988) builds on approaches by Dorothy Emmet (1956), Edward Shils (1961, 1965), and S. N. Eisenstadt (1968; cf. Weber 1968), among others, who sought to refine the Weberian categories of charisma and institution to accommodate empirical perceptions of charismatic and prophetic activity *within* central institutions, within the routine aspects of the social order. Robert R. Wilson's important *Prophecy and Society in Ancient Israel* (1980) worked along similar lines, presenting some prophets as central authority figures, and others as peripheral. Long's neo-Weberian revisionism readily suggested itself as an aid in constructing an alternative re-reading of these postexilic prophets as bearers of charisma in multiple social locations, going beyond Wilson's suggestive treatment. To my knowledge, Long's admirable work has not been utilized by scholars of Israelite and Judean prophecy until now.[1]

A fourth impetus came by way of Michael H. Floyd's 1999 survey of Zechariah research. Why is it, he asked, that no recent commentators have attempted to reconstruct the sociohistorical matrix of the book or its ideational unity (262)? Petersen (1995) and Meyers and Meyers (1993) readily assume multiple authorship and then move on. Floyd contributes his own answer to the matrix question in his 2000 FOTL volume on the Minor Prophets: a mantic scribal group devoted to prophetic texts two centuries removed from the historical Zechariah (456). Floyd's answer is possible, but I think there is a more plausible hypothesis: a prophetic tradent group in the early Persian period, with perhaps a single principal author.

Haggai and Zech 1–8 share a social location and historical context at the very center of Jerusalemite institutions in the early years of Darius the Great, 522–486 B.C. It was their shared concern for temple restoration that provided the social catalyst for the achievement of the rebuilding project, a program embraced—according to the biblical texts—by both Joshua the high priest and Zerubbabel the governor, as well as by the general populace. As Meyers and Meyers have argued, this prophetic material was very probably redacted together

---

[1] Theodore E. Long's work receives favorable use elsewhere in Frans H. Kamsteeg's 1998 study of *Prophetic Pentecostalism in Chile: A Case Study on Religion and Public Policy*, providing his foundational definition for "prophetic" (10, 16).

into a composite unity by 515 B.C. with a view toward temple completion. However, this centralized social context is not present in Zech 9–14. The social location indicated for the prophet figure(s) in chs. 9–14 is the social periphery, with evidence of heavy marginalization especially concentrated in the shepherd passages of 10:1–3, 11:4–17, and 13:7–9. How did material from such differing social locations, and exhibiting such divergent social roles for the prophetic figure(s) involved, come to be gathered together into its present interconnected fourteen-chaptered form?

Differences in social location and role are usually considered as powerful evidence against literary unity. However, my research in the relevant sociological, anthropological, and ethnographic literature leads me to conclude that a single prophetic claimant and a single prophetic movement may indeed occupy a wide variety of social locations in the course of its activity in relatively brief spans of time. This thesis is demonstrable from studies of prophet-led religious movements, especially the prophetic religions of twentieth-century Africa. African prophetic religions arguably provide the closest contemporary base for ethnographic comparison, for the construction of typologies, and for sociological models applicable to the study of ancient Israelite and Judean prophecy.

The demonstrably divergent social locations of the prophetic figure(s?) and tradent group(s?) responsible for the prophetic literature now present in Zech 1–8 and Zech 9–14 thus constitute no definitive argument against reading this prophetic material as the remains of a single generation of prophet/tradent activity. Since such differences in social location are usually considered (if they are considered at all) as strong evidence against such socioliterary unity, my research represents a significant step in a new direction. Something must explain the present redactional unity of this material in the Book of the Twelve. My hypothesis is that a single prophet or prophetic tradent group in a social location trajectory from center to periphery allows us to account for the present shape of the book and its redactional unity under one prophetic name.

The investigation began as a sociological and redactional analysis of Haggai/Zechariah/Malachi in the Book of the Twelve, but soon shifted: the matter under investigation was no longer the redactional connections of the smaller literary units; it was the social location trajectory of a prophetic movement, a movement now represented in the canon by these three concluding prophetic books. The research then sharpened its focus to the question of the social matrix of the book of Zechariah as a whole.

My procedure in the present work is to examine sociological theory on the social location of prophecy, then to explore the social typology of religious movements, especially prophet-led religions. Next, I develop several case studies of prophets and prophet-led movements, mainly from twentieth-century Africa, which demonstrate that their social locations can change in relatively brief spans of time. I call these changes *social location trajectories*, a conceptual tool developed for the first time in this work. I then apply *social location trajectory analysis* to the exegesis of the book of Zechariah, unit by unit. Finally, using the results of the social location analysis of the book of Zechariah, I reconsider the question of the book's redactional and authorial unity.

This investigation raises larger questions regarding the Book of the Twelve and the Second Temple period. What social matrix accounts for the present concluding trilogy of the Book of the Twelve, what Ronald W. Pierce called "the Haggai/Zechariah/Malachi corpus" (1984a, 1984b)? What were the social matrix and redactional processes that led to the completion of the Twelve on one scroll? The research also serves to broaden biblical scholarship's methodological repertoire in its approach to the issues of prophetic roles, social location, social history, and redaction history. Prophets and their tradent groups may follow many different roads; this dissertation seeks to reconstruct that steep and stony but serviceable road followed by one such prophet/tradent group in early Persian period Yehud.

1

THE SOCIOLOGICAL STUDY OF THE PROPHETS: PROPHECY, CHARISMA, AND SOCIAL LOCATION IN THE WEBERIAN TRADITION

MAX WEBER AND CHARISMATIC AUTHORITY

Social scientists rightly tell us that religion is an expression of culture, a socially organized system of beliefs and practices that seeks to make sense out of life (Segal 2003, 19). These socially constructed systems of meaning are ways in which humans respond to the sacred (Durkheim 1947) or the divine (Livingstone 1993, 11).[1] Religions are systems of transcendent symbolic order. Prophetic religions—the general area of study in this work—can be defined as religions founded or led by persons who perceive themselves, or are perceived by others, to be responding to a divine call or mandate (Ray 2000, 81). They mediate the divine by speaking a divinely given message (Bowen 2005, 216). As a cultural system, a prophetic religion needs to be analyzed as part of a cultural whole (Lambek 2002, 2–3). This study accordingly attempts to see the prophetic book of Zechariah as an expression of a sociocultural system in Persian period Yehud.

Serious sociological investigation of prophetic religious movements began with Max Weber (1864–1920). Weber's most important contributions to the subject can be found in *Das Antike Judentum* (1921), translated as *Ancient Judaism* (1952), and in his posthumous *Wirtschaft und Gesellschaft* (1921), translated as *Economy and Society: An Outline of Interpretive Sociology* (1978). David L. Petersen noted "minor points of disagreement" on this subject between the two works, stemming in part from the different purposes and perspectives of each (1979, 143–44 n. 9).[2] A review of Weberian sociology is in order here to set the stage for the present investigation.[3] Following this review I will discuss

---

[1] The problem of the definition of religion is eruditely addressed by anthropologist James M. Donovan, who explores several proposed definitions (2003).
[2] The major section of *Wirtschaft und Gesellschaft* on religion (1978, 399–634) was first published in English under the title *The Sociology of Religion* (1963). The chapter on "The Prophet" from the sociology of religion section is reprinted in Petersen (1987, 99–111).
[3] For critical discussions of Weber and charisma or Weber and prophecy see Philip Abrams (1982); Peter L. Berger on the social location of Israelite prophecy (1963);

some important revisions that have been proposed to Weber's system, which have significant implications for the study of prophetic movements, including those of ancient Israel and Judah. The chapter concludes with an inclusive model of prophetic social roles and social location analysis that will serve as an analytic tool for the rest of the dissertation.

Weberian sociology's so-called "three types of authority" are actually three ways in which domination seeks to legitimate itself in society (1978, 212–16; cf. Lang 1983, 65–67, and Petersen 1981, 12–13). According to Weber these three ways, which he called "pure types," never appear in their pure forms in any historical cases. Social reality is, of course, elusively more complex than our theoretical models.

The three pure types have to do with authority, which for Weber means the accepted legitimacy of social domination, or "the probability that certain specific commands (or all commands) will be obeyed by a given group of persons" (1978, 212). The authority structure seeks "to establish and to cultivate the belief in its legitimacy" (213). Every form of domination that depends upon such claims of legitimacy implies a need for some degree of voluntary compliance; but the types of legitimacy claimed vary fundamentally, with fundamentally different consequences.

Weber's three pure types of authority are: (1) *legal authority*, (2) *traditional authority*, and (3) the one that interests us here, *charismatic authority*: a claim to legitimacy "resting on devotion to the exceptional sanctity, heroism or exemplary character of an individual person, and of the normative patterns or order revealed or ordained by him" (215). Charisma remains today one of the most important Weberian concepts in the anthropology of religion (so Keyes 2002, 248).

Each of the three pure types displays its own tendencies in regard to the means in which it implements domination. Legal authority with its rational basis implements its domination through bureaucracies—professional classes qualified by technical expertise and arranged in a hierarchy of official positions (Weber 1978, 217–26). Traditional authority with its basis in ancient custom implements its domination through gerontocracies, kinship structures, or fealty relationships (226–41). Charismatic authority with its apparent basis in exceptional personality implements its domination through the acceptance and

---

Joseph Blenkinsopp (1995, 115–18, 145–46; 1996, 34–35); Charles E. Carter and Carol L. Meyers (1996, *passim*); S. N. Eisenstadt (1968, ix–lvi); Dorothy Emmet (1956); H. H. Gerth and C. Wright Mills (1946, 1–74); Charles F. Keyes (2002); Bernhard Lang (1983; 1984, 156–65); Rodney R. Hutton (1994, 104–7); Theodore E. Long (1986; 1988); Patrick D. Miller (2000, 177); A. D. H. Mayes (1989); Talcott Parsons (1947, 3–86; 1965, 171–75); David L. Petersen (1979; 1981; 1987, 1–21); and F. Raphaël (1971, 297–336, especially 309–18).

validation of charismatic claims by followers or disciples. This voluntarism sets the latter apart from the first two: "What alone is important is how the individual is actually regarded by those subject to charismatic authority" (242; cf. 241–54). Hence, Bryan R. Wilson speaks of "charismatic demand," a state in which public conditions are conducive to bestowing such recognition (1975a, xiv).

The prophet is Weber's ideal exemplar of charismatic authority. His study of Israelite prophecy in particular held special meaning to him and contributed to his formulation of charismatic authority in *Wirtschaft und Gesellschaft* (Gerth and Mills 1946, 27). Accordingly, his definition of "prophet" centers on the charismatic promulgation of a divine mandate: a prophet is "a purely individual bearer of charisma, who by virtue of his mission proclaims a religious doctrine or divine commandment" (Weber 1978, 439).

These three pure types of legitimation weigh heavily in Weber's philosophy of history and social change. Weber's social change is caused by the dynamic between bureaucratic or traditional institutions and charismatic movements. Traditional authority, rationalization, and bureaucratization are social forces that act for continuity. But these processes are not constant; there is a punctuated equilibrium at work.[4] Charisma, the principal force for discontinuity, is in Weber's words "a certain quality of an individual personality by virtue of which he is set apart from ordinary men and treated as endowed with supernatural, superhuman, or at least specifically exceptional qualities" (1111; cf. Gerth and Mills, 1946, 51–52; Keyes 2002, 235–36, 247). Where the routine and the rational disintegrate in the face of growing social tension, charismatic authority may arise with new and revolutionary demands.

Weber's views have probably contributed to the perpetuation of romantic ideals in historiography, where "the monumentalized individual becomes the sovereign of history" (Gerth and Mills 1946, 53).[5] Put more objectively, charisma and bureaucracy serve as mutually balancing concepts. Put in caricature, the routine aspects of history are overseen by faceless bureaucrats or tradition-bound patriarchs; the dynamic episodes (which by their very nature bear the most interest), by exceptionally endowed charismatic leaders: the prophets, miracle-workers, robber barons, and military heroes of the world (1946, 52).

---

[4] I have borrowed the term "punctuated equilibrium" from the Harvard paleobiologist Stephen Jay Gould (1982). Despite the term's biological coinage, it well describes Weber's dynamic between social stability and social change (1978, 987).
[5] For a dissenting view see Bendix (1960, 327–29 and 329 n. 30).

THE ROUTINIZATION OF CHARISMA

For Weber the three types of legitimation never appear in their pure forms in real societies. This idea leads Weber to the next step, the routinization of charisma. In this regard there are three important points:

1) [charisma] is a source of legitimate authority;
2) it is a revolutionary force, tending to upset the stability of institutionaized orders;
3) in the nature of the case it cannot itself become the basis of a stabilized order without undergoing profound structural changes. As a result of these changes it tends to become transformed into either the rational-legal or the traditional type. (Parsons 1947, 66; Weber 1978, 246–54; Keyes 2002, 249)

Talcott Parsons elaborates:

> The initial source of [charisma's] revolutionary character lies in setting up the authority of an individual against the established order, the office or traditionalized status of those originally in authority. But if the "movement" secures sufficient recognition to have the prospect of permanent organization the successors of the original leader cannot in the nature of the case base their claim to legitimacy on the same grounds. Hence the problem of succession, both of who shall succeed and of the pattern of determination of the legitimacy of his status, is crucial to all charismatic movements. (1947, 66)

Hence, Weber introduced the idea that charisma may become routinized. Contact charisma is charisma routinized through ritual transmission from one charisma bearer to another, which may become *Amtcharisma*, the charisma of office; *Gentilcharisma*, charisma of kinship, may become, more specifically, *Erbcharisma*, hereditary charisma; or there may be "succession by an unbound process of individual succession" (Parsons 1947, 66; Weber 1978, 246–49; Eisenstadt 1968, xxi). Such steps are ordinarily necessary if the charismatic movement is to maintain its authority.

A case in point is the life-and-death struggle for leadership succession in early Islam between 'Ali, who as both Muhammad's cousin and his son-in-law had family claims to the succession, and supporters of Mu'awiya, the Umayyad governor of Syria, who had strong ties to the earliest caliphate. At the end of his caliphate, Mu'awiya successfully introduced hereditary succession on behalf of his son (Holt, Lambton, and Lewis 1970, 54, 57–72). 'Ali's party is represented today by the Shi'ites, who still claim loyalty to him; Mu'awiya's party became the Sunnis.

Charismatic routinization well describes this transformative phase in the early Islamic community. The title Caliph—from the Arabic *khalifa*, "successor"—bear this out. *Khalifa* denotes an office, not of prophet, but of guardianship of the prophet's teachings and of the politico-military administration of the Islamic community (Denny 1987, 130). In Islam, Muhammad was the last of the prophets, but not the last of the charismatically endowed leaders.

Extraordinary states of religious dynamism or social disruption cool off and are thus replaced by incipient institutions. Hence, Weber's emphasis upon the charismatic individual as a social force does not minimize the social power of institutions. Rather, "by tracing out the routinization of charisma, [he] is able to assign a heavy causal weight to institutional routines" (Gerth and Mills 1947, 54). Charismatic movements may be thus transformed into either of the other two types of authority.

Such routinization does not necessarily remove the charismatic element. Rather, Weber held that charisma may become dissociated from the individual and embodied in institutions. Successors then exercise their charismatic authority "at second remove as it were, by virtue of an institutionally legitimized status or office" (Parsons 1947, 67).

At this point in the theory, problems appear. Weber wrote,

> Charismatic authority is sharply opposed to rational, and particularly bureaucratic, authority, and to traditional authority, whether in its patriarchal, patrimonial, or estate variants, all of which are everyday forms of domination.... The charismatic type is the direct antithesis of this.... Within the sphere of its claims, charismatic authority repudiates the past, and is in this sense a specifically revolutionary force. (1978, 244)

This antithesis of charisma against all other forms of legitimation leads to a fundamental tension in Weber's sociology. Weber's charismatic authority stands opposed to both the authority of tradition and the authority of bureaucracies. Yet charismatic authority may also be transformed in traditional or bureaucratic directions without losing the charismatic element. Moreover, charismatic authority exists at a basic level in every system of action (Parsons 1947, 75–76). This tension raises some questions: can charismatic authority and other authority types be more closely interrelated than Weber thought? Can charismatic movements operate as traditional or bureaucratic authority structures? Can charismatic movements arise within such routine structures and remain within them? Can charismatic movements indeed nurture such routine structures?

WILSON, PETERSEN, AND VON RAD

It was difficulties such as these that led Robert R. Wilson in his 1980 *Prophecy and Society in Ancient Israel* to refrain from using the category of charisma. He wrote,

> Our reluctance to use the concept of charisma does not necessarily stem from doubts about its potential usefulness but rather is due to the recognition that proper use of the concept would require more discussion of psychological and sociological theory than is possible in this brief treatment. (57)

Petersen went much further, at least in regard to Israelite prophecy: "Charisma, if Weber's seminal formulations are to remain our guide, represents a kind of authority which simply is not present among Israel's prophets" (1981, 9). Petersen's denial stems from his understanding of Weber's prophets as charismatic *authority bearers* who exercise newly created leadership over a particular group. Such leadership, for Petersen, is at least implicitly anti-establishment and revolutionary. Petersen questioned whether the prophets should be viewed as leaders at all (1981, 10–11).

It seems to me that Petersen's pessimism about the concept is unjustified. Later writers such as Rodney Hutton (1994), Joseph Blenkinsopp (1995, 1996), and Patrick D. Miller (2000) continued to treat charisma as a useful concept in understanding Israelite and Judean prophecy. An important element is the observation—present in Weber's idea of routinization—that charisma transforms itself toward the social center. This movement may not be "the most common emphasis in Weber's … work" (so Eisenstadt 1968, xxix), yet it is nonetheless present. The question then is: can charisma be defined in such a way as to account both for its distinctiveness from the routine and for its interrelationship with the routine? Edward Shils attempted to bridge the gap between the two by redefining it in this way:

> The charismatic quality of an individual as perceived by others, or himself, lies in what is thought to be his connection with … some very central feature of man's existence and the cosmos in which he lives. The centrality, coupled with intensity, makes it extraordinary…. [Charismatic qualities] may also become resident, in varying degrees of intensity, in institutions—in the qualities, norms, and beliefs to which members are expected to adhere or are expected to possess—and in an attenuated form, in categories or strata of the members of a society. (1965, 201–2; cf. 1961)

Eisenstadt commended Shils's proposal: "Here the gap between the charismatic as an extraordinary event or quality and as a constituent element of any orderly social life is at least partially bridged" (1968, xxvi). We may even say that every society seeks its own legitimation by asserting values and symbols it holds to be central; hence in Shils and Eisenstadt's estimation every society has a charismatic core.

If charisma can function at the social center, validating or guiding the direction of a particular society alongside other authority-types, then one of Petersen's reasons for denying Weberian charisma to Israel's prophets is removed. Thus in *Ancient Judaism* Weber argued that in Israel the charisma of prophecy could be validated by (among others criteria) adherence to the Torah, Israel's expression of traditional authority par excellence (1952, 395). For Weber "the Torah is always the completely self-evident presupposition of all prophecy" (295). Prophets who were thus validated were bound to continue to recognize such traditional authority, and to operate in some manner alongside it, lest they promote their own rejection.[6] Yet this mode of validation did not prevent Weber from saying in the same context that "the scripturally learned rabbis naturally lived in a state of tension" with prophecy (395). Elsewhere in the same work Weber spoke of both free prophets and court prophets as exercising charisma (105–06). While the former could engage in risky and radical polemics against the royal court, the later typically functioned in a manner that validated the king's charisma as Yahweh's anointed (102–04). Thus, not all prophets were prophets of doom for Weber. For example, he viewed the Israelite אִישׁ הָאֱלֹהִים ("man of God") as "one who communicated the will of the god of the covenant to the holders of political power," at first mainly positively, in answer to inquiries by the authority, but later in unsolicited and often negative ways, which could lead to rejection (108). Hence, we see in Weber a variety in the social functions and social locations of prophetic charisma, from center to periphery.

This variety does not apply solely to Weber's views on prophetic charisma. It is part of his general approach to the issue of charisma in society. One might imagine that Weber would describe Israel's hereditary leaders as bearers of traditional, patriarchal authority. Such is undoubtedly true. However, regarding early Israel's social organization, Weber described the נָשִׂיא ("chief, prince, minor king") as "a hereditary *charismatic* city prince" and noted that "a permanent charismatic preference seems to have been accorded to one or several sibs constituting the magistracy." This interlacing of charismatic authority and traditional authority is further seen in Weber's description of the חֹרִים ("nobility"), a hereditary traditional authority in Israel, as holding a "charismatic position ... [dependent] ... on its military strength, and ... its wealth" (16–17). Weber's charisma is thus seen as present within established traditional authority struc-

---

[6] This is precisely the strategy of charismatic validation which the Pharisees are presented as employing against Jesus in John 9:16—οὐκ ἔστιν οὗτος παρὰ θεοῦ ὁ ἄνθρωπος, ὅτι τὸ σάββατον οὐ τηρεῖ, "This man is not from God, for he does not keep the Sabbath."

tures. Anthropologist Charles F. Keyes points out that sometimes charismatic outbreaks "have contributed to the establishment of a new, perhaps even more rationalized order" (2002, 249).

As for Petersen's doubt that Israel's prophets were leaders of groups (1981, 10), I think that unless one views the words and actions of prophets as requiring no social validation whatsoever, and hence, requiring no audience whatsoever, then some concept of leadership seems necessary. The barest necessity here, it seems, is the leadership implicit in the concept of social validation itself. Prophets need not be leaders of mass movements, but some people, however few in number, must receive the prophetic claim as valid. The production and survival of Israel's prophetic literature seems evidence enough that sufficient social validation took place regarding the prophets of the Hebrew Bible, or we would not know about them at all.

A similar exposition of the interlacing of charisma with other types of authority, based upon his reading of Weber, was carried out by Gerhard von Rad in a chapter entitled "Sacred Office and Charisma in Ancient Israel," in volume 1 of his *Old Testament Theology* (1962, 93–102). There von Rad began with the proposition that both office and charisma "were but the prolongation of the arm of Jahweh himself" who was "present in person" within both, and "for whom it was an easy matter to break with even the most legitimate institution or the best-attested *charisma*" (93). Sacral office and prophetic charisma for von Rad related sometimes by way of cooperation, sometimes by opposition, and sometimes by compromise.

Von Rad's analysis traces out diachronically, in effect, a social location analysis of charisma in Israel. He wrote, "as a general principle, the prophets never disputed the legitimacy and necessity of, for example, the kingdom, or the priests, or the judicial office of the elders. Indeed they took these ... as organs of the will of Jahweh" (99). Kings themselves were legitimated as Yahweh's anointed ones by the "royal charisma," however curtailed this may have become in the official functioning of the court (96; cf. 323).[7] In ninth-century Israel, von Rad discerned the "still comparatively harmonious cooperation between prophecy and military leadership," such that a prophet "gave the order to attack" and even "determined the part of the army which was to advance" (1 Kgs 20:13–22). However, as "the unhappy result of an emergency" in the eighth and seventh centuries there came about an "antagonistic isolation vis-à-vis all state and sacral offices alike" in which "prophecy regarded itself, by virtue of its free charismatic commission, as the one and only authority mediating between Jahweh and Israel" (98–99). Later the Deuteronomic tradition, with its assertion that more prophets

---

[7] See also H.-J. Kraus's exposition of charismatic kingship (1986, 119–23). For an exposition of the bureaucratic Solomon and the Judean dynasty as bearers of charismatic kingship, see Gösta W. Ahlström (1968); cf. Thomas W. Overholt (1984).

"like Moses" would arise, sought to place Israel "explicitly under charismatic leadership," while later still the Priestly Document left "absolutely no place" for the charismatic element. In the postexilic era, charisma reasserted itself through the temple-based activities of worship and instruction carried out by Levites and in the teaching of the sages (101–02). Von Rad's chapter concludes with the unequivocal assertion that charisma "was an absolutely constitutive factor in Jahwism," present in many forms in Israel, including the oracles of holy war, the words of the prophets, the songs of the Levites, and the counsel of the sages (102).

Von Rad's analysis of sacral office and charisma, so dependent upon Weber for its formulations, still holds up rather well, and shows von Rad's successful and multivalent use of Weber's category of charisma. In this regard Thomas W. Overholt writes:

> In my opinion Weber's ideal type "charisma" has been a productive concept in critical biblical studies, one which has by no means outlived its usefulness.... [I]n the future the insights it suggests will have less to do with the personal qualities of the charismatic individual than with the nature of the relationship between such individuals and various groups within their societies at large. (1984, 299)

THEODORE E. LONG:
REDEFINING THE SOCIAL LOCATIONS OF PROPHETIC CHARISMA

Overholt's 1984 perceptions about future research showed themselves to be well founded. In a pair of articles entitled "Prophecy, Charisma, and Politics: Reinterpreting the Weberian Thesis" (1986) and "A Theory of Prophetic Religion and Politics" (1988), Theodore E. Long attempted to renovate the Weberian charisma thesis by redefining the social location wherein charisma operates. In this regard his study is similar to earlier ones by Dorothy Emmet (1956), Edward Shils (1961, 1965), S. N. Eisenstadt (1968), and more implicitly, Gerhard von Rad. However, Long pursued the question more systematically. We may indeed ask if his work constitutes the kind of analysis Wilson sensed was needed.

Long asked three questions to lead us into his redefinition of charisma's social location:

1) What is the sociological character of prophecy, especially in relation to charisma?
2) What is the social location of prophecy?
3) What is the social and political relevance of prophecy? (1986, 4)

The key problem Long sought to address is that modern sociological scholarship seemed to have settled on one rigid interpretation of Weber in answer to these questions, whereas—as we have already seen—alternative readings are possible. The rigid and orthodox Weberian approach sees prophecy as "a special form of leadership which gains significance as an agent of social change" (4). Its answers to the above three questions run as follows:

1) Prophecy is the *prototype of charismatic authority* and leadership.
2) Prophecy arises *outside the routine institutional order* as a political response of the alienated to societal crisis.
3) Prophecy is a *revolutionary force* which challenges existing authority to institute major socio-political changes. (4, emphases original)

Long thought that these answers were not without merit, but were misleading and incomplete. His revised analysis is founded on reconsideration of the link between prophecy and charisma "which conventional wisdom has overextended toward the equation of prophecy with charismatic authority" (4).

For instance, Long found it mistaken to make revolutionary social force a part of the definition of prophecy. Even Weber's own work on Israel's prophets "exposes the empirical flaw" here. Since for both Weber and Long "no one recognized their charisma as a valid claim on social authority" (6), Israel's prophets could hardly constitute such a revolutionary force. The prophets were not necessarily agents of social change, and Weber's own studies "do not justify the 'effectual' definition of the prophet as charismatic authority or agent of change" (Petersen 1979, 136).

Long then introduced a distinction between "personal charisma" and "charismatic authority," between the "quality of charisma and the social role proffered in recognition of it" (1986, 6). He found this distinction inherent in Weber, for the concept of routinization recognizes the manner in which charisma can be detached from the individual bearer and woven into the fabric of routine authority structures (Weber 1978, 1121). For Long, this "constitutes *de facto* recognition of that distinction" (1986, 7). A social group may recognize charismatic giftedness, yet not confer a leadership role upon the charismatic individual; prophets are not necessarily leaders. If personal charisma may be detached from any necessary role of leadership, a leadership that in the Weberian analysis arises outside of routine authority structures, then prophecy need not make revolutionary claims to authority and revolutionary demands for social change. Rather, a wide variety of social roles for prophets and social locations for prophetic activity become available.[8]

In three propositions Long summarized the sociological implications of this reassessment of Weber. The three propositions correct and supplement the usual interpretation of Weber given in the three Weberian answers listed above:

1) *Prophecy may arise within established groups and institutions* rather than just among the alienated and marginal.
2) *Prophecy need not always await internal societal crisis* but may also arise as an expression of group solidarity.
3) *Prophecy is primarily a religious phenomenon, not a political one*, originating in and primarily directed toward the religious life of a people. (1986, 7, emphases original)

As Jeffrey Hadden and Anson Shupe put it, prophets "can arise within 'routine structures' and establishment institutions"; they "need not be 'marginal men' or without 'legitimate' credentials or resources"; "they can just as likely emerge from a bureaucracy as from a wilderness, from times of societal disorganization or crisis as much as from times of relative stability" (1986, xvii–xviii).[9] Weber recognized that "prophetic action can be institutionalized, built into the ordinary functioning of religion (and politics)" (Long 1986, 8). That capability is central to Weberian routinization. But if "prophetic charisma may also arise within the established structure of power," then "a person who holds or gains organizational power may later be recognized as a prophet by virtue of unusual acts" (8).[10] Thus there can both be a prophecy of alienation, the usual interpretation of Weber, as well as a prophecy of reform, and a prophecy of the social center.

Prophecy, then, may arise anywhere within the social fabric and not merely from the periphery; it may arise during times of relative peace and stability "in the service of social solidarity" (9), and not merely during times of crisis. While Weber's idea of the crisis-situation may often govern the conferring of leadership roles on prophets, prophecy itself does not depend upon crisis situations or the leadership thus conferred. Significantly, Weber thought that prophecy appeared in

---

[8] "If it is personal charisma alone which defines the prophet, then it becomes possible for prophecy to arise within the routine social structures of ordinary life" (Long 1986, 8).

[9] See the comparable thought in Bernhard Lang: "The prophetic charisma is to be understood as a power of renewal which breaks out in the middle of traditional structures that are transcended without being destroyed" (1983, 113).

[10] See also D. F. Barnes's historical analysis of charisma and religious leadership (1978, 1–18). Barnes attempts to demonstrate empirically that such various social origins are possible for prophets and prophetic movements.

Israel (and for that matter in the ancient Near East as well) not in response to the internal conditions of their own societies, specifically not for social reform itself, but in response to international politics, which "constituted the theater of their god's activity" (1978, 443): "Except for the world politics of the great powers which threatened their homeland and constituted the message of their most impressive oracles, the prophets could not have emerged" (1952, 268; cf. Long 1986, 9).

Another point in Long's analysis is that prophecy is not principally a political phenomenon. Rather, it "first and foremost ... is a religious phenomenon; whatever political significance it may have is secondary to and derivative from its religious mission" (1986, 10). Weber emphasized this point (1952, 275), however forgotten it may be in the current literature and popularizations of the Weberian thesis.[11] However, Long observes that the "religious message is often implicated in political issues of the day, and its very proclamation may actually become a political phenomenon" (1986, 10).

Weber's own precision may help focus the discussion more tightly here. Weber's charisma may be a revolutionary force, and even a revolutionary force in the political realm. However, politicization of prophetic claims is not inherent in Weber's exposition of charisma: "*Within the sphere of its claims*, charismatic authority repudiates the past, and is in this sense a specifically revolutionary force" (1978, 244, emphasis mine). That is, Weber's charisma is specifically revolutionary only within a certain sphere, the sphere of its claims. The claims may be vast or quite circumscribed. Weber's observation about possible limits to charisma's claims, however, opens up a wide range of social locations where charismatic claims may be exercised, and a similarly wide range to the sphere of its societal impact. Long maintains that prophecy remains a revolutionary force. "The prophet is an agent of revolutionary change" (1986, 11). However, rarely do prophetic movements achieve sudden political change:

> Prophecy is a cultural phenomenon which makes its revolutionary force felt as a diffuse resource of a community, often through religious organizational vehicles. Rarely are its consequences felt directly in social structure in the short run; instead, it works primarily to build or reconstruct cultural communities over the long run. (11)

Prophets' activities may not create social movements; when they do, such movements may not be politicized; and prophetic movements that are politicized

---

[11] But see sociologist Peter L. Berger's refreshing comment, "Weber explicitly rejects the notion that these [canonical] prophets are to be understood as spokesmen of a social protest movement of underprivileged strata. Their concern is religious, though there are ethical and social implications to this concern" (1963, 941).

may even align themselves "with the reigning powers ... to build up solidarity [rather] than to disrupt or radically transform" (14). Accordingly, *"prophecy carries a variety of possibilities"* (14, emphasis original), and movements of social solidarity, movements that build or rebuild central institutions, movements emanating from the social center, and movements that enunciate core values from the center may now be considered candidates for the social role of prophecy. Long's article concludes with a call to apply this theory of prophecy and politics to particular historical circumstances (17). Accordingly, this dissertation attempts to apply Long's ideas to prophecy in the book of Zechariah in Persian period Yehud.

Long's reassessment was anticipated in some ways by sociologist Peter L. Berger's article, "Charisma and Religious Innovation: The Social Location of Israelite Prophecy." Berger wrote, "It is no longer possible to understand the prophets as isolated individuals opposed to the established religion of the priesthood. This suggests a modification of the theory of charisma that would de-emphasize the latter's non-institutional character" (1963, 940) "Charismatic innovation need not necessarily originate in social marginality. It may also originate within the traditionally established institutions" (950). Unfortunately, Berger based his reworking of Weberian charisma on an overly positive assessment of the scholarship on cult-prophecy such as Sigmund Mowinckel's *Psalmenstudien* III (1923), A. R. Johnson's *Cultic Prophet in Ancient Israel* (1962 [1944]), A. Haldar's *Associations of Cult Prophets among the Ancient Semites* (1945), and A. Gunneweg's *Muendliche und schriftliche Tradition der vorexilischen Prophetenbuecher* (1959). He thought the impact of the Uppsala school shifted the discussion to create "a measure of consensus" which now regarded the canonical prophets *as* cultic prophets, albeit radicalized. J. Williams (1969) was severely critical of Berger. Berger was mistaken on the matter of consensus, despite his attempts to restrict the claim, but nonetheless provides a valuable reading of mid-century biblical scholarship from his perspective as a sociologist. He does follow the right empirical hunch, namely, the observation that prophets operate from a variety of social locations. A serious drawback is his move to place the prophets (yet again) in one social location, the cult in this case.

In view of this broadened range of social locations, Long offered a revised definition of prophet. Weber, it will be remembered, defined prophet as "a purely individual bearer of charisma, who by virtue of his mission proclaims a religious doctrine or divine commandment" (1978, 439). Long distinguished between the personal characteristic of charisma and the variable social roles that may accompany it. He defined prophecy as *"the charismatic proclamation/demonstration of divine claims and judgments on human life or institutions by one who feels called to that mission"* (1988, 5, emphasis original); and the principal task of the prophet "is to proclaim or demonstrate a divine message in the hope of submitting all of human life to a transcendent system of meaning" (4). Varied responses, such as recognizing charismatic authority or granting a prophet a leadership role, and varied social locations from the periphery to the social center can then be recognized as social variables accompanying the phenomenon of prophecy, not part of the phenomenon of prophecy itself.

Long's definition, in somewhat humbler form, is found largely to agree with Lester Grabbe's: "a prophet is a mediator who claims to receive messages from a divinity, by various means, and communicates these messages to recipients" (1995, 107). My preferred definition of prophet draws upon both: *a prophet is someone recognized to be charismatically empowered who speaks or otherwise demonstrates the will of deity to recipients.*

PETERSEN ON THE SOCIAL ROLES OF PROPHECY

Long's reassessment of the Weberian thesis stands as an important corrective. This dissertation makes use of the model, but complements Long's analysis of charisma with elements of role theory drawn from Petersen (1981). Role theory provides a behavioral model that frees the researcher from the impossible demand of assessing charismatic states. Those who enact prophetic roles make an implicit claim to personal charisma. Personal charisma need not constitute a claim to charismatic leadership. Personal charisma cannot be empirically assessed directly, but role enactment can. Personal charisma, then, may remain a theoretical consideration behind the enactment of prophetic roles.

Earlier I quoted Petersen's criticism of biblical scholarship's using Weber's concept of charisma. It is necessary now to return to his critique and to incorporate an important insight into the present study. Petersen wrote, "Charisma, if Weber's seminal formulations are to remain our guide, represents a kind of authority which is simply not present among Israel's prophets" (9). Petersen's interest here is to move beyond certain stereotypes that in his estimation no longer serve usefully in the study of Israel's prophets. Hence he entitled the chapter where he gives this critique, "Beyond 'Charisma' and 'Office.'"

The old dichotomy advanced by Martin Noth between charisma and office is no longer helpful (1967, 229–49). Walther Eichrodt used this dichotomy in a programmatic way in his *Theology of the Old Testament*, where under the rubric of "The Instruments of the Covenant" the "charismatic leaders," including the רֹאִים ("seers," "visionaries"), נְזִרִים ("nazirites"), שֹׁפְטִים ("judges," "deliverers"), נְבִיאִים ("prophets"), and the classical prophets, are sharply distinguished from the "official leaders"—Israel's priests and kings (1961, I:8–9; 289–456). This dichotomy, while hearkening back to Weberian terminology, lacked from its inception the more nuanced approach found in Weber's three-fold legitimation model. It failed to explain, for example, how the notion of office—which in Weberian terms is a rational-legal concept—relates to a traditional society. Weber's own use of the term *amtcharisma* (office charisma) belies any simple separation between the two categories. As we have seen, von Rad's treatment of charisma and sacral office also rejects any strict dichotomy (1962, 93–102).[12]

Petersen's role enactment model attempts to replace the bureaucratic notion of office and the notion of charismatic authority with sets of behavior patterns that generally follow various courses of societal expectation. The sets of behavioral patterns may be implicitly perceived or explicitly learned. The one who enacts the role may be validated in that role by a social group, depending upon a wide variety of social conditions. Prophets need not be leaders of groups, but they do conform to certain social expectations to be validated as prophets. Petersen's study concludes that neither office nor ecstasy[13] nor charismatic authority adequately describe Israel's prophets:

> those who rely on these categories presume one characteristic mode of prophetic behavior and thereby tend to ignore the many ways in which Israel's prophets acted as prophets.... [W]e have discovered that the prophets performed their roles in many ways ... [and] acted at several different levels of behavioral involvement. (1981, 98)

A study of the role labels given prophet figures in Israel reveals this variety. Petersen gives a cogent analysis of the prophetic role labels רֹאֶה ("seer"), אִישׁ־(הָ)אֱלֹהִים ("man of God"), נָבִיא ("prophet"), and חֹזֶה ("seer," "visionary"). According to his study, the חֹזֶה ("seer," "visionary") was an urban resident

---

[12] While acknowledging the activity of cult prophets, Eichrodt speaks of "an extremely loose connection between [these] prophets and the sanctuary" and cites A. Jepsen's observation (1934, 161) that the thirty biblical texts in which prophet and priest are closely linked all derive from Jerusalem or Judah, where "special conditions [may have] obtained, possibly connected with the Deuteronomic reform" (1961, I:315). Conditions in the Persian period also had a special character according to Eichrodt: for Haggai and Zechariah, incorporation into a guild of Temple prophets "was something to be taken for granted" (1961, I:339 n. 3).

[13] There is little clear evidence for the practice of ecstasy among Israel's classical prophets. There are however various levels of behavioral involvement, ranging from ritual acting, engrossed acting, classical hypnotic role taking, to histrionic neurosis (Petersen 1981, 20–25). On ecstatic religion in general, see Lewis (1981 [1971]). On ecstasy among Israel's prophets, see Lindblom's famous assertion of it (1962) and Heschel's well-known marginalizing of it (1962, 2:131–46). For other discussions of prophetic ecstasy, see Robert R. Wilson (1979, 321–37) and Petersen (1981, 25–30). Perhaps the most explicit biblical account of anything like prophetic ecstasy appears, oddly enough, in the wisdom book of Job, in Eliphaz's opening speech (4.12–17; cf. von Rad 1962, 101). Evidence for ecstasy is more discernible for Israel's pre-classical prophets (cf. Num 24:4; 1 Sam 10:5–13).

sacrificial-cult functionary who was available as a consultant-diviner for a fee. The אִישׁ־(הָ)אֱלֹהִים ("man of God") was an itinerant and peripheral holy man who enjoyed the support of particular urbanite groups, the בְּנֵי הַנְּבִיאִים ("sons of the prophets"). The terms נָבִיא ("prophet") and חֹזֶה ("seer," "visionary") both refer to the central morality prophet (for which see Lewis 1989), "a prophet who regularly legitimates or sanctions the central values and structures of the society and who venerates a deity of distinct moral quality, a deity who is perceived as central to the social order" (Petersen 1981, 99; cf. 2002, 5–14; see also Blenkinsopp 1995, 124–26, for a similar review of the terms).[14] The unifying point for Israel's prophets, then, was not one social role, behavior pattern or social location, for these are widely variable, but service as spokespersons for the one deity, Yahweh of Israel. But one need not discard charisma, as Petersen does, in favor of social role analysis. The categories of charisma and role enactment complement each other.

AN INCLUSIVE MODEL

Petersen's role enactment approach seeks to interweave several branches of the family tree of biblical scholarship on prophecy. Roots of this tree may be traced back at least as far as Hölscher's proposals (1914) about the urban and itinerant settings of ecstatic prophetism as well as to the moral interpretation of Ewald (1867), which Wellhausen later cultivated (1983 [1883]). This inclusiveness has a considerable advantage over the older models that failed by their inability to account for competing and complementary prophetic roles to the particular role each had isolated and identified.

The sociological model central to this dissertation is one that displays a similar diversity—prophetic activity in various or changing social roles and social locations. As we will see in chapter three, prophetic claimants and prophetic groups sometimes display dramatic shifts in social role and social location. The model is drawn from current ethnographic and historical data on prophets and prophetic movements. Thus there can be prophets of the center, prophets of reform, and prophets of the periphery, all engaged in the charismatic proclamation or demonstration of divine claims. I use this inclusive model here as an analytic tool for understanding the production of the prophetic book of Zechariah.

---

[14] I am not convinced, however, that the terms נָבִיא ("prophet") and חֹזֶה ("seer," "visionary") represent distinct geographic traditions, one northern and the latter southern, as both Petersen (1981, 50–63) and Robert R. Wilson (1980, 136–38; 254–56), following James Muilenberg (1965), think. See the strictures on a separate Ephraimite prophetic tradition given by Blenkinsopp (1996, 3–4).

It is widely recognized that Proto-Zechariah, chs. 1–8, derives from a prophetic figure who embraced and was embraced by central authorities and his audience society in early Yehud (Cook 1995, 138–44). Deutero-Zechariah, chs 9–14, derives from a prophetic figure or group who was rejected by central authorities and the populace of Yehud (162–65). Yet both literatures, Proto- and Deutero-Zechariah, are part of one book. Why?

I take this literature as representative of a single prophetic tradent group, and perhaps a single prophetic figure, Zechariah ben-Berechiah ben-Iddo. This movement displays a shift in social location which I am calling a *social location trajectory*, a trajectory similar to the trajectories that are demonstrable for other prophetic movements observed by ethnographers, cultural anthropologists, and historians. It is to the topic of social location trajectories and the typology of prophetic religious movements that we now turn. This step shall serve the forthcoming social location analysis of the book of Zechariah, and the consideration of the social matrix that gave birth to its perplexing fourteen-chaptered form.

2

SOCIAL LOCATION TRAJECTORIES OF PROPHETS AND PROPHETIC MOVEMENTS: A SOCIOETHNOGRAPHIC MODEL

OF MODELS AND METHODS

In chapter one I surveyed the literature in the sociological theory of prophecy, charisma, and social location. I drew upon insights from Max Weber (1952; 1978) and Theodore E. Long (1986; 1988) to suggest a workable basis in social theory for investigating actual prophetic figures and prophetic movements, including those of Persian period Yehud. Prophetic charisma, we concluded, need not confine itself to socially peripheral groups, but may arise anywhere within the social fabric, and prophetic claimants may appear at any point along the spectrum of social locations, from periphery to center. As Joseph Blenkinsopp observed back in 1983, "the idea of the prophet as a radical, a religious individualist pitted against the 'establishment,' a proponent of a new morality, is in need of a revision" (25). Thirteen years later Blenkinsopp was still calling the community of biblical scholars to "reconsider common assumptions about the prophet as a radical innovator preaching a radically innovative ethic" (1996, 15). It is just such a reconsideration that my research is laboring to construct.

As background for the social location trajectory analysis I employ in this work on the book of Zechariah and its social matrix, the present chapter shall consider the sociological issue of ideal types, some of the hazards and benefits of constructing such theoretical social models, some of the biblical research that employs social location analysis, and some of the implications of this research. Finally I shall explain why prophetic religions in sub-Saharan African tribal contexts provide a usable comparative base for analyzing prophetic religion in Persian period Yehud. Following this discussion, chapter three presents a series of case studies that yield empirically derived models of social location trajectories for prophets and prophetic groups. The book of Zechariah shall then be analyzed in light of these social location trajectories.

As defined in chapter one, social location trajectories are the routes through social locations followed by the bearers of tradition within a particular society. Any diachronic change in social location can be described as a social location trajectory. Such trajectories can be discerned in some prophetic texts, in other historical sources pertaining to prophetic movements, and in the field reports and studies of contemporary prophetic movements produced by sociologists, cultural anthropologists, and ethnographers.

For a discussion of types and typology in social-scientific research, Max Weber's classic approach creates abstract generalizations of social action (i.e., types or models) based on concrete historical phenomena (1978, 19–22; 57–58 n. 5 and the literature listed there). James Farganis explains, "Social theorists construct models or ideal types that explain the interrelationships of relevant key elements of the social world" (1996, 110). For a definition of models in social-scientific research in ancient Near Eastern cultures, I turn to a helpful analysis of the issue:

> In the social scientific approach to the Ancient Near East, a model is a pattern which is used to illuminate poorly understood aspects of the ancient culture. The model is formed from general laws derived from examining more accessible societies in order to determine those aspects which are inherent to a situation for a particular type of society. Sociological models tend to be generalizing in that by relying on comparison they will lessen the uniqueness of aspects in a society. (Wood 1991, 5)

Wood's point is significant for the present work. Israelite and Judean prophetism can no longer be directly observed. All that remains is indirect observation through the lens of the surviving texts, which evidence but a part of the social dynamic inherent in the original situation. We may register a modest dissent from some uses of the notion of "general laws" in social-scientific research. Nevertheless the concept itself is not to be rejected, provided one understands that such "laws" are tools of the mind to classify various types of social behavior. Human behavior is sometimes anomalous, since "people, unlike inanimate objects, do not always follow predictable patterns" (1991, 7).

Nonetheless, cultures and societies can be analyzed as dynamic systems whose inherent characteristics carry recognizable patterns (Clarke 1978, 39). Analysis of the particular social dynamics within more accessible societies can provide sufficient data to construct generalizing hypotheses. The comparative method of sociological analysis using models allows the researcher to fill in the gaps in the ancient evidence, utilizing these hypotheses, which can be tested by their interpretive success or failure, their heuristic power. Those models which provide an account of more of the textual data than their competitors will be considered successful. As Wood writes, "Any reconstruction which attempts to achieve historical knowledge is a process of grouping data in a way that best explains all the relevant data" (1991, 7). Models assist in grouping data in ways analogous to actual cases observed elsewhere.

For this reason I do not accept the usual critique of the method of modeling made, for example, by C. S. Rodd (1981). Rodd wondered whether antiquity could ever be susceptible to sociological analysis. The accidents of time have inevitably destroyed an unknown but large amount of the data relevant to any particular hypothesis. Hence, Rodd says, the process of data collection so essential to the scientific method will inevitably and hopelessly be skewed. Thomas W. Overholt replied to Rodd's criticism:

> Theories about basic social phenomena widely "tested" in more contemporary cultures would be found to have some degree of applicability to biblical times as well.... To the extent that the basic patterns can be observed for, say, charismatic leadership or prophetic intermediation in a wide variety of cultures and periods of time, it would seem reasonable to hope that such patterns might aid us in understanding aspects of life in biblical times. (1984, 292–93)

If we are to understand anything at all of the social world of biblical antiquity, something like the modeling method seems inevitable. It is better to construct such models self-consciously, aware of the danger of misplaced generalization and stereotyping, than to operate with the unexamined models of sociologically naive scholarship.

David L. Clarke lists three general types of models: iconic, analogue, and symbolic. Most modeling in the social sciences is analogical, and this is the type employed here. "Analogue models represent observed attributes by substituting other kinds of 'analogous' attributes whose consequences are congruent to those of the observed attributes." They are "the most common and most tantalizingly dangerous form of model" (1978, 31–33). In Wood's discussion (1991) the major argument is that historical reconstruction inevitably requires the use of models of some kind, either implicitly or explicitly. Despite the risk, he argues that it is better to use models explicitly, recognizing their weaknesses as well as their interpretive abilities. The chief weakness and danger is their tendency to distort data through overgeneralization. Their chief strength, conversely, is their ability (if rightly used) to correlate congruently a number of specific social situations for generalized analysis.

Even successful models do not lead to epistemological certainty. As Wood again points out,

> Despite how thorough a reconstruction may be, in each case a certain amount of data will stand as evidence against that reconstruction. Thus historical knowledge is a process of weighing evidence.... [E]very reconstruction is in some manner uncertain because it has a certain amount of evidence which weighs against it. (1991, 7)

The model derived from the typologies of our present study will be tested by its ability to account for the material now represented in the units recognized so widely as Proto-Zechariah and Deutero-Zechariah. As I shall contend in the chapters to follow, it is this model, based on these empirically derived social location and social location trajectory typologies, that helps make my overall hypothesis tenable, that in Persian period Yehud a single prophet/tradent group in a single generation of social location change was responsible for producing and preserving the prophetic material now contained in the redactionally interconnected book of Zechariah. This hypothesis can be used to produce a reasonably congruent exegesis of these texts in an alternative and holistic reading.

PROPHETS AND SOCIAL LOCATION

Robert R. Wilson in his groundbreaking *Prophecy and Society in Ancient Israel* (1980) called for a concertedly sociological scholarship on Israelite prophecy. After more than a century of critical study, Wilson rightly claimed, most of the social dimensions of prophecy remained unclear. Part of his call was for nuanced approaches in the socioliterary study of the prophets. Form critics such as Claus Westermann, Wilson wrote, had ignored the social locations of the very prophetic speech forms they were investigating (cf. Westermann 1967; Robert R. Wilson 1973). It now became evident that there was no necessary identity between the social location of the prophet and the social matrix of his language. Thus "a prophet who delivers oracles in the temple court may not employ speech forms that originated in the temple" (1980, 11). Scholars now recognized these deficiencies, Wilson reported, and were poised to address the complexity of the relationships between the biblical prophets and their societies. He called for future research to proceed along these lines. As he then noted,

> Treatments of the problem of prophecy and society must take this complexity into account. It seems increasingly likely that not all of the Israelite prophets were related to their societies in the same way. In addition, different relationships may have existed at various times in Israelite history and this historical dimension must also be considered. (1980, 13–14)

Since Wilson's 1980 work, many sociologically oriented studies in the prophets, or including the prophets, have appeared.[1] The present study also seeks

---

[1] Some of the more notable monographs among them include David L. Petersen's analysis of the prophets' social roles (1981; cf. 2002), Joseph Blenkinsopp's history of Israelite prophecy (1983; 1996), his exploration of Israelite religious and intellectual leadership (1995), Bernhard Lang's work on Israel's "prophetic minority" (1983), Norman Gottwald's *The Hebrew Bible: A Socio-Literary Introduction* (1985), Paul D. Hanson (1986), Thomas W. Overholt's cross-cultural analysis of prophecy (1986), his work on the social dynamics of the prophetic process (1989), his book on *Cultural Anthropology and the Old Testament* (1996; cf. Culley and

to respond to this scholarly agenda, with a focus on the social location trajectories of prophets and prophetic movements and Zechariah.

Despite the influence of Wilson's nuanced sociological approach, and of many who published in his wake, monochromatic and stereotyped approaches persist in the scholarly world. Theologian Rosemary Radford Ruether writes:

> Like the liberation theologian, the prophet was a figure who generally stood outside the institutional power elite of society, but within the covenant of the Biblical community. The prophet and the liberation theologian speak a judgmental word of God against the sins of the community in order to call it back to faithfulness to the radical foundations of the faith of the covenant, contextualized in the contemporary situation.... The prophetic stance presupposes a relationship between faith and society that is in tension with established religion.... Prophetic faith ... sets God in tension with the ruling class by having God speak, through the prophet, as advocate of the poor and the oppressed. (1990, 24–33)

While there is much here about individual prophets that is true, Ruether's working definition of *prophet as opposition figure* ignores the discussion carried on by Wilson and others. She categorizes prophetic movements as social protest movements, stereotypes prophecy as countercultural and oppositional, and privileges prophetic modes of religion as superior to priestly religion and to other institutionalized modes. Similarly, Donald C. Smith's *Passive Obedience and Prophetic Protest: Social Criticism in the Scottish Church 1830–1945* readily equates prophetic criticism with social criticism (1987, 5–8), and uses this equation as the starting point for its analysis of the social conscience of the Church of Scotland. More recently Frans H. Kamsteeg in his study of Chilean Pentecostal base communities seems to use "prophetic" as a synonym for social protest and resistance (1998, 87, 90–91, and 106 n. 24; for older examples, see Köbben 1960; Lanternari 1965). Resistance against tyranny is certainly in keeping with the high moral conscience of the biblical prophets. Walter Brueggemann thus

---

Overholt 1982), Daniel L. Smith's *Religion of the Landless* (1989), J. Andrew Dearman's work on Israelite religion and culture (1992), Walter Brueggemann's *Social Reading of the Old Testament* (1994), Rodney R. Hutton's work on charisma and authority in Israel (1994), Jon L. Berquist's sociohistorical approach to Persian period Yehud (1995), Stephen L Cook's book on the social setting of postexilic prophecy and apocalyptic (1995), Lester L. Grabbe's work on religious specialists in Israel (1995), David W. Baker (1999), and J. David Pleins on *Social Visions of the Hebrew Bible* (2001). Notable collections of sociologically oriented exegetical articles, many on the prophets, include those edited by A. D. H. Mayes (1989), Robert P. Gordon (1995), and Charles E. Carter and Carol L. Meyers (1996).

waxes eloquent on the work of Moses as "the paradigmatic prophet who sought to evoke in Israel an alternative consciousness" to the tyranny of the Egyptian empire (1978, 15), with its "politics of oppression and exploitation" (17). Yet there is more to the work of the prophet than this task, noble as it is. As Petersen recently wrote, "Many popular understandings of Israel's prophets have placed them in the latter [disenfranchised] setting. Rarely, however, was that the case, either in Israel or throughout the ancient Near East" (2002, 13). My explorations will distance themselves somewhat from these monochromatic approaches in favor of a nuanced, multivalent perspective.

Prophets and prophetic movements typically produce meaning-laden symbols throughout their trajectories in the various social roles and social locations available to them. Such meaning-laden symbols, produced as word or deed, will frequently evidence the particular social role and social location of the prophet/group at the time of their production. Such symbols may be preserved in oral tradition or in written form. Literary remains of prophetic movements, created over spans of time, frequently bear witness to social transformations. It may even be that the static or steady-state social location is the rarity, not the rule, for such figures and movements.

In the Hebrew Bible the career of Isaiah of Jerusalem, for example, may show a discernible trajectory in social location. As J. Kselman suggests,

> [Isaiah] may have been a central prophet, condemning Judah's enemies and reaffirming such traditional Jerusalemite views as the inviolability of the city, and urging a return to traditional values. However, when his critique of King Ahaz became too demanding, he was pushed to the periphery, surrounded only by a small support group (Isa. 8:16–18). Isaiah moved back to the center and to social maintenance functions as a result of Hezekiah's reforms. (1985, 123; cf. Carroll 1979, 140–41)

While we may question whether rejection by the monarch constituted complete marginalization for the prophet,[2] and the sufficiency of the evidence that his support group was indeed few in number, Kselman's reading is probably generally correct.

The book of Amos may also evidence the social dislocation of the eighth century prophet. Although he does not use the terminology of social location trajectories, Robert R. Wilson hypothesizes a particular social location change for Amos:

---

[2] Robert P. Carroll, citing Isa 8:11–13, surmised that the prophet's marginalization resulted from "the futile struggle to persuade Ahaz to trust Yahweh and the strong antagonism between prophet and people" (1979, 140).

Amos was a member of the Judean establishment, although probably not part of the central cult in Jerusalem.... The identity of his support group is unclear, although if he did function as a central prophet in the south, then he may have been supported by members of the Judean establishment. However, he clearly functioned as a peripheral prophet in the north, where he tried to reform the social and religious systems along Judahite lines. (1980, 270)

After public rejection and deportation from the north, Wilson suggests Amos "may have then functioned as a central prophet in Judah" (270). This social location trajectory—from the social center of one public, Judah, to the periphery of another, Israel, and back again—may do much to account for the present redactional shape of the book. As Kselman proposed,

Amos the eighth-century prophet may have been a central prophet in Judah and a peripheral prophet in Israel whose work was transmitted and preserved by other subsequent central prophets associated with the Jerusalem elite. (1985, 124)

S. N. Rosenbaum argues a contrary view of Amos's social history. He proposes that Amos was not a Judean, but an Israelite and professional civil servant whose thorough acquaintance with Samaritan social abuses led to his strident denunciations, his rejection by his northern public, and his subsequent exile to the south (1990, 67; *passim*). Rosenbaum offers, in effect, a different social location trajectory for the figure of Amos.[3] For my present purpose it is not essential to adjudicate the disagreement between Wilson and Rosenbaum. The significant point for my purpose is that both of these readings of Amos utilize social location analysis and implicitly suggest particular social location trajectories for the figure of Amos. Social location analysis and social location trajectory analysis ought to be considered significant tools for the biblical scholar.[4]

This type of analysis is not only significant for studying the prophetic figures themselves. The process of literary preservation may also leave evidence of the social locations of the later tradents themselves, as Robert Coote's (1981) study of Amos and his redactor, or Grace Emmerson's (1984) study of Hosea and his redactor argue. Coote, for example, proposes a highly specific social location

---

[3] Other Amos interpretations that attempt sociohistorical reconstruction include John H. Hayes's unitary eighth-century reading (1988) and M. E. Polley's sociopolitical reading (1989).

[4] Wilson observes that "central authority intermediaries may once have been members of peripheral social groups," but he does not develop the thought (1980, 69).

for his hypothesized Judean redactor. This stage of the book, the second of three redactional stages according to Coote,

> was composed in Jerusalem late in the seventh century, by a scribal adjunct to the ruling elite; through writing and the art of literature he expresses and preserves on behalf of the ruling elite the desire to maintain the status and power of Jerusalem as a sociopolitical center, and the motivation to put this power to use in a program of customary and juridical reform.... [T]he elite must try to appropriate the prophetic voice not to consolidate their own controlling power but to tap its liberating power. (1981, 102–03)

When the redactions can be traced diachronically—and I do not suggest that they always can—the presence of social location trajectories may be evidenced.[5] In the chapters to follow I shall propose an alternative reading of Zechariah in its origins through a particular hypothesized social location trajectory.

A Methodological Correction

Sociologists in this century have exhibited a tendency to focus their analytical powers on studies of social change and of social anomalies. This tendency is natural for empirically based endeavors which require scientific observation and control, but nonetheless results unfortunately in a lopsided body of conclusions, a bias away from the investigation of social centers, social consolidation, and the techniques of tradition maintenance in society. My investigations indicate that this tendency exists also in respect to research on prophetic religions. As we have seen, the stereotype of the marginalized social protest figure persists. However, as Theodore E. Long has intimated and as I shall demonstrate below, prophets may also function in tradition maintenance and social-consolidation roles.

In writing about the sociology of orthodoxies, Thomas C. Oden observes:

> The premise of the sociology of any orthodoxy (Islamic, Skinnerian, Marxian, psychoanalytic, Jewish, Protestant, and so on) is this: If social processes are to achieve multigenerational continuity, they require legitimization and careful tradition-maintenance. Without any authorized definition of a movement's teaching, it cannot span the generations or even assess the validity of potential misinterpretations. A religious tradition dissipates rapidly if it cannot distinguish itself in relation to its cultural alternatives. The attempt to provide clear and authoritative doctrinal

---

[5] According to S. N. Rosenbaum, *contra* Coote, Amos's book "suffered little editing at the hands of later Judean editors" (1990, 67); similarly, Marvin Sweeney's synchronic reading of Amos (2000).

definition in order to sustain the cohesive basis of the community is called orthodoxy. Although this process has been poorly understood sociologically, it exists in every human community that has intergenerational aspirations and certainly in all the great religious traditions.... [O]rthodoxy is ... a living tradition of social experience. (1990, 151-52)

In light of Oden's observations, and of Theodore E. Long's social theory of prophecy, I have worked to explore the multivalent social dynamics of prophets and prophetic movements. This is an important corrective which needs to be further exploited and tested in sociological and biblical research.[6] Sociological analysis of prophetic movements needs the ability to assess the tradition-maintenance functions of prophetic figures, as well as their functions in challenging tradition and transforming society.

As the next chapter shall demonstrate, single prophetic figures and movements may indeed occupy wide varieties of social locations and roles within the course of their trajectories. The tradition of historical-critical biblical scholarship, however, has neglected this empirically demonstrable observation. In historical criticism, differences in social location behind the literary collections that comprise certain biblical books are typically seen as evidence of multiple authorship and diverse sources. This dissertation calls this methodological assumption into question. There are several grounds for the methodological correction proposed here.

First, while the hypothesis of multiple authors or sources may satisfactorily account for differences in social location in a literary work, it is not the only explanation possible. It is all too often our ignorance about the lives of the creators of ancient literary materials that renders single explanations credible, like the multiple-author, multiple-source hypotheses. Such an approach is naively monothetic, not polythetic (David L. Clarke 1978, 35-40).[7] Even when multiple

---

[6] Other works exploring tradition maintenance in societies include J. Alan Winter's *Continuities in the Sociology of Religion: Creed, Congregation and Community* (1977), Hans Mol's *Identity and the Sacred* (1976), and George Bond, Walton Johnson, and Sheila S. Walker's *African Christianity: Patterns of Religious Continuity* (1979). Robert Bellah's *Habits of the Heart* (1985) does the same on a popular level.

[7] Monothetic and polythetic are terms used in systems theory in archaeology, which I have adapted for use in socioliterary analysis. "An aggregate of entities or systems are said to be monothetic if the possession of a unique set of attributes is both sufficient and necessary for membership of the aggregate.... An aggregate of entities or systems are said to be polythetic if each individual possesses a large but unspecified number of the attributes of the aggregate, if each attribute is possessed by large numbers of these individuals, and no single attribute is both sufficient and necessary to the aggregate membership" (Clarke 1978, 492-93). In my argument above, mono-

authors and sources can be reasonably inferred, the question of the socioliterary relationship of the authors and sources to each other still remains. Increasing subtlety in the sociology of knowledge and the socioliterary study of the Hebrew Bible brings to light alternative and competing explanations. The increased subtlety brought to biblical studies by sociological perspectives has shown that we have known much less about the origins of this literature than historical criticism has typically claimed. It also shows multivalent sociohistorical possibilities for explanation that now must be explored by the community of scholarship. This dissertation is one such socioliterary experiment.

Second, the now-passing isolation of biblical historical criticism within the academy has protected its regnant orthodoxies from scrutiny by other disciplines and perspectives. The multiple-author, multiple-source approach to social location differences is such an orthodoxy, with a pedigree tracing back to Wellhausen and de Wette.[8] The rise of interdisciplinary studies in the Hebrew Bible has challenged historical criticism's long-standing hegemony over the biblical text. Such interdisciplinary studies frequently offer holistic readings of biblical materials, and perhaps this tendency is not accidental. This holistic trend is an important corrective to the fragmented readings of the literature given by some in the tradition of historical criticism. The interdisciplinary approach attempted in this dissertation participates in this holistic trend. But rather than avoiding the question of origin, as do many holistic readers,[9] it seeks to account for the creation of this literature by proposing a single prophet or prophetic movement in social transformation. It propounds a holism of a single community of origin. Of course, such a reading, like other holistic readings, must in turn undergo criticism by the community of biblical scholars.

---

thetic descriptions bear a higher burden of proof than polythetic ones. Change in social location cannot, in itself, be viewed as sufficient evidence to support the conclusion that a textual unit has a different community of origin.

[8] The power of Julius Wellhausen's Documentary Hypothesis lies not only in the multitude of textual observations that the theory correlates, but also—and perhaps especially—in the social hegemony he attributed to the parties responsible for each successive documentary strand. J, E, D, and P represent each the successive central social institutions of their times. This powerful sociohistoric and textual synthesis rendered Wellhausen's formulation superior to the hypothesis's earlier form under de Wette. Alternative approaches today should labor equally hard to present credible sociohistoric and textual syntheses.

[9] For example, Robert Alter in his otherwise brilliant *Art of Biblical Narrative* (1981), and even more so Regina Schwartz in *The Book and the Text: The Bible and Literary Theory* (1990). Alter's *World of Biblical Literature* (1990) corrects this deficiency somewhat. In Zechariah studies, both Edgar Conrad (1999) and Mark Cameron Love (1999) avoid drawing conclusions about the social situation outside of the text.

Third, it seems to me that historical criticism has not taken with sufficient seriousness the observation that rhetoric is an agent of social transformation. The social agency of rhetoric pertains both to the liberalizers and the conservatizers of a given society, both to the rhetors of revolution and of counter-revolution. To dissuade from change *is* to change. Since Israel's prophets typically engaged in public discourse, students of prophecy ought to be aware of the possibility that the literary remains of their rhetoric show evidence of social changes induced by their rhetoric. Rhetorical visions not only reflect social realities; they create them. As rhetorical theorist Ernest Bormann put it, "words *are the social context*" (1972, 400, emphasis his). This conclusion, overstated though it is, nonetheless calls into question monochromatic assumptions about the careers of the authors and tradents of the literary material under review here, and clears the way for more polychromatic explorations. A single prophetic movement may create new social situations and may operate in multivalent ways. Some of these ways may serve the interests of tradition maintenance and social consolidation. These interests may even persist in the face of radical social rejection, perhaps awaiting future vindication. This scenario may be the case with the postexilic prophetic material that concludes the Book of the Twelve, the Haggai/Zechariah/Malachi corpus.

This correction of historical criticism, it seems to me, is not without its own methodological difficulty, however—one that may be disturbing to those, like myself, who have been trained in the tradition of historical criticism. This difficulty is the issue of falsifiability. In the scientific method, hypotheses are formulated to be tested. Such testing assumes their ability to be verified or falsified. If divergent social locations in literature can be accounted for by a variety of hypotheses, how can these competing hypotheses be tested? The social locations themselves cannot serve as criteria for falsifiability: they are the variables to be accounted for by the hypothesis. Similarly, shifts in rhetoric do not constitute evidence for falsifiability of the hypothesis. In sociohistorical research on ancient documents, rhetorical analysis is a principal means of determining social location, and changes in rhetorical stance are a principal evidence of changes in social location. Methodologically, this observation means that social location differences and differences in rhetorical stance may become functionally equivalent. It also means that those components that comprise the evidence of change in rhetorical stance—differences in vocabulary, syntax, tone, style, audience—may no longer be considered secure indicators of different authors or sources. They may be, on the contrary, concomitants of the social location shifts themselves. This correlation of rhetoric and social location means that these components of rhetoric and the components of social location cannot be viewed as secure criteria for falsifying hypotheses of social location trajectories in literature. To do so commits the researcher to methodological circularity. Such criteria may need to be found elsewhere. Future research ought to address questions about the relationship between social location change in the rhetors and writers of prophecy and changes in the rhetoric of prophetic speech and written texts.

The principal criteria used in this dissertation's methodology are ethnographic analogy, exegetical consistency, tradition history, historical linguistics, and general plausibility. I do not claim to have demonstrated that my reading of these texts in a single generation's social location trajectory is the correct reading. I merely claim that it makes for a plausibly consistent reading of the texts, perhaps even probable, based on what we know from the sociological study of prophetic movements elsewhere, and the exegesis of the texts themselves. This claim is for a chastened sociohistorical reconstruction that may be read alongside other reconstructions, which may also be plausible and consistent. Future research may provide greater precision and nuance to the reading of these texts to verify or falsify my hypothesis. Either outcome is to be welcomed.

THE TYPOLOGY OF RELIGIOUS MOVEMENTS

In order to facilitate the sociological analysis of postexilic Judean prophetic religion, it is necessary to employ conceptual tools that enable the analyst to compare that religion to others of similar type. Such conceptual tools are called typologies or ideal types. They stand as conceptual generalizations that permit diverse social phenomena to be usefully assessed as aggregates.

> The ideal type is a rational construct that helps to orient us to the confusing infinity of social facts. The model is not the reality; it provides a framework with which to observe and determine how social processes deviate from the ways in which the rational model organizes them. (Farganis 1996, 110)

Because the type is an idealized generalization, social reality always differs from the type to some degree. Nonetheless, without the type, comparison is impossible. One must compare like things to like things.

Typology, moreover, must operate on a sound theoretical foundation. Definitions of types must be built upon attributes rather than correlates. "Attributes are features present in all instances of a phenomenon. Correlates occur in only some instances" (Stark and Bainbridge 1996, 16). The sociological method of comparative typology is a hallmark of the work of Max Weber (1978).

The sociological classification of religious movements, including prophetic religious movements, is indebted not only to Weber, but also to Ernst Troeltsch (1968 [1911]), H. Richard Niebuhr (1957 [1929]), Ralph Linton (1972 [1943]), Joachim Wach (1962 [1944]), Bengt G. M. Sundkler (1961), James Fernandez (1964), Harold W. Turner (1967), Anthony F. C. Wallace (1969a [1956]), Bryan R. Wilson (1973), Bennetta Jules-Rosette (1979a; 1979b; 1987), Rodney Stark (1985), Stark and William Sims Bainbridge (1985; 1996), James C. Livingston (1993), and Jeffrey K. Hadden (1999; 2000), among others. All of these sociologists, anthropologists, and scholars of religion have contributed to the development of what Weber called ideal types. A complete review of the enormous literature on the subject of the sociological typology of religious movements is neither possible nor necessary here. But some points about such sociological typologies need to be made as background for our study of prophetic religion and its social location.

Various social typology systems regarding religious movements have been proposed based on various principles. Some are based on the degree of a group's institutionalization, others on the kind or degree of a group's social deviance, others on theological deviance, others on the axis of natural *versus* voluntary organizational structures, others on the nature of a group's supernaturalist response to the evil of the world, and others on past *versus* future orientations of ideology. Still other systems abound, too numerous to discuss here. One must note that although typologies have been employed in ways that impede good theorizing or mask radical differences, most of these typologies remain useful to some degree. This study makes use of typology for the purpose of assessing the social locations and social location trajectories of prophet-led movements

Social location analysis plots the relationship of a social group to the social center of a particular society. As Theodore E. Long reminds us, "prophecy may arise within established groups and institutions rather than just among the alienated and marginal" (1986, 7). Analysis of social centers and social peripheries, accordingly, is a crucial element in social location analysis (Shils 1961; Long 1986; 1988). Social centers can be conceived in multiple variables: politically, in terms of *de jure* governing authorities and centers of power; ethnographically, in terms of *de facto* relationships in the exercise of social power, or theologically, in terms of the transcendent values held by powerful members of a particular society. There may be very real differences between *de jure* authority and *de facto* authority, and such authority can be held by rival members of a society. Thus the social location of a particular group may exist at more than one point simultaneously, depending upon the variable chosen for analysis as the social center. One group may be peripheral to governing authority, but central to popular consciousness; or a particular group can be peripheral to one elite, but central to a competing elite; or a particular group can be central to the collective elites of a society, but peripheral to the masses; and so on. These differentials are important to the African colonial and postcolonial situation in several of the case studies to be considered here. Considerable care must be exercised in discerning social centers and social peripheries of particular societies, and in defining the specific social forces that constitute a social center.

Moreover, the social location of a particular group can change over time. The plotting of social location change over time yields the phenomenon that I have called "social location trajectories." The concept of social location trajectory derives in part from points made by Walter Brueggemann (1994), Michael L.

Mickler (1986), and Robert R. Wilson (1980, 69). In an essay entitled, "Trajectories in Old Testament Literature and the Sociology of Ancient Israel" (1994), Brueggemann speaks of "trajectories running through the tradition," embedded in cultures and social praxis, and of "continuities that flow between various pieces of literature":

> As a result of social value, use, and transmission, continuities both in terms of cultural context and in terms of theological perspective become decisive for interpretation.... The Mosaic tradition tends to be a movement of protest that is situated among the disinherited and that articulates its theological vision in terms of a God who decisively intrudes, even against seemingly impenetrable institutions and orderings. On the other hand, the Davidic tradition tends to be a movement of consolidation that is situated among the established and secure and that articulates its theological vision in terms of a God who faithfully abides and sustains on behalf of the present ordering. (1994, 14)

Mickler's essay focused on two case histories of what he called "charismatic leadership trajectories" (1986). Wilson, following I. M. Lewis's work on central and peripheral intermediaries (1971, second edition 1989), noted that prophets may originate at the periphery, but move to occupy the social center (1980, 69). Social location trajectory analysis as applied to the Old Testament is a development out of tradition history, wherein the traditions are envisioned as embodied in social movements engaged in particular long-term projects in theological witness. It is an attempt to give flesh and blood to tradition history, through socioliterary and sociohistorical interpretation.

Given sufficient evidence, social location trajectories can be derived empirically to describe the historical experiences of prophets and prophet-led movements through time. These trajectories can be generalized into an ideal typology, a typology akin to the processual typologies developed by social scientists such as Anthony F. C. Wallace (1969a; 1969b), James Fernandez (1964), or Bennetta Jules-Rosette (1979a, 1979b). The research presented here will show that there can be steady-state situations as well as radical changes in social location for prophetic groups over relatively brief periods of time. Social location trajectories are a useful tool in the sociohistorical analysis of recent prophetic movements, and can be usefully applied as a modeling tool for the study of the biblical witness to Israelite and Judean prophetic phenomena.

Various social location trajectories are possible for prophetic movements. Such movements may be marginal at the outset and become centralized, or central at the outset, to become marginalized. Or they may represent movements of religious or social reform which in course may become either centralized or marginalized. Trajectories toward the social center or toward the social periphery may be only partial. Or steady-state conditions may persist in a particular set of social relations, maintaining a prophet or tradent group in a particular social location.

Social location shifts can be demonstrated to occur both multigenerationally or within a single prophetic figure's career.

In social settings in which two or more social groups encounter each other in cultural clash, a further nuance in social location analysis is necessary. When one society dominates another, the dominant group's social institutions will appear to be central; the weaker group's will appear to be peripheral. However, from an *endogenous* perspective, a group's institutions will appear to be central to that group (Cook 1995). Marginalization and centralization trajectories can be plotted for any prophetic figure or movement from both an endogenous perspective and an exogenous perspective.

As we have seen, the stereotypical image of the prophet is as a marginalized figure. Such marginalization is well attested in case studies of prophetic figures and movements. Elijah, Amos at Bethel, Jeremiah, the theorized figure or group behind the Deutero-Zechariah literature, Jesus, and Montanus are all frequently portrayed as marginalized prophets (but see the strictures in Petersen 2002, 13).

Marginalization of a prophet or prophetic group may be produced by popular resistance or enforced by some central authority, or it may be self-imposed. It may result from a process involving aspects of both official and popular resistance by the social center as well as self-imposed rejection by the prophet or tradent group. On the other hand, centralization cannot entirely be self-imposed; not even when the prophet or tradent group becomes the governing authority, as happened in early Islam. Centralization requires strong popular or official consent; but marginalization does not require popular or official resistance.

Every society is made up of social strata and subgroups. A prophet and his tradent group may be peripheral to the larger society, yet central to a particular strata or subgroup. Each subgroup may also be analyzed as a society. Hence, a prophet/group may display quite dissimilar trajectories simultaneously, when viewed from the perspectives of two or more subgroups of a society. Acceptance of a prophet or tradent group by a previously rival group may in turn alienate that particular prophet or tradent group's first supporters. This observation about subgroups leads to a further complication: prophetic groups themselves sometimes fragment, with various social location trajectories available to each of the splinters. In the ethnographic case studies that follow in chapter three, I have tried to present clear cases that illustrate (1) prophetic figures and movements in diverse social locations, and (2) prophetic figures and movements in particular social location trajectories. A *prophet*, as we have seen, is someone recognized to be charismatically empowered who speaks or otherwise demonstrates the will of deity to recipients, usually a particular social group. *Prophetic religion* at the primary level is the religion—the system of transcendent symbolic order—of groups led by prophets. At a secondary level, prophetic religion is religion founded by prophets who may no longer be alive or active in guiding their established religious groups, movements and institutions. In this work I use the term *prophetic religion* mainly as a referent for the former variety.

OUT OF AFRICA

In this work I shall employ primarily African prophetic religions as a sociocultural base for the comparative study of Yehudean prophetic religion in the book of Zechariah.[10] Why is it constructive to use the African experience as a base for comparative study? Several answers pertain. First, Africa abounds in prophetic religions; there is no lack of raw material. Second, these religions have been subjected to extensive observation and analysis by field researchers, ethnographers, cultural anthropologists, sociologists of religion, and historians. There is no lack of analyzed data for many of these religious groups and movements. Thirdly, while there are many differences between sixth- and fifth-century B.C. Yehudean prophetic religion and nineteenth- and twentieth-century A.D. African prophetic religions, African prophetic religion bears the strongest general religiocultural parallels to Yehudean prophetic religion known to me.

Among these parallels are, first, the recent abandonment of local nature-deities for the worship of the high, creator God. In most of the African cases studied here, the high God, the creator, was once viewed as remote and relatively unconcerned with human beings, who were, accordingly, more strongly related to the local nature deities and ancestral spirits thought to dominate the governance of the nonheavenly world (Mbiti 1970). This circumstance comports well with the recurrent African legend that the high creator God was once nigh at hand, but, offended by bad human behavior, he went far away (Johnson 1994, 167–68).

In Yehud, the popular religion of earlier generations mixed Yahwism with the cults of the baal-deities, local spirits associated with fertility. Yehud's recent abandonment of the baal-deities—an act associated with the penitential character of the exilic era—parallels the African prophetic religionists' abandonment of the local deities for the worship of the high creator God. In both of these cases, the local nature deities have been recently displaced by the religious reassertion of the high, creator God in newly formed, or newly reformed prophetic religion.

Secondly, Yehud's traditional social organization as a tribal network of real and supposed clans and families is similar to sub-Saharan African tribal social organization. Roland de Vaux's astute definition of "tribe" is suggestive of both the utility of the term and its ambiguities: "A tribe is an autonomous group of families who believe that they are descended from a common ancestor" (1961, 4). A person's identity within a well-defined extended-family heritage and a

---

[10] On the problems and prospects of such cross-cultural comparisons, see Overholt (1982; 1986; 1989).

multigenerational genealogy are highly prized features of both the Judean and the African experiences (Malamat 1973; de Vaux 1961, 4–13; Gottwald 1979, 293–337; Dearman 1992, 27 and n. 75; but see the cautions in Fiensy 1987).[11]

Thirdly, Persian period Yehud's sociopolitical situation as a colonial outpost of the mighty Persian Empire bears parallels to the modern African neocolonial and postcolonial experience. Both experiences occur under the domination of a politically and militarily superior entity, an entity that sets the general conditions for social and economic interaction. For these reasons, comparisons "out of Africa" have merit for the study of Yehudean prophetic religion.

One of my cases is derived from historical sources, and hence, requires historical-critical reconstruction; others derive from contemporary sociological and ethnographic observation. My sampling cannot, of course, purport to be comprehensive. Such coverage would require, perhaps, several lifetimes of research. Nor can it purport to be systematically selective, for I have not discovered any systematic method to produce a representative sample from the vast number of religious movements active now and in the past. There are, then, unavoidable elements of both randomness and bias in my selection. Perhaps, however, these factors will prove to be assets rather than liabilities, for I did not find it difficult to discover these examples, and all were referenced in mainstream sociological, ethnographic and anthropological literature. I prefer to think that my selection of cases is not unrepresentative of prophetic religious movements as a whole. Future researchers may determine whether or not my preference is valid.

The current study applies the method of social location trajectory analysis to the prophetic materials in what is widely recognized as Proto-Zechariah and Deutero-Zechariah, discerning in them the literary remains of a single generational prophet/tradent group, perhaps the product of a single principal prophetic author, in changing social locations in early Persian period Yehud.

---

[11] A number of these issues are helpfully discussed in Gottwald's *Tribes of Yahweh* (1979, 293–337); cf. his treatment of the terminology for primary, secondary and tertiary divisions of the Israelite tribes (1979, 245–92); cf. Malamat (1973).

3

FIVE CASE STUDIES IN SOCIAL LOCATION TRAJECTORIES OF PROPHETS AND PROPHETIC MOVEMENTS

In the first two chapters I established a basis in sociological theory for seeing a wide range of social locations in the operation of prophetic charisma. This work provided the basis for my proposal about social location trajectories for the analysis of the social matrix that gave birth to the book of Zechariah. But social-scientific studies of religion must not remain a theoretical or an "armchair" matter. Weber worked from published historical texts in producing his *verstehenden Soziologie*, but Clifford Geertz (2002 [1973]) emphasized fieldwork, especially in small scale societies—villages, schools, marketplaces. The social-scientific study of religion today still bears much of the stamp of Geertz, locating large-scale cultural change "in specific towns and villages and with respect to specific people" (John R. Bowen 2005, 20). I am not a fieldwork researcher, but I have used the work of fieldworkers in producing my social location trajectory analyses of prophetic claimants and prophetic movements. Here follows then a series of case studies, mostly African and mostly twentieth century, in the careers of prophetic claimants and the prophetic movements they have spawned. My case studies are about Simon Kimbangu in the Belgian Congo; Isaiah Shembe, the Zulu prophet in South Africa; Muhammad, the founder of Islam, my sole premodern example; Tomo Nyirenda, the Nyasa prophet; and Alice Lenshina, the Bemba prophetess in Zambia.

I: SIMON KIMBANGU

The exceedingly brief public career of Simon Kimbangu (1889–1951) led to the creation of one of the foremost religious organizations in the Democratic Republic of Congo (formerly Zaire). The two most important studies of Kimbanguism in English are those by Efraim Andersson (1958) and Marie-Louise Martin (1975). Martin's seems the more accurate, since she had access to many Kimbanguist documents unavailable to Andersson. For briefer studies, see Bryan R. Wilson (1975b, 70–82), George B. Thomas (1977), and Benjamin C. Ray (2000, 172–77).

Simon Kimbangu's public prophetic career lasted no more than six months, from April to September of 1921, half of it in hiding. Simon came from the Kikongo-speaking peoples of the lower Congo (Andersson 1958, 9). He professed faith in Jesus Christ as a young man, through the ministry of an English Baptist mission in 1915, in what was then the Belgian Congo. Within a short time he was serving as a teacher in the mission school at Ngombe-Lutete; later Kimbangu worked as an evangelist in the nearby village of N'Kamba.

It is said that for three years, starting with the 1918 influenza epidemic that killed thousands in the Congo, he resisted the call to be a prophet. Prophetism frequently is defined in Africa as including (and sometimes consisting mainly in) the power to heal (Oosthuizen 1992). It is said that on April 6, 1921, while going to market, he entered the house of a critically ill woman, laid his hands on her and healed her in the name of Jesus Christ. This event—seen as the foundational event of Kimbangu's prophetic call—is re-enacted every April 6 by a Kimbanguist theater group in N'Kamba. Further healings and miracles are reported in the days and weeks following. Kimbanguist liturgy still memorializes these events "In the name of the Father and of the Son and of the Holy Spirit who descended upon Simon Kimbangu." Soon a ministry of preaching followed. His basic message: cast your fetishes aside and trust in God alone; practice monogamy, modesty, and sexual purity.

Hundreds of people—from many clans and tribes—made pilgrimage to N'Kamba to witness the strange events. Some white settlers believed a revolt was breaking out, as occurred the previous year in Sankuru. The travelers aroused the suspicion of the Belgian colonial authorities, who sent the local administrator, Léon Morel, to investigate. Morel's report also contains the suspicion that Kimbangu may have been seeking to organize a rebellion. It was evident at this time that Kimbangu was not acting under the authority of the Baptist mission. Morel reports that he tried in vain to interrogate Kimbangu, only to receive in reply prayers, Bible readings, speaking in tongues, and ecstatic hymnody.

Kimbangu himself was completely apolitical in his activities. Nevertheless, his prophetic movement spread so rapidly that it came to be seen as a political threat by the Belgian colonial administration. No other movement had unified members of so many clans and tribes before. They decided to suppress it immediately and severely. On June 6 Morel returned to N'Kamba, this time with a group of soldiers, to arrest him.

He fled, and continued to carry out short preaching and healing tours from hiding. Many Kimbanguists and associates of other prophetic claimants were arrested in the following months. On September 21 Kimbangu returned to N'Kamba, reportedly in obedience to a divine revelation. He gave himself up voluntarily, after exhorting his followers to abstain from violence.

After a peremptory military trial, he was sentenced to death on October 3, on a charge of sedition and hostility to whites. After the intervention of some missionaries, his death sentence was commuted to life in prison, the sentence to be served far away in Elizabethville (now Lubumbashi). After a hasty farewell to his family, he was taken away a hundred miles across the Congo. He never saw his family again. He had virtually no subsequent contact with his followers, and spent most of the next thirty years in solitary confinement. He died in prison on October 12, 1951. Nevertheless, as sociologist Bryan R. Wilson observed, "his acclaim was such that his name eventually came to provide the basis for a national Congolese religious movement" (1975b, 70). Many groups—some pacifist, others revolutionary—came to revere him as the African messiah. Numerous popular sects and cults, documented by Efraim Andersson (1958), grew up around Kimbangu-like figures, some orthodox Christian, some heterodox, some traditional African, and some revolutionary. Thaumaturgical activity dominated many of these groups.[1]

Thus he became a key figure for African nationalist consciousness and messianic speculation—all this without his knowledge or consent. In 1959, the Congolese nationalist independence leader Joseph Kasavubu was even rumored to be Simon Kimbangu reincarnated (Edgerton 2002, 183). Indeed, shortly before Kimbangu's 1951 death, one of his former followers was able to visit him in prison, and, informing him of these developments, heard his emphatic denial: "I was, and am simply a servant of Jesus Christ and nothing more" (1975b, 75).

Banishment and deportation of Kimbanguists was standard Belgian policy for more than thirty years, from 1922 to 1957. Some 100,000 people suffered in this way over these years. Nevertheless, the movement grew. No movement before Kimbangu had so joined competing tribes together, thus transforming natural religious communities in the tribes into a much larger trans-tribal, voluntary religious community of the type described by Joachim Wach (1962 [1944]) and James C. Livingston (1993, 138–47). This community can well be described as a nativistic *revitalization movement* of the kind described by Anthony F. C. Wallace (1969a).[2] A great turning point came in 1957. By this time

---

[1] In his typology of religious movements, Bryan R. Wilson classifies thaumaturgy, the claim to work miracles, as one of eight supernaturalist responses to the perceived evil of the world. Thaumaturgical movements emphasize miraculous healing. "The individual's concern is relief from present and specific ills by special dispensations" (1973, 24). The term derives from the Greek word for "wonder" or "miracle," *thauma*. Thaumaturgy is concerned with specific afflictions and their alleviation and finds the solution to such problems in "the direct appeal to supernatural powers" for healing, restoration, and guarantees of physical and spiritual security (Livingston 1993, 154).

[2] A revitalization movement is a type of reformist religious cult, "a deliberate, organized, conscious effort by members of a society to construct a more satisfying culture ... a special kind of culture change phenomenon" (1969a, 31–32). Revitalization is a processual model involving five identified stages: (1) a "steady state," in which social and psychological stress are ... at manageable levels; (2) "a period of increased

Kimbanguists were established secretly, but not maliciously, in various positions in the colonial administration. Joseph Diangienda, one of Kimbangu's own sons, served as secretary to the Belgian Governor-General Pétillon. A delegation met with Pétillon bearing this letter, signed by six hundred Kimbanguists:

> We are suffering so much. Whenever we meet for prayer we are arrested by your soldiers. In order not to burden the police with added work we shall all gather—unarmed—in the Stadium, where you can arrest us all at once or massacre us. (Quoted in Martin 1975, 106)

Faced with the prospect of so many arrests, and receiving assurances of their nonviolent, and even nonpolitical, intentions, Pétillon caved in. By December 1959, amid political turmoil and pro-independence rioting, legal status was formally granted to the Kimbanguist church by the Belgian Senate. When Zaire declared independence in 1960 under the ill-fated regime of Joseph Kasavubu and Patrice Lumumba, Kimbanguism was already well established as a popular religion, rivaling in numbers the traditional Catholic and Protestant churches of the region. *L'Église de Jésus Christ sur la Terre par le Prophète Simon Kimbangu* is one of only four religious groups possessing official government sanction in the country. This is the organization that possesses the best claim to legitimacy as the Kimbanguist church, since it was led by the three sons of the prophet. This Kimbanguist church became a full member of the World Council of Churches in 1969 (170). By the 1970s, millions claimed the name of Kimbanguist.

We saw, then, that the movement's first step was the almost purely charismatic character of Simon Kimbangu's brief career. Then followed the generation-long institutionalization plainly evident in the Kimbanguist ecclesial organization, administered by the prophet's sons who also served as government officials. Third came the 1960 change to Congolese national independence that permitted Kimbanguism to emerge from the shadows of a tolerated existence to become a national religion, the "Church without Whites" (Martin 1975). Fourth is its continued rapid growth in independent Zaire/Congo. The Kimbanguist

---

individual stress," in which the usual societal and habitual patterns of behavior and stress-management no longer appear to be effective; colonialism is the frequent catalyst of increased stress; (3) a "period of cultural distortion," in which social and psychological stress levels dramatically increase and in which the elements of the culture "are not harmoniously related, but are mutually inconsistent and interfering"; (4) a "period of revitalization," in which there comes to be some innovative solution to the stress proposed and accepted by a large number of people in the culture, leading to cultural adaptation and change; and lastly, (5) a new steady state, in which the innovations of the previous stage have been successfully routinized and passed on in what are perceived to be new, viable patterns of behavior (1969a, 36–45). An historical example can be found in his *Death and Rebirth of the Seneca* (1969b).

church is the largest AIC—African Indigenous Church—in all of Africa.[3] Barrett reports that "the growth of the denomination has accelerated considerably since Independence in 1960" (2001, 213). By 1970 there were about 3,500,000 Kimbanguists in Zaire/Congo; and by 1995, there were about 7,500,000 in 12,000 congregations (2001, 213). Thus about 15% of the Congolese are affiliated with this church.[4]

The social location trajectory of Kimbanguism thus goes from extreme to extreme within the brief span of forty years, from a marginalized, persecuted movement under the Belgians to a large, successful, and nationally recognized church under the independence government. Sociologist Bryan R. Wilson thus speaks of Kimbanguism as an excellent example of "steady institutionalization" (1975b, 70; cf. 1975a), moving from its origins as a sect to become a church.[5] In the generation since 1960, it has remained in a steady-state condition, at the social center.[6] Thus Kimbanguism is one nativistic revitalization movement that most notably succeeded. It continues to carry out its witness amid the untold sorrows of Congolese life in this "troubled heart of Africa" (Edgerton 2002).

II. ISAIAH SHEMBE AND THE *AMANAZARETHA*: A CULTURAL SANCTUARY FOR A DYING WORLD

*"Arise Africa, Seek a Saviour,
Today you are the laughingstock of the nations"*
—Isaiah Shembe[7]

Isaiah Shembe (c. 1870–1935) was the prophet and founding figure of the *amaNazaretha* Church, the church of the "Nazarites," also known as the Nazareth Baptist Church, among the Zulu in South Africa.[8] The Shembe movement is an

---

[3] For the AIC designation, see Harold W. Turner (1967), David Barrett (1968), Edward Fasholé-Luke et al. (1978), and Francis Kimani Githieya (1997).
[4] Charles H. Cutter's 2004 estimate is somewhat smaller: 10% of a population of more than 56,600,000, or about 5.6 million (116). Barrett's number seems to be more authoritative than Cutter's.
[5] For the church/sect/cult typology first proposed by Ernst Troeltsch (1968 [1911]), see H. Richard Niebuhr (1957 [1929]), and Stark and Bainbridge (1985).
[6] For new steady-state conditions as the outcome of a successful revitalization movement, see Wallace (1969a, 45).
[7] Quoted in Vilakazi 1986, 127.
[8] Other names for the group are *Iblanda lamaNazaretha*, "The Church of the Nazarites," and *Isonto lamaNazaretha*, "The Church of Nazareth" (Vilakazi 1986, xi; 23).

example of an indigenous Zulu prophetism that became widely influential in the tribe, even among the Zulu chiefs, and then shifted to the social periphery.

Swedish missiologist Bengt G. M. Sundkler (1961), who did extensive field work in the study of Shembism and knew many of the early Shembites, reported that the Zulu accorded more prestige to Isaiah Shembe during his lifetime than to any of his Zulu contemporaries (1961, 111). Shembism thus represented one of the major Zulu religions, with adherents from every social strata, including the highest levels. The Shembe religion swiftly became a centralized prophetic movement, heavily institutionalized, that sought to articulate selected values from the old Zulu world, and employ them for the renewal of Zulu society in South Africa. It serves as an excellent exemplar of the "nativistic movement" type, described by anthropologist Ralph Linton (1972 [1943]),[9] the "revitalization movement" type, described by Anthony Wallace (1969a [1956]), as well as the Zionist type of AIC, described by Sundkler.[10] In its first generation, the *amaNazaretha* reached the Zulu social center; in its second and third generations, it has been pushed to the periphery. This movement serves well as a base for sociological comparison for the centralized Jerusalemite prophetic movement represented in the books of Haggai and Zech 1–8, and perhaps also in its later phases for the marginalized prophet/tradent group represented in Zech 9–14.

---

[9] In a classic essay, anthropologist Ralph Linton described nativistic movements as "any conscious, organized attempt on the part of a society's members to revive or perpetuate selected aspects of its culture" (1972, 497). Nativistic movements typically arise, according to Linton, in situations of cross-cultural contact, in which one group perceives itself to be inferior to, or dominated by, the other. Nativism is common in colonial and postcolonial Africa. However, nativistic movements can also arise within dominant groups as well, as they did among the Mongol conquerors of China and among the Gothic conquerors of Italy (1972, 500–02). Nativism is a strategy of reasserting a group's cultural ascendancy against perceived threats from the outside.

[10] Sundkler's ground-breaking field study, *Bantu Prophets in South Africa* (1961 [1948]), identified two main types of groups among black independent churches. The first, the Ethiopian type, originated as breakaway groups from the traditional mission churches that had been founded by whites, seceding over the issue of apartheid to form wholly self-governing organizations. Sundkler's second type, the Zionist churches, are charismatic healing groups led by prophets. They practice an African variant of an originally black American Pentecostalism. Sundkler chose the Zionist name for this second type because a very large number of these churches bear names using the words Zion or Jerusalem, and many of them resurrect Old Testament regulations (1961, 41, 48). See also Oosthuizen (1992, 1–3), and in relation to biblical scholarship, Daniel L. Smith (1989, 69–90), where leadership patterns in Bantu Zionist churches provide "mechanisms for survival" for oppressed minority groups.

Zulu identity was profoundly important to Isaiah Shembe and remains so for the movement he instituted. The Zulu are one of the southeastern Bantu peoples of Natal in South Africa; the term denotes their particular Bantu language as well.[11] The Zulu comprise the most numerous and coherent of the many tribal groups among the Bantu.[12]

Zulu cohesion, however, is a relatively recent innovation, dating from the early nineteenth century, when European civilization did not yet pose a direct threat. It was the warrior-king Shaka (1787?–1828) who created it, almost out of nothing. Shaka became chief of a small group in 1816, and ruled—brutally but effectively—for a mere twelve years, forcibly assimilating conquered peoples and molding them into an efficient military-based multitribal nation, which took its name from an eighteenth-century eponymous ancestor whose name meant "the heavens" (Morris 1965, 43; Sundkler 1961, 287). Using innovative weapons and military techniques, uncannily similar to classic Roman warfare, Shaka led the way in what the Zulu call the *Mfecane*, the "Time of Troubles," provoking a series of bloody wars and massive migrations.[13] After battle, the surviving women of the vanquished were married off into Zulu families loyal to the king; the surviving men were incorporated into the *impis*, or regiments, of the army (M'Timkulu 1977, 14). Slight infractions received the severest penalties, and executions were a daily occurrence at Shaka's kraal. Perhaps up to two million Africans died in the upheavals of that era (Morris 1965, 108).

Zulu supremacy did not long endure. Shaka himself was assassinated by rival kinsmen in 1828. The kingdom survived two generations of incompetent kings. Dingane ruled until his own assassination in 1840, in the aftermath of a disastrous defeat by the Boers in 1838 at the Buffalo River. The Boers long celebrated the day of their victory, December 16, as a holiday of national deliverance, calling it Dingane's Day. Significantly, the *amaNazaretha* was the only indigenous church that also celebrated this day—but as a day of mourning. Observance was discontinued after the government renamed the holiday "Day of the Covenant" (Vilakazi 1986, 156; 143–44).

In their struggle to maintain independence the Zulu demonstrated great courage. Alone of all aboriginal peoples, the Zulu managed to wipe out an entire division of the well-armed British army, prompting Rudyard Kipling's grudging admiration in these poetic lines from *Barrack Room Ballads*:

---

[11] The word *Bantu* refers to the indigenous black tribes of equatorial and southern Africa, as well as to the general group of indigenous languages spoken there; the term derives from the word for "people."

[12] The diversity of tribal groups among the Bantu is discussed by A. F. Steyn and C. M. Rip (1974, 62) and more fully by Donald R. Morris (1965).

[13] For the *Mfecane's* effects upon Zulu religion, see M'Timkulu (1977, 13–14).

> We took our chanst among the Kyber 'ills,
>   The Boers knocked us silly at a mile,
> The Burman give us Irriwaddy chills,
>   An' a Zulu *impi* dished us up in style. (1968, 444)

Thus in the Battle of Isandhlwana on January 22, 1879, the main *impi* of the Zulu forces—some twenty thousand warriors—overran the central encampment of the invading British forces. They killed about 800 British soldiers and at least 470 of their Kaffir allies. Zulu losses, estimated as at least 2,000, stunned the kingdom (Morris 1965, 387). The victory was shortlived. Wooden assegais, leather shields and the plundered rifles of Isandhlwana could not prevail against the well-prepared and sizeable British forces which soon arrived. Within six months the Zulu were defeated at Ulundi, the site of the Zulu king Cetshwayo's own kraal, and incorporated into Queen Victoria's empire. The once-great civilization tumbled into the long anarchy that Morris called the "ruin of Zululand" (1965, 596; cf. Davenport 1977, 111–12); but the memory of the Zulu's brief glory lived on.[14]

This sociohistorical context provides the background for Isaiah Shembe's prophetism and the rise of the *amaNazaretha* church, one of the most interesting and influential of the indigenous religious movements in South Africa.[15] Shembe was born around 1870, perhaps as early as 1867 (Sundkler 1961, 110; Vilakazi 1986, 23). The Zulu's sudden loss of independence in 1879 must have been a formative influence on the boy. It is for this reason, in part, that sociologists of religion treat the *amaNazaretha* church as a classic example of deprivation theory. Thus Vilakazi wrote that the Shembe church and movements

---

[14] Britain restored Cetshwayo to kingship in 1883, but he failed to generate support among the feuding clans and a brief civil war broke out. Cetshwayo died soon after (Morris 1965, 603–07; Davenport 1977, 111). Morris gives a full history of Shaka and the rise and fall of the Zulu empire (1965); Davenport provides a detailed account of the geopolitical and economic contexts of the key events (1977).

[15] The standard works on Isaiah Shembe include Bengt G. M. Sundkler's *Bantu Prophets in South Africa* (1961); his Shembe article in the *Encyclopedia of Religion* (1987); and the Zulu anthropologist Absalom Vilakazi's *Shembe: The Revitalization of African Society* (1986). Limited reference can also be found in Bryan R. Wilson's *Magic and the Millennium* (1973, 136–40); and in D. M'timkulu (1977). A general study of prophet-figures in Zion-type churches can be found in Gerhardus C. Oosthuizen's *The Healer-Prophet in Afro-Christian Churches* (1992). Oosthuizen has published numerous works on the subject and on Shembism. See also the three-volume collection of Shembe stories and texts edited by Irving Hexham and Oosthuizen (1996; 1999; 2002), entitled *The Story of Isaiah Shembe*. For those who read Zulu, J. L. Dube's *uShembe* (1936) provides a biography of the prophet, based on personal acquaintance.

like it, "were responses of the colonized peoples to the conquering and oppressive impact of European sociocultural domination over small traditional societies" (1986, x; Wilson 1975b, 130–42).[16] Like other nativistic revitalization movements, it preserved selected features of the old Zulu way and held these out as the divinely ordained pattern for achieving the future world. Vilakazi reported that "the people in this church belong to the old and dying Zulu cultural world. They find in the Shembe Church cultural sanctuary where the old values are still respected" (1986, 54).[17]

Little is reported about Shembe's early life, and some of these reports contain conflicting details. One of these reports tells of an auditory experience while he was praying in a cattle kraal during a thunderstorm. Lightning flashed, and a heavenly voice warned the youth to "flee fornication." Later he was commanded to climb a mountain where he had a visionary experience, accompanied again by lightning, in which he saw his own putrefying corpse and was warned by a voice again to "flee fornication" (Sundkler 1961, 110; Vilakazi differs in some details, 1986, 24–26). He woke up claiming to have "seen Jehovah" (Sundkler 1987, 239). Later, after his marriage in traditional Zulu polygamy, a third revelation commanded him to leave his four wives. Shembe was so troubled by this and by further dreams and visions that his family believed him to be mad, and he may have attempted suicide. In a final encounter, lightning struck, killing his best ox and burning Shembe on the thigh, leaving a scar. It is reported that God healed

---

[16] For "deprivation theory" and "relative deprivation theory," see Ralph Linton (1972 [1943]); Anthony F. C. Wallace (1969a [1956]); David Aberle (1972); and J. Milton Yinger (1967). For the theory in a Marxist form, see Peter Worsley (1968). For critical discussion see Bryan R. Wilson (1973, 287–292; 498–502); and Yinger (1970, 420–25). Biblical scholar Thomas W. Overholt makes implicit use of deprivation theory in his book *Channels of Prophecy* (1989, 27–51; *passim*), and Robert R. Wilson discusses the topic in his *Prophecy and Society* (1980, 76–78). Bryan R. Wilson, however, cautions us by observing that in the colonialized situation, religious authority may be the only effective authority structure remaining in the indigenous culture. Hence, the hypothesis of deprivation through colonialization may not provide a correct explanation for the surge of religiously based movements in such societies. In some colonial situations, indigenous religious movements may flourish because colonialization may curtail or remove certain indigenous barriers or competing authority structures from the society (1973, 289; 132).

[17] Vilakazi lists among these values "respect for seniority; parental authority over children; the subordinate role of women; and the acceptance of polygamy" (1986, 54). Significantly, he lists exclusively aspects of Zulu clan-based social structure.

him, and he then received power to heal others (Sundkler 1961, 110). The Nazarites view these experiences as his call to be a prophet.[18]

According to one version of the story, Isaiah Shembe was already well known as a healer and preacher when, in 1906, he was baptized and ordained by the Reverend W. M. Leshenga of the African Native Baptist Church (50), a church patterned after the European-type Baptist mission churches.[19] It was apparently in connection with his baptism and ordination that Shembe began to devote his attention to the Bible, especially the Old Testament. In the Bible, however, Shembe encountered a culture whose tribal ways were much like those of the Zulu and less like those of the European-type churches (Vilakazi 1986, 28). In 1911 he founded his *amaNazaretha* church (Sundkler 1987, 239); some sources report the date as 1910 (David B. Barrett 1968, 304). Differences with his former affiliation included his shifting sabbath observance from Sunday to Saturday, the issue which caused the rift with the African Native Baptists, and other Old Testament distinctives. For example, he interpreted the selected features of Israel's law—and especially statements about Israel's Nazirites—as applying to his own people. He forbad his followers to cut their hair, to drink beer, or to eat pork; further, he permitted polygamy, basing it on Old Testament precedent and Zulu tradition, but enjoined a strict separation of the sexes before marriage (Sundkler 1961, 111; Vilakazi 1986, 119–122; 32–34). Most significantly, Shembe began to incorporate traditional Zulu tribal practices into the religion. The Old Testament Nazirite and kosher customs must have served effectively to sever the *amaNazaretha* from outsiders

In 1912 Shembe again is said to have had a visionary experience on a mountain called Inhlangakazi, near the port city of Durban. After resisting various temptations, angels brought him heavenly bread and wine. Coming down from the mountain, Shembe "knew that he had acquired a new identity and was now a new man" (Sundkler 1987, 239). According to this version of the story, he validated this new identity among his people by performing his first exorcisms and healings. Such activity became so prominent among the *amaNazaretha* that there was scarcely anyone in the church during Shembe's lifetime who did not claim to have been healed or exorcised by him. In this way Shembe presented himself

---

[18] Oosthuizen's questionnaire-based research on Zion-type church prophet-healers in South Africa lists illnesses, dreams, visions and purification experiences as virtually essential features of the call-experience of the prophet-healer (1992, 22–31). Shembe's vision of his own corpse with the command for sexual purity fits the pattern of a purification experience; and although it does so in an unusual way, his lightning injury fits the pattern of illness. The other features of the typology are also present. It may be asked how much of this pattern now so commonly encountered in the AICs was created by Shembe, and how much was inherited from the past.

[19] Sundkler labeled this type of African church the Ethiopian type.

as "the Servant" whom God had sent to the Zulu, just as Moses and Jesus had been sent to the Jews (240).

Shembe appears to have purposely structured his movement in part as an economic response to economic deprivation. This deprivation had it roots, as we have seen, in the ruin of Zululand in the aftermath of 1879. In the 1890s the colonial governor exercised almost total power over the Zulu, dismissing chiefs at will, enforcing a hated labor tax, and imposing *corvée* on one in every ten men (Davenport 1977, 153). Further tensions arose almost every year: in 1905, when the Delimitation Commission set aside forty percent of Zululand for white settlement; in 1906, with the imposition of a poll-tax, which led to an armed Zulu rebellion; in 1907, with a labor dispute in which whites restricted black laborers to menial jobs in the minefields; and so on. The years 1910 to 1924 saw increasing restrictions on black labor and land rights under the Botha and Smuts administrations (153; 176–80). That the *amaNazaretha* was well constructed to address economic problems shows from the momentum it gained during the Great Depression.[20] Growth continued throughout the 1930s, 1940s and 1950s, especially among semi-urbanized people (M'Timkulu 1977, 27). As one writer notes,

> [Shembe's] particular emphasis was to find some salvation for his people during the difficult times.... Initially his movement contained several aspects of the traditional prophet movements. His concern, however, was not so much to preach the gospel or to establish a new church, as to provide a measure of economic security for his people. The essential basis of the Shembe group was a cooperative one. They banded together, first of all, to buy land in order to gain more security at a time when individual purchase of land was being steadily denied to Africans. They would also live as a communal group.... Theirs was an entirely new structure centered in the kind of world that Shembe knew well—the world of employment. His common sharing meant a pooling of wages. Everyone living in the common village worked and contributed his wages and the head of this common family [Shembe] was able to buy land which then the members of the group really owned. They would not be pushed around by the white man any more. (M'Timkulu 1977, 25)

"A MUSEUM OF OLD AFRICAN CUSTOMS"

As we have seen, nativistic movements such as the *amaNazaretha* preserve selected features of indigenous tradition and incorporate them into innovative

---

[20] South Africa had already faced a depression in 1920–22 (Houghton 1964, 42).

patterns for coping with social upheaval and cultural disorientation. As is common with prophet-founder figures in the African setting, Shembe's role was constructed in ways analogous to the role of African tribal chief. Followers consulted him on many seemingly personal decisions, such as the choice of marriage partners and details of business deals. He purchased a large plot of land on the hills of Ohlange, about ten miles north of Durban, constructing upon it a large village, housing some 5,000 people. This village, named Ekuphakameni, "The High Place," was established in 1916 and serves as Zion, the cultic center of Shembism (Sundkler 1961, 111; 349; Vilakazi 1986, 161 n. 22). Administrative decisions for the village devolved upon the prophet as if he were a chief. The *amaNazaretha* congregations themselves, and preeminently the one at Ekuphakameni, are organized much like the Zulu were during Shaka's rule.

In Shaka's day an *impi* was formed from all the males born in a certain year. They were raised together, trained together, and they served together in their military unit in wartime. Each *impi* possessed its own distinctive regalia in clothing and shield design. The permission to marry came to each *impi* as a group from Shaka himself. Some of the *impis* were even denied this privilege until their forties. Girls, too, were organized into age groups for their training and upbringing (Morris 1965, 50–53).

The similarity among the Shembites is seen especially on ritual occasions at Ekuphakameni. There the whole assembly, divided into groups pertaining to age, gender and martial status, performs slow and solemn dances in traditional Zulu dress; these were often led by Shembe himself (see the photograph in Sundkler 1961, facing page 190). The age, gender and marital status groups each have distinctive clothing styles and regalia, which is regimented by church tradition; nor may the men discard or sell any of their ceremonial dress and regalia as long as they live. The practice of wearing traditional dress even increased among the church's people in the 1980s. In 1986 Vilakazi reported that the *amaNazaretha* were the only AIC to encourage distinctively African dress and to employ African dance in worship. The other indigenous churches typically disparage these practices as pagan (148–50; 154). Shembe thus sacralized and preserved distinctive aspects of the old Zulu way. Vilakazi noted that the village, "which is geographically in the centre of a very progressive community and surrounded on all sides by missions, is like a museum of old African customs and practices" (1986, 45).[21]

Another evidence of the nativistic role that Shembe and the *amaNazaretha* played in black South African society is their strong relationship with the heredi-

---

[21] The Zulu musicologist Bongani Mthethwa offers a musicological analysis of Shembe's hymn-tune melodies based on traditional Zulu categories in Vilakazi (1986, 134–52). Sundkler called these melodies "solemn, simple, and searching" (1987, 239).

tary chiefs of the Zulu people. This trend also shows that the movement became for a time a centralized, not a marginalized, religion. A number of chiefs favored the main separatist churches—including especially the *amaNazaretha*—with their support and membership. No less than fifteen of the prominent chiefs were members of the group by 1961, and in those years many more attended the two annual pilgrim festivals, at Ekuphakameni in July, and at the mountain Inhlangakazi in January. The chiefs also routinely conferred with the prophet about political affairs during the July festival (Sundkler 1961, 312). Sundkler once met a young chief at Ekuphakameni who had come there "not in order to become a Nazarite, but to study the ways of imposing *inhlonipho* (Zulu word for respect) on his people" (1961, 111).

In 1961 Sundkler observed the "considerable sociological significance" of the fact that "the chiefs' clans claiming seniority to the royal, Zulu, clan, are prominent members of Shembe's Church; thus the Mtetwa[22] and Qwabe" (*sic*, 312–13). Before his death in 1935 the prophet's cattle were farmed out in their wards, a privilege accorded only to the Zulu king in the past. The Shembites even called him *inkosi*, "king," although this was not meant politically (Vilakazi 1986, 41; 112). Chiefs still take the opportunity to address the *amaNazaretha* today (Buthelezi 2001).

Sundkler noted that even before he founded the *amaNazaretha*, Isaiah Shembe was "closely related to Meseni Qwabe," one of the militant leaders in the 1906 Zulu rebellion, which had been led by "the great nationalist leader Bambata Zondi" (1987, 239; 1961, 311). After the rebellion failed, Meseni (or Messen) Qwabe was deported to St. Helena. Sundkler gives this account of the events that followed:

> [On the island of St. Helena] he saw a vision of a prophet dressed in white. Six years after his death, his widows recognized Isaiah Shembe as this very prophet. When Shembe came to Messen's grave, they exclaimed: "There is Jehova (*sic*) dressed in white." The prophet arranged a great remembrance in Messen Qwabe's honour and announced: "I am going to revive the bones of Messen and of the people who were killed in Bambata's rebellion." The great Messen had five sons, all of whom became members of the Church which their revered father had thus posthumously joined. It is here taken for granted that any Qwabe, illiterate or literate, should become a member of this church. (1961, 313)[23]

---

[22] Bongani Mthethwa is apparently a member of this clan (1986, xv).
[23] Most Shembites then were illiterate. By the early 1980s literacy had significantly increased among the Shembites (Vilakazi 1986, 118).

This incident shows Shembe's Zulu nationalism in a number of ways. He implicitly validated Meseni as friend and national leader; he in turn was validated as a prophet by the Qwabe clan, and especially the five sons who figuratively fulfilled the prophecy by joining the *amaNazaretha*; and he validated the Zulu practice of honoring the spirits of the ancestors, represented here by the 1906 rebellion's honored dead (Barrett 1968, 120).

Such honor as the Zulu accord to the ancestors is now accorded to the spirit of the dead Shembe (Sundkler 1961; Vilakazi 1986, 52).[24] He is viewed as watching over the church, and revelations are typically reported in his name (Vilakazi 1986, 52). Sundkler reports one such Shembite claim:

> I had a dream. A voice told me: You are called. — By whom? You are called by the Man of God [meaning Isaiah Shembe]. I saw the Man of God. He looked very sad. But he gave me the Key. We are here to buy the Key, so that we will be able to enter. If you have not the Key, you cannot enter. (1961, 188; cf. 329)

This form of experience is especially significant since Isaiah Shembe's son, Johannes Galilee Shembe, also known as Shembe II, a university-educated man, was often seen as lacking his father's charisma. Early in his tenure as the group's leader, the charismatic functions once exercised by Shembe I were partly assumed by several women. In one example, hymns published by the church have their author listed as Isaiah Shembe "after his resurrection from the dead." They were published this way — according to Johannes Galilee Shembe — because several women had received the hymns in revelatory visions and auditions from Isaiah Shembe (Sundkler 1961, 284). This form of prophetic activity, in which revelations are viewed as mediated through Isaiah Shembe, still continues among the *amaNazaretha*. Thus *Erbcharisma* or *Amtcharisma* is not as powerful as Shembe's original charisma.

For reasons like these — the use of tribal dance, indigenous hymnody, Zulu nationalism, the adaptation of the ancestor cult, and the strong relationship with the old Zulu patrimonial system — Sundkler concluded that the *amaNazaretha* church was more intentionally nativistic in its approach than other groups of the Zionist type (1961, 49).

This intense nativism can be seen in the *amaNazaretha* approach to the traditional Christian doctrine of the Trinity. In the Zulu patrimonial system, fathers are superior to sons. If, as explained by Vilakazi, the father is a chief, one might approach the father by means of the son's good offices; but one must never equate the two, lest insult be given; so it is with God and Christ. *AmaNazaretha*

---

[24] On ancestor worship among the Zulu see Vilakazi (1986, 11–17; 76) and M'Timkulu (1977, 18–25).

Christology is a Zulu Christology and therefore subordinationist and unitarian. Traditional Zulu values thus exercise considerable ideological power over the form of theology adopted by the *amaNazaretha* (Vilakazi 1986, 74; Sundkler 1961, 283).

Membership figures vary widely for the Shembe church, but nonetheless are substantial. In the early 1970s Bryan Wilson reported figures of 50,000 given by Sundkler in 1948; 10,000 by Katesa Schlosser in 1958; and by others up to 80,000 (1973, 138). In 1961 Sundkler said that any attempt to estimate its membership would be "sheer guesswork," since the church itself keeps few written records, and many attenders may also participate in other competing religions (131). M'Timkulu, writing in about 1970, reported the size between 120,000 and 150,000 (1977, 28). In 1982 David Barrett's first edition of the *World Christian Encyclopedia*, which generally had the most accurate figures available for such movements, reported a membership of 200,000 adult members, and a total of 430,000 people affiliated (1982, 625). Barrett's 2001 second edition reports 700,000 affiliates as of 1995, in 300 congregations (2001, 681). More recent figures, reported informally, put the membership at close to 1 million. If so, roughly 12% of South Africa's eight million Zulus have some affiliation with the *amaNazaretha*.

Isaiah Shembe functioned as a central authority prophet throughout virtually his entire career. In my social location analysis model, Shembe's prophetic claims were quickly validated by the Zulu. He had come from a well-placed Zulu family, had friendships among the Zulu tribal leadership before he founded the *amaNazaretha*, and continued successfully to cultivate such relationships throughout his life. The membership of the *amaNazaretha* came from every stratum of Zulu society. He became the confidant of and advisor to chiefs, and one of the noblest of clans, the Qwabe, maintained a special relationship with him and with the *amaNazaretha*. He enunciated certain core values of Zulu tradition at a time when such values were failing, placing them in the new context of an indigenous Zion-type church organization, which became substantially successful. From this organizational and ideological base, he created a new way of living within the ruins of Zululand. In 1961 Sundkler wrote, "There is very probably no Zulu in modern times who has had such an intense influence over such a large number of people as Shembe" (110).

In more recent years, the social location of Shembism has drifted to the periphery of Zulu society. Entrenched in a traditional way of life, eschewing doctors, medicine, western clothing, the cutting of hair, and many features of technological society, and growing primarily among the most impoverished of South Africa's blacks, the *amaNazaretha* has become a church of the poor. Its current geographic center, called Ebuhleni, "The Place of Beauty," a few kilometers from Ekuphakameni, has been overrun by the ugly urban sprawl of the city of Durban. Most Shembites live in Inanda, the Durban-area township where both

Ekuphakameni and Ebuleni are located. Living conditions in Ebuhleni are desperate: dependable sources of drinking water, public sanitation, and paved roads are lacking; houses are made of mud, plastic, and cardboard (Mkhize 2000). Nonetheless, Zulu chiefs still address gatherings of church members, and speak warmly of their close ties to the family of Isaiah Shembe.[25] A small educated class of Shembites, drawn from converts from mission churches, and from younger, upwardly mobile Shembites, lives in tension with their more traditional co-religionists (Vilakazi 1986, 118–19). But this element has not stopped the steady marginalization of the *amaNazaretha* in Zulu society. The church was also weakened by the sharp succession struggle after the death of Johannes Galilee Shembe in 1976 between Bishop Amos Shembe (1907–1986), a younger brother of Johannes Galilee, and Londa Shembe (1944–1989), a grandson of the founder, who titled himself Shembe III. Amos retained the majority, while Londa led out a splinter group. Londa was later assassinated (Nxamalo 2005). The main branch is now led by Mbusi Vimbeni Shembe (1933–).

A generation after the death of Johannes Galilee Shembe (1904–1976), the *amaNazaretha* social location trajectory has moved from a place in the social center, as exemplified in the career of Isaiah Shembe, to occupy the periphery. Shembism is now a marginalized religion of the poor, a museum of a dying culture.

III. MUHAMMAD

"Islam appears to be a cement of empires."
—Ernest Gellner (1969, 128)

If the traditional Muslim sources are to be believed, one of the most dramatic historical cases of social location change within a single lifetime is the case of the prophet from Mecca, Muhammad (ca. 570–632 A.D.). The sources are difficult, and there is not unanimity on their reliability. I have chosen to follow what may be called the majority view regarding the historical value of the primary biographical sources on Muhammad. This general view is ably represented by W. Montgomery Watt (1961) and Maxime Rodinson (1957; 1980 [1961]), and promoted more recently by Karen Armstrong (1992). Watt's biographical works on Muhammad are still widely regarded as the most important critical studies in English. However, a different school of historical-critical biography has grown up around the work of historian John Wansbrough, who published in the 1970s and who offered a tentative reconstruction of emergent Islam based on a quite skeptical assessment of the traditional Islamic sources, since they were

---

[25] For one example, see Buthelezi (2001).

written long after their subject's death. This latter approach, followed by Andrew Rippen (1990) and Ibn Warraq (2000) among others, would render it difficult if not impossible to speak of a biography of the prophet, but not many have followed them into this seemingly extreme path. What then do these traditional sources tell us? I offer the following tentative scenario.

In course of time a caravaneer, then trusted steward of a wealthy widow's caravans, then husband of this former employer, Muhammad did not take up the role of prophet until the age of forty, it seems. Watt surmized that his prophetism arose partly in response to the moral threat introduced by the new and highly successful mercantilism controlled by the leading clans of the dominant Quraysh tribe (1961; cf. Rodinson 1980, 38).

Situated between the great powers of Byzantium in the Greek-speaking north and the Sasanids in the Persian east, Mecca had become the center of a growing trade. The sudden influx of wealth disrupted the long-stable community. The sanctions of the old polytheistic desert religion proved no longer adequate to direct the course of public life. The old tribal humanism based on honor, kin-group allegiance, and protection of the weak had begun to collapse. "Individuals tended to group themselves more according to their own interest within the framework of the new economic structures than according to tribal affiliation" (Rodinson 1957, 38). Hence, some of the earliest passages in the Quran give emphatic directions about using wealth for social benevolence (Watt 1961, 33). *Zakat*—the requirement of almsgiving—would become one of the five pillars of Islam (Armstrong 1992, 93). One of Muhammad's earliest self-designations is "Warner" (*nadhîr*), one who bears witness to his brothers about the coming of Allah's Day of Judgment, when one's acts of generosity will help him gain salvation (Rodinson 1957, 38). As Bryan S. Turner observed, "Islam took the major concepts of tribal humanism— generosity, courage, loyalty and veracity—and gave them a new, religious content" (1974, 35). The new religious community would cut across blood ties and social prestige to build a new super-tribe based on faith in Allah and in Muhammad as his messenger. This faith would provide the social stability now disintegrating in the old blood-based tribal system.

Although he was from the Quraysh tribe (albeit one of its lesser clans, the Hashim), Muhammad faced opposition for ten years from powerful Qurayshi families. The majority of modern critical biographers, as well as the traditional Islamic biographers, typically accept as persuasive the evidence of substantial persecution in Muhammad's early years as prophet (Bodley 1946; Rodinson 1957; Watt 1961; Armstrong 1992; cf. the Iranian Shi'ite S. Mujtaba Musawa Lari's 1990 biographical sketch; for critical discussion of the difficulties in the early biographical sources, see Rippen 1990, 30–43). In the early years he drew only a small number of disciples, mostly from his own family and clan, from the rebellious young men of some leading families, and among people of mixed ages from various weaker groups, including foreigners and freedmen. Early Islamic sources describe the movement as consisting of the young and the weak. Weak means "without good clan protection" (Watt 1961, 37). Watt analyzed a list of the names of the earliest Muslims, apparently originating from the first few months of the movement. His analysis identified (1) names of young men from the most influential families of the powerful Quraysh tribe; (2) names of young men from less influential tribes; (3) names of men from outside the Meccan clan system. He concluded, "as we move down the scale to the weaker clans and families, we find among the Muslims men of greater influence within clan and family" (36). Opposition was directed by the prominent men of the most prominent Qurayshi families.

Rejecting the polytheism of the powerful clans and denouncing the injustices of the wealthy in language reminiscent of Amos and Jeremiah, his persecution in Mecca intensified over the years. Responses to this opposition included the emigration of some of his followers to Ethiopia, and the now infamous incident of the "Satanic Verses." Eventually he lost even the protection of his own clan, and only with some difficulty received a pledge of protection from another. In 620, invited to settle a blood-feud two hundred miles away in Yathrib,[26] Muhammad seems to have barely escaped Mecca with his life. Tradition reports that the prominent young Qurayshi, Abu Jahl, Muhammad's chief persecutor, recruited well-connected young men from each clan to kill Muhammad together. Since all the tribes would share the blood-guilt, no blood-feud would occur. Muhammad's clan would have to be satisfied with the payment of blood-money, for they could not fight the whole tribe (Armstrong 1992, 152). Watt doubted some details of the traditional story of Muhammad's *hijrah* (emigration) to Yathrib, but accepted the basic point that the prophet's life was endangered (1961, 82).[27]

Once safely in Yathrib, Muhammad validated his prophetic claims by negotiating a swift settlement between the warring parties. United under his leadership, the Yathrib community became the first Islamic state. After ten years of raids, intermittent warfare, negotiations, and a broken truce, Mecca capitulated to forces led by the prophet in 630. The negotiated settlement included Meccan submission to Islam. Even the men of the leading clans— including some whom the prophet had condemned to death—one by one made peace with him and submitted to Islam. Most of Arabia soon followed peaceably. By 650 much of North Africa and the Near East lay under the control the Islamic state, heir to both the Sassanid and the Byzantine empires (Esposito 1988, 7–13; Noss 1974, 511–16; Holt, et al. 1970, 54, 57–72; Turner 1974, 64).

---

[26] Yathrib is now known as Medina, from *Madinat an nabi*, "City of the Prophet."

[27] Watt surmised that in leaving Mecca, he would forfeit his protection and could be killed without the reprisal of a blood-feud (1961, 90–1).

Muhammad's career and his movement present the sociologist with a trajectory from marginalization to centralization. "It was the function of the Prophet to be, not only a spiritual guide, but also the organizer of a new social order with all that such a function implies" (Nasr 1966, 68). Role recognition as a prophetic claimant brought him validation by the few and opposition by the many; both of these responses brought him opportunity to increase the social circle of validation, yet his persistence in prophetic activity similarly brought about intensified persecution. The geographic move to Yathrib led to a swift centralization of him and his movement. Yet to his former Meccan public, he remained a rejected figure. Thus centralization by one public accompanied marginalization by another. Yet even this state of affairs was temporary. Military campaigns and skillful negotiations eventually brought even Mecca's leading Quraysh to accept his prophetic claims as the transcendent center of the emerging Muslim society. Seyyed Hossein Nasr, the Muslim historian of religion, wrote, "The spirituality of Islam of which the Prophet is a prototype is not the rejection of the world but the transcending of it through its integration into a Centre" (1966, 77).

In Bryan R. Wilson's typology, early Islam may be characterized as expressing both a conversionist response[28] and a reformist response[29] to the perceived evil of the world. Muhammad's career apparently moves from a conversion-

---

[28] The conversionist response is Wilson's second of eight types of supernaturalist responses to the perceived evil of the world: "the world is corrupt because [people] are corrupt; if [people] can be changed, then the world will be changed" (1973, 22). Conversion here is not a synonym for recruitment to the movement. The prevailing metaphor is change of heart. In the face of evil, change of heart, a transformation of the self by divine aid, is the real necessity. Such a transformation involves a subjective change in relation to the evil of the world, a change that transcends evil.

[29] Wilson's seventh response to the perceived evil of the world is the *reformist* response. This response "recognizes evil but assumes that it may be dealt with according to supernaturally given insights about the ways in which social organization should be amended" (1973, 25). Reformist cults produce a critique of a given tradition or society and apply some divinely sanctioned prescription about amending that tradition or society. The assessment of the evil of the world is less extreme than that of Wilson's introversionist or revolutionist responses. Human beings have some power to achieve social salvation, but they cannot do so "without the prompting of supernatural agencies" (25). Sometimes such groups may cooperate with secular reform movements, and are relatively more open and accommodating to the surrounding culture than several of the other response types. According to James C. Livingston, the reformist cult "often begins as a revolutionist and introversionist movement but, while maintaining its structure, over time modifies its response to the outside world" (1993, 154).

ist/reformist response that is rejected and marginalized in Mecca, to centralization in Medina, to a more powerful centralization back again in Mecca, all within the brief span of about twenty years.

IV. TOMO NYIRENDA, THE *MWANA LESA* IN NYASALAND

One case history of a prophet and a political leader working in tandem—albeit with ominous results—is the case of the Nyasa prophet Tomo Nyirenda. Information on this movement is scant, but it is clear that in 1925 Tomo Nyirenda took the title *Mwana Lesa*, "God's Child" or "God's Son," as many earlier African traditional prophets in Nyasaland (now Malawi) had done (Taylor and Lehmann 1961, 26; Johnson 1979, 104). Allied with the Nyasa chief Shaiwila, Mwanalesa Nyirenda became his witch-finder. Fear of witchcraft is a well-documented aspect of African life (Mbiti 1970, 258); and this attitude characterized the tribes of the region. Indeed, Taylor and Lehmann reported that "fear of witchcraft and a corresponding use of protective charms" was the most prominent aspect of tribal religion in this area (1961, 271).[30] With loose ties with the Watchtower societies, or perhaps merely sharing some of the Watchtower doctrines that had originated with the American sect, the Jehovah's Witnesses,[31] Nyirenda conducted a brief but extensive work of itinerant preaching and baptizing, immersing thousands. His particular innovation was to use the baptism rite as a witch-finding technique. Those who did not submerge deeply into the baptismal waters were marked out as witches and subject to ransom by their families or execution. According to Taylor and Lehmann, it was in this way that Chief Shaiwila rid himself of his enemies (1961, 26, 229).

Nyirenda preached a form of imminent millennial expectation drawn from Watchtower sources, adding to it the teaching that whites and leaders of organized churches were "snakes." His preaching drew large audiences of both Christians and followers of traditional tribal religions in Nyasaland.

Early in 1926 the colonial administration tried and executed the Nyasa chief Shaiwila and his prophet Tomo Nyirenda. But by then the chief and his prophet

---

[30] In conversation with African evangelical Christians I found a similar tendency. Whereas western evangelicals often speak of forgiveness of sin as the principal benefit of their religion, evangelicals from villages in Ghana and Nigeria that I have questioned typically speak instead of Christianity's power to deliver them from the witches. The Harrist movement (Haliburton 1971; Walker 1983; 1987) and Alice Lenshina's Lumpa Church (see below) also preached emphatically against witchcraft and claimed the power to oppose it successfully.

[31] The name Watchtower is derived from the sect's publishing house in New York City, The Watchtower Bible and Tract Society. The sect was founded by C. T. Russell in the United States in 1874.

had already killed as witches many people, especially from among the rival Lala and Lamba tribes (1961, 26). There is some dispute about the number of their victims. Taylor and Lehmann put the number at more than thirty (1961, 26). Walton Johnson reports that 200 people were killed in this way (1979, 104).

In my social typology of prophets, I categorize Tomo Nyirenda as a central authority prophet within Nyasa tribal society, in a nativistic revitalization mode. Supported by a Nyasa chief, and locating witches among rival tribes, his social function served to validate and consolidate local Nyasa power, as expressed in the person of Shaiwila, over against the perceived or invented threat of the Lala and the Lamba. This social function, carried out as it was at the supreme expense of the so-called witches, was criminalized by the colonial administration, a nonindigenous social structure militarily more powerful than the Nyasa tribe. Hence, Nyirenda's effort at validating and consolidating Nyasa supremacy failed. The prophetic-millennialist movement in the region continued, however.

In 1935 the colonial administration banned the Watchtower societies' printed literature. But in this move the Europeans did not act alone. In a few districts the chiefs themselves carried out campaigns of suppression, and burnt down Watchtower meeting enclosures. Watchtower groups were radically marginalized. The chiefs' actions in part responded to the new influx of Watchtower adherents fleeing from a 1934 government crackdown in the neighboring Congo. Some Watchtower groups as a result built their own separate villages where they could live removed from the oppression by the tribal villages (Taylor and Lehmann 1961, 27). In this case, social marginalization was literally as well as metaphorically true: the new villages comprising tribally mixed groups united by religion operated on the fringes of the region's tribal-based village system.

Thus the marginalized groups of prophetic adherents, joined by like-minded outsiders from the north, but opposed by both colonial authority and indigenous tribal leadership, created new and separate social centers in which they could operate with relative autonomy. The social location trajectory within this brief span of years is accordingly complex. First appears a pattern of centralization under Mwanalesa Nyirenda's alliance with Chief Shaiwila. Then follows a phase of criminalization[32] by the colonial authority, and marginalization of the movement by the remaining chiefs. Finally, the marginalized groups achieved a qualified recentralization. They achieved this by relocating in their own separate villages, constituting themselves as new dominant local groups even as they remained marginalized in relation to the larger tribal-based society.

---

[32] For a sociological study of the criminalization of charismatic movements, see Mickler (1986).

V. ALICE LENSHINA AND THE LUMPA CHURCH

> *You who love the land of darkness,*
> *let us break through, be saved.*
> *He will help us in everything,*
> *he will take us out of evil,*
> *when, when?*[33]
> —From the hymns of Alice Lenshina

One of the most tragic stories of twentieth century African religious history took place among the Bemba, the dominant ethnic group in Zambia's Northern Province, in 1964. The Bemba cherish a strong warrior tradition (Bond 1979, 140). In the period under review, 1953–1978, most Bemba lived in remote rural areas. Before the 1964 transition from British colonial administration of the territory as Northern Rhodesia to African nationalist administration as Zambia, most Bemba men worked either as farmers or as migrant miners in central Africa's mineral-rich Copperbelt. It was in this social situation of fledgling nationalism and advancing industrialization that a prophetic claimant arose among the rural Bemba, Alice Lenshina Mulenga Lubusha (c. 1919–1978).

At its peak, Lenshina's movement, taking the name the "Lumpa Church," attracted somewhere between 50,000 to 100,000 adherents (Bond 1987, 513; Van Binsbergen 1981, 288; cf. Barrett 2001, I:820), drawn not only from the Bemba of Northern Province, but from tribes throughout the Copperbelt, into Tanzania (then known as Tanganyika), north into the Congo, south into Zimbabwe (then known as Southern Rhodesia) and southeast into Malawi (then known as Nyasaland). In 1956, western observers counted up to 1,000 pilgrims a week coming to Lenshina's remote village (Taylor and Lehmann 1961, 250; Van Binsbergen 1981, 289). This was the church that would enact a violent insurrection against the fledgling nationalist government of independent Zambia, resulting in the deaths of between 700 to 1,500 people, mostly Lumpa, and the banning of the Lumpa Church (Brockman 1994; Van Binsbergen 1981, 266).

Alice Lenshina, a nearly illiterate peasant woman, was the daughter of a minor administrative official in the Chinsali district of Northern Province. She grew up near the Lubwa mission of the Free Church of Scotland, a conservative Calvinist denomination. The Zambian name for the Free Church's Northern Rhodesian mission was the United Church of Central Africa (Bond 1979, 141).[34] Despite the remoteness of her home area, Lenshina grew up and lived amidst

---

[33] Quoted in Roberts (1970, 529).

[34] For a history of the Lubwa Mission, see Ipenburg (1992), but note the criticisms in Musambachme (1998).

substantial western contact and had received some education in the local mission school.

Like many prophetic claimants, her call came through an experience of physical crisis. It was in the midst of an illness in 1953 that Lenshina claimed to receive the first of her visions and the divine call to become a prophetess (Bond 1987, 513; Wilson 1973, 94). Avowing that she had returned from the dead, she reported that she had been to heaven, where she was told to return to earth and do God's will. According to a 1956 presbytery report, Lenshina is quoted as saying, "When I was ill and died, I was carried by angels. Jesus said, 'Let her go back and live in her village.' But I stayed there three days and nights, and angels came and Jesus came and talked to me" (Taylor and Lehmann 1961, 250). In another account, it is reported that in her death experience, Jesus called her to a river where he said, "'Send her back. Her time has not yet come." Jesus then told her to visit the white people, who would have a message for her" (Roberts 1970, 523). She and her husband, Petro Chitankwa, reported her experiences to the local minister, the Scottish Reverend Fergus MacPherson. Roberts gives the date of Lenshina's first meeting with MacPherson as September 18, 1953, when she was a young woman of about age 33 (1970, 522–23).

Completing her catechumenate under MacPherson's leadership, she was baptized in November of 1953 and given the name Alice (Roberts 1970, 524). MacPherson treated her with kindness, but with no special deference. For some months she seems to have been content with her situation as a member of the Lubwa Protestant United Mission. She regularly spoke at the mission church services, and began composing new Bemba-style hymns, which revolutionized the mission church's singing (Taylor and Lehmann 1961, 255–56).[35]

News of her death-experience spread quickly; soon large numbers of people were attending the mission church's services. There they heard her speak powerfully against such behaviors as theft, deceit and adultery. She was especially insistent that they give up their magic charms and fetishes. Her hymns proved to be compelling to her African following. In these ways she came to be widely recognized.

In November of 1954 MacPherson went on leave (Roberts 1970, 524). Soon Lenshina began independent activities, giving to local farmers seeds that she had blessed for planting, leading church services of her own, and baptizing. Mission church leaders viewed these baptisms as a serious breach, especially since many of those whom Lenshina baptized had already been baptized in their own or in other churches (Taylor and Lehmann 1961, 250). Rebaptism meant

---

[35] For samplings of Lenshina's hymn-texts see Taylor and Lehmann (1961, 256–59) and Roberts (1970, 528–29).

schism. MacPherson's departure may have been an element in Lenshina's disaffection with the mission church (so Bryan R. Wilson 1973, 96).

By 1955 it was clear that she had broken away, preaching her own message and baptizing. Her message was judged to be heretical by the leaders of the Lubwa Mission and by the White Fathers of the nearby Roman Catholic mission at Ilondola (Roberts 1970, 524 and n. 30). However, according to Taylor and Lehmann's interviews with Lenshina, her message contained nothing new:

> I cannot teach you anything. You know it (God's Law) just as well as I do. There is killing all over the world, and greediness and selfishness; that is the responsibility of the leaders. In the Lumpa Church the people find a special power to resist in temptation. In other churches people, even the teachers, are weak. They still possess forbidden things. The people who follow me understand what it means to throw away charms. I want them to follow the commandments which you also know. (1961, 255)

Essentially, Lenshina exhorted people to do the same things the Scottish mission church had taught. The content was a simple evangelistic message, with emphasis upon strict obedience to the Ten Commandments and to Lenshina's moral exhortations. Bryan R. Wilson suggests that the Lumpa's rules were "an intensification of the moral ideals" taught by the Scottish mission church (1973, 96). There were some differences; in particular, baptism—of both adults and infants—was the only sacrament of the movement. Converts in areas far removed from Chinsali district had to wait for Lenshina's arrival in order to be baptized, or to come on pilgrimage to see her.

The flood of her followers came from many tribes, from patrilineal and matrilineal groups, from urbanized workers of the copper industry as well as traditional farmers, and from a range of social classes. The work of the large Roman Catholic mission at Ilondola was nearly destroyed by defection to Lumpa (Roberts 1970, 533; Wilson 1973, 96). Proximity to the railroad helped the movement spread to rural settlements along the rail line as well as to urban areas. The core group, however, comprised rural Bemba farmers and their families (Van Binsbergen 1981, 289). At its peak in 1958, the Lumpa Church commanded the loyalty of between 70% to 90% of the local population in Chinsali district (Van Binsbergen 1981, 289; Wilson 1973, 96; Taylor and Lehmann 1961, 252; Roberts 1970, 533).

By 1958 the new movement had achieved a substantial organizational structure, in imitation of the mission church model. Lenshina's movement became known as the "Lumpa Church." Bond reports that *lumpa* is a Bemba word meaning "excelling" or "most important" (1987, 513; cf. Taylor and Lehmann, 1961, 253). The name carried a negative critique of other churches. In some ways the Lumpa Church did excel all others; western witnesses expressed amazement at how thoroughly Lumpa members obeyed the strict moral code that Lenshina enjoined upon them (Van Binsbergen 1981, 291).

Lenshina claimed that she could protect followers from the power of witchcraft. For indigenous Africans, this feature stood in stark and favorable contrast with the teachings of the missionaries of the Free Church of Scotland, who denied that witchcraft even existed. Witchcraft is a most prominent aspect of the African world-view (Bond 1987, 513).[36] Roberts suggests that, with the decline of the chiefs, whose power was traditionally thought to limit sorcery, fear of witchcraft was on the rise (1970, 518). Witchcraft was a sensitive subject for the governing colonial authorities, who had outlawed witch-finding in the aftermath of murderous movements like the *Mwana Lesa*'s (Taylor and Lehmann 1961, 251; cf. 26–27; Bryan R. Wilson 1973, 83–84). Unlike the *Mwana Lesa*, Lenshina did not engage in witchcraft accusation. Such activity would have quickly brought about criminal charges against her. Instead, people willingly came to her, confessing their involvement in sorcery, and giving up the paraphernalia of their craft. Lenshina preached repentance from both the practice of witchcraft and from the practice of defense against witchcraft; her followers had to give up all (Wilson 1973, 98–99).

As a prophet-speaker, Lenshina would play a a reed pipe or flute and then announce, "Come, hear what God is telling you.... Bring your magic, horns and charms, then you will be saved in God's judgment." These objects she would collect and store in vast quantities in huts (Taylor and Lehmann 1961, 250–51), proof that such objects had no power over her (Wilson 1973, 98). The discarded objects even included Roman Catholic crucifixes and Methodist hymnals (Barratt 2003, 5, with photographs).

Lenshina's movement was also characterized by an emphasis on healing. Bryan R. Wilson accordingly classifies Lumpa as a thaumaturgical cult (1973, 100). Curiously, however, Lenshina engaged in no particular healing rituals or prayers. She did not lay hands on people or touch them in any way. Instead, the sick and troubled would come and tell her of their illnesses or difficulties. Some would receive counsel before departing. Afterwards, they would claim to have found healing or relief (Taylor and Lehmann 1961, 263).

Another important feature of the movement, one that proved to be effective in drawing a large following, was the singing of Lenshina's hymns. Compared to the often poorly translated versions of western hymns, and the often lackluster

---

[36] John S. Mbiti writes, "Every African who has grown up in the traditional environment will, no doubt, know something about this mystical power, which often is experienced, or manifests itself, in magic, witchcraft, divination and mysterious phenomena that seem to defy even immediate scientific explanations" (1970, 253–54).

singing of the mission churches, Lenshina's Bemba-style hymn-texts, sung vigorously to traditional Bemba melodies, ignited interest throughout the region. Taylor and Lehmann asserted that "the most important medium in the Lumpa congregations [was] not the spoken but the sung word" (255).

Lenshina established headquarters at a village near the Lubwa mission named Kasomo, which she re-named *Sioni* (Zion). Sioni became the center of pilgrimage, with the villagers playing host to thousands. Pilgrims came with tribute objects and monetary gifts, and they contributed labor in Sioni's fields, growing food to support the large numbers of people now present in the district. They also gave tribute labor to build what became known as the Lumpa Cathedral, "one of the largest church buildings in Central Africa" (Van Binsbergen 1981, 289).[37]

Sioni also became the center of an expansive network of church-related activities, including a church-operated chain of stores, traveling choirs, and a fleet of cars and trucks (Bond 1979, 143; Van Binsbergen 1981, 292). By 1959 there were 148 Lumpa congregations, with most of these in Chinsali district (Bond 1979, 143).

In 1957 or 1958, the Lumpa Church presented the colonial government with a document called "The Laws of the Lumpa Church," which attempted to present Lumpa as a peaceful, law-abiding church. The document declared that Lumpa was "not an organization to make unruly behavior with the laws of the country." Although some members displayed suspicion of westerners, the laws called for no racial discrimination. The laws exhorted members to refrain from "coveting, witchcraft, stealing, sorcery, witches, drunkenness, bad songs and all primitive dances." The laws also forbade polygamy and the veneration of ancestors, and such practices as beer-drinking. The use of tobacco was discouraged, but not forbidden (Taylor and Lehmann 1961, 253).

In the now-independent association, Alice Lenshina's role as prophet-founder and leader of Lumpa was unquestioned. Taylor and Lehmann's reported: "Lenshina was the undisputed head of the group. 'We have to ask Mama' repeatedly proved the answer to a request" (254). In most respects, Lenshina's leadership role appeared to be similar to that of a high Bemba chief. People began bringing her their legal disputes, thus by-passing the hereditary chiefs as well as the administrative authority of the colonial government. Very substantial donations poured in from branch churches, along with a steady stream of pilgrims. This chief-like status, and the fact that between 70%–90% of the people of Chinsali district now professed allegiance to the Lumpa Church, brought her into conflict

---

[37] For a photographic essay on the now long-abandoned site of Sioni and its cathedral, see Barratt (2003). For additional photographs of Sioni and the cathedral, as well as contemporary newspaper accounts on a website, see *The Lumpa Uprising* (2003). The cathedral is depicted in the articles dated 31 July and 1 August.

with Bemba Senior Chief Nkula, who came to view Lumpa as a rival to his own authority (Wilson 1973, 96).

Despite the Lumpa law against racial discrimination, there was a strong anti-western orientation. The local Protestant and Roman Catholic missions were considered, if not false churches, then at least ineffectual ones. Church meetings were used to promote the United Nationalist Independence Party (UNIP), the party that would comprise the postcolonial Zambian regime in October of 1964. UNIP was founded in 1959 by Kenneth Kaunda, also of Chinsali district, the son of a Free Church evangelist and schoolteacher at the Lubwa mission (Bond 1979, 143). In 1961 Taylor and Lehmann reported that the African National Congress (ANC) had gone on record declaring the Lumpa Church as "the only real African church suitable for their members" (1961, 254).

Taylor and Lehmann also reported that "the most active of [Lumpa's] priests in the Copperbelt happened to be the brother of an ANC secretary" (1961, 254). This remark refers to Robert Kaunda, brother of Kenneth Kaunda, who had been an ANC activist before he founded UNIP. Kenneth Kaunda would go on to become the first president of independent Zambia (Wilson 1973, 99; cf. Alexander 1998, 360–61). The Kaunda family was from the same district as Alice Lenshina, Kenneth Kaunda had even gone to school with her, and his father, David Kaunda, had been the founder of the Lubwa Mission (Musambachme 1998). Thus the founders of both Lumpa and UNIP had roots in the same Lubwa mission church. Unfortunately, this positive relationship with UNIP would suffer reversal, with dire consequences.

OPPOSITION TO LUMPA

Lenshina's prophet-movement began within the confines of the Scottish mission church, but as we have seen, it did not remain so. Taking an implicitly anti-western stance, Lumpa claimed superiority over the western mission churches, both Protestant and Roman Catholic. Thus the mission churches constituted the first opposition to Lumpa. Opposition also arose from the British colonial government. Colonial authorities were suspicious of Lumpa in part because of its similarity to the disruptive and illegal witch-finding movements of the recent past. In 1956 a visiting Roman Catholic priest was accused by a Lumpa member of being a witch. The colonial authorities quickly arrested the accuser. The arrest, however, was protested by a number of Lumpa leaders, including Petro Chitankwa, Lenshina's husband. In the public disturbance that followed he and sixty-four others were arrested; Petro was sentenced to two years imprisonment at hard labor (Roberts 1970, 534; Van Binsbergen 1981, 294; Bryan R. Wilson 1973, 96). Moreover, by 1958 it was clear that Lenshina had no intention of registering the Lumpa Church with the colonial government as an approved church (Brockman 1994).

More opposition arose from the rivalry between Lenshina and the local chiefs, including the Bemba's Senior Chief, Nkula. When large numbers of Lumpa moved permanently into Chinsali district, they began to erect their own villages without authorization from the chiefs, who viewed such activities as under their exclusive control (Van Binsbergen 1981, 289). Moreover, Lumpa members in the region became increasingly separatistic, withdrawing into their own unauthorized villages. As charismatic, theocratic authority began to displace traditional authority, the prophetess increasingly became the center of her followers' political, as well as religious, lives. The unauthorized settlements became a major source of tension not only with the local chiefs, but also with the non-Lumpa people of the region. Further tensions with the non-Lumpa arose when Lenshina attempted to lease land in the district, presumably for settlement purposes. The non-Lumpa likely feared Lumpa's dominance in their district. The first violent clashes with the police arose over these unauthorized settlements in 1959 (Van Binsbergen 1981, 293; 307).

At the same time that these tensions surfaced, Lumpa began to experience a sharp decline in membership. In the years 1958–1964, Lumpa dropped from about 70%–90% of the rural population in Chinsali district, to about 10% of the rural population (Bryan R. Wilson 1973, 96; Van Binsbergen 1981, 289). Meanwhile, local membership in the mission churches and in UNIP was on the rise. The reasons for Lumpa's precipitous decline are not clear. Perhaps the demands of tribute labor were perceived as unreasonable—it was in 1958 that the Lumpa Cathedral was completed, at the cost of enormous amounts of tribute labor, donated building supplies, and financial gifts. Moreover, villagers in the Chinsali district complained of the great demands upon their hospitality made by the large numbers of pilgrims. Perhaps the emphatically theocratic governance of Lumpa alienated many members. Perhaps the increasingly separatist stance vis-à-vis the traditional authority of the chiefs was negatively perceived. In any case, Lenshina's movement came to be regarded with more and more hostility by more and more Bemba.

In 1962, as the prophetess arrogated more authority for herself, she forbade her members to participate in UNIP. Lenshina's new separatist prohibition took place when, returning home from a year's journey visiting urban Lumpa congregations, she discovered her own congregation in decline and local UNIP membership on the rise. She swiftly staged a public burning of UNIP party cards, and issued Lumpa membership "tickets" instead. Participation in nontheocratic government was interpreted as sin; all government was to be theocratic government; and Lenshina was the prophetic voice of divine authority. Thus, neither the local chiefs, nor the colonial authorities, nor the rising UNIP could be recognized or legitimated. UNIP was evil. Accordingly, when in 1962 UNIP activists were killed in conflict with the colonial authorities, Lenshina declared that they would be damned (Van Binsbergen 1981, 294).

In the same year, the Lumpa of various districts flatly refused to obey the laws of the chiefdoms or to observe kinship obligations. The denial of kinship obligations is remarkable, given the strong ties of extended family relationships in most African social contexts, "one of the strongest forces in traditional African life" (Mbiti 1970, 135). The denial of kinship obligations indicates that the remaining Lumpa now viewed their new faith-created communities as a new family or tribe under a new chief, Alice Lenshina. Lumpa was closing in on itself, becoming increasingly autonomous, moving toward social implosion.[38]

Violence now broke out between Lumpa and UNIP. Despite the Gandhian principles held by Kenneth Kaunda (Van Binsbergen 1981, 268), local UNIP members in Chinsali district seem to be the instigators. Van Binsbergen concluded that UNIP members started the violence, and did more violence than Lumpa members (295 and Table 8.1). UNIP also responded violently to members of other nonpolitical religious groups who refused membership, such as the Watchtower societies (Bryan R. Wilson 1973, 100 n. 60).

By 1963 Lumpa members refused to obey the laws of the colonial government, a move that represented a radical break from the stance represented in the "Laws of the Lumpa Church" (Bond 1987, 513). 1963 was also an election year, marked by increased activity by UNIP, aggressively recruiting members and eliciting voters. Both UNIP and Lumpa were pressing for membership.

It was at this time that Lumpa took on a new, radical feature—imminent millennialism. Millennialism had hardly been apparent in Lumpa's earlier years. Now Lenshina sent messages to Lumpa congregations and villages, declaring that the end of the world was at hand; the Lumpa should leave their worldly goods and homes behind, and build holy villages exclusively for themselves as they awaited the end (Bond 1979, 151). By 1964, Chinsali district alone had twenty-two illegal settlements; Kasama district had six, Isoka district had three, and Lundazi district had six, for a total population of more than 6,700 adults. One reason for the rise of these settlements was fear of UNIP. UNIP had won the elections; Lumpa now feared retaliation (Bryan R. Wilson 1973, 100 n. 60).

In 1964 Lenshina now forbade Lumpa parents to send their children to school. Lumpa's separatist anti-education stance must have proved deeply offen-

---

[38] Social implosion occurs when "part of a relatively open social network becomes markedly more closed.... Implosion is a kind of schism, except that it represents secession from society in general rather than merely from a religious organization" (Stark and Bainbridge 1996, 185). "The primary consequence of a social implosion is to reduce greatly the group's stakes in conformity ... to the conventional moral order" (192).

sive to UNIP leadership, since UNIP's political program called for an intense focus on public education as the chief solution to central Africa's problems. Violence again broke out (Van Binsbergen 1981, 295). In that year it became clear that Lumpa would refuse to acknowledge any outside authority whatsoever (Bond 1979, 151). Kenneth Kaunda, who would soon become the prime minister of the new government, issued an ultimatum that the Lumpa dismantle their unauthorized settlements and return to their home villages. Instead, the Lumpa fortified them. Social implosion was nearly complete. These villages became holy ground to the Lumpa; protecting them became a holy calling.

In July of 1964 Kaunda's ultimatum's deadline arrived. Police officers visited a Lumpa village in Chinsali district. The villagers assumed that they had come to dismantle the village; the Lumpa attacked and killed two of them. Seventeen Lumpa villagers were also killed in what newspaper accounts called a "pitched battle" (*The Lumpa Uprising* 2003, 1–2; Van Binsbergen 1981, 293). This battle proved to be the beginning of a mass insurrection by the Lumpa. Lumpa groups staged numerous attacks against non-Lumpa villages, killing even the women and children. When confronted by police or government troops and told to surrender, they fought ferociously, despite their primitive weapons. Both men and women alike fought for Lumpa. Many believed that their baptisms would render them invulnerable to bullets. Battles raged from July until October, the very month that Zambian independence took effect (*The Lumpa Uprising* 2003). Kaunda gave orders that troops were to spare human life whenever possible. He later confessed to Van Binsbergen that the decision "to use force against the Lumpas ... was the hardest decision of his life" (1981, 267).

Massacre was inevitable. Spears, arrows and a few muzzle-loaders were no match for the automatic weapons wielded by government troops. Bond reports:

> As the Lumpa attacked they shouted, "Jericho!" in the belief that the walls of evil would tumble down and that they would triumph in battle. As they were shot they shouted, "Hallelujah!" in the belief that they would be transported directly to heaven, only to return to rule the world. (1987, 513)

Soldiers stated that the Lumpa fought with a ferocity they had never seen before. Nonetheless, the Lumpa were defeated. Many fought to the death. Lenshina herself came out of hiding in August and surrendered to the authorities. Sioni was destroyed and its cathedral left desolate. The Lumpa Church was banned. Its prophetess and many of its surviving people went to prison. Estimates of the number of people killed range from 700 (Bond 1987, 513) to 1,500 (Van Binsbergen 1981, 266).

AFTERMATH

In the years after the defeat, the Zambian government had to face the difficult task of reintegrating former Lumpa members into society. Bond's study of the Lumpa uprising included a focus on the resettlement of Lumpa survivors (1979, 153–55). He noted that urban Lumpa did not participate in the insurrection and some Lumpa groups in other rural districts also remained peaceful. Participation was heaviest in Chinsali district. Some of the Lumpa groups outside Chinsali district were taken into custody despite their nonviolent behavior. The Zambian authorities decided to resettle most of the former Lumpa in their home districts under their original chiefdoms. Resettlement plans were only partly successful. After their release, many Lumpa loyalists fled north to the Congo, where just across the border a remnant of the Lumpa Church maintained a tenuous existence. Among these fugitives were many of the agnate kin of Lenshina. By 1968 the Lumpa remnant numbered some 19,000 (154).

In 1968 the Zambian government declared an amnesty for all returning Lumpa, but few responded. Lenshina herself remained in prison until 1975. Her release was intended as a gesture of conciliation toward the Lumpa, but the church remained a banned organization in Zambia, and Lenshina's movements were restricted (Mulenga 2003, 1). Two years later, after leading an illegal worship service, Lenshina was arrested again. By that time, however, "the movement was effectively dead" (Brockman 1994). Most Lumpa had either rejoined their old churches, or joined new movements. Having rejoined a mission church herself, Lenshina died in 1978, disgraced and discredited by most of her former followers.

SOCIOLOGICAL ASSESSMENT OF THE LUMPA CHURCH

Several sociological typologies describe the Lumpa Church of Alice Lenshina. Lumpa can be considered a *nativistic* cult, but because of its strict proscription against polygamy, witchcraft-protection and the cult of ancestors, Lumpa cannot be considered a purely nativist movement. Lumpa combined both European and traditional African elements. Elements of old-culture revival are seen, for example, in the thaumaturgical reponse regarding sickness and witchcraft, and in the replacement of European hymns by Bemba hymn-texts and melodies. Much of the Lumpa value-system was imported from Europe; but Lumpa separated itself from selected manifestations of western culture, such as the mission churches, the white missionaries, Methodist hymnals, and the like. Nativism, then, describes some important features of Lumpa. Its nativism enabled it to become, for a time, the center of social power in rural Chinsali and elsewhere in Northern Province. Lumpa syncretistically adapted the mission-church faith and social organization to traditional African concerns such as witchcraft protection and thaumaturgy, and adapted the worship practices of Scottish Presbyterians to express Bemba traditions and values more completely.

Bryan R. Wilson considered Lumpa a *thaumaturgical* cult, but an unusual one (1973, 94–100). It was unusual among thaumaturgical movements in that it developed an effective organization over a large territory. Lumpa was a thaumaturgical cult with a substantial social organization, in imitation of the model of the western mission church, controlled from the center—Lenshina's holy village of Sioni.

As an intensification of the teachings of the Presbyterian Free Church of Scotland, Lumpa can also be considered a *reformist* cult. In contrast to the Scottish mission at Lubwa, Lumpa demanded—and obtained—a purer form of obedience than is usually seen in the social context of the mission church. But as Lumpa withdrew, it turned more revolutionist. The revolutionist response, according to Wilson, expects a supernaturally wrought destruction and re-creation of the world, thus eliminating evil forever (23). Alienated from the centers of social power in new-born Zambia, and withdrawn into its own barricaded villages in social implosion, it awaited its own salvation from on high and the destruction of all else.

Lumpa can also be considered a *revitalization* movement. Lumpa, however, is a revitalization cult that failed; it did not produce a new steady-state culture. Lumpa did experience a period of revitalization, but not all the tasks of revitalization were accomplished.[39] The last years of Lumpa's trajectory are years of steady marginalization; and Lumpa's adaptive strategies, instead of leading to a new steady state, brought about its violent demise at the hands of UNIP and the Zambian military. As such, Alice Lenshina's Lumpa Church movement is one of the most spectacular examples known to history of a failed revitalization movement.

In certain respects the rise of the Lumpa Church is analogous to the rise of Islam in the generation of Muhammad. Both were social movements led by prophetic claimants; both took place in a social context of detribalization; both were revitalization movements; both movements became militarized in the face of perceived threats to their survival. A key difference lies in the fact that the fledgling Islamic *umma* of Medina won its military struggle against the Meccans. If UNIP had been armed only with the spears, axes and arrows of the rural Bemba, Lumpa may have proven victorious in Northern Province and become the center of a new religiously based empire, like the Islamic empire of the late seventh century. But Lumpa, as we have seen, was defeated and radically delegitimated by the UNIP-led government.

---

[39] Wallace described the stages of the revitalization processual type (1969a, 36–45).

The social location trajectory of the Lumpa movement thus begins with an ordinary Bemba woman, Alice Lenshina, who claimed extraordinary experiences of divine revelation. She became the center of a movement that could not or would not be contained by the Lubwa mission, and took a social role both as prophet-speaker and as *de facto* chief of the new multitribal community network of the Lumpa Church, centered at Kasomo/Sioni village in Chinsali district. Receiving massive legitimation[40] from Bemba and non-Bemba alike, she became the single most powerful individual in Chinsali district, and one of the most powerful individuals in Northern Rhodesia. Lenshina was, for a time, the very center of a new society that transcended traditional tribal limitations and that trumped traditional authority structures. Among the Bemba and other Copperbelt tribal peoples, Lumpa sought to supplant the long-legitimated loyalties of family, kin, tribe, and chiefdom with its own new, radical redefinitions. At the same time, UNIP was also casting its net, seeking support and legitimation in the same geographical areas as Lumpa, and from the same peasant class (Van Binsbergen 1981, 296).

Lumpa's ascendancy was not to last. Perhaps the movement declined through its own sheer weight—its extreme demands upon loyalty, time, tribute labor, gifts, and hospitality. Perhaps the natural ties of family and tribe proved too strong for the voluntarist ties of the Lumpa Church to survive. Perhaps there were other circumstances within Lumpa that rendered it such that it could not be sustained by its thaumaturgical mode or sustain its revitalization stance. Or perhaps the reason for Lumpa's failure lies in forces external to it: the rise of Zambian nationalism and UNIP's determined opposition to apolitical religious groups. Perhaps it was for all of these reasons that Lumpa failed. The ultimate answer need not concern us.

Anthony Wallace's revitalization theory—published originally in 1956, several years before the Lumpa Church crisis of 1964—could well have served as a prediction of the disaster. Regarding the "adaptation" task of his processual model, Wallace wrote:

> The movement is a revolutionary organization and almost inevitably will encounter some resistance. Resistance may in some cases be slight and fleeting but more commonly is determined and resourceful, and is held either by a powerful faction within the society or by agents of a dominant foreign society. The movement may therefore have to use various strategies of adaptation [including] force.... In instances where organized hostility to the movement develops, a crystalization of counter-hostility against unbeliev-

---

[40] For the concept of legitimation in society, see Adams and Mikelson (1987).

ers frequently occurs, and emphasis shifts from cultivation of the ideal to combat against the unbeliever. (1969a, 44)

But Lumpa lost membership in a decline nearly as swift as its sudden rise. Ordinary Bemba in rural villages lost faith in Lenshina as a true prophetess, and lost faith in Lumpa as a valid alternative to the mission churches.

By 1962 Lumpa had become a marginalized endogenous minority religion. By the middle of 1964 Lumpa had become a barricaded group, living apart in its own walled-off, armed villages in social implosion. By August the church was officially banned, and its prophetess imprisoned. By October it was decimated, defeated, and discredited by the vast majority of Bemba and by other Zambian tribes. Thus, the movement that once attained central-authority status among the Bemba now lost all claim, except to a relatively small group of close supporters dominated by those with matrilinear family ties to Lenshina herself. The social location trajectory of Lumpa, from rise to apex to decline to nadir—or from periphery to center to periphery—took eleven years, from November 1953 to October 1964. Alice Lenshina remained a discredited figure until her death in 1978.

CONCLUSION TO THE FIVE CASE STUDIES

As these case studies of various prophetic figures and movements have shown, prophetic claimants indeed occupy a widely variable range of social locations. Prophetic claimants operate at the social center, or along the social periphery, or at points along the spectrum. Prophetic charisma cannot be restricted to the margin, as an outside force for social disruption, agitating for revolutionary change. Prophetic charisma may appear anywhere. The data from sociologists of religion, cultural anthropologists, and ethnographers about prophetic claimants and their movements confirms the theoretical stance about charisma and prophecy set out by the revisers of Weber. As Theodore E. Long had written:

> *Prophecy may arise within established groups and institutions* rather than just among the alienated and marginal.... *[P]rophecy need not always await internal societal crisis* but may also arise as an expression of group solidarity. (1986, 7, emphases original)[41]

---

[41] Bernhard Lang similarly wrote, "Prophetic charisma is to be understood as a power of renewal which breaks out in the middle of traditional structures that are transcended without being destroyed" (1983, 113).

The five case studies stand as evidence. Isaiah Shembe was born into a noted Zulu family, and when he claimed a prophetic calling, was embraced by Zulu culture. Enshrined at Ekuphakameni, the Zulu Zion, Shembism preserved selected features of traditional African life, transformed the lives of innumerable Zulu, and attracted the loyalty of chiefs. However, Shembism became "a museum of old African customs" (Vilakazi 1986, 45). Later, and likely in part as a result this cultural isolation, Shembism would become a marginalized religion of the poor, where it has remained for at least a generation.

Tomo Nyirenda likewise arose at the social center of Nyasa society. He became the central authority prophet for a nativist Nyasa witch-finding movement at the expense of rival Lala and Lamba tribes, but was eventually criminalized and executed, along with his ally and chief, Shaiwila.

Simon Kimbangu, on the other hand, arose in the obscure village of N'Kamba in the lower Congo, but became the focus of a highly institutionalized religion that looks to him as its founding prophet. As a nativistic revitalization movement that succeeded in establishing a new steady-state, Kimbanguism's trajectory moved from periphery to center in the space of forty years. Over its second forty years, it maintained a steady-state social location at the center, despite the turmoils of Congo history.

Muhammad, if the traditional Islamic sources are correct, came from a family with poor clan-protection, but became a respectable caravaneer and merchant. Soon after claiming a prophetic calling, he found himself ostracized by mainstream Meccan society. In Yathrib, however, he attained the social center, from whence he eventually came to dominate the center of Meccan society as well. Muhammad accordingly moved from his status in Meccan commerce, to ostracization over his prophetic claims and demands, to centralization in Yathrib, to a new centralization in Mecca, all in the space of about twenty years. As Seyyed Hossein Nasr wrote, "It was the function of the prophet to be ... the organizer of a new social order with all that such a function implies" (1966, 68). Thus Islam became "the cement of empires" (Gellner 1969, 128).

Like Tomo Nyirenda, Alice Lenshina, too, became criminalized, but only after a meteoric rise in Chinsali district and far beyond. In this she was able to present a considerable challenge to the likewise-rising UNIP-led independence government of her former schoolmate, Kenneth Kaunda, vying for control of the social center of Zambia's Northern Province. Her Lumpa Church movement thus moved from periphery to center and back to the periphery, a failed revitalization movement.

Some of these prophetic figures and movements display or achieve periods of steady-state social location, a kind of homeostasis. These remain at the social center, such as Kimbanguism since the 1960s, or at some degree of critical distance from the center, or at the periphery, such as the *amaNazaretha* in recent years, and are able to maintain their existence in these steady state social locations.

Some prophetic movements arise in complex societies, those in which more than one culture is strongly represented. As we have seen, a single prophetic group or claimant may display different social locations simultaneously, depending upon whether social location is evaluated from endogenous or exogenous perspectives. Muhammad was ostracized at Mecca, but embraced at Medina. This complexity can exist whether in situations of colonial or neocolonial imperialism, or in conditions where rival groups from the same society vie with one another for dominance. Thus Alice Lenshina's Lumpa prophet-movement vied with UNIP for domination in Northern Province of Rhodesia/Zambia, only to collapse in social implosion and massacre.

Steady-state equilibrium cannot account for the social dynamics of all prophetic movements and individuals. Field researchers have traced single prophetic movements within single generations shifting from center to periphery, such as the *amaNazaretha* in recent decades, or from periphery to center, such as Muhammad and Mecca, or from mid-point circumstances to either extreme. These are the changes that I have called social location trajectories. Such trajectories are observable for individual prophetic claimants, and sometimes within impressively brief spans of time.

Because sociologists, cultural anthropologists and field ethnographers have observed such wide variabilities in social location and social location trajectories for modern-day prophetic social dynamics, *it is no longer safe to assume continuity of social location for the biblical prophets and their associated movements*. Nor is it safe to assume that when changes of social location can be discerned in the Bible's prophetic materials, such changes require a change of speaker or author, support group, tradent community or audience society. The biblical data themselves can now be seen to require of us a flexible and polythetic set of potential explanations. These explanations can now exploit a broader range of hypotheses, based upon *prophecy's observable social dynamics,* derived from case studies and the typologies they suggest. Instead of the monothetic hypotheses based on the assumption of change of speaker, author, or tradent, interpreters should now add to their explanatory repertoires *changes in any of the relationships* among speaker(s) or author(s), tradent(s), support group(s) and audience society(ies).

Equipped now with a theoretical base for understanding the operation of prophetic charisma in varying social locations, the examples of the case studies we have examined, mainly from the modern African tribal neocolonial situation, and the new tool of social location trajectory analysis, we are now ready to examine the book of Zechariah, and to determine the social location analysis of the units of the book. Walter Brueggemann writes:

> Pieces of literature should not be studied in isolation nor in terms of mechanical dependence and relationship through a literary process.... [S]pecial attention should be paid to the continuities that flow between various pieces of literature. As a result of social value, use, and transmission, continuities both in terms of cultural context and in terms of theological perspective become decisive for interpretation. (1994, 14)

He adds later:

> A history-of-traditions approach must include a sociological analysis so that we are aware of the social function of each of the traditions, the authority assigned to it, the claims made for it, and the power and social vision deriving from it. (38)

Brueggemann's socially embodied history-of-traditions approach calls forth the social location trajectory analysis contemplated here. It leads to the question raised at the beginning of this dissertation, the issue raised by Michael H. Floyd in 1999 about the sociohistorical matrix that gave birth to the strange fourteen-chaptered form of the book of Zechariah (262). Can a coherent reading of Zechariah be achieved by means of social location trajectory analysis? That is the next stage of the investigation.

4

HAGGAI AND ZECHARIAH: TWO PROPHETS AND TWO BOOKS?

I. THE SOCIOHISTORICAL SETTING

A coherent reading of the book of Zechariah requires us for at least two reasons to pay some attention to Haggai and the book that goes by his name. First, Zechariah the prophet is identified in company with Haggai in Ezra 5–6; there they are together credited, along with certain unspecified "elders," with getting the destroyed Jerusalem temple rebuilt, no mean achievement. Second, the book of Haggai begins with a redactional frame that is continued in Zech 1–8; as Meyers and Meyers argued in their impressive 1987 commentary, the two portions likely once circulated together as a single composite book. The present chapter shall examine both issues: the persons Haggai and Zechariah, along with other identifiable persons and social circumstances in Yehud; and the redactional framework of Haggai–Zech 1–8. Because I have published my views on Haggai elsewhere (Curtis 2003), my treatment of persons and social circumstances here shall come in summary form.

In the study of the social dynamics of prophecy in Persian period Yehud, the book of Haggai finds an important place. Unlike longer books such as Hosea, Micah, or Nahum in which sociological data is slight, the brief Haggai provides us with some valuable evidence regarding the prophet, his intended audience, and, it seems, the actual effect his words had upon his audience society. The presence of an editorial framework (Hag 1:1; 1:15; 2:1, 2:10; 2:20) also gives us some evidence about the redaction history of the document. The linking of Haggai with Zechariah, not only in the historical reminiscences about them in Ezra 5–6, but also in the interwoven editorial framework that I shall discuss below, joining Hag 1–2 to Zech 1–8 as a single composite unity, further provides us with information about the reception history of this prophetic book. Haggai with its editorial framework presents us with a book of oracles in the form of a historical narrative, complete with the names of Yehudean officials and dated to the second regnal year of Darius the Great. Placed within this framework are the five oracles of the prophet.[1] As Petersen writes, "there is sufficient prose to justify the con-

---

[1] On the narrative framework of Haggai, see below, and also Peter R. Ackroyd (1951); W. A. M. Beuken (1967); Rex Mason (1977); and John Kessler (2002, 31–57).

tention that Haggai is fundamentally a narrative that includes a number of prophetic utterances" (1984, 35).[2]

---

[2] Despite its brevity, there is a wealth of literature on this book. Important premodern commentaries include those by Theodore of Mopsuestia (350–428) and John Calvin (1509–1564). Selections from Theodore's commentary are available in Alberto Ferriero's *Twelve Prophets* (2003) in the *Ancient Christian Commentary on Scripture* series. The whole of Theodore's commentary has also recently been published (2004). Calvin's is in need of a modern critical edition, but exists in English (n.d.). Useful commentaries from the nineteenth century include, among others, those by Thomas V. Moore (1856), C. F. Keil (1975 [1868 original]), E. B. Pusey (1892) and George Adam Smith (1928 [1898]). Julius Wellhausen's *Kleine Propheten* (1898) supplies helpful text-critical notes and brief interpretive suggestions. In the twentieth century useful commentaries include those by Hinckley G. Mitchell in ICC (1912), Douglas R. Jones (1962b), Joyce G. Baldwin (1972), Wilhelm Rudolph in KAT (1976), Samuel Amsler in CAT (1981), David L. Petersen in OTL (1984), Ralph L. Smith in WBC (1984), Carol L. Meyers and Eric M. Meyers in AB (1987), Pieter A. Verhoef in NICOT (1987), Carroll Stuhlmueller (1988), Hans Walter Wolff (1988), Henning Graf Reventlow in ATD (1993), Eugene H. Merrill (1994), Paul L. Redditt (1995), J. Alec Motyer (1998), Michael H. Floyd in FOTL (2000), and Marvin A. Sweeney (2000). The most important of these in English are the ones by Mitchell, by Petersen, and by Meyers and Meyers. Significant monographs that discuss Haggai at length include those by T. Chary on Haggai and the Jerusalem cult (1955), Beuken on the tradition-history of Haggai in its alleged pre-Chronistic and Chronistic forms (1967), Ackroyd on temple-building, eschatology, and popular response in Haggai (1968), Paul D. Hanson on the social location of Haggai as an alleged advocate of a Zadokite priestly program (1979), Daniel L. Smith on the sociology of Haggai and the question of the identity of the "impure people" of Hag 2:14 (1989), Janet E. Tollington on tradition and innovation in Haggai (1993), and Jon L. Berquist, who reads Haggai against the backdrop of the impending march of the Persian army through southern Palestine on its way to stop the Egyptian revolt of 519 B.C. (1995). Peter R. Bedford's *Temple Restoration in Early Achaemenid Judah* (2001) provides a sociohistorical analysis of early Yehud as background for Hag and Zech 1–8. John Kessler's *Book of Haggai: Prophecy and Society in Early Persian Yehud* (2002) has conclusions similar to those I advocate here. Significant articles and briefer studies include those by Paul F. Bloomhardt on the "poems" of Haggai (1928), Peter Ackroyd on the editorial framework and selected historical issues (1951, 1952, 1956, 1958), Leroy Waterman on a messianic conspiracy theory involving Haggai, Zechariah, and Zerubbabel (1954), F. S. North on a proposed critical reconstruction of the text of Haggai (1956), Georg Sauer on Zerubbabel (1967), Herbert G. May on the possible identification of "this people" and "this nation" in Hag 2:14 as Samaritans (1968), Rex Mason on the editorial framework of Haggai and on the restoration era (1977, 1982a), Eric M. Meyers on the meaning of priestly *torah* in Hag 2:11 (1983), Richard J. Coggins on the history of Haggai scholarship (1987), Joseph Blenkinsopp on general issues of history and interpretation (1996), and Robert B. Chisholm (2002).

THE EXILIC ERA, 587 B.C.–538 B.C.

To understand Haggai's and Zechariah's roles and social locations in Yehudean life, we must look to the material and social conditions that prevailed in Yehud at the end of the exilic era and during the early years of the return. After their final reprisal raid against Judah in 581 B.C., the Babylonians neglected Judah. There is no literary evidence for a continuing Babylonian presence in the ruined land. The archaeological record likewise reveals virtually no new building projects of any kind in the land for the period from Jerusalem's destruction in 587 B.C. to the time of the first return in about 537 B.C. (Stern 1982; 2001, 348–50). The land, however, was not empty. It was very likely an era of subsistence farming by peasants in a depressed economy, lacking fortified cities and notable leadership, and without the economic means to do much to better their situation. Hence, the first returnees to Yehud entered into quite bleak conditions.

THE ERA OF RETURN, 537 B.C.–432 B.C.

According to the Bible, the events of what we may call the Era of Return depend mainly upon the actions of Persian kings and the efforts of Judeans from exile in the east. Our main historical sources for this period are the prophetic books of Haggai and Zechariah, and the composite historical work, Ezra–Neh.[3] The book of Ezra reports Persian royal activity this way, linking the work of rebuilding to the decrees of kings and to the command of Israel's God:

> The elders of the Jews continued to build and prosper under the preaching of Haggai the prophet and Zechariah, a descendent of Iddo. They finished building the temple according to the command of the God of Israel and the decrees of Cyrus, Darius and Artaxerxes, kings of Persia.[4] The temple was completed on the third day of the month of Adar, in the sixth year of the reign of King Darius.[5] (Ezra 6:14–15)

Many more studies could be cited here. Charles E. Carter's detailed ethnoarchaeological study of Yehud (1999) gives important insights into the social conditions of the Persian period in Palestine.

[3] For discussion of biblical and nonbiblical sources for the period, as well as other historical issues, see Widengren (1977), and more recently Albertz (2002, 112–38).

[4] The mention of Artaxerxes I (465–424 B.C.), whose rule commenced fifty-one years after temple completion, probably refers to royal-sponsored acts of temple maintenance or temple expansion, rather than temple building. The decree in Ezra 4:17–23 is the likely basis for the inclusion of his name here.

[5] That is, March 12, 515 B.C.

The biblical texts also stress the role of exilic Jews. The Judean "prince" Sheshbazzar, the governor Zerubbabel, the high priest Joshua, the prophet Zechariah, the priest-and-scribe Ezra: each of these men arrived in Yehud from Mesopotamia. The "cupbearer of the king," Nehemiah, arrived from the Persian capital Susa. These contributed significantly to the important works of architectural rebuilding or social reconsolidation or religious renewal so necessary to Yehudean life. Compared to the Palestinian Jews, these Jews from exile often had more in the way of material means to stage a "restoration."

SHESHBAZZAR AND ZERUBBABEL

The Ezra–Nehemiah narrative is often maddeningly unclear about chronological order and historical detail. Just who is Sheshbazzar? After introducing him as the "prince"/"noble" of Yehud in Ezra 1:8 (נָשִׂיא לִיהוּדָה),[6] the later historical reminiscence in Ezra 5:14 mentions him as a prior "governor" (פֶּחָה, cognate to "pasha" in Persian) of Yehud. We know nothing more of him, and the attempts to identify him as the Shenazzar of 1 Chr 3:18 have not garnered much support in the past.[7] Even the word "prince"/"noble" (נָשִׂיא) need not denote a Davidide. In Haggai and in Zech 1–8 Zerubbabel is named repeatedly as governor (פֶּחָה) of Yehud, but though named in Ezra–Neh, he never possesses this title there; instead it is borne by Tattanai (Ezra 5:3, 6; 6:6, 13), the governor (פֶּחָה) of Abar-Nahara, Trans-Euphrates, the western administrative district of the large satrapy headed in Babylon.[8] The two names Sheshbazzar and Zerubbabel appear in close proximity in Ezra 1:11 and 2:2, but it is never clearly stated in those texts that the latter succeeded the former as governor of Yehud. Nonetheless, by Ezra 3:2 Zerubbabel seems to be in charge of the civil administration, while his colleague Joshua serves as high priest. Sheshbazzar appears no more except as a memory in 5:14, where at last the title פֶּחָה appears for him.

Despite such problems, the probable meaning of the term פֶּחָה in Haggai–Zech 1–8 is to denote the leader of a subprovince within Abar-Nahara (Briant 2002, 488). Accordingly, Sheshbazzar and later Zerubbabel seem to have been answerable to the governor of Abar-Nahara, who in turn was answerable to the satrap of Babylon. It was very likely at this time that Judah was renamed in

---

[6] H. G. M. Williamson quite plausibly relates the title נָשִׂיא to its use in Num 7, where it appears programmatically to denote the various tribal "princes" who bring offerings, often of silver and gold, for the dedication of the Tabernacle (1985, 18).

[7] James C. VanderKam has recently argued in favor of the identification, citing Greek spellings of Sheshbazzar as Σαναβασσαρος in support, a spelling more akin to Shenazzar, LXX Σανεσαρ, in 1 Chr 3:18 (2004, 6–7).

[8] Thus the title פֶּחָה has a range of meanings in Persian imperial practice, as Pierre Briant has shown (2002, 487–88).

Aramaic, "Yehud," to reflect its rank as a subprovince of the expanding Persian Empire.⁹

Zerubbabel, on the other hand, is well attested. Whether as a son of Pediah (1 Chr 3:19), or as a son of Shealtiel (Hag 1:1, 12, 14; 2:2, 23), both of whom are named in the Davidides' genealogy of 1 Chr 3, it is certain that Zerubbabel was a descendent of Jehoiachin in the line of David, and thus a likely choice as a leader for Yehud. In the event that Sheshbazzar is to be understood as the Shenazzar of 1 Chr 3:18, then Zerubbabel would be his nephew; there would be the beginnings of a once-royal family line in succession as governors of Yehud, a situation the Persians employed elsewhere in their administration. In the next generation, as it seems from the evidence of a seal impression, Zerubbabel's daughter Shelomith, the only Persian period woman mentioned in the Davidide geneaology in 1 Chr 3 (vs. 19), is named "אמה of Elnathan," "maidservant of Elnathan." On another seal in the same cache Elnathan is named as governor (Meyers 1987, 518 n. 8). The title אָמָה denotes either a high official answerable to the governor, or it denotes Shelomith as the Davidide wife of Elnathan, in which case there is a Davidide gubernatorial dynasty in Yehud for at least two generations.

Another matter of debate regarding Sheshbazzar and Zerubbabel is whether Ezra 1–6 narrates a story of one return to Yehud, with Zerubbabel in the company of Sheshbazzar and under his authority, or a story of two returns, with the second one led independently and some years later by Zerubbabel. In my earlier publication on Haggai, I defended the latter view (Curtis 2003, 305–06), based partly on the evidence from Hag 1:2–4 about much new building of residences in the year 520 B.C., and partly on the account in 1 Esdras 5:1–6, where, unlike the murky account in Ezra 1–2, Zerubbabel's return is clearly a second event. Based on this evidence, Zerubbabel's commission under Darius likely took place no earlier than 521 B.C. If so, then Zerubbabel would have been a carefully scrutinized candidate for this office, seeing that his appointment came so soon after the massive revolts that shook the empire upon the accession of Darius in 522 B.C., as attested in the famous Behistun Inscription.¹⁰ During Zerubbabel's tenure in Yehud, Tattanai was the administrative official over Trans-Euphrates (so Ezra 5:3, 6; 6:13), and Hystanes (*Ushtannu*) was the satrap over Babylon and Abar-Nahara (Olmstead 1948, 139; Yamauchi 1990, 156). Olmstead assigns the outset

---

⁹ Following Meyers and Meyers (1987:13–16); but see McEvenue (1981, 353–64) and Stern (1982, 213), who think that early Persian period Yehud was governed from Samaria, and that not until Nehemiah's coming did Yehud gain subprovince rank.
¹⁰ For a photograph and description of the Behistun Inscription, see Yamauchi (1990, 131–34). For the Old Persian text and translation, see Kent (1953, 116–34). For historical-critical analysis of the text see Briant (2002, 99–138).

of Zerubbabel's governorship to 520 B.C. (1948, 136). Haggai's significance begins soon after this second return.

YEHUD: SIZE AND POPULATION

The Yehud in which Haggai and Zechariah carried out their function as prophets was necessarily a smallish place, and probably not well-populated. While both Yehud's boundaries and population size have been debated in recent years, the majority view favors both of the above conclusions. Williamson, considering primarily literary data, concluded that Yehud was less than half the size of the preexilic Kingdom of Judah (1992); Charles E. Carter, relying primarily upon an ethno-archaeological approach, thinks it even smaller than Williamson, lacking the trio of northwestern coastal plains towns of Lod, Hadid, and Ono named in Ezra 2:33, and the Shephelah towns of Gezer, Azekah and Ain Shems (1999, 91; cf. 1994). In either case, the subprovince is no more than about twenty-five to thirty miles wide (40–50 km). In the north Yehud possessed Gibeon, Mizpah and Bethel, but no farther; in the south Yehud did not even possess Hebron or Lachish (Williamson 1992).

As for population, we are likely not to take as definitive the figures totalling about 50,000 people given in Ezra 2:64–65. John Kessler, among others, suggests that the numbers of Ezra 2's population count may well be cumulative over a long period of time, and thus not representative of the period of Zerubbabel (2002, 95). This approach accords well with the results of Carter's meticulous ethno-archaeological study of Persian period Yehud, the most detailed study of its kind (1999). Carter very provisionally suggests a figure of about 13,350 for Persian I, and about 20,650 for Persian II (201). These numbers are a far cry from Joel P. Weinberg's 200,000 minimum (1992), an excessively high number with little basis either in texts or archaeology. For Jerusalem itself, Carter suggests a small population of about 1500 (1999, 321).[11] Even if Carter's numbers for Yehud and Jerusalem are too small, we are ill-advised to alter them radically upward, unless there is new evidence from the ground.

A small and ill-populated Yehud, then, means that attempts to read Haggai and Zechariah as anti-Persian subversive literature, supportive of messianic conspiracy and revolt, are ill-founded. Yehud was incapable of offering any real resistance to Persian power, and everyone knew it (so Briant 2002, 115–16). Secondly, a small Yehud was likely an impoverished Yehud, incapable of mounting a significant system of commerce with the outside world, and incapa-

---

[11] Neh 7:5 notes that Jerusalem, even in 445 B.C., had "few people in it." Later Nehemiah attempted to remedy this situation by drafting one out of every ten men to establish homes inside Jerusalem (11:1).

ble of achieving rapid economic growth. Poverty was widespread, and the payment of taxes a hard burden. Even those who had made the trip from a prosperous Babylon likely expended much or all of their capital on the long journey. Thirdly, inner-community strife was still possible in such a small society, and more likely than active contention over Persian control, but social cohesion may also have been more achievable, as the response to the preaching accounted for in the books of Haggai and Zech 1–8 indicates. Accordingly, it is to this Yehud that Haggai speaks in the second year of Darius, 520 B.C.

HAGGAI THE PROPHET

We possess very limited evidence about the individual named Haggai. Not even a patronym is given, either in this book or in Ezra–Neh. This latter fact may indicate that Haggai derived from the non-*golah* community of Palestinian Jews, the subsistence farmers of forsaken Judah. He is quite well acquainted with the agricultural conditions of the land, a point that leads Beuken to suppose non-*golah* origins as well (1967, 197, 216–17). Rural agrarians who had never been severed from their land were perhaps less likely than the exiled *golah*-Jews to use patronyms. However, Haggai, as his speeches show, was an articulate and perhaps well-educated man. He need not have been literate to produce the stirring speeches now recorded in his book. The address in Hag 2:4 to "all the people of the land" (כָּל־עַם הָאָרֶץ) is, in any case, no respecter of persons. Both *golah* and non-*golah* Jews are included by it, and there is yet no indication of community disruption between the two groups at this time. Haggai addresses all.[12]

This prophetic book is most emphatic that Haggai is a genuine prophet faithfully conveying Yahweh's own message to his people in Yehud. Twenty-six prophetic-word formulae pepper this brief book of less than forty verses, an unusually high density of occurrences.[13] This fact may indicate either that the prophetic word had been lacking for some time, or that there was competition between prophetic claimants, leading to public doubt about their claims. The former view is the far more likely one, given the evidence. Haggai seems to be presented as a new prophet speaking a new word from Yahweh, in a place where there had been long absence of such a word.

---

[12] *Contra* Morton Smith (1971, 113–14) and Hanson (1979, 240–46), but following Meyers and Meyers (1987, 50–51). The book of Ezra–Neh may indicate a later breach.
[13] See the comparative chart in Boda (2000, 298).

HAGGAI'S MESSAGES

Haggai's book contains five oracles given over the space of four months in the second year of Darius, 522 B.C. The five oracles appear at 1:2–11; 1:13b; 2:2–9; 2:11–19; and 2:21–23, introduced by and interlaced with the historical narrative frame. I need discuss only three of them briefly.

The historical context of recent revolt in the empire (522–521 B.C.) supplies a possible motive for these Yehudeans to believe that "the time has not yet come for Yahweh's house to be rebuilt" (Hag 1:2). Perhaps an overly fearful population thought construction efforts would be construed as fortifying the city for a revolt, as was insinuated in Tattenai's letter-report to the king in Ezra 5:7–17. In any case, Haggai sternly confronted this conviction in his first oracle, delivered on the first of Elul, in that second year of Darius, August 29, 520 B.C.:

הָעָם הַזֶּה אָמְרוּ לֹא עֶת־בֹּא עֶת־בֵּית יְהוָה לְהִבָּנוֹת׃
הַעֵת לָכֶם אַתֶּם לָשֶׁבֶת בְּבָתֵּיכֶם סְפוּנִים וְהַבַּיִת הַזֶּה חָרֵב׃

> This people says, "The time has not yet come for Yahweh's house to be rebuilt." Is it time for you yourselves to be living in your paneled houses while this house remains a ruin? (Hag 1:2, 4)

The response to Haggai's stern message was everything the prophet wished. Despite the risky rhetoric, and addressing governor, high priest, and people as a whole, Haggai found himself validated and legitimated as a true prophet. The whole community obeyed his word, and resumed the long-abandoned task of temple reconstruction (Hag 1:12).

It is this very success that led Hanson to speak of the "ignominious path upon which the prophetic office was sent by Haggai and Zechariah" (1979, 247). But this position assumes that good prophets must always stand outside the social center, that prophetic charisma is an outside, revolutionary force. It assumes an idealized view of prophets, that the prophetic task can never be substantially achieved within history by real communities of people. For Hanson, such success means betrayal of office. This is a false assumption. Haggai is an example of a prophet whose social vision prevailed for a time within human society. As such, Haggai shifted from his original stance as a reformist prophet, speaking in rebuke, to become what Robert R. Wilson called a "central intermediary" (1980, 40, 83). He worked for social and religious consolidation of a weak community.[14] As Walter Brueggemann observed:

---

[14] This point is quite overlooked in J. David Pleins's "social visions" discussion of Haggai (2001, 397–99).

Prophetic faith is aimed, in the first instance, at *reconstruction of social reality*. It believes that the world of social transaction is redeemable and subject to change. It affirms, moreover, that human agents can make a difference in the shape of the world.... [T]he prophets are in the first instance *reformist*. (1989, 13, emphases original)

As a reformist prophet, Haggai laid himself open to the risk of rejection and marginalization. But Haggai's work shows that the prophetic word can be embraced by its audience society. Thus, out of reformist beginnings, Haggai's social location trajectory moved to the social center, and he became a central authority prophet. Yet even as a central authority prophet, Haggai maintained the capability of rebuking his community, as is seen in Haggai's fourth oracle.

In Haggai's fourth message (2:11–19), delivered the twenty-fourth day of Kislev (December 18, 520 B.C.),[15] Yahweh commands Haggai to request two priestly rulings regarding matters of ritual defilement.[16] The two rulings provide Haggai with an opportunity once more for stern rebuke:

כֵּן הָעָם־הַזֶּה וְכֵן־הַגּוֹי הַזֶּה לְפָנַי נְאֻם־יְהוָה
וְכֵן כָּל־מַעֲשֵׂה יְדֵיהֶם וַאֲשֶׁר יַקְרִיבוּ שָׁם טָמֵא הוּא

So it is with this people,
and so it is with this nation before me—Yahweh's oracle—
and so it is with all the work of their hands
and whatever they offer there;
it is unclean! (Hag 2:14)

If we take the general context seriously, "this people" (הָעָם־הַזֶּה) and "this nation" (הַגּוֹי הַזֶּה) cannot denote the Samaritan community or other non-Yehudeans in the vicinity,[17] as several interpreters have held, but the Yehudean community itself. Here we see the prophet's independence of judgment, a judgment against his own community when necessary.

---

[15] Sweeney (2000, 550) puts forth the intriguing thought that "the Maccabean rededication of the Temple altar on the twenty-fifth of Kislev" may have been seen "as a fulfillment of Haggai's prophecy."
[16] The NIV misconstrues 2:11, when it says to ask the priests "what the law says." The better interpretation of שְׁאַל־נָא אֶת־הַכֹּהֲנִים תּוֹרָה is that the prophet is requesting a priestly *ruling* on an unresolved question (Meyers, 1983, 71).
[17] *Contra* Wolff (1988, 92–94), representing a long tradition of German scholarship. The same view is found in Olmstead's *History of the Persian Empire* (1948, 137–38), but this interpretation requires a substantial, speculative recasting of the text. See also the exegetical discussions in May (1968) and Daniel L. Smith (1989, 180–97).

Perhaps Haggai, as Meyers and Meyers suggest, "regards the people as 'unclean' or 'defiled' because the temple is not yet completed and because the uncleanness that abounds cannot yet be restrained" (1987, 57; also Sweeney 2000, 2:351). Whatever the correct solution to this interpretive puzzle may be, Haggai is far from incapable of critiquing his community. The sternness we saw in Haggai's first oracle we see again in his fourth.

Haggai's last oracle anticipates the eschatological shaking of heaven and earth. The much-contested oracle announces the election of Zerubbabel to status as a servant of Yahweh with an eschatological role. As Meyers and Meyers rightly point out, this "naming of a historical personage to figure in God's eschatological purpose is unique in Hebrew prophecy" (1987, 68):

בַּיּוֹם הַהוּא נְאֻם־יְהוָה צְבָאוֹת
אֶקָּחֲךָ זְרֻבָּבֶל בֶּן־שְׁאַלְתִּיאֵל עַבְדִּי נְאֻם־יְהוָה
וְשַׂמְתִּיךָ כַּחוֹתָם
כִּי־בְךָ בָחַרְתִּי נְאֻם יְהוָה צְבָאוֹת

"On that day"—oracle of Yahweh of the heavenly armies—
"I will take you, Zerubbabel, son of Shealtiel, my servant,"
—oracle of Yahweh—
"and I will make you like a signet ring,
for I have chosen you,"
—oracle of Yahweh of the heavenly armies. (Hag 2:23)

Leroy Waterman took this text as evidence of Zerubbabel's involvement in an anti-Persian messianic conspiracy in Yehud (1954). A. T. Olmstead, only a little more soberly, took Haggai as a fanatical zealot stirring up revolt, only to be rebuffed by the *Realpolitik* of a cautious and cagey Zerubbabel (1948, 135–41). John W. Betlyon writes that Zerubbabel and Haggai both disappeared because they "flirted with nationalistic zeal, a move that must have angered" the Persians (2006, 21). John D. W. Watts suggested that the suffering servant of Isa 53 was actually Zerubbabel himself, wrongfully executed by the Persians in response to messianic hopes like those perhaps expressed in Hag 2:23 (1987, 222–32).

Paul F. Bloomhardt's reconstruction (1928), that Zerubbabel headed a full-fledged Judean revolt against Persia in the aftermath of the death of Cambyses and amid the turmoil of widespread anti-Darius insurrection, like these other proposals, fails on chronological grounds. With the exception of Egypt, which was not subdued until 519 B.C., the revolts were all suppressed by November 27, 521 B.C., a date well in advance of Haggai's earliest oracle, given on August 29, 520 B.C. The day of Haggai's allegedly rebellious fifth oracle, December 18, 520 B.C, was more than a year after Darius had secured the empire. As we have seen, a small and ill-populated Yehud could scarcely raise the resources to stage a revolt, and against an empire that was already well-consolidated. They had trouble enough building a temple.[18]

These revolt-oriented interpretations also overlook two important features of the text. First, in Hag 2:21, Yahweh's command for the prophet to address Zerubbabel appears not with his good Yehudean patronym, but with his official Persian-bestowed title: אֱמֹר אֶל־זְרֻבָּבֶל פַּחַת־יְהוּדָה לֵאמֹר, "Speak to Zerubbabel, Governor of Yehud, saying...." The address, accordingly, presupposes Persian loyalty. Second, and as we shall see more about below, the editorial framework with its Darius-era dating also presupposes Persian loyalty. Hence, both the redactor and the prophet agree that Persian loyalty characterized the time, a loyalty all the more likely if Yehud is indeed small. The oracle then affirms Yehudean loyalty to Persia, but looks beyond to a time when Yahweh shall enact the events of the eschaton.[19] As Meyers and Meyers suggest in this regard, "the rebuilding of the temple meant the reestablishment of the kingdom of God and not of man" (1987, 82). In that day Zerubbabel shall become "like [Yahweh's] signet ring" (חוֹתָם), reversing the negative judgment on the Davidides announced in Jer 22:24. Zerubbabel, the Persian-loyalist governor, is the one in whom Yahweh reclaimed the Davidic line for service in the mysterious eschaton.

AFTERMATH

The fate of Haggai is unknown. After his fifth oracle he drops out of the picture without another word. There is the prospect, however, of one further piece of knowledge. Two months after Haggai's first oracle and in the month before his last, Zech 1:1 reports that Yahweh's word came to Zechariah in the eighth month of that year. The two prophets' oracles thus intersected in Jerusalem for at least three weeks and perhaps as many as seven, and in much the same cause. Though Zechariah has more concerns than Haggai's book demonstrates, they both shared a passionate commitment to the great project of temple reconstruction.[20] This constellation of careers and concerns naturally suggests the prospect that Haggai commenced a Jerusalemite prophetic movement, one in

---

[18] Sweeney thinks Haggai's meaning to be that once Yahweh has overthrown the Persians, Zerubbabel would sit on the Davidic throne, throne of a world empire (2000 2:553–55). This interpretation has the benefit of placing the destruction of Persian rule not in Zerubbabel's hands, but in Yahweh's.

[19] For discussion of the difficulties of defining eschatology in studies of the Old Testament, see Magne Saebø (1998, 209–18). For a book-length development of Old Testament eschatology, see Donald E. Gowan (1986).

[20] But see Mark Boda (2003), who sees in Zechariah, especially Zech 7–8 a critical distancing from the temple-construction project.

which Zechariah became a willing partner or disciple. What, then, do we know about Zechariah?

Zechariah 1:1 identifies him as Zechariah ben Berechiah ben Iddo. Ezra 5:1 and 6:14, on the other hand, identify him as Zechariah ben Iddo, a different patronymic. Iddo, we know, was a chief priest, one among several who returned with Joshua the high priest and with Zerubbabel the governor, as Neh 12:4 indicates. Nehemiah 12 goes on to name the high priest and chief priests of the next generation in vss. 12–21. There the priestly successor to Iddo is not Berechiah, but Zechariah. Perhaps Berechiah died young, and Zechariah was raised by his grandfather, and hence was known as ben-Iddo. As I have argued previously (Curtis 2003, 319), the indication that his grandfather Iddo was serving as a chief priest in 520 B.C. suggests that Zechariah was still a young man in that year. A number of commentators over the years have even supposed that he was "that young man" (הַנַּעַר הַלָּז) of Zech 2:8's third night vision (so Merrill 1994, 115), though this view seems unlikely, and the term seems to apply to an angel within the vision, rather than to the prophet. As Reventlow writes, "den zweiten Engel übermittelten Botschaft ist nicht Sacharja ... sodern der Mann im Bild" (1993, 47). Nevertheless, the data about Iddo and Zechariah in Neh 12 strongly indicate that Zechariah would have been a young man when he began his prophetic career in 520 B.C.

That conclusion suggests the further thought that Zechariah likely outlived Haggai and thus became his prophetic successor. This supposition may also provide the reason why we have no more words from Haggai after December 18, 520 B.C. Perhaps Haggai died soon after, leaving Zechariah as successor prophet and tradent in Jerusalem. The hypothesis of Zechariah as tradent for Haggai may then help account for the joint redaction of their two works, Hag 1–2 and Zech 1–8, as one composite book. This thesis gains some force when we notice that some of the editorial framework in Zech 1–8 appears unexpectedly in first-person form, as in Zech 4:8, 6:9, 7:4, and 8:18, and that some passages in Zech 1–8 are clearly dependent upon Haggai, as in Zech 8:9–12, and remark favorably upon his role in Jerusalem's temple-building project, as in Zech 8:9.

The close personal connection between these two prophets in Yehud may now be reflected in the composite literary connection in Haggai–Zech 1–8, a token of how they came to be embraced as central authority prophets by their audience society and its leaders, and how their prophetic walk took them both together, for a time, up the steep and stony road of Zion's hard obedience.

II. ESCHATOLOGICAL EXPECTATION AND THE DATE FORMULAE IN HAGGAI AND ZECHARIAH

The books of Haggai and Zechariah appear in a unique form in the Hebrew Bible. They are the only prophetic books to share the same narrative framework.

This narrative framework is characterized by (1) *introductory formulae* to the units of prophetic oracles and visions, and (2) unusually specific *date formulae* that typically report each unit's year, month and day. These dates are keyed to the regnal years of the Persian monarch Darius, and can be precisely calculated to the period from August 29, 520 B.C. to December 7, 518 B.C.[21] The date formulae, found in Hag 1:1, 15–2:1, 2:10, 2:20 and Zech 1:1, 1:7 and 7:1, frame all the Haggai material and half the Zechariah material, up through chapter 8, and it is these formulae that this half of the chapter analyzes.

As is well known, these two prophetic units, Hag 1–2 and Zech 1–8 also share a prevailing interest in the restoration of postexilic Jerusalem, and specifically in the project of temple-restoration. These two phenomena, one literary (the framework) and the other ideological (the temple-building interest), set this block of prophetic material apart from the preceding prophetic material—the preexilic and exilic prophetic collection that forms the early corpus of the Book of the Twelve—as well as from the concluding block of postexilic prophecy now found in Zech 9–14 and Malachi. These observations, coupled with the observation that Zech 9–14 lacks both of these characteristics, form the basis for the now common view that both Hag 1–2 and Zech 1–8 once circulated together as an independent book, in a composite editorial unity.[22]

The characteristic date formulae read, with modest variations, as follows:

CHART 4.1
DATE FORMULA IN HAGGAI–ZECHARIAH

בִּשְׁנַת X לְדָרְיָוֶשׁ הַמֶּלֶךְ בַּחֹדֶשׁ X בְּיוֹם X לַחֹדֶשׁ
הָיָה דְבַר־יְהוָה בְּיַד־X הַנָּבִיא לֵאמֹר:

In the X year of Darius the king
in the X month
on the X day [of the month]
Yahweh's word came by/to X the prophet, saying:

The variations appear as expansions, contractions, and changes in the order of elements, but the formula remains nonetheless recognizable throughout the corpus, giving the whole an overarching unity in literary style. It is in this form

---

[21] Dates have been calculated using the tables in Parker and Dubberstein (1942).
[22] Hans Walter Wolff's Haggai commentary (1988) ignores this important issue.

that Haggai–Zech 1–8 come down to us, augmented by the later prophecies now found in chs. 9–14, which were added to the earlier composite work.²³

DATE FORMULAE IN THE PROPHETIC BOOKS

What purpose could be served by arranging Haggai–Zech 1–8 in such a chronologically defined form?²⁴ This question can be answered only after a review of chronological notation in the Hebrew prophetic books.²⁵ I omit discussion of the more general types of chronological notices found, for example, in the opening headings of the eighth-century prophetic books of Hosea, Amos, Micah, and Isaiah (for which see Freedman 1987, 9–26). Chronological headings for particular oracles and events appear for the first time in Isa 1–39 (6:1; 7:1; 20:1; 36:1; 38:1; 39:1). These six headings present only generic chronological information, sometimes with and sometimes without the regnal year formulae: "the year that King Uzziah died" (6:1), "the fourteenth year of King Hezekiah" (36:1), and "In those days Hezekiah became sick" (38:1). Aside from the ones listed above, no such notations appear elsewhere in these books.²⁶

Like Hosea, Amos, Micah, and Isaiah, the book of Jeremiah begins with a formulaic introductory notice, dating the book to the reigns of Judean kings:

דִּבְרֵי יִרְמְיָהוּ . . .
אֲשֶׁר הָיָה דְבַר־יְהוָה אֵלָיו בִּימֵי יֹאשִׁיָּהוּ . . . בִּשְׁלֹשׁ־עֶשְׂרֵה שָׁנָה לְמָלְכוֹ
וַיְהִי בִּימֵי יְהוֹיָקִים . . . עַד־תֹּם עַשְׁתֵּי עֶשְׂרֵה שָׁנָה לְצִדְקִיָּהוּ . . .
עַד־גְּלוֹת יְרוּשָׁלִַם בַּחֹדֶשׁ הַחֲמִישִׁי ס

The words of Jeremiah ... to whom Yahweh's word came in the days of Josiah ... in the thirteenth year of his reign. It also came in the days of Jehoiakim ... and until the end of the eleventh year of Zedekiah ... until the captivity of Jerusalem in the fifth month. (1:1–3).

---

²³ Proposed dates for Zech 9–14 now bring this corpus into the early Persian Period, making possible new proposals regarding its relationship to Haggai–Zech 1–8. Andrew Hill's historical-linguistic investigation of the Deutero-Zechariah corpus yields a date of "ca. 520–450 or better 515–458 b.c. (sic)" (1982, 32); Freedman's (1976; 1991, 60) canonical investigations led him similarly to propose ca. 500 B.C. I shall discuss these proposals in chapter eight.
²⁴ For an alternative to the proposal given below, see Mason (1977).
²⁵ To my knowledge, no comprehensive discussion of this subject exists. See Beuken (1967, 21–26) for a brief review of the issues, and Kessler (2002, 42–44) for a different view than that given above.
²⁶ No date formulae of any kind appear in Isa 40–66, nor in Joel, Obadiah, Jonah, Nahum, and Habakkuk. Zephaniah's heading (1:1) relates the book to "the days of Josiah." The remaining prophetic books with date formulae are discussed below.

At least two new features appear here, however. (1) For the first time in the prophetic canon the opening heading specifies *particular regnal years* for the prophet's career. (2) For the first time in prophetic chronology a particular month is mentioned, the month of Jerusalem's capture.

Like Isaiah, but unlike Hosea, Amos, and Micah, the book of Jeremiah also introduces subsequent sections by date formulae; and unlike Isaiah, they are quite frequent, appearing twenty times. However, these notations are now also keyed to particular years of Judah's kings. Some, moreover, display another new element: the inclusion of synchronisms to *Babylonian* regnal years. The book of Jeremiah's Babylonian datings appear in those oracles and narratives that pertain to the disaster of Nebuchadnezzar's victory and Judah's exile (24:1; 25:1; 32:1; 34:1; 52:12, 28, 29, 30, 31). The book of Jeremiah's date formulae serve an interpretive purpose. They contribute the concreteness of time and situation to Jeremiah's oracles and sermons, and thus create a specific dramatic emphasis in the narratives recounting the last years of Judah.

For example, the oracle in Jer 25:1–14 ominously bears the first regnal year of Nebuchadnezzar in its date formula;[27] it is also the first prophetic text in the Hebrew Bible dated to the reign of a non-Israelite king; and it contains the book's earliest announcement of a seventy-year desolation for Judah. Readers who note the unprecedented Babylonian date may be reminded of the book's opening heading, dating Jeremiah's prophetic activity "until the captivity of Jerusalem" (1:3). The interpretive function is clear. For its original post-destruction readers and hearers, and for us as well, the chronological framework roots oracle, sermon, and narrative into the well-known story of Jerusalem's fall. The early readers and hearers of Jeremiah's collected prophecies knew, as we do, the date of Jerusalem's destruction.[28]

Of the extant preexilic prophetic writings, the Jeremiah material exhibits the greatest interest and specificity in chronology. It is little recognized, however, that its chronological formulae increase in specificity as the great date of destruction draws nearer in the narrative framework.[29] Of the twenty dated chronological headings in Jeremiah, ten give the *year only* in the formula, five exhibit a *year+month* formula, four more give a *year+month+day* formula, and one gives a *month+day* formula where the year has already just been mentioned.[30]

---

[27] The date is lacking in the Septuagint.

[28] Seitz (1985, 1989) argues persuasively for an exilic redaction of the book.

[29] Seitz noticed the specificity in Jeremiah's chronological formulae, but failed to mention its tendency to point to the destruction date (1989, 231). I have found no mention of this tendency in the scholarly literature.

[30] The book of Jeremiah's narrative order differs from its chronological order (cf. 24:1 and 25:1). I assume the date formulae to be archival in origin and therefore authentic,

The general flow of the date formula is from general to particular, and from relative paucity of date formulae to relative abundance. These two observations gain force if one brackets out of consideration the section of "Oracles against the Nations" collected in the Massoretic Text as chs. 46–51. In Septuagintal text forms, this material appears after 25:13, which may be the original placement.[31] The year-only formulae persist throughout the book, but are augmented by the year+month formulae, and then by the year+month+day and month+day formulae which dominate in the last chapter.[32] See the following table for the references:

CHART 4.2
LOCATIONS OF THE DATE FORMULAE IN JEREMIAH

Year-only:	1:2; 25:1–3; 32:1; 36:1; 45:1; 46:2; 51:59; 52:28, 29, 30
Year+Month:	1:3; 28:1; 28:17; 36:9; 39:1
Year+Month+Day:	39:2; 52:4, 12, 31
Month+Day:	52:6 (with the year mentioned in 52:5)[33]

YEAR+MONTH FORMULAE

The year+month formula appears five times in Jeremiah, and in significantly negative contexts. (1) The first year+month date form appears in the heading of the book (1:3), in its reference to Jerusalem's capture in the fifth month of Zedekiah's eleventh year (=August, 587 B.C.), which is said to con-

---

but shaped in their degree of specificity and in their placement by a post-destruction promulgator of Jeremiah's oracles (ca. 560) in retrospect of the destruction in 587 B.C. Except for 1:1–3, all the remaining date formulae in Jeremiah appear in the "Baruch Memoirs" (chs. 25–45) or in the historical appendix (ch. 52).

[31] See the discussion in Otto Eissfeldt (1965, 348–350) as well as the commentaries by William Holladay (1989) and William McKane (1986).

[32] Even if the book once concluded at ch. 39, as some think, based in part on the dates in 1:3 and 39:1–2 (McKane 1986, 1), this tendency in the date forms remains. Against this reconstruction, however, stands the fact that Jer 39 does not mention the fifth month, the closing date for Jeremiah's activity in 1:3, but the fourth month, the date of the breach in Jerusalem's wall. The reader must wait until 52:12–13 for mention of the crucial "fifth month," which both serves to relate the time of the destruction, as well as to give closure to the chronological sequence begun in 1:3.

[33] Other types of chronological markers appear in Jeremiah; I do not include them here because they are either not calendrically dated (24:1, "After Nebuchadnezzar ... had taken into exile....") or not part of the framework itself (25:3, within an oracle).

clude Jeremiah's prophetic activity. As even the casual reader of Jeremiah will know, the prophet is presented as surviving the destruction and prophesying again. Perhaps this heading, then, is interested in something more than the dates of Jeremiah's career: the date formula of 1:3 serves to highlight not the prophet alone, so much as the object of the prophet's concern, Jerusalem, and the prophet's fateful role in its end. (2) Jeremiah 28 narrates Hananiah's opposition to Jeremiah's seventy-year prediction of Babylonian ascendency. This unit's heading in Jer 28:1 appears in the year+month form (=July/August, 594 B.C.). (3) Hananiah's death notice (28:17), dated a mere two months later is presented as confirming Jeremiah's sterner word of doom. (4) The earliest date given in all the year+month formulae is found in Jer 36:9, noting the date of the city's fast for its deliverance, a fast proclaimed by Jehoiakim in the ninth month of his fifth year (= November/December, 604 B.C.), when Nebuchadnezzar's army was advancing against neighboring Ashkelon. This fast provides the occasion for Jehoiakim's burning of Jeremiah's scroll (36:23). (5) Last of this type, Jer 39:1, dates the year and month beginning Nebuchadnezzar's siege of Jerusalem (= December 589/January 588).

YEAR+MONTH+DAY FORMULAE

The first year+month+day formula in Jeremiah stands at 39:2, immediately after the final appearance of the year+month formula. It is most significant that this highly specific date form in 39:2, the first of its kind to appear in prophetic literature, introduces the narrative of Nebuchadnezzar's breach of Jerusalem's wall and the city's surrender. No other date formulae in the preceding prophetic materials display such chronological exactitude, and no other dates in the preexilic prophets match this exactitude except for those in ch. 52, the historical appendix to the Jeremiah collection (cf. the editorial notice concluding Jeremiah's words at 51:64), drawn from 2 Kgs 24–25.

In the appendix no less than three year+month+day formulae occur, in 52:4, 12 and 31, to which we may add the month+day formula in vs. 6 where the year has just been mentioned. Of these four date formulae, 52:4 and 6 record Jerusalem's siege and surrender. 52:12–13 alters the basic formula by a significant change:

וּבַחֹדֶשׁ הַחֲמִישִׁי בֶּעָשׂוֹר לַחֹדֶשׁ
הִיא שְׁנַת תְּשַׁע־עֶשְׂרֵה שָׁנָה לַמֶּלֶךְ נְבוּכַדְרֶאצַּר מֶלֶךְ־בָּבֶל
בָּא נְבוּזַרְאֲדָן רַב־טַבָּחִים עָמַד לִפְנֵי מֶלֶךְ־בָּבֶל בִּירוּשָׁלִָם
וַיִּשְׂרֹף אֶת־בֵּית־יְהוָה וְאֶת־בֵּית הַמֶּלֶךְ
וְאֵת כָּל־בָּתֵּי יְרוּשָׁלִַם וְאֶת־כָּל־בֵּית הַגָּדוֹל שָׂרַף בָּאֵשׁ

> In the fifth month, on the tenth day of the month—which was the nineteenth year of King Nebuchadnezzar, king of Babylon—Nebuzaradan the captain of the bodyguard who served the king of Babylon entered Jerusalem. He burned Yahweh's house, the king's house, and all the houses of Jerusalem—every great house he burned.

The extended formula introducing this narrative is notable since it pinpoints the date of the disaster with a synchronic formula relating the preceding Judean chronology of the narrative (cf. 52:5) to a particular regnal year of the *Babylonian* king. The formula resembles the month+day formulae noted earlier, except for the extended and now concluding clause containing the Babylonian year.

Three additional year-only formulae follow, noting the dates of various deportations (52:28, 29, 30), keyed now *only* to *Babylonian* regnal years. Significantly, none of the three deportations—dated so generically—coincide with the city's capture and destruction. Two of them precede it, and the last represents Babylon's 581 B.C. reprisal following Gedaliah's assassination.

The final date formula in Jeremiah introduces the narrative of Jehoiachin's release, in the now familiar year+month+day style. The year now, however, is the thirty-seventh year of *Jehoiachin's captivity*, which the text then synchronizes to the first year of Amel-Marduk (561 B.C.). This last chronological notice, in a new exilic-year synchronic formula, closes the book of Jeremiah on an optimistic note: it is a token of future mercy.

What was the source of these dates? Was it perhaps an official archive? If, as I surmise, this was so, then the archival dates can be considered to be "politically correct," that is, they are keyed to each successive dominant power. This hypothesis may account for the series of regnal date-types found in the book: first, those that are solely Judean in form, then those that are synchronous, giving both Judean and Babylonian dates, then those that are solely Babylonian, and lastly the synchronous form of the notice reporting Jehoiachin's relegitimation.

The point of view of the creator of Jeremiah's chronological framework is clear: the time of Jerusalem's capture (39:2; 52:6) and of its destruction (52:12), even down to the very day, must "forever live in infamy." Regnal date formulae are declarations of political loyalty and legitimation. The chronology itself assists the prophetic proclamation that Yahweh rules over the nations and plays no favorites, not even in the case of a chosen people. The book's dates accede to what the sermons of Jeremiah demanded: surrender to a foreign legitimacy.

Chronological interest continues unabated in Ezekiel. Aside from the enigmatic reference to the "thirtieth year" (1:1), which does not fit the pattern, this book contains sections persistently dated to "the $\underline{X}$ year of our exile" (33:21, 40:1). The formula exists in less specific variations, such as "in the twelfth year" (32:1), but the attentive reader knows that such abbreviated formulae refer not to the regnal year of any king, nor to the year of Jerusalem's destruction—which occurs in Ezekiel's twelfth year of exile—, but to the exilic years of Ezekiel's community, or more specifically, to the exilic years of the king they had accompanied to Babylonia in 597 B.C., King Jehoiachin (Albright 1942a, 54). Ezekiel's date formulae appear in the first person plural: the prophet speaks poignantly for himself and for his displaced community (Davis 1989, 59–60). Like the strokes on the wall of a prisoner's jail cell, these chronological markers serve an interpretive purpose, reminding the book's readers and hearers of the disaster of landlessness that lies behind Ezekiel's every word. The book's consistently first-person plural date formulae, keyed to exilic years, have no precise analogies in the Hebrew Bible (Beuken 1967, 23).

Ellen F. Davis characterizes the oracles introduced by date formulae as "archival speech," with analogies in the writing of Babylonian legal transactions (1989, 59). Citing Zimmerli's comment that Ezekiel's dates serve as an authenticating device (1979, 113), she observes that Ezekiel "was moving prophecy in the direction of archival speech, marking and filing the evidence, documenting the case that the divine word was indeed delivered in due time, though the warning was not heeded" (1989, 59).

Of the fourteen datelines in Ezekiel, twelve contain a year+month+day formula.[34] As in Jeremiah, this formula can be extended in order to emphasize particular events, thus exposing the interests of the narrative frame. However, the single example of such expansion in Ezekiel lies in the introductory formula to the temple vision found at the outset of chs. 40–48:

בְּעֶשְׂרִים וְחָמֵשׁ שָׁנָה לְגָלוּתֵנוּ בְּרֹאשׁ הַשָּׁנָה בֶּעָשׂוֹר לַחֹדֶשׁ בְּאַרְבַּע
עֶשְׂרֵה שָׁנָה אַחַר אֲשֶׁר הֻכְּתָה הָעִיר בְּעֶצֶם הַיּוֹם הַזֶּה הָיְתָה עָלַי יַד־יְהוָה

> In the twenty-fifth year of our exile, at the beginning of the year, on the tenth day of the month, in the fourteenth year after the city was conquered, on that very day, the hand of Yahweh was upon me. (40:1)

The manner of the formula's expansion is worth noting. First comes the conventional Ezekielian date formula, relating the ensuing vision to "the twenty-fifth year of our exile." Then a second and synchronous dating appears, relating the vision to the fourteenth year of Jerusalem's subjugation. This second form is then filled out by an emphatic clause about the day: "on that very day." We have here, in effect, a double date for the temple vision, both of which hearken back to disaster: the disaster of exile for Ezekiel's community in 597, and the disaster

---

[34] 1:1, 2; 8:1; 20:1; 24:1; 26:1; 29:1,17; 30:20; 31:1; 32:1, 17; 33:21; 40:1. Of these, only 1:2 and 26:1 are incomplete. In 1:2, the missing month has already been supplied in 1:1, and so is omitted; in 26:1 the name of the month is inexplicably missing in the MT.

of Jerusalem's defeat in 587. Both serve to root the vision of the new temple into the tensions of Jerusalem's and its people's present desolation.[35] But the prophet serves notice that God will yet act on their behalf.

With the probable exception of Joel, which bears no dated formulae at all, only three of our present canonical prophetic books—the books of Haggai, Zechariah, and Malachi—were wholly produced after the promulgation of Jeremiah's and Ezekiel's prophecies.[36] As we have seen, only the composite book Haggai–Zech 1–8 continues using the year+month+day formulae in its narrative framework; in Zech 9–14 and in Malachi no chronological formulae of any kind appear. A consistent pattern emerges in this survey of prophetic chronological formulae. With Jerusalem's conquest as narrated in Jeremiah, the year+month+day formula-types become characteristic.[37] This Jeremiah usage continues as standard practice in Ezekiel, and then in Haggai–Zech 1–8. Afterwards in the prophetic canon, date formulae cease altogether.[38]

It is my contention that the impetus for specific dating, the motive that instigated the use of the year+month+day formula, arose from a similarly specific theological decision on the part of prophets and prophetic tradents in the post-destruction and exilic communities, one perpetuated by prophetic tradents in the returned community: a decision to memorialize Jerusalem's fall and the temple's destruction, a decision to grant to this history of judgment and grievous loss a

---

[35] Various calendrical ambiguities render the month of the ch. 40's heading uncertain: is it the first month of the spring calendar, Nisan, and hence, preparation for Passover; or is it the first month of the autumnal calendar, Tishri, and hence, a Fall new year's festival? Is it perhaps also the midpoint (so Zimmerli 1983, 346–47) or the conclusion (so Greenberg 1983, 11) of a Jubilee period? Any one of these views underscores the tension inherent in the date of Ezk 40:1 (Davis 1989, 123). Davis (1989, 59–60) points out that Ezekiel's date formulae, with the single exception of 40:1, appear among the doom speeches.

[36] I leave open the vexed questions of the manner of promulgation of preexilic and exilic prophetic books, and the form in which they were read by their postexilic successors. The essential point for the present argument is that this material was available in some form to the postexilic prophets, and that their dependence upon it can be demonstrated, as Mason, among others, has done (1976; 1982b; 1990; 2003).

[37] Not surprisingly, especially for those who think that the redaction of prophetic books occurred in a Deuteronomic setting, 1 and 2 Kings display an identical tendency in their date forms. The only exception to this pattern occurs in 1 Kgs 6:38. Significantly, this formula marks *the time of the first temple's completion*. In the Hebrew Bible, nearly every account of temple building, temple desecration, temple repair, and temple reform is narrated with acute chronometric interest (see for example, 1 Kgs 6:1, 37, 38; 8:2; 14:25; 2 Kgs 25:8; 2 Chr 3:2; 15:10; 29:3, 17; Ezra 3:1, 8; 4:24; and 6:15).

[38] But note the year-only formulae in Daniel (1:1; 2:1; 7:1; 8:1; 9:1; and 10:1).

formative power for this people's continuing life in the world. This viewpoint explains both the formula's point of origin in Jer 39:2 and its disappearance after Zech 7:1.

Two influential treatments of the narrative framework and date formulae of Haggai–Zech 1–8 are those of Beuken (1967) and Mason (1977). Both agree that the dated framework is a late editorial production, composed a century or two after the original oracles, although Mason is open to earlier datings. Beuken, noting its interest in the priestly and political leaders, among other traits, sees it as arising from the circle of the Chronicler (1967, 42). Mason argues more generally for a theocratic group behind the framework, and that such a group promulgated Haggai's and Zechariah's oracles in this form to emphasize the realized eschatological fulfillment of some of the prophets' claims, while they awaited the fulfillment of the rest. Meyers and Meyers have noted, however, the pervasive chronologically specific interest in temple-restoration in the framework, and its lack of any date for the temple's completion, which appears only in Ezra 6:15. As they conclude: "The fact that nowhere in either prophetic work is the rededication of the temple mentioned surely means that their combined literary work was completed prior to that event" (1987, xl). Our survey of prophetic chronological notices adds weight to the Meyers's thesis of a composite redaction for Haggai–Zech 1–8 before 515 B.C. One need not look to a late Chronistic milieu for the narrative frame or its date formulae.[39] My contentions are (1) that Haggai–Zech 1–8's date formulae framework is best seen in the light of chronological notation in previous prophetic books, not in the Chronicler; (2) that the book of Jeremiah's year+month+day formulae, which are synchronized with pagan regnal years, memorialize temple-desolation, and are produced in the exilic era, provided the specific model for those of Haggai–Zech 1–8, which are year+month+day in form, keyed to pagan regnal years, and point towards temple-completion.

Hence, I disagree with Davis, who thinks the date forms of Haggai–Zech 1–8 are imitative of Ezekiel's (1989, 150 n. 27).[40] There may be influence here

---

[39] Kessler writes, "the most probable assumption is that the dates in Haggai were formulated as a point close to the time indicated by the dates themselves" (2002, 49). He, however, rejects the thesis that Hag 1–2 and Zech 1–8 comprised a composite book (56).

[40] Regarding Ezekiel's dating system, Davis writes, "That such a system of dating was recognized as a mark of authenticity in prophetic speech is indicated by its imitation in Haggai and Zechariah" (1989, 59 n. 27). "Because it was unsafe for the exiles to flaunt their loyalty by dating from Jehoiakin's regnal years, they dated from his captivity; for a postexilic editor to have invented such a system would have been absurd" (59). Davis also notes Albright's defense of Ezekiel's dates: "not only the exiles but

from the more pervasive chronological organization of the Ezekiel material, but the formulae themselves stand closer to Jeremiah's form, keyed to non-Israelite regnal years. Since the last date in Jeremiah is also an exilic year of Jehoiachin (52:31), the first of this type to appear in the order of the prophetic canon, Ezekiel's exilic-year date formulae may also be dependent on the book of Jeremiah.

THE NEO-BABYLONIAN CHRONICLES (747 B.C.–539 B.C.) AND THE DATE FORMULAE IN THE PROPHETS

Some confirming evidence of this hypothesis appears in the chronographic procedures followed by the scribes in the texts known as the Neo-Babylonian Chronicles (Glassner 2004).[41] The pertinent texts, dating from 747 B.C. through 539 B.C., are the first extant texts in Babylonian literature that systematically employ precise dating procedures—sometimes in year+month+day formulae—to record certain types of events.[42] These precise dating procedures were only now favored because of the new correlation between the old Babylonian lunar calendar and the solar year, a correlation likely made in 747 B.C. (Parker and Dubberstein 1942, 1). Only a few types of events are routinely so memorialized in the chronicles. Taking the first known Babylonian Chronicle, which A. K. Grayson classifies as Chronicle 1 (=BM 92502 + BM 75976; =Glassner's Chronicle 16)[43]

---

also the Babylonians regarded Jehoiakin as the legitimate king of Judah, 'held in reserve for possible restoration if circumstances should seem to require it'" (Albright 1942a, 49–55). See also Freedy and Redford, on "The Dates in Ezekiel in Relation to Biblical, Babylonian, and Egyptian Sources" (1970, 462–85).

[41] Glassner has the most complete series of Mesopotamian chronicle texts, with introductions, transcriptions, and translations (2004). For good photographs, as well as transcriptions, translations, and detailed commentary, see also Grayson (1975), and for some of these texts, Wiseman (1956). For translations of representative texts, see *ANET* (301–07); older presentations can be found in Luckenbill (1924) and Rogers (1912, 208–19). For brief discussion see Freedman (1975).

[42] Wiseman lists eight major chronicle texts extant, some of which are linked in series: 1. Sargon of Agade–Kastiliasu (ca. 2350–1600 B.C.); 2. The Babylonian Chronicle: Nabonassar–Shamashumukin (747–648 B.C.); 3. Esarhaddon Chronicle (680–667 B.C.); 4. Chronicle of the Years 680–626 (B.C.); 5. Nabopolassar–Nebuchadnezzar II (626–595 B.C.); 6. Neriglissar, Year 3 (556 B.C.); 7. Nabonidus (555–539 B.C.); 8. Various Seleucid Chronicles and King Lists (306–175 B.C.) (1979, 398). The first of these, the so-called Sargon Chronicle, carries only the most generic chronology—a list of successive events and kings—and no date formulae whatsoever (*ANET*, 266–67). All of these, except #6, as well as other types of annalistic texts, appear in *ANET*.

[43] Grayson understood BM 75977 to belong to Chronicle 1 (1975, 69); Glassner takes it to be a separate, partly parallel account (2004, 202), listed as Chronicle 17.

as a typical example, I have somewhat arbitrarily categorized the dated events according to a few general subjects: events in the royal house, such as the accessions and deaths of kings; revolts and executions; military events, such as departures of major expeditions; and events in temples and shrines, such as the plundering and restoration of the images of the gods. From the point of view of the Babylonian chroniclers these were the significant items to record for the royal court with chronometric precision.

Several interesting parallels appear between the prophetic date formulae and those of the roughly contemporary Neo-Babylonian chronicle literature. These parallels strengthen our case that we are not to look to a late Chronistic milieu (so Beuken 1967, and similarly, Mason 1977) for the origin of precise date formulae in the latter prophets, but to an earlier phase of biblical history, the era of Neo-Babylonian ascendancy. These parallels also suggest that the chronographic formulae found earliest in Jeremiah, but also in Ezekiel and Haggai–Zech 1–8, as well as the date formulae in 1 and 2 Kings, especially those within the narrative of Jerusalem's destruction, show dependence upon Neo-Babylonian chronometry. The argument that follows thus suggests that it was not only the Jewish calendar that came under Babylonian influence—as is widely acknowledged (Bickerman 1984, 60; de Vaux 1961, 185)—but also the chronographic conventions of Yehud's prophets, redactors, and tradents.[44]

The chronometric capabilities of Mesopotamian culture substantially increased in the mid-eighth century when the Babylonians stabilized their lunar calendar. Parker and Dubberstein surmized that it was in the reign of Nabonassar (747–734 B.C.) that Babylonian astronomers recognized that "235 lunar months have almost exactly the same number of days as nineteen solar years" (1942, 1). Before this time, a thirteenth lunar month was intercalated irregularly, as needed, to prevent the new year from falling too far from the time of the vernal equinox. By 747 B.C. these intercalations were rationalized: seven lunar months were to be added during each nineteen-year cycle. By the fourth century B.C. a standardized time was set to intercalate each added month within the nineteen-year cycle (1942, 2; Finegan 1964, 30–31). The eighth-century system simplified chronometry and quickly came into use in official documents such as the so-called Babylonian Chronicle.

---

[44] It was probably during the reign of King Jehoiakim (609–598 B.C.) that the Babylonian calendar came into use in Judah (de Vaux 1961, 185, 192), and not after 587 B.C. as Bickerman asserts (1984, 60). Jehoiakim became a vassal to Nebuchadnezzar in 605 or 604 B.C.; and biblical texts' dates given during his reign, all of which fall late in or after 604 (Jer 36:9, 22), conform to the Babylonian pattern. Dates given under Zedekiah's reign similarly conform (Jer 28:1, 17; 39:1, 2; cf. 1:3; and 2 Kgs 25:1, 3).

BABYLONIAN CHRONICLE 1, 747 B.C.–667 B.C.

In the eighth century and after, systematic and detailed calendrical notations, down to the month and day, appear frequently in chronicle and annalistic texts. The longest and perhaps best example among these is the so-called Babylonian Chronicle (BM 92502 + BM 75976), which records events from 747–667 B.C.[45]

This document, preserved on a very large four-columned tablet and a smaller broken duplicating fragment, provides the principal evidence for the stabilization of the calendar during Nabonassar's reign.[46] Hellenistic astronomers recognized the Nabonassar era as a time of great advances in science, and it is from this era that an almost continuous record of astronomical observation was made and preserved down at least to the time of Ptolemy (Hallo and Simpson 1971, 144, 169; Bickerman 1980, 23). The Ptolemaic Canon's dated list of kings begins with Nabonassar's reign (for text see Bickerman 1980, 110–11).

The Babylonian Chronicle contains ninety-one date formulae within 184 lines of text, enumerating at least 137 dated events. Twenty of the date formulae are concluding summaries giving the totals of years in each given king's reign and using the formula, "PN reigned X years in country Y." Seventeen give the year only. Three supply more detailed information. The first of these three gives the regnal total as "one month and two [?] days" (I.17). The second one reports the total as "one year—(precisely) six months" (III.6). The third gives the total as "ten months" (III.15). Presumably the less-than-one-year brevity of these three reigns justified the scribe's departure from his usual year-only formulae.

The remaining seventy-one date formulae provide the chronological groundwork for the text. These formulae open each narrative unit, and often each sentence within the unit. They almost invariably use the following syntax, in Chart 4.3 below:

CHART 4.3
THE DATE FORMULA IN THE BABYLONIAN CHRONICLE

Sattu V (ilu) Nabu-nasir
In the fifth year of Nabonassar.... (I.9)

---

[45] For this text, transliteration, and translation see Glassner (2004, 193–202) or Grayson (1975, 69–87); cf. Luckenbill (1924); *ANET* (301–3). For later annalistic texts with similar chronometry, see also Wiseman (1956); *ANET* (303–7; 563–64), and the further bibliographies there. Hallo and Younger's important anthology of texts (2003) omits the Neo-Babylonian chronicles series, probably since they were well published elsewhere.

[46] For photographs, see Grayson (1975, plates XII, XIII, and XIV).

Twenty-six of these formulae, such as the one quoted above, give the year only—the once-standard form in Mesopotamian annalistic texts. Now, however, this year-only form is in the minority. Twelve more formulae name the month, and thirty others give the month and day as well. Such extended chronographic precision is unprecedented in Mesopotamian historiography.

In earlier annalistic texts, events may occasionally be dated to specific months and days of the given year. For example, the so-called Monolith Inscriptions of Shalmaneser III (858–824), record a major military expedition departing in the king's first year, "in the month Aiaru, the 13th day" (*ANET*, 277). Few events are dated down to the month and fewer still to the day. The one quoted above may be dated so because it is the first in the series of significant expeditions by Shalmaneser III—expeditions which now became commonplace, an almost annual event, and the main subject of the so-called Eponym Chronicle which records the major events, mostly military, of each year (Hallo and Simpson 1971, 127). Pritchard has collected a number of annalistic texts of this nature from Shalmaneser III's ninth-century reign (*ANET*, 276–81), as do Hallo and Younger from Neo-Assyrian inscriptions (*COS* 2:261–306), and from Neo-Babylonian sources (*COS* 2:306–14). Typically, expeditionary departures or other significant events are recorded with year-only formulae, standard procedure for the scribes:

> In the sixth year of my rule, I departed from Nineveh. (*ANET*, 279)

Only rarely does any further calendrical detail follow, as in the example below, recording the same event:

> In the year of (the eponym[47]) Daian-Ashus [= Shalmaneser's sixth year], in the month Aiaru, the fourteenth day, I departed from Nineveh. (*ANET*, 278)

This is the expedition which battled the huge western alliance at Qarqar in 853 B.C.[48] Thus, the second example above displays the unusual year+month+day formula to mark this significant battle.

In the Babylonian Chronicle, however, there appear to be several more kinds of events that merit detailed chronometric reporting. Chart 4.4 below shows the number and kind of events dated by each of the formula-types found in the chronicle, and Chart 4.5 displays texts with dated events regarding shrines.

---

[47] For examples of the several eponym-year lists, see Glassner (2004, 160–76), and *ANET* (269–71); for brief discussion see Oppenheimer (1977, 145–46, 233), and Bickerman (1980, 63–67).

[48] The alliance included Aram's Ben-Hadad II and Israel's Ahab, who made peace with each other in order to face Assyria (Hallo and Simpkins 1971, 127; cf. 1 Kgs 20).

CHART 4.4
DATE FORMULAE AND EVENTS IN THE BABYLONIAN CHRONICLE

Event	Year	+Month	+Day	Totals
Royal House				
King enthroned	19	1	3	23
King captured/killed/dies	8	5	9	22
King dethroned	1			1
King ill	1		2	3
No king	1			1
King's wife dies			1	1
King's family/nobles captured			1	1
King/nobles exiled	2	2	2	6
Palace captured	1		1	2
Subtotal	*33*	*8*	*19*	*60*
Military				
Battle	6		1	7
Battle not joined	1			1
Expedition against place X	11	1		12
Place Y captured/plundered	10		6	16
City not taken	1			1
Captives/plunder arrive		1		1
Inhabitants held for ransom			2	2
Massacre of inhabitants	1	1	3	5
Selection of inhabitants	2			2
Retreat/flight	6			6
Subtotal	*38*	*3*	*12*	*53*
Shrines				
Gods plundered/deported	1			1
Gods held for ransom			1	1
Gods restored		2	3	5
Ritual not observed	1	1	1	3
Gods in unknown event		1		1
Subtotal	*2*	*4*	*5*	*11*
Revolts and Executions				
Official/noble executed	2	1	1	4
Revolt	1		4	5
Subtotal	*3*	*1*	*5*	*9*
Miscellaneous				
Unknown event	1	2		3
Tablet dated by scribe			1	1
Subtotal	*1*	*2*	*1*	*4*
Totals	77	18	42	137

CHART 4.5
THE BABYLONIAN CHRONICLE:
DATED EVENTS REGARDING SHRINES

Y = year-only formula Y+M = year+month formula
Y+M+D = year+month+day formula M+D = month+day formula

Nabonassar (747–734 B.C.)
I.1, 5: "In the third year (of the reign of) Nabonassar ... [Tiglath-Pileser (III)] ... deported the gods of Shapazza." Y

Asshur-nadin-shumi (699–694 B.C.)
II.35–40: "In the sixth year (of the reign) of Asshur-nadin-shumi.... King Hallushu-(Inshushinak) of Elam went to Akkad; at the end <of the month> of Teshrit he entered Sippar and massacred the inhabitants. Shamash did not leave Ebabbar."[49] Y+M

Nergal-ushezib (693 B.C.)
II.45–III.1: "In the first year (of the reign) of Nergal-ushezib.... In the month of Teshrit, the first day, the Assyrian army entered Uruk. It held the gods and inhabitants of Uruk for ransom." Y+M+D

Eight-year lapse in the Babylonian kingship (688–681 B.C.)
III.28–29: "The eighth year when there was no king in Babylon, in the month of Dumuzi, the third day, the gods of Uruk returned from [Assy]ria (!) to Uruk." Y+M+D

Esarhaddon (680–669 B.C.)
III.39; 44–46: "In the first year (of the reign) of Esarhaddon ... in the month of Elul Ishtaran and the gods [of Der] went from [...] to Der." Y+M
IV.9–10: "In the sixth year, the King of Elam entered Sippar. There was a massacre. Shamash did not leave Ebabbara." Y
IV.16–18: "The seventh year ... in the month of Adar, Ishtar of Akkade and the gods of Akkade came from Elam; they entered Akkade in the month of Adar, on the tenth day." Y+M/M+D

Shamash-shum-ukin (667–648 B.C.)
IV.34–36: "In the year of the accession of Shamash-shum-ukin, in the month of Iyyar, Bel and the gods of Akkad left Asshur; they entered Babylon in the month of Iyyar, the [four]teen/twenty-[four]th (?) day." Y+M/M+D

---

[49] The text means that because of the invasion, the image of the god did not process from the temple in the annual ritual (*ANET*, 301). The E-barra, or Ebarbar, was a major temple in Sippar (Oppenheim 1977, 277). The above translations are from Glassner (2004, 193–203), although the transliterations of names are presented without his diacriticals.

From Chart 4.4 above it is evident that only a few types of events are routinely memorialized in the chronicle. The chart employs five general subjects, the Royal House, Military, Shrines, Revolts and Executions, and Miscellaneous. From the point of view of the Neo-Babylonian chroniclers such events were worthy of recording for their archives. For them, the precise form of chronology giving the very day was appropriate especially for several kinds of events, among which were events regarding temples. Enormous interest was paid to events regarding the royal house, with no less than sixty such events chronicled, nineteen of them with the +day formula. With only slightly less interest did the chroniclers regard the military, with fifty-three such events dated, nineteen of them with the +day formula. Activities regarding shrines and the images of the gods occupy the next place in the chronometric interest of the scribes, with eleven such events listed, five of them with the +day formula. These entries in the Babylonian Chronicle are shown in Chart 4.5, above.

The main conclusion demonstrated by Chart 4.4 and Chart 4.5 is that Mesopotamian scribes became keenly interested in preserving precise chronometric data in regard to temple activity.[50] They tended to record these activities in year+month formula or year+month+day formulae. This tendency is particularly true for the record of the restoration of the images of the gods to their shrines. Not all such shrine-related activities are recorded in this precise manner, but the data indicate an impressive tendency in this direction, for Mesopotamian scribal practices from the mid-eighth down through the seventh centuries B.C.

The same chronometric practice appears in the so-called Akitu Chronicle, recording selected events involving the interruption of the New Year's festival from 689 B.C. to 626 B.C. (Glassner 2004, 212–15; Grayson 1975, 131–32). A similar practice is found in inscriptions regarding temple-rebuilding in the Neo-Babylonian period. Regarding Nebuchadnezzar's restoration of E-Urimin-Anka, the ziggurat of Borsippa, one text says, "since remote days [it] had fallen in ruins … In a propitious month, on an auspicious day, I began to repair [it].… I built it anew as in olden times" (*COS* 2.122B:310). Similarly, regarding Nabonidus's restoration of the temple Ehulhul in Harran, one text tells how the king was commissioned by Marduk to rebuild. This text then relates: "For rebuilding Ehulhul, the temple of Sin … in a propitious month, on an auspicious day, which Shamash and Adad revealed to me … I cleared its foundations and laid the brickwork.… I built [it] anew" (*COS* 2.123A:311). Likewise Nabonidus is said to have begun the rebuilding of the temple Ebarbar in Sippar "in the month

---

[50] Grayson collates Chronicle Text 1C into the Babylonian Chronicle, containing the following addition for the regnal report of Nabonassar: "The fifteenth year [of Nabonassar]: On the twenty-second day of the month of Teshri, the gods of the Sea-Land returned [to] their shrines" (II.4–5), another example of the Y+M+D date form associated with shrines.

Tashritu, on an auspicious day, which Shamash and Adad revealed to me" (*COS* 2.123A:312).

Roland de Vaux has shown that it was after the reign of Josiah, and likely in the reign of Jehoiakim (609–598 B.C.) that the Babylonian calendar was adopted in Judah (1961, 185, 192). This most likely took place in 605 or 604 B.C., the time when Judah passed from Egyptian to Babylonian vassalage. I suggest that it was not merely the Judean calendar that came under Babylonian influence. The "politically correct" Babylonian dates of Jeremiah's oracles, in which appear the year+month+day formulae, also depend directly upon the current Babylonian scribal practice as witnessed in these chronicle texts. These parallels strengthen the case that we are not to look to a late Chronistic or late theocratic milieu, as Beuken and Mason respectively proposed, for the origin of the date formulae used eventually in Haggai–Zech 1–8, but to an earlier phase of biblical history, the era of Neo-Babylonian ascendancy, and to the book of Jeremiah, which first employed the precise date formulae.

THE BOOK OF JEREMIAH'S SEVENTY YEARS

Confirming evidence also appears in the specific manner in which the seventy-year tradition of chastisement appears in various prophetic books and contexts. As Ackroyd suggested, the seventy years represents a complex and fluid tradition (1958, 23–27). Several versions of the tradition can be traced in the book of Jeremiah with its repeated announcements of seventy years, or more generally, of three generations of exile. (1) The tradition first appears in Jer 25:11–12, in an oracle cross-dated to Jehoiakim's fourth year and to Nebuchadnezzar's first year, 605 B.C. (25:1). There Jeremiah stunned his audience by announcing a seventy-year desolation for the land of Judah. The announcement comes after Babylon's similarly stunning victory over Egypt at Carchemish in June of that year. From that time to Babylon's fall in October 539 B.C. lies a period of some sixty-six years—close enough by ancient conventions (or even certain modern ones) to be rounded off as seventy.[51] (2) Jeremiah's letter to the recently deported exiles in ch. 29, while again predicting "seventy years," formulates it as a period of Babylonian ascendancy: "seventy years for Babylon" (29:10). This speech can be dated to about 595 B.C.—ten years after the oracle of 25:11. From which date were its exilic addressees to calculate the time? (3) The oracle of 27:1–7 speaks in much more general and universal terms: the period of

---

[51] This oracle is probably the one inferred in Dan 9:2. Daniel's "seventy sevens" (9:24–27) are an apocalyptic elaboration of the Jeremiah tradition in a schematic pattern of eschatological delay.

Babylonian rule for the ancient Near East will last for three generations: "All the nations shall serve him and his son and his grandson, until the time of his own land comes" (27:7).[52] Still another formulation of the tradition appears in 2 Chr 36:21, where the Chronicler quite specifically dates the period to the time of the land's "desolation" (587 B.C.), in order for it to "enjoy its Sabbaths … to fulfill seventy years."

Bearing in mind this flexibility in the Jeremiah tradition, one should not be surprised that the recipients of the tradition after the return from exile treated it with a similar flexibility. Given earlier prophets' extravagant promises about the return from exile, the early restoration period in Jerusalem was a time when eschatological hopes could reasonably expect perhaps even dramatic fulfillment. But, disillusioned by their paltry fortunes and unrelieved misfortunes, and disappointed in the meager trickle of returnees, the returned community in Haggai–Zech 1–8 saw itself as *still living under a chastisement of seventy years*.[53] The first night-vision of Zech 1:7–17 clearly indicates this opinion for the prophet himself, when his interpreting angel cries out:

יְהוָה צְבָאוֹת עַד־מָתַי אַתָּה לֹא־תְרַחֵם אֶת־יְרוּשָׁלִַם
וְאֵת עָרֵי יְהוּדָה אֲשֶׁר זָעַמְתָּה זֶה שִׁבְעִים שָׁנָה

Yahweh of the heavenly armies, how long will you withhold mercy from Jerusalem and the cities of Yehud, which you have cursed these seventy years? (1:12)

This vision is dated in 1:7 with a variant of the familiar year+month+day formula,[54] and can be assigned to February 15, 519 B.C., 68 years after the destruction.

That this assessment of the times was widely shared in Yehud is indicated in the introductory narrative to the oracle in Zech 7. There the issue pertains to fasting. A delegation from Bethel inquires of "the priests … and the prophets": "Should I mourn and fast in the fifth month, as I have done for so many years?" (7:3). The prophet's oracular reply recasts the time as seventy years:

כִּי־צַמְתֶּם וְסָפוֹד בַּחֲמִישִׁי וּבַשְּׁבִיעִי וְזֶה שִׁבְעִים שָׁנָה
הֲצוֹם צַמְתֻּנִי אָנִי

---

[52] The textual problems in 27:1's date formula are considerable. See Holladay (1989, 115) for a proposed solution: Zedekiah's fourth year (594 B.C.).

[53] For a recent review of the role of Babylon in the book of Zechariah, see Boda (2005).

[54] See Meyers and Meyers for a striking interpretation of the arrangement of elements in the date formulae of Haggai–Zech 1–8 (1987, xlvi–xlviii).

When you fasted and mourned in the fifth month and in the seventh for these seventy years, was it for me that you fasted? (7:5)

In all probability these two fasts related to the temple's destruction in the fifth month of 587 B.C. and Gedaliah's assassination in the seventh month of (perhaps) 587 B.C. Once more the narrative introduction is clearly dated, to the equivalent of December 7, 518 B.C. (7:1).

Why should such a question be asked at such a time? The answer lies in the background of the impending completion of the temple (cf. 8:9–13, with the resumption of the fasting issue in 8:19). The understandable result for these fast-observers at such a time is to question the continued propriety of mourning. Zechariah answers, in effect, when the temple is completed (accompanied by social justice—Zech 8:14–19) national fasting will become international feasting. The seventy-year chastisement, *a chastisement of temple-desolation*, is soon to be ended:

כֵּן שַׁבְתִּי זָמַמְתִּי בַּיָּמִים הָאֵלֶּה לְהֵיטִיב אֶת־יְרוּשָׁלַםִ
וְאֶת־בֵּית יְהוּדָה אַל־תִּירָאוּ

"So again I have purposed in these days to do good to Jerusalem and to the house of Judah: fear not!" (8:15)

CONCLUSION

To repeat the key question: what motive might our editor have had in compiling this material in such a chronologically defined form? We now have sufficient data to provide a satisfactory answer. It was the impending conclusion of the seventy-year chastisement, seventy years of temple-desolation as calculated by the returned exiles, that engendered both great eschatological hopes and great frustrations. For Haggai and Zechariah, hope could hardly prevail without the restoration of the cosmic center, the center of both sacred space and sacred time, Yahweh's temple (Meyers and Meyers 1987, 245; Levenson 1988, 75–99). Only then could fertility and blessing prevail in the renewed land (Hag 2:17–19; Zech 8:12–13).

Haggai's preaching proved to be the necessary catalyst. Pent-up frustrations and discouragements gave way before the power of Haggai's proclamation to a tremendous release of energy—energy now directed toward the one great task of temple reconstruction. Eschatological hope, freed now from the inertia of despair and aided by the emergence of the prophet Zechariah, now ruled the day.

It was this theological-historical environment, leading to the imminent completion of the second temple, which prompted the promulgation of Haggai–Zech 1–8 as a composite unity. The community still needed the oracles that had provided the catalyst for the great reaction still at work. Hence, they were preserved and memorialized in a chronologically defined narrative framework that would explain their purpose, providing still further encouragement to the community so heavily engaged in the work of building. It is in this interpretative chronological framework, harkening back especially to the date formulae in the book of Jeremiah's accounts of defeat and destruction, that Hag 1–2 and Zech 1–8 appear; only now the borrowed formulae serve to narrate the reversal of past disasters and the reestablishment of cosmic order. Just as in Neo-Babylonian scribal practice, temple desolation and temple restoration are memorialized down to the very day. In this dated framework, in imitation of and counterbalance to the date forms of Jeremiah that memorialized the temple's loss, we find the returned community's eschatological and imminent expectation of the end of seventy years' chastisement.

Since the temple concern is the single overriding concern of Haggai, and a central concern of Zechariah, it would be only natural for them to describe in glowing terms its completion and dedication. Such is not the case. Detailed chronological interest in the temple characterizes nearly every account of temple building, repair, reform, and desecration in the Hebrew Bible.[55] Since both these interests, temple and chronology are paramount to the editor of Haggai–Zech 1–8, it would be difficult to hold that the temple's completion date was omitted from the record—if it had already occurred. This omission renders it most probable that the editor worked prior to that time. The chronological interest in the concluding collection of oracles of this composite work, Zech 7–8, adds confidence to this conclusion, independently of the arguments employed by Meyers and Meyers (1987). The question about fasting for "these seventy years" (7:5), dated to the fourth year of Darius (518 B.C.) and the continuing encouragement to "be strong" so that "the temple might be built" (8:9) contextualize all the collected oracles of Zech 7–8 to the situation before the dedication. The entire composite collection, then, still looks forward in restless anticipation of the great event.[56]

I take this viewpoint as most probable, given this evidence: as the construction neared its completion, sometime between 518 B.C. (Zech 7:1) and 515 B.C. (Ezra 6:15),[57] our editor—perhaps Zechariah himself, as indicated by the first-person pronouns that appear late in the editorial framework at 4:8, 6:9, 7:4, and

---

[55] 1 Kgs 6:1, 37, 38; 8:2; 14:25; 2 Kgs 25:8; 2 Chr 3:2; 15:10; 29:3, 17; Ezra 3:1, 8; 4:24; 6:15.

[56] Meyers and Meyers (1987, xl, xliii) see the collection as prepared for the dedication ceremony of the finished temple in 515 B.C. I see it as prepared and circulating before that event.

[57] See Ackroyd (1958, 23, 27) for discussion of the reliability of the date in Ezra 6:15.

8:18—selected material from the body of oracles and visions produced in restoration Jerusalem by Haggai and Zechariah, arranging them in the chronological narrative framework that distinguishes these two bodies of prophecy from all other.[58] It was in this form that the oracles and visions were then circulated as "tracts for the times" in Persian period Yehud. For these prophets and their promulgators, figures to be associated with central authority in Jerusalem, a new era of realized eschatological fulfillment was at hand.

I have now concluded my two-part examination of the sociohistorical context and the narrative framework in which Haggai–Zech 1–8 is presented. With these conclusions in mind, I now turn to the reading of the book of Zechariah itself, the main issue at hand. I have examined sociological theory about prophets, charisma, and social location. I have also presented five case studies in the careers of actual prophets in their audience societies, and derived from them a model of social location trajectory analysis. I now apply this model to the reading of the book of Zechariah. What can a social-location reading of Zechariah contribute to the interpretation of this enigmatic book?

---

[58] On the possible role of Zechariah in compiling and redacting Haggai–Zech 1–8, see Meyers and Meyers (1987, 433).

5

HISTORY, LITERATURE AND SOCIAL LOCATION
PART ONE: ZECH 1–8

The book of Zechariah perplexes. What is the reader to do with this bizarre book? Jerome called it *"obscurissimus liber,"* "the most obscure book" (quoted in Lamarche 1961, 7 n. 1), and Childs adds, few Old Testament books reflect such a chaos of conflicting interpretations" (1979, 476). Mark Cameron Love's recent monograph despairs over making sense of Zechariah; his book's title denotes "the evasive text" and "the frustrated reader," and at last he comes to ask, "Why is Zechariah unreadable?" (1999, 230). In the Middle Ages, Abarbanel complained, "the prophecies of Zechariah are so obscure, that no expositors, however skilled, have 'found their hands'[1] in their explanations"; Rabbi Jarchi concurred: "we shall never be able to discover their true interpretation until the teacher of righteousness[2] arrives" (quoted in Hengstenberg n.d., 958).

Difficulties abound in this text; nonetheless, many writers have attempted to explain its meaning.[3] Paul D. Hanson's treatment in his *Dawn of Apocalyptic*

---

[1] I.e., exercised skill, cf. Ps 76:5.

[2] Cf. הַמּוֹרֶה לִצְדָקָה in Joel 2:23, according to a common medieval rabbinic (and Qumran) interpretation. Modern translations generally render מוֹרֶה as "rain."

[3] Useful commentaries on Zechariah from the nineteenth century include, among others, those by Thomas V. Moore (1856), C. F. Keil (n.d. [1868]), C. H. H. Wright (1980 [1879 original]), E. B. Pusey (1892), and George Adam Smith (1928 [1898]). Moore, Keil, Wright and Pusey are intent upon the defense of unitary authorship for Zechariah. Julius Wellhausen's *Kleine Propheten* (1898) supplies helpful text-critical notes but only brief interpretive suggestions. Ernst W. Hengstenberg's *Christology of the Old Testament*, (n.d., 1829–35 German original) provides almost a full commentary on all fourteen chapters, albeit with interpretive excesses. In the twentieth century useful commentaries include those by Hinckley G. Mitchell in the ICC (1912), David Baron (1972 [1919]), Paul Lamarche (1961, on Zech 9–14 only), Douglas R. Jones (1962b), H. C. Leupold (1971 [1956]), Joyce G. Baldwin (1972), Wilhelm Rudolph in KAT (1977), Samuel Amsler on Zech 1–8 in CAT (1981), André Lacocque on Zech 9–14 in CAT (1981), David L. Petersen in OTL (1984, 1995), Ralph L. Smith in WBC (1984), Carol L. Meyers and Eric M. Meyers in AB (1987, 1993), Carroll Stuhlmueller (1988), Cody Aelred (1990), Henning Graf Reventlow in ATD (1993), Eugene H. Merrill (1994), Paul L. Redditt (1995), Brian Tidiman (1996), Thomas McComiskey (1998), Edgar W. Conrad (1999), Michael H. Floyd in FOTL

(2000), Marvin A. Sweeney (2000) and Barry Webb (2003). As is the case with the book of Haggai, the most important recent commentaries are those by Petersen and by Meyers and Meyers. Again, as with Haggai, important premodern commentaries include those by Theodore of Mopsuestia (350–428) and John Calvin (1509–1564). Didymus the Blind, Cyril of Alexandria, Theodoret of Cyrus and Jerome all wrote commentaries on Zechariah, and these are still extant (Robert C. Hill 2006, 1–6; Al Wolters 1999, 685); Didymus on Zechariah is now published in English (2006), as is Theodore of Mopsuestia's on the Twelve Prophets (2004). Those by Rashi (1040–1105) and David Kimchi (ca. 1160–1235; English translation 1837) also deserve mention. Significant monographs or lengthy studies on Zechariah include those by Bernhard Stade on the Hellenistic dating of Deutero-Zechariah and other interpretative questions, one of the most important studies of Zech 9–14 ever published (1881; 1882a; 1882b), George L. Robinson in defense of unitary authorship (1895–96), Benedikt Otzen on Deutero-Zechariah (1964), W. A. M. Beuken on tradition history in Zech 1–8 (1967), Peter R. Ackroyd on the history and literature of the exile and restoration periods (1968), Paul D. Hanson on Zechariah and the origins of apocalyptic literature (1979), Rex Mason on temple preaching in Zech 1–8 (1990), and on inner-biblical allusion in Zech 9–14 (2003), Mike Butterworth on the structure of Zechariah (1992), Raymond F. Person on the possibility of a Deuteronomic redaction of Zech 9–14 (1993), Janet E. Tollington on tradition and innovation in Zech 1–8 (1993), Katrina Larkin on mantological wisdom and eschatology in Zech 9–14 (1994), Stephen L. Cook on millennial social groups in power and Zechariah (1995), Wolter Rose on *Zemah and Zerubbabel* in Zech 1–8 (2000; cf. 2003), Meredith G. Kline on the night visions in Zech 1–6 (2001), and Peter R. Bedford on temple building and Achaemenid polity in Zech 1–8 (2001). Significant articles or books incorporating briefer studies of Zechariah include those by John J. S. Perowne (1875), Julius Wellhausen (1903), Emil G. H. Kraeling on Zech 9 (1924), George L. Robinson (1965 [1926]), Abraham Malamat on Zech 9 (1950–51), M. Delcor on inner-biblical "borrowing" ("*emprunt*") in Zech 9–14 (1952), Leroy Waterman on Zerubbabel and the messianic conspiracy theory (1954), T. Chary on postexilic prophets and the cult (1955), Douglas R. Jones on a Syrian provenance for Zech 9–11 (1962a), Georg Sauer on the different approaches to Zerubbabel in Haggai and Zechariah (1967), Walter Harrelson on the celebration of the Feast of Booths in Zech 14 (1968), E. Lipinski on various exegetical issues (1970), Rex Mason on the relation of Zech 9–14 to Zech 1–8, on intertextuality in Zech 9–14, and on other issues (1976; 1982a; 1982b; 1984), Andrew E. Hill on the historical linguistics of dating Zech 9–14 (1982), Ronald W. Pierce on a Haggai/Zechariah/Malachi corpus (1984a; 1984b), Donald E. Gowan on the eschatology and theology of Zechariah (1986; 1998), Paul D. Hanson on the community of the people of God and on postexilic religion (1986; 1987), Richard J. Coggins, who gives an able review of Zechariah scholarship (1987), Paul L. Redditt on the two shepherds of Zech 11 and on historical and redactional issues in Zech 9–14 (1993, 1994, 1996), Jon L. Berquist on Persian period history and society in Zechariah (1995), Joseph Blenkinsopp on historical and literary-critical questions in Zechariah (1996), Michael H. Floyd on recent com-posits a sharp literary break and an ideological contradiction between Zech 1–8 and Zech 9–14 (1979). The first half of the book, he surmised, arose from prophets who had uncritically endorsed a powerful and centralized priestly Zadokite party; the second half arose from a disenfranchised and marginalized apocalyptic protest group. Wellhausen wrote, "Passing from chaps. 1–8 to chaps. 9 ff., we at once feel ourselves transported into a different world" (1903, 5393). Soggin can even say that "chs. 9–14 have nothing to do with chs. 1–8 of

---

mentary-writing on Zechariah (1999), R. David Moseman on a unitary reading of Proto- and Deutero-Zechariah (2000), Mark J. Boda on crowns and thrones in Zech 6, on penitence in Zech 1–8, and on Persia and Babylon in Zech 1:7–6:15 (2001; 2003; 2005), Robert B. Chisholm on the structural exegesis of Zechariah (2002), and James C. VanderKam on the postexilic priesthood (2004). As we have seen, the study that does the most thorough analysis of ethno-archaeological materials for the reconstruction of Yehudean society is the one by Charles E. Carter (1999; see also in brief, 1994). Also notable in historical reconstruction are Sean D. McEvenue's analysis of the political structure of Yehud (1981), Ephraim Stern's essential archaeological summaries of the Persian period in Palestine (1982; 2001), numerous chapters in volume one of W. D. Davies and Louis Finkelstein's *Cambridge History of Judaism* (1984), John W. Betlyon on the Yehud coins and their evidential value for understanding Yehud's provincial government (1986), Eric M. Meyers on the Yehudean restoration (1987), Joseph Blenkinsopp on temple and society in Yehud (1991), Bryan Beyer on Zerubbabel (1992), H. G. M. Williamson on numerous historical questions about Yehud (1992; 1999), Robert North on postexilic Yehudean officials (1992), Jon L. Berquist on postexilic religion and society (1995), Peter R. Bedford on temple and society (2001), and the successive volumes of *Second Temple Studies* (Phillip R, Davies, editor, 1991; Tamara C. Eshkenazi and Kent H. Richards, editors, 1994; Philip R. Davies and John M. Halligan, editors, 2002). As previously noted, Meyers and Meyers (1987) and Williamson (1992) disagree with McEvenue (1981) and Stern (1982; 2001, 580–81) about the separate existence of a province of Yehud before the governorship of Nehemiah. McEvenue and Stern, following Albrecht Alt, think that Yehud was under Samaritan administration until 445 B.C. For the Persian imperial context, Pierre Briant's *From Cyrus to Alexander: A History of the Persian Empire* (2002; see also 1992) is now essential, and replaces A. T. Olmstead's 1948 history. Lisbeth S. Fried's *The Priest and the Great King: Temple-Palace Relations in the Persian Empire* (2004) argues the novel thesis that there was no local autonomy in the Persian imperial system, that Yehud had no theocracy, and that the high priest had no real power. Only Persians and Persian appointees had power. She explains the Yehud coins as evidence of brief periods of liberty, when Persian officials were drawn away from Yehud because of intermittent warfare. She suggests it was only under the Maccabees that Yehud achieved anything like independence. This thesis seems extreme. Many more books and articles dealing with Zechariah and its related issues could be cited here.

the book" (1976, 347). In his *Introduction to the Old Testament*, Soggin even places his chapter discussion of Zech 9–14 after his chapter on Malachi, thus further separating the two sides of the book. Gottwald seems to have been in such doubt over its interpretation that he did not even devote a single section of his *Socio-Literary Introduction* to the discussion of Zech 9–14 (1985).

HISTORY OF SCHOLARSHIP

How did this situation in scholarship—the division of the book of Zechariah—come about? Critical discussion can be traced back to the early seventeenth century, when Joseph Mede (1586–1638), also spelled Mead, first expressed an opinion regarding different authorship for part of Zech 9–14.[4] Mede's opinion, published posthumously in 1653, piously attempted to explain the reference to the prophet Jeremiah in Matt 27:9–10's citation of Zech 11:12–13: "Then what was spoken by the prophet Jeremiah was fulfilled: 'They took thirty pieces of silver, the price set on him by the people of Israel, and they gave them for the potter's field, as the Lord had commanded me.'" Mede then argued that Zech 9–11 came from the hand of Jeremiah, and thus was preexilic.

Henry Hammond, court preacher and chaplain to Charles I, soon followed Mede in 1653, and some thus look to Hammond as the "father of English biblical criticism" (Hooper 1922), but the preexilic view did not draw much attention until the early eighteenth century, when Richard Kidder in 1700, an Anglican bishop, and William Whiston in 1722, a Cambridge professor better known for his translation of Josephus, both extended the proposal to include all of Zech 9–14 as preexilic. In reply, J. C. Carpov in 1728 wrote a vigorous defense of the traditional view. The matter seemed to rest until the latter part of the century. At that time the pious B. G. Flügge in 1784 introduced Mede's ideas into Germany, while English Archbishop William Newcome in 1785 divided Zech 9–11 from 12–14, arguing that they were two separate fragments, the former from before the fall of Samaria and the latter from the time between Josiah's death and the fall of Judah. H. Corrodi in 1792 attacked these views, and in so doing boldly proposed a post-Zecharian date for the whole (Mitchell 1912, 250).[5]

---

[4] My account of the early history of the scholarship on Zech 9–14 is dependent upon Robinson's account given in his published Leipzig dissertation (1895–96, 7–12), as augmented by Mitchell (1912), Hanson (1979), Meyers and Meyers (1993), Wolters (1995), and Floyd (1999).

[5] Early in his article, George L. Robinson lists Hugo Grotius (1583–1645) as the first to propose a post-Zecharian origin for 9–14 (1895–96, 4). This is not correct, and Mitchell points out the error (1912, 250). However, later Robinson clarifies his point: Grotius was speaking hypothetically that "if he were compelled to dissent from the traditional view and determined the date of Zech. 9–14 by the clear references

Interpreters soon parted into three schools of thought: those advocating (1) a preexilic date for Zech 9–14, (2) an early postexilic date with unitary Zecharian authorship, and (3) a late post-Zecharian date. L. Bertholdt in 1814 opted for the preexilic date, followed by Wilhelm Gesenius. J. G. Eichhorn, after wavering, came to advocate a late Greek/Maccabean date in 1824.[6] Wilhelm M. L. de Wette also wavered, at first declaring for the preexilic view in 1817, but shifting to the unity of Zechariah in 1833. In 1836 Hengstenberg also defended unitary authorship, as did C. F. Keil in 1853 (1975; cf. 1884), John J. S. Perowne (1875), and, in book length, C. H. H. Wright in 1879. In 1835 J. H. W. Vatke advocated a post-Zecharian origin. Eichhorn's view was to become familiar to many: Zech 9–10 described Alexander the Great's conquests of 333 B.C. Less known was his interpretation that Zech 13:7–14:21 lamented the death of Judas Maccabaeus in 161 B.C. and that the intervening material, Zech 11:1–13:6, fell between these two events, all in the Greek period.

With Bernhard Stade's three-installment article in the founding volumes of ZAW, entitled "Deuterozacharja: eine kritische Studie," greatly elaborating Eichhorn's 1824 proposals, a new era of Zechariah scholarship ensued (1881; 1882a; 1882b). The weight of critical opinion now began to shift toward a late postexilic date (so Robinson 1895–96, 10). This shift did not happen all at once. As late as 1903 Wellhausen could still write, "most recent critics make the second part [Zech 9–14] older" than Zech 1–8 (5394). Stade argued that Zech 9–14 derived from the period of the struggle of the Diadochoi for control of Alexander's empire, placing specific portions of the book at intervals between 306 B.C. and 278 B.C. (1882b, 305). Stade declared that the reference to the sons of Yavan in 9:13 was alone ("*allein*"!) sufficient to show an origin for these chapters after 333 B.C. (1882b, 290). Moreover, the references to Assyria and Egypt in Zech 10:10–11 were to be interpreted not of the preexilic powers that had threatened Israel and Judah, but of the Seleucid and Ptolemaic empires (1882b, 290–96), at the end of the wars of the Diadochoi and at the outset of the five Syrian Wars (301–198 B.C.). Stade's arguments *against* the preexilic date, largely based on Hengstenberg (so Leupold 1971, 12), eventually carried the day. Stade's argument *for* a late post-Zecharian date also became widely influential. Even if his proposals for specific dates were not persuasive, many scholars were willing to follow him into the Greek period in general for the origins of Zech 9–14.

Others, such as Wellhausen, pushed the time limits further. Noting the distinction between Judah and Jerusalem made in Zech 12:2–7, he suggested that

---

to the facts of history, these prophecies would have to be assigned to a period not earlier than the time of the Macabbees" (1895–96, 57).

[6] In overlooking Corrodi, Meyers and Meyers are mistaken in their statement that Eichhorn was the first to propose a post-Zecharian date for chs. 9–14 (1993, 53).

this distinction "seems to indicate the Maccabean period," when deliverance for the city came from the people of the countryside–the Maccabean warriors (1903, 5394). This observation pertained to Zech 12–14; chs. 9–11 were perhaps slightly earlier, dating from the period of Seleucid domination in the first third of the second century B.C., since in these chapters Assyria, the code-word for Seleucid power, "takes precedence" over Egypt (5395). Much twentieth century interpretation was taken up with promoting either Alexander/Diadochoi settings, or a Maccabean setting for Zech 9–14.

Stade's argument was taken up by Mitchell in his important ICC volume (1912), a work that did much to promote the Deutero-Zechariah thesis in the English-speaking world. However, Mitchell did not accept Stade's Diadochoi-era proposals. According to Mitchell, Zech 9:1–10 are "a distinct prophecy written soon after the battle of Issus" (333 B.C.), anticipating Alexander's victorious march through Syro-Palestine; Zech 9:11–11:3, however, "dates from the reign of Ptolemy III" (Euergetes, 246–221 B.C.), who is the first of the two shepherds in 11:4–17 (1912, 303). Zechariah 11:4–17 with 13:7–9, a "pessimistic" text, dates from a time "soon after the battle of Raphia" in 217 B.C., when Antiochus III suffered defeat at the hands of the Ptolemaic army, leaving a reputedly tyrannical Ptolemy IV Philopater (r. 221–204 B.C.) in charge of Syro-Palestine (1912, 258–59; 256).[7] At about the same time another writer, one "with apocalyptic tendencies" added Zech 12:1–13:6 and 14:1–21 to the work to complete the whole (259).

In reply to Stade, George L. Robinson wrote his Leipzig dissertation in defense of unitary authorship for Zech 1–14 (1895–96), the last lengthy defense of the matter in English. Robinson held that multiple authorship was possible, but unitary authorship far more likely, "almost conclusive" (92). Some of Robinson's arguments for authorial unity were quite weak, but others are telling, and some of them will receive mention in chapter eight. For much of the twentieth century the published arguments did not advance very far beyond the range exhibited by Stade, Wellhausen, and Mitchell on the one hand, and by Keil, Pusey, C. H. H. Wright, and Robinson on the other. Twentieth century literary-critical scholarship almost unanimously endorsed the multiple-author thesis, while at the same time conservative scholarship mostly held to unitary authorship.

Benedikt Otzen's 1964 treatise on Deutero-Zechariah, which includes a thorough review of the history of scholarship, discussed at length numerous interpretations for the shepherd pericope in Zech 11. Similarly, Jones (1962b) and Mitchell (1912) both mention at least forty proposals for the identity of the three wicked shepherds. Interpretive despair was setting in. Critical scholarship largely agreed on a Greek or Maccabean date for Zech 9–14, though some, such

---

[7] 3 Maccabees gives an exaggerated description of Philopater's atrocities against the Jews of Judea and Alexandria. See especially 3 Macc 3–5.

as Otzen, continued to hold out for preexilic dates for much of the material, and a few, such as A. F. Kirkpatrick (1915) and Joseph Klausner (1955, 200), held to an early Persian period date, ca. 485 B.C. The late postexilic majority, however, could find no consensus on any more specific social setting, or on which historical events lay behind the text. Was it Alexandrian, or the time of the Diadochoi, or the beginning of the five Syrian Wars, or the end of the Syrian Wars, or the Maccabean era? And who were the three worthless shepherds of Zech 11:8? The array of proposals regarding Hellenistic-era identities is nothing short of bewildering. Identifications include the Seleucid-era high priests Jason, Lysimachus, and Menelaus (so Rubinkam and Marti); Jason, Menelaus, and Alcimus (so Oesterley); Judas Maccabaeus and his brothers Jonathan and Simon (so Abarbanel); Pharisees, Sadducees, and Essenes (so Lightfoot); Antiochus III, Seleucus IV, and the usurper Heliodorus (so Mitchell, 1912, 307); Seleucus IV, Heliodorus, and Demetrius (also suggested by Mitchell); Antiochus IV, Antiochus V, and Demetrius (so C. H. H. Wright); and the list goes on.[8]

Other interpreters had their own proposals: Moses, Aaron, and Miriam (so Jerome); kings, priests, and prophets (so Theodoret of Cyrus); the northern kings Zechariah, Shallum, and perhaps Menahem (so Maurer, Hitzig, and Ewald); Assyria, Babylonia, and Persia (so Kliefoth; Mitchell 1912, 306–07); rulers, priests, and prophets (so Baron 1919, 397); Jehoahaz, Jehoiakim, and Jehoiachin (so Person 1993, 128); nameless false prophets (so Meyers and Meyers 1993, 265); Jehoiakim, Jehoiachin, and Zedekiah (so Merrill 1994, 293–94); and Cyrus, Cambyses, and Darius (so Sweeney 2000, 678), In light of such discord, Baldwin (1972, 183), Redditt (1993), Meyers and Meyers (1993), and Petersen (1995), among others, understandably refrain from naming names.

New exegetical methods and interests arose in the second half of the twentieth century, and these had their due impact upon Zecharian studies. Lamarche (1961), in a study that anticipated later holistic literary-critical developments, found an alleged chiasm that grandly structured all of Zech 9–14 and highlighted its messianic interest, though few have followed him in these claims.[9] Beuken discerned a tradition history and redaction history in Haggai–Zech 1–8 that led from a pre-Chronistic level of the text in the late sixth century to a Chronistic redaction in the mid- or late Persian period (1967). Ackroyd, also employing a traditio-historical method, and well armed with newly available knowledge of the Persian period, discerned a common core in Haggai and Zech 1–8 regarding "the temple, the new community and the new age, and the people's response," but was not convinced of Beuken's "chronistic" milieu for the redaction (1968, 171; 152 n. 58; cf. Beuken 1967, 331–36).

---

[8] Baldwin presents a useful discussion of the possibilities (1972, 181–83).
[9] Baldwin (1972) is a notable exception.

Soon a new movement in sociological exegesis, long dormant, arose, resulting in works such as Hanson's *Dawn of Apocalyptic* (1979 [1975]) and Robert R. Wilson's groundbreaking *Prophecy and Society in Ancient Israel* (1980). Hanson, who shall be discussed at length below, applied social location analysis, tradition history, redaction history, and genre history to Zechariah, to construct a detailed story of internecine conflict in Persian period Yehud. Meanwhile, canonical approaches to the Hebrew Bible/Christian Old Testament emerged, headed by works such as Childs's *Introduction to the Old Testament as Scripture* (1979), which attempted to read Zech 1–8 and Zech 9–14 as part of one canonical book, despite the plurality of authorship, separate redaction histories and conflicting theologies for the two parts. The work of Mason (1976), based on his only recently published 1973 dissertation (2003), drew numerous thematic ties between the two parts of the book, and proved important for the canonical criticism of Childs and others as they discussed the book of Zechariah.

Out of canonical criticism grew a new movement in Zechariah studies, one devoted to a unitary reading of the Book of the Twelve, including Zechariah as part of the larger work. Both D. A. Schneider (1979) and Ronald W. Pierce (1984a, 1984b) discerned a Haggai/Zechariah/Malachi corpus with its own literary unity. For Schneider, this corpus was the fourth and final piece to be added to a "book of the nine" to become the Book of the Twelve. Schneider's dissertation attracted significant attention, and it was instrumental in the creation, first, of the SBL Formation of the Book of the Twelve Consultation (1993–1997), and later, the SBL Seminar on the Formation of the Book of the Twelve (1998–2002). James D. Nogalski's Zurich dissertation (published as two volumes in BZAW, 1993a, 1993b), also attracted significant attention both to the issue of the Book of the Twelve, and to the SBL's program units devoted to that topic.[10] The meetings of these scholarly associations led to three published collections of essays, *Forming Prophetic Literature*, edited by James W. Watts and Paul R. House (1996), *Reading and Hearing the Book of the Twelve*, edited by Nogalski and Sweeney (2000), and *Thematic Threads in the Book of the Twelve*, edited by Paul L. Redditt and Aaron Schart (2003). The new movement was not without its dissenters: Ehud Ben Zvi (1996) cautioned that the scholar's assumption of certain types of intentionality in redaction may lead one to read what is not there in the text: we assume unity, and so we find unity (142).

Meanwhile two major paired volumes of commentaries were to appear in the 1980s and 1990s that would significantly alter the consensus of opinion regarding the social setting of Zechariah: Petersen's OTL volumes, *Haggai and Zechariah 1–8* (1984) and *Zechariah 9–14 and Malachi* (1995), and the Meyers and Meyers massive Anchor Bible volumes, *Haggai, Zechariah 1–8* (1987) and

---

[10] Nogalski, however, concluded that Zechariah had less demonstrable connections with the rest of the Twelve than he found for other books.

Zechariah 9–14 (1993). The two projects shared many features in both method and outcome. Both exegeted Haggai and Zechariah in dialogue with the material culture of the period, in light of recent archaeology. Both assumed the authorial break between Zech 1–8 and 9–14 without attempting any major demonstration. Both viewed Haggai and Zech 1–8 as closely related texts, with minimal later redactional layering, though Petersen is more open to later editing. Meyers and Meyers in particular pressed the thesis, mentioned above, that Haggai and Zech1–8 once circulated together in a redacted form as a composite book prepared for use in the dedication ceremony of the completed temple, and hence, by 515 B.C. Both gave prominence to the presence of intertextuality in Zechariah, or inner-biblical exegesis, though this feature of the text had already been examined by Stade, Robinson, Delcor (1952), and meticulously by Mason (1982b; cf. 2003), and would be examined in more detail by Nogalski (1993a, 1993b). Both also viewed Zech 9–14 not as a product of the Hellenistic or Maccabean periods, *contra* the consensus, but as a product of the early or middle Persian period. Both also resisted the temptation to deduce specific historical personages behind the cryptic allusions of texts like Zech 11:8. Petersen makes the justifiably sharp remark that "in no instance is such an identification proposed in this commentary" (1995, 5).[11]

The Persian period setting proposed by these commentators, supported by the historical linguistic analysis of Andrew E. Hill (1982), has been well received by many in the scholarly community, undermining the prior consensus. Support for Hellenistic dating persists (Nogalski 1993b, 216 and n. 24; Schmidt 1995, 278; Steck 2000, 110 and n. 152; and Floyd 2000, 315–16, among others), but it is less common now than at any time since Mitchell (1912).

Meanwhile there were some twentieth-century and contemporary scholars who followed in the footsteps of Hengstenberg, Keil, Wright, and Robinson, attempting to defend unitary authorship. Among them stand Van Hoonacker (1902), Baron (1919), Young (1949), Klausner (1955), Baldwin (1972), Merrill (1994), Tidiman (1996), Kline (2001), and Webb (2003), who, among others, admits the possibility of later redactional work. Albright too saw no reason why most of the oracles of Zech 9–14 should not be credited to the historical Zechariah (1942b, 121). J. Stafford Wright (1965) and R. K. Harrison (1969) made cautious cases for unitary authorship, but believed that multiple authorship was still possible. Some of their arguments will be considered in chapter eight.

---

[11] Otto Eissfeldt's 1965 comment regarding such identifications is notable: "We do not know, and … so far as we can see, we are unlikely ever to know" (439).

RECENT UNITARY READINGS OF ZECHARIAH

Another move, one in postcritical and canonical exegesis, has very recently come to the fore. As we have seen, in his 1999 review article on Zechariah research, Floyd noted that "it is odd that no recent commentaries have attempted to grasp either the ideational concept or the sociohistorical context forming the matrix of the book as a whole." He continues: "For whatever reason, interpreters seem reluctant to confront the fact that the editors who put the prophetic corpus in its canonical form regarded all fourteen chapters of Zechariah as constituting a distinct prophetic book" (262).[12]

Shortly after the time when Floyd raised his point, several Zechariah commentaries were to appear that attempted a unified literary reading of the book: Conrad's radical postcritical *Zechariah* (1999), which abandons all attempt to root the text in real history; Webb's modest *Message of Zechariah* (2003), which takes the chronometric heading of 7:1 as determinative not only for chs. 7–8, but also as inclusive of chs. 9–14; Sweeney's similar strategy in his *Twelve Prophets* (2000); similarly, Floyd's own *Minor Prophets, Part 2* contribution to the FOTL series (2000), which, like its literary brethren, offers a form critical reading of the successive units, including the macro-unit of the book as a whole; and Kline, who argues for his own peculiar Zecharian macrostructure (2001). Sweeney even thinks that the prophetic biography of Zech 11:4–17 "may well be derived from Zechariah himself" (2000, 566). Such an admission by a major scholar may signal a break in the scholarly consensus regarding this book. But if we are to accept the early Persian period date promoted by Hill, Meyers and Meyers, and Petersen, we should expect to see a reappraisal of the role of the historical Zechariah for Zech 9–14. Strangely, Meyers and Meyers and Petersen do not broach the subject.

Floyd himself (2000) considers that the original Zechariah's prophetic texts (essentially chs. 1–8 and perhaps other original material) were preserved by a scribal school of tradents, who studied them along with other prophetic texts, and who made them the basis for further literary work in similar vein. A *massa'*, according to Floyd, is a genre that involves the "reinterpretation of previous revelation" (306; following Weis, 1992). Taking their cue from how Yahweh had acted for Yehud in the early Persian period, as proclaimed by the historical Zechariah, these prophetic tradents (Floyd calls them "scribes") proclaimed what

---

[12] One modest attempt in this direction—to find an unifying ideational center for the book—is found in Thomas McComiskey's 1998 commentary (perhaps this volume appeared too late to be considered by Floyd), which sees the ideational core as the dialogue between divine sovereignty and human responsibility, a dialogue signaled by the angel's anguished question in 1:12, "How long?" (1016). This proposal seems too general to give much guidance.

they saw as Yahweh's work in their own period, ca. 330–300 B.C. (315). Thus the two *mas'ot* of chs. 9–11 and 12–14 are scribal restatements of Zechariah's insights, designed for the new challenges Yahweh had constructed in his world in the Hellenistic era (308). Hence Floyd finds literary and theological unity in Zech 1–14, despite plurality of authorship and diverse sociohistorical settings. This is an intriguing proposal.

Sweeney, on the other hand, places Zech 9–14 in the early Persian period, and makes the bold claim that "Zechariah 7:1–14:21 constitutes a narrative report concerning the transmission of YHWH's word to Zechariah on the fourth day of the ninth month, i.e., Kislev, in the fourth year of King Darius of Persia" (2000, 634). Further he writes, "In the absence of such independent information [regarding setting or addressees], Zechariah 9–11 and 12–14 must be considered as structurally subordinate in the first instance to Zech 7:1, which provides the necessary information" (636). He then notes, "whereas Zech 8:18–23 indicates that the nations will ultimately recognize YHWH in Jerusalem, Zechariah 9–11 and 12–14 provide a detailed scenario of the process by which this recognition will take place" (636). This last comment reflects a point that has long been recognized in more traditional commentaries, and it provides a fruitful way to understand the theological and literary unity of Zech 1–14. Nonetheless, like Floyd, Sweeney sees the unity as one that is editorially constructed: "Although both Zechariah 9–11 and 12–14 were apparently composed by a writer or writers other than the prophet Zechariah, they are currently presented as the prophet's 'pronouncements' concerning YHWH's future actions" (656). Is it possible to assert a more forceful version of Zecharian unity than Sweeney's and Floyd's?

Kline attempts just such a proposal. He recognizes the explicit structure of the book as outlined by its three date-forms and two *massa'* headings, but believes there is a parallel structure, more subtle, indicating a unity for the whole at the compositional level. That unitary structure involves positing a "diptych" of 1:1–6:8, plus 7:1–14:21, which frame a central "hinge" at 6:9–15. Further, each of the two side panels of this diptych is in turn a diptych of its own, with hinges at 3:1–10 and 11:1–17. The identification of the three hinges depends upon his exegesis of each of these three units as involving the prophet in "a coronation, and investiture to theocratic office" (2001, 241). "Such a curious overall structuring is rather clearly to be attributed to an original master plan for the whole work" (2001, 256). Crownings are certainly in mind in 3:9 and 6:11; however, the alleged parallel in 11:1–17 stumbles. First, it is not at all clear that 11:1–17 is a single unit of text, since 11:1–3, addressed to "Lebanon" (11:1), is widely regarded as poetry, while the so-called Shepherd Allegory in 11:4–16, involving the union of Israel and Judah (11:14), is clearly prose, and 11:17's "Woe to the worthless shepherd" is again poetical. Second, it seems excessively subtle to call upon the reader to detect a coronation in the action of taking up a shepherd's staff (11:7). The reading of 11:15 as a reference to donning shepherd's *clothing* (כְּלִי רֹעֶה, itself a doubtful interpretation)—and making this action a royal investiture—seems forced. Shepherds are often royal figures in prophetic literature, but would the readers and hearers of the book detect such a correlation among these three passages? A priestly turban, a royal crown, and a shepherd's crook do not seem like a convincing triplet. Many interpreters see the shepherding task in Zech 11 as a prophetic/pastoral one, not royal. The interpretation of 11:4's word to the prophet (כֹּה אָמַר יְהוָה אֱלֹהָי) as denoting access to the heavenly throne room—symbolized also in the vision of 3:1-10 and represented by the earthly temple in 6:9-15—is a clear case of over-interpretation. Could an alternative proposal regarding the unity of Zechariah be sustained? To do so, we must first survey the book to discover its overall character.

THE SHAPE OF THE BOOK

Scholarly opinion about certain features of the shape of the book of Zechariah enjoys a wide consensus, a consensus that spans the divisions between schools of thought. There are generally agreed to be five sections, joined together by a redactional framework, minimally, at 1:1, 1:7 and 7:1. The first unit is Zech 1:1-6, an opening oracle on repentance which is viewed as providing the introduction to the subsequent section or sections or book as a whole. Next comes Zech 1:7-6:8, the series of night visions, with their accompanying oracles, generally seen as providing hope and encouragement to the paltry community of restoration-era Yehud. The coronation scene with its accompanying oracle in Zech 6:9-15 is typically seen as concluding the night vision episode.[13] Then follows a new unit, Zech 7:1-8:23, a collection of oracles focused on social justice and eschatological hope for Jerusalem, announced in answer to a question about ritual fasting. Each of these units of material so far is dated explicitly, as we have seen, to the second or fourth year of Darius the Great, often down to the day. Then comes the undated material: two sections each headed as a מַשָּׂא, "an oracle," Zech 9-11 and Zech 12-14. The content of these sections is more difficult to determine, but can generally be described as pertaining to the destiny of Jerusalem and its ultimate deliverance from the power of sin and evil enemies, both within and without. In the most common approach to the material, the major division is seen as coming between Zech 1-8 and Zech 9-14, between the dated and the undated material, or, for many, between the prophetic material of Zech 1-8 and the proto-apocalyptic material of Zech 9-14. Chart 5.1 below shows the book's outline:

---

[13] Stephen L. Cook, among others, takes 6:9-15 as an early redactional addition to the vision reports of 1:7-6:8 (1995, 134).

CHART 5.1
THE STRUCTURE OF ZECHARIAH

The Editorial Frame:	Zech 1:1; 1:7; 7:1; 9:1; 12:1
Part One	
Unit One: 1:1–6	Introduction to the Book
Unit Two: 1:7–6:15	The Night Visions and Oracles
Unit Three: 7:1–8:23	Question & Answer
Part Two	
Unit One: 9:1–11:17	The First מַשָּׂא
Unit Two: 12:1–14:21	The Second מַשָּׂא

SURVEY OF THE CONTENTS OF THE BOOK:
PART ONE: ZECH 1:1–8:23

THE EDITORIAL FRAME

As I have indicated in chapter four, Hag 1–2 and Zech 1–8 share a common editorial framework, a framework characterized by oracular introductory formulae and date formulae, dated to the reign of Darius the Great, the Persian monarch. The dates in Haggai and Zech 1–8, which are often given precisely down to the day, interlock, with the first date in Zechariah (1:1) preceding the final date in Haggai (2:10, 20) by about a month. The interlocking pattern, and their common themes and diction (Meyers and Meyers 1987, xlv–xlviii), make it probable that Haggai and Zech 1–8 once circulated as a single composite book, focused on abetting the great project of temple restoration envisaged by the prophets and the restoration community of Yehud (xl). As I have shown, detailed chronometric interest often accompanied temple-related activity in Babylonian texts. The same is true in the Latter Prophets. In Haggai–Zech 1–8 chronometric precision continues from Hag 1:1 through the heading in Zech 7:1, which introduces the question and oracular answers now found in chs. 7–8. With the completion of the temple in 515 B.C., I suggest that chronometric interest waned. The expanded form of Zechariah is organized by its *massa'* headings at 9:1 and 12:1; no more date formulae appear.

Haggai–Zechariah 1–8 announces the reestablishment of Yahweh's presence in Zion and calls the returned community and all Yehudeans to a life of ritual purity and social justice. In essence the message is, "Yahweh's kingdom in Zion has returned!—hope is alive; live accordingly!" It also includes the message to those still in exile, "Return to Zion!" The expanded version of Zechariah, which includes chs. 9–14, takes the Yehud community through a future of struggle until it reaches the victory of Yahweh's worldwide kingdom in Zion. That struggle-filled future is, as one writer put it, the "death and transfiguration of the holy city" (Leithart 1995).

The fact that no further date forms appear in Zech 9–14 is often taken as evidence that Zechariah was not the author of these two *mas'ot*. However, our evidence from Babylonian scribal practice regarding the link between precision dating and temple-related activity renders another explanation preferable. Once the temple was completed, there was no more perceived need for chronometric precision in recording prophetic oracles. The temple reestablished not only sacred space, but sacred time as well. Yahweh again sat enthroned in his temple; all was right with the world (or soon would be).

PART ONE, UNIT ONE: 1:1–6
INTRODUCTION TO THE BOOK

The first recorded word of Zechariah's oracles is קָצַף, "was angry," a verbal root emphatically repeated in noun form at the end of the opening line to form a compact *inclusio*:

קָצַף יְהוָה עַל־אֲבוֹתֵיכֶם קָצֶף

"Yahweh was very angry with your ancestors!" (1:2)

This is a daring opening. Here I assume that this book's literary form reflects the occasion of public discourse the prophet as speaker used with his intended audience.[14] Unlike the night visions, the first oracle (1:2–5) assumes a spoken, rather than a written, original. According to 1:2, Zechariah addresses his words to the descendents of those with whom Yahweh had been so angry. In these words he places himself at risk of rejection because of a threatening message. Like Muhammad in Mecca, and like the prophet Haggai before him, Zechariah courts the possibility of social marginalization because of the implied prospect of divine judgment. Yahweh's wrath once blazed against the ancestors; would his wrath break forth against their present-day descendents as well?

שׁוּבוּ אֵלַי נְאֻם יְהוָה צְבָאוֹת
וְאָשׁוּב אֲלֵיכֶם אָמַר יְהוָה צְבָאוֹת

---

[14] *Contra* Carroll (1990), Conrad (1999), and others.

"Turn to me,"—oracle of Yahweh of the heavenly armies—
"and I will turn to you!"—says Yahweh of the heavenly armies. (1:3)

Four times in the opening oracle the key root שׁוּב appears, twice in 1:3; once each in 1:4 and 1:6; "turn!" "repent!"—quoting the message of the former prophets. The term has a double referent: just as the ancestors were exhorted to "turn," so Zechariah's own audience is exhorted to turn. The שׁוּבוּ command may also have a bearing upon the exiles: "Return" to Zion, and Yahweh "will return to you." Verse 6 apparently likewise has a double reference: some of the ancestors did "turn" and repent, presumably during the exile. Zechariah's present hearers also responded favorably to the oracle, a rare occurrence for the prophets:

וַיָּשׁוּבוּ וַיֹּאמְרוּ כַּאֲשֶׁר זָמַם יְהוָה צְבָאוֹת לַעֲשׂוֹת לָנוּ כִּדְרָכֵינוּ
וּכְמַעֲלָלֵינוּ כֵּן עָשָׂה אִתָּנוּ

Then they turned and said, "Just as Yahweh of the heavenly armies has planned to do to us, according to our ways and according to our deeds, so he has done with us." (1:6)

With the notice in 1:6 about repentance enacted, Zechariah has been validated as a legitimate prophet by his audience society; the prime occasion of risking marginalization is ended, but a prophet never ceases to bear this risk. Upon every occasion when a prophet attempts to communicate the will of the deity, he or she is subject to renewed scrutiny by the audience society, and may be rejected and marginalized.

PART ONE, UNIT TWO: 1:7–6:15
THE NIGHT VISIONS AND RELATED ORACLES

Unit Two, the Night Visions, is a well organized series of vision reports, with the visions explained to the visionary prophet Zechariah by an interpreting angel, who appears in most of the visions. The origin of the material is most likely literary, rather than oral. Connected to the vision reports are a series of oracles that may in some cases briefly postdate the vision reports, added as interpretive commentary upon the visions. The interpretive oracles nonetheless are presented as Zechariah's inspired speech, and there is no reason to doubt the attribution. Often the oracles serve to clarify the meaning of, or to focus attention upon, key elements in the vision reports. Hanson claims that the set serves to promote a "propagandistic message" in support of "the hierocracy" (1979, 256), a claim that I shall evaluate after a review of the set's contents.

There is debate as to the number of vision reports. Meyers and Meyers and others count the vision report of the filthy priest of Zech 3 as an addition to an original seven-fold composition (1987, 179), which, oddly enough, "plays an integral role in the overall scheme of the visions" (1987, 191). Others hold that the vision report of the flying scroll in Zech 5:1–4 continues through the rest of Zech 5 to include the material about the woman in the ephah (5:5–11), thus comprising one complex vision report (5:1–11). Kline takes the text in that way, as about first the dispossession of apostates in Yehud, and then the deportation of those apostates from Yehud (2001, 177–202).

Despite these minority reports, it seems best to take the visions as they come, as a series of eight. The vision of the filthy priest in Zech 3, fourth in the series, plays an integral role because it is paired at the center with the fifth in the series, the vision of the menorah and olive trees in 4:1–14. Both of these central visions pertain to the leaders of Yehud, the high priest and the governor. The vision reports in Zech 5 are separated into the traditional two units by means of the formulaic reference to "lifting up" the eyes and "seeing" (שָׂא נָא עֵינֶיךָ וּרְאֵה, 5:5; cf. 5:1, וָאֶשָּׂא עֵינַי וָאֶרְאֶה), a feature shared with visions two (2:1, ET=1:18), three (2:5, ET=2:1), and eight (6:1).

What then is the content of the vision reports and related oracles? And what is their import for the social location of the prophet? The night vision reports and oracles disclose that Zechariah became and was received as a central authority prophet for fledgling Yehud, in close but not uncritical support of Joshua the high priest and Zerubbabel the governor. The vision reports and oracles of 1:7–6:15 focus not merely on the rebuilding of the temple, although that labor was of vital importance to the prophet and his tradents, but on the political and theological consolidation of Yehud as a Yahwistic theocracy under Persian imperial rule. Their purpose was to help prepare for the arrival of a future Davidide royal figure named the *Zemah*,[15] the "Branch" or the "Shoot," whose reign would supercede that of the Persian kings.

Thus the restoration envisioned by Zechariah was only in part a return to the Judean past. Elements of continuity with the past included the role of the high priest; the function of the temple as a center for ritual purification, moral renewal, and doxological activity; the return of the line of David in authority in Yehud; the reestablishment of Jerusalem as the cultic center of the society, and the renewal of the claim that Yahweh in some sense "dwelt" on Mt. Zion.[16]

---

[15] Following Wolter H. Rose (2000, 16), I have settled on using the English spelling *Zemah*, without diacritical marks, as the most convenient way of rendering the transliteration of the Hebrew צֶמַח.

[16] The frequently heard opinion that Isa 66:1–2 stands in criticism of the temple-building project endorsed in Haggai and Zech 1–8 (so Hanson 1986, 260; and Berquist 1995, 77, among others) must be tempered by the observation that, a few lines later, Isa 66:6 may speak of Yahweh's voice "*from* the temple" (קוֹל מֵהֵיכָל קוֹל יְהוָה, emphasis mine). Even if this reading is not followed, more generally it is clear that

Elements of discontinuity include the loss of kingship, the loss of sovereignty, the loss of territory, and the loss of population (Carter 1999). Other elements of discontinuity include the social and cultural differences between the *golah*-community of returnees and those Judeans who had remained behind in the land. Hanson, Berquist, and others have made much of this distinction, but the evidence of the books of Haggai and Zechariah is decidedly against any kind of major rift between the two groups yet (Meyers and Meyers 1987, 50–51; Ackroyd 1968, 150, n. 50). Such rifts are perhaps attested later, in the period of Ezra and Nehemiah (Ezra 9; Neh 5; cf. Blenkinsopp 1988, 66–69).

It is into this concrete situation that Zechariah wrote his vision reports, and into which they were then promulgated as authoritative direction from Yahweh of the heavenly armies. The visions came, the prophet tells us, on the night of the twenty-fourth of Shevat (February 15), 519 B.C.

VISION REPORT #1, THE ANGELIC HORSEMEN, ZECH 1:8–17. Zechariah the visionary sees a "man" riding a red horse stationed among myrtle trees in a deep dell; the "man," it later appears, seems to be the *mal'ak yahweh* (1:11), to whom other angelic riders, riding different colored horses, report. An interpreting angel, who shall accompany Zechariah through most of his visions, identifies the riders: like the Persian monarch's mounted couriers, the riders are Yahweh's scouts, sent out "to patrol the earth" (1:10). The horsemen, perhaps four in number, are representations of Yahweh's exercise of universal dominion. Their report, that "all the earth is at peace" (1:11) accords with the recent end of military hostilities in the Persian Empire—nine failed revolts that broke out at the *coup d'état* staged by Darius that made him emperor in 522 B.C., as recounted in the Behistun Inscription. The scouts' response evokes an anguished cry from the *mal'ak yahweh*: "Yahweh of the heavenly armies, how long will you withhold mercy from Jerusalem and from the cities of Yehud, which you have cursed these seventy years?" (1:12). The *mal'ak*'s question presupposes that Yehud is still under the punishment begun with the Babylonian exile, as announced by the prophet Jeremiah (25:11; 29:10). The nations are at peace, but Yehud is still in distress. Here the seventy years are understood, as we have seen, not as years of exile but as years of temple desolation. Yahweh replies with "good and comforting words" (1:13), and the prophet is commanded to proclaim the message that Yahweh has returned to his city, that the temple shall be rebuilt, that prosperity will again abound in Yehud, and that Yahweh "will again choose Jerusalem" (1:17). The oracle reasserts the Zion theology of the Davidic

---

Isa 56–66 does not abandon Zion theology. Childs warns, "The attempts to gain great historical specificity by various reconstructions ... run the danger of going beyond the intention of the biblical text itself" (2001, 540).

and Isaianic traditions. In the vision's setting of the worldwide purview of the angelic horsemen's patrol, comes the assurance of Yahweh's deep concern for Yehud and its capital city.

VISION REPORT #2, FOUR HORNS AND FOUR BLACKSMITHS, ZECH 2:1–4 (ET=1:18–21). Zechariah sees four horns and four craftsmen. The interpreting angel identifies them as the evil powers that have "scattered Judah, Israel and Jerusalem" (2:2; ET=1:19). Hence, they include Assyria and Babylonia. Unlike the fourfold beasts of Dan 7, the four horns take their number not from the *number* of kingdoms that took part in the scattering, but from the traditional ancient Near Eastern *ideology* of kingship. That ideology is expressed in typical "boilerplate" terminology, for example, by Ashurbanipal's (668–633 B.C.) royal titles found in the Rassam Cylinder inscription:

> Ashurbanipal, the great king, the legitimate king, king of the world, king of Assyria, king of (all) the four rims (of the earth), king of kings, prince without rival." (*ANET*, 297)

The title "king of (all) the four rims (of the earth)" means "universal king." The Assyrian and Babylonian kings claimed this title, a title dating far back to Sumerian times. The four "rims" of the earth, sometimes translated as four "quarters," cover the four directions. Thus the horned powers claim universal sovereignty.

The vision's blacksmiths are Yahweh's agents raised up to counteract the force of the horns. The Hebrew term translated in some versions as "blacksmith," חָרָשׁ, can denote a craftsman of any kind. According to Holladay's lexicon, it denotes a stoneworker in Exod 28:11, a carpenter in 2 Kgs 12:12, and a metalworker in 1 Sam 13:19 (1988, 118).

The choice of "blacksmith" for the translation here depends in turn upon the assessment of the horns as metallic objects, probably arrayed on one or more helmets in the vision.[17] The two exegetical decisions, that the horns are metal, and that the craftsmen are blacksmiths, are mutually reinforcing, and assist the reader in construing the vision of horns and craftsmen as a unity. The prophet

---

[17] Suggested as a possibility in Meyers and Meyers (1987, 136). An alternative view is expressed by Petersen and by Conrad, who see them as the horns of the rebuilt horned altar (1984, 165; 1999, 77–78). Sweeney's similar interpretation suggests that the horns are derived from the rebuilt altar, because it was Yahweh who had "brought about Israel's punishment in the first place" (2000, 582). This attempt reads too much into the vision report, and seems to present Yahweh opposing Yahweh, since both the horns and the smiths are ultimately representations of divine power. Boda, alternatively, sees the חָרָשִׁים as "ploughmen," who drive off horned cattle, a view that is lexically possible (2005, 25).

speaks of blacksmiths, armed with hammers, beating back or beating down the horns of the metalled helmets.

The text requires us to discover a meaning that pertains to a power that "cast down" the powers that "scattered Judah, Israel and Jerusalem." The best candidate for such a power is Persia, which under its founding emperor Cyrus took over the Babylonian Empire. In postexilic biblical texts, Persia is often treated favorably (Ezra 6:14). As we have seen, Joshua the high priest and Zerubbabel the governor were almost certainly Persian loyalists, as were other notable postexilic leaders, such as Ezra and Nehemiah. The first of Zechariah's night-visions also seems to present a favorable view of the Persian Empire, newly pacified by Darius the Great (r. 522–486 B.C.), when it presents all the earth as "resting peacefully" (1.11).

The overall meaning of the vision is that Yahweh in kindness has used the Persian empire to cast down oppressive political powers, and to reverse the "scattering" effect of the exile. Under the new Persian policy, Jews are returning to their ancestral land to rebuild the ruined cities and to restore the institutions of Yahweh's religion. The second night vision of the prophet Zechariah thus portrays the Persian Empire (550–331 B.C.) as a benevolent, protective force raised up by Yahweh to assist his ancient people in their exilic plight.

VISION REPORT #3, THE MEASURE OF JERUSALEM, ZECH 2:5–17 (ET=2:1–5). So far Zechariah has served only as witness to the visionary actions. Now he enters into the action directly: he sees a "man" with a measuring line and asks, "Where are you going?"—"To measure Jerusalem" is the reply. Such measuring would have been a common procedure in reconstructing the city. Here the measuring is to be done by an angel, denoted both as "man" (אִישׁ, 2:5) and as "young man" (הַנַּעַר הַלָּז, 2:8), but he is interrupted by another angel with a pressing message: "Jerusalem shall be inhabited as an unwalled city because of the great number of people and cattle within her" (2:8). Moreover, reminiscent both of Elisha's vision at Dothan (2 Kgs 6:17) and of Exodus-Sinai traditions (Exod 14:20; 40:38), the angel proclaims that Yahweh himself will be "a wall of fire" around her and "glory within her" (2:8).

Three additional oracles are attached, not necessarily of the same compositional level as the vision report, but nonetheless integrated into the whole and part of the final canonical form of the text. The first (2:10) urges exiles to return. The second (2:11–13) predicts the plundering of the Yehud's political oppressors, past and present, and presents the fulfillment of this prediction as proof of the genuineness of Zechariah's prophetic call. The third, a prophetic call for rejoicing (Floyd 2000, 636–37), invokes Yahweh's beloved Zion-Daughter to rejoice—because Yahweh will again dwell in Zion, because foreign nations will become one with the Yehudean people of God, because in so doing, Zechariah will be further confirmed as a true prophet, and because Yehud will become

Yahweh's own inheritance "in the Holy Land" (אַדְמַת הַקֹּדֶשׁ 2:16).¹⁸ The report ends with a liturgically derived call for an awed silence before the awesome Yahweh, "for he has roused himself from his holy dwelling" (2:17 NRSV).

Amid the second oracle appears the first use of a key thematic word in Zechariah, עַיִן, "eye" (2:12), aside from its repeated formulaic use in the introductions to the visions. הַנֹּגֵעַ בָּכֶם נֹגֵעַ בְּבָבַת עֵינוֹ, "Whoever touches you touches the pupil/ball of his [Yahweh's] eye." The term will appear nineteen times in Zech 1–14, six times in the vision report formulae, and six times of Yahweh's eye(s)—here in 2:12 and in 3:9, 4:10, 8:6, 9:8 and 12:4. In three of these the sense is of Yahweh's protection over Yehud (2:12; 9:8; 12:4). I shall later return to this unifying Zecharian theme.

VISION REPORT #4, THE FILTHY PRIEST, ZECH 3:1–10. The vision report begins in a unique way in the series: וַיַּרְאֵנִי, "and he showed me" (3:1), a point which leads some to consider the fourth report an addition. This conclusion overlooks the lack of absolute uniformity in the opening lines of each vision, and makes too little of the consistent use of a form of ר.א.ה in each incipit.

Now Zechariah enters deeper into the visionary world and closer to the core issues facing fledgling restoration-era Jerusalem. The vision takes the form of a trial scene in the divine council, with the *mal'ak yahweh* as the presiding judge, and Joshua the high priest as the accused. It is the second and final appearance of the *mal'ak yahweh* in the vision reports. As in Job 1–2 it is not שָׂטָן, Satan, but הַשָּׂטָן, "the satan," or better, "the accuser," a heavenly prosecutor figure, who stands at Joshua's right hand (cf. Ps 109:6) to accuse him. The vision's content may reflect doubts among the Yehudeans about Joshua's fitness for high-priestly service, born as he was in Babylonian exile, without benefit of the temple and its ritual purity. The *mal'ak yahweh*, however, permits no accusations. The accuser is silenced and Joshua is pronounced "a brand snatched from the fire" (3:2), the fires of evil and the unclean land of exile.

Joshua, it is now noted, is disgustingly dressed in filthy, dung-covered clothes (בְּגָדִים צוֹאִים), in violation of ritual purity, *en flagrant*. But this "is no obstacle" (Moore 1856, 154). The heavenly council itself proceeds to disrobe Joshua and to invest him with the clean ceremonial robes of his high-priestly office. Again Zechariah enters the action of the vision: "Put a clean turban on his head." The heavenly court complies. Then the *mal'ak yahweh* judge charges the newly invested priest for the performance of his high office, in divine oracular speech: "Walk in my ways … then you will have charge of my courts … and I will give you access among those standing here" (3:7). Remarkably, this priest

---

¹⁸ This text is the earliest attested occurrence of the phrase "the Holy Land," and the only one in the Hebrew Bible (Meyers and Meyers 1987, 170).

is promised access not merely to the restored earthly sacred court, but, like a prophet (Jer 23:18–22), to the heavenly court as well.

Further instruction promises the coming of the man called צֶמַח, *Zemah*, the "Branch," or "Shoot," denoted as עַבְדִּי, Yahweh's "servant" (3:8), perhaps reminiscent of Isa 4:2, בַּיּוֹם הַהוּא יִהְיֶה צֶמַח יְהוָה לִצְבִי וּלְכָבוֹד, the "beautiful" and "glorious" Branch of Yahweh," but more clearly evoking the book of Jeremiah (Rose 2003, 178):

הִנֵּה יָמִים בָּאִים נְאֻם־יְהוָה וַהֲקִמֹתִי לְדָוִד צֶמַח צַדִּיק וּמָלַךְ מֶלֶךְ
וְהִשְׂכִּיל וְעָשָׂה מִשְׁפָּט וּצְדָקָה בָּאָרֶץ

"See! Days are coming"—Yahweh's oracle—"when I will raise up for David a righteous Branch; he will reign as king and will deal wisely, and will do justice and righteousness in the land." (23:5)

בַּיָּמִים הָהֵם וּבָעֵת הַהִיא אַצְמִיחַ לְדָוִד צֶמַח צְדָקָה
וְעָשָׂה מִשְׁפָּט וּצְדָקָה בָּאָרֶץ

"In those days and at that time I will cause to sprout forth for David a righteous Branch, and he will do justice and righteousness in the land." (33:15)

This promise is reminiscent also of the "shoot" of Isa 11:1 (חֹטֶר מִגֵּזַע יִשַׁי) and 53:2 (וַיַּעַל כַּיּוֹנֵק לְפָנָיו וְכַשֹּׁרֶשׁ מֵאֶרֶץ צִיָּה), who also is denoted as עַבְדִּי, "my servant" (52:13). The *Zemah*-expectation tradition that Zechariah received from the earlier prophets is thus decidedly a royal, Davidic one.

Remarkably, the *Zemah* prediction is not spoken to Zerubbabel the current Davidide, but to Joshua the high priest, suggesting that the *Zemah* will have priestly functions. This surmise is further suggested by the sign-value of Joshua's priestly associates, who are said to be אַנְשֵׁי מוֹפֵת, "men of portent" of things to come (3:8), namely the coming *Zemah*. This priestly function of the *Zemah* is further suggested by the oracular line in 3:9 accompanying the prediction: וּמַשְׁתִּי אֶת־עֲוֹן הָאָרֶץ־הַהִיא בְּיוֹם אֶחָד, "and I will remove the iniquity of that land in a single day." This line seems to be the inscription that shall be carved on the strange seven-eyed stone of 3:9, a stone likely denoting both divine omniscience and messianic promise.[19] Following Mitchell, Petersen, and Kline, the stone may well be the metal plaque attached to the front of the high priest's tiara, which in Exod 28:36 is said to bear the inscription, קֹדֶשׁ לַיהוָה, "holy to

---

[19] For another stone serving as messianic symbol, see Ps 118:22. The messianic-stone motif is prominent in New Testament texts. Elsewhere in Zechariah, other stones appear, sometimes perplexingly. See 4:7, 10; 5:4, 8; 9:15, 16; and 12:3.

Yahweh" (1912, 157–58; 1984, 211–12; 2001, 122–26).[20] The coming of the *Zemah* is thus associated with the removal of sin, a priestly function in ancient Israel. That this removal shall occur on a single day" (בְּיוֹם אֶחָד) evokes the Day of Atonement functions of the high priest (Lev 16). Here the Davidide associations of the righteous ruler of Isa 11:1 and Jer 23:5 and 33:15 are combined with priestly associations of atonement for sin. The vision report concludes with a further oracular line, promising peace, prosperity and hospitality in Yehud, under each man's vine and fig tree.

The priestly functions of the *Zemah* point distinctly away from identifying this figure as Zerubbabel. Wolter H. Rose (2000, 140–41; 2003) concludes that the *Zemah* of Zech 3 and 6 is not Zerubbabel, *contra* Hanson and many others (1986, 262), but a future royal figure. This conclusion is entirely sound. The future expectation expressed in Zech 3:8 is thoroughly inappropriate for referring to Zerubbabel, a figure who is already *present* in Yehud.

To sum up, the fourth vision "serves to justify not only the role of high priest but a specific person to fill it" (Petersen 1988, 748). Against all doubts, the investiture of Joshua grants him greater divine access than any priest before him. He and his priestly associates, moreover, are signs of the future—the coming of the *Zemah*, who shall fulfill for all time the priestly function of sin-removal, a function now carried out by Joshua. Peace and prosperity shall characterize that day.

With the first four vision reports, Zechariah has brought the reader from the worldwide scope of the angelic horsemen to one of the core values of Yehudean life, the temple and the high priesthood. The next four visions will, inversely, take the reader from inner-Yehudean concerns back to a worldwide scope (so Meyers and Meyers 1987, lvi; and, in a way, Floyd 2000, 330).

VISION REPORT #5, THE GOLDEN MENORAH AND THE TWO OLIVE TREES, ZECH 4:1–14. In the fifth vision, again addressing inner-Yehudean concerns, Zechariah is awakened by his interpreting angel. The text is unclear as to whether the prophet was literally awakened, or whether the awakening was from one level of visionary experience to another. Zechariah sees a golden menorah flanked by two olive trees. The olive trees are somehow linked by pipes to the menorah's oil bowl; thus the trees continuously feed the menorah with fresh oil, fueling its lamps. The lamps are either seven in number, like the traditional Tabernacle menorah, or perhaps forty-nine in number, with each

---

[20] As in Zech 5:8, perhaps 4:10, and elsewhere in the MT, stone is sometimes not differentiated from metal.

of the seven branches bearing seven wicks in its lamp.²¹ If forty-nine, then we have a "Jubilee" menorah, a menorah intensified.

The light of the menorah represents the light of Yahweh's presence, as mediated by the temple, wherein the menorah was to be located. The sevenfold branches with their lamps represent the "seven eyes" of Yahweh (3:9; 4:10b), denoting divine omniscience. Thus two olive trees flank a symbol of the deity. The flanking motif is reminiscent of cylinder seal iconography. The two trees symbolize two persons. The fact that the lights of the menorah are supported by the oil coming from the two trees suggests that the restoration of Yahweh's presence in Yehud is facilitated by two human leaders, namely, the high priest Joshua, the subject of the fourth vision report, and the Davidide governor, Zerubbabel, who shall be spoken of remarkably in the interpretive oracle that accompanies this fifth vision report (4:6b–10a).²²

Yet the work of the high priest and the governor is not a matter of human power. Trust in such power is disavowed, perhaps denounced, by the motto-like declaration of Zech 4:6b, לֹא בְחַיִל וְלֹא בְכֹחַ כִּי אִם־בְּרוּחִי אָמַר יְהוָה צְבָאוֹת, "'not by might, and not by power, but surely by my Spirit!'—says Yahweh of the heavenly armies." The work of restoration is not one of synergistic force, but of monergistic enabling. There is, nonetheless, a "symbiosis" depicted in the divine-human relationship (so Petersen 1984, 234). The symbolism appears not to be one of anointing, but one of enabling; hence the unusual phrase, בְּנֵי־הַיִּצְהָר, "sons of oil" (4:14), using the less common word for oil, יִצְהָר, not שֶׁמֶן, the word used in all contexts in the MT involving anointing. These two, servant-like yet majestic, הָעֹמְדִים עַל־אֲדוֹן כָּל־הָאָרֶץ, "stand before the Sovereign of all the earth" (4:14). As Petersen concludes, "This vision suggests a rather specific form of leadership structure for the restored community, namely, civil and priestly leaders who depend upon Yahweh for their power" (1988, 748).²³

The important oracle of 4:6b–10a remains to be commented upon. It seems an obvious interruption in the narrative flow of the vision, which leaves an unanswered question hanging in 4:4; the answer is delayed until 4:10b. Many therefore attribute the oracle to a later redaction. This supposition may well be the case; however, the oracle balances the twin visions reports of 3:1–10 and 4:1–14 with content to and about Zerubbabel parallel to that which is revealed to

---

[21] The issue depends upon whether the second of the three appearances of the word שִׁבְעָה in Zech 4:2 is treated as a dittography or not. See Meyers and Meyers (1987, 235–37) for a full discussion.
[22] *Contra* Kline (2001, 165), who takes the trees as anointers, and therefore as prophets (though, strangely, not as Haggai and Zechariah); Boda (2001), who suggests Haggai and Zechariah; and Rose (2003, 182–84), who sees them as heavenly beings.
[23] But see Rose (2003, 182–84) for a different view of these "two sons."

Joshua in the divine speech of 3:6–10. Without this oracular material, the fifth vision report seems incomplete. Moreover, in 4:6b–10a the temple is still incomplete; its composition must come from the same time period as the vision reports and the work of temple reconstruction, 519–515 B.C.

In the oracles, first, Zerubbabel is addressed with the motto about power; those who think that Zerubbabel is a messianic contender, leading revolt against Persia, and those who think that Haggai and Zechariah are wild-eyed prophets fomenting rebellion (so Olmstead 1948, 136–42; Waterman 1954; more modestly, Hanson 1979, 247, 439; and Betlyon 1986, 640 and n. 29),[24] should consider the quietism of the motto. As Bryan E. Beyer observes:

> What happened to [Zerubbabel] is unknown. Some scholars have proposed that [he] fell into disfavor with Persian authorities and was then either deposed, taken to Persia, imprisoned, and/or put to death. Such theories, however, are based upon arguments from silence. Simply because a person is not mentioned after a certain time, we cannot conclude that this indicates his death or removal from office. Zerubbabel is probably not mentioned in the biblical narratives after the completion of the temple because he no longer played a role in the biblical writer's overall purpose. (1992, 1086)

To return to the oracle, Zerubbabel is then announced as having a key role in the reconstruction of the temple. The apparently great obstacle posed by הַר־הַגָּדוֹל, a "mighty mountain," shall become a level place!—perhaps an exaggerated reference to the rubble-covered top of Mt. Zion, which shall become the platform for the new temple—or a metaphorical description of the seemingly insurmountable problems posed by the project (Conrad 1999, 106).[25] Zerubbabel

---

[24] Berquist argues convincingly against any such messianic conspiracy theory involving Zerubbabel (1995, 61–68).

[25] Petersen take the "mighty mountain" as a metaphor for Zerubbabel, in stark contrast to the mere "plain," denoting, perhaps, Joshua the high priest, or Tattenai the sub-satrap of Trans-Euphrates, who then is being admonished to leave temple-building to the Davidide Zerubbabel. In this case the point of view of the redactor—decidedly pro-Zerubbabel—lies at odds with the point of view found in the original vision reports, which favor equality between the governor and priest (1984, 239–40, 244). This view overplays the evidence, and relies on an unlikely textual reconstruction of the הַר־הַגָּדוֹל phrase in 4:7. Moreover, the purpose of the oracles in 4:6b–10a is not to exalt Zerubbabel at the expense of Joshua, but to provide Zerubbabel with explicit divine authorization for the temple-building project, a project ordinarily carried out by kings, a mandate parallel to the one enjoyed by Joshua in 3:7–10. As Meyers and Meyers have argued (1987, 268) the material in the oracular insertion, since it is about temple-construction, can hardly have originated after 515 B.C. If it ever existed independently of the vision reports (which they doubt), it

shall then bring forth הָאֶבֶן הָרֹאשָׁה, "the first stone," perhaps a reference to a ceremonial stone reclaimed from the old building, reused in temple-rebuilding ceremonies in the ancient Near East (so Ellis 1968; followed by Meyers and Meyers 1987, 246–48; and Petersen 1984, 240–41). Both Merrill (1994, 161) and Stuhlmueller (1988, 87) think this stone is the "top stone," that is, the final stone of the building, which is certainly possible. If so, then the whole building process from start to finish is in view in Zech 4:6b–10a. Is this stone perhaps the same stone referred to in 4:10a, and there called הָאֶבֶן הַבְּדִיל, "the tin stone"? More likely it seems that the "tin-stone" is an object used as a foundation deposit, also common to ancient Near Eastern palace- and temple-founding ceremonies, as documented from the archaeological record by Ellis (1968; so also Meyers and Meyers 1987, 253–54; and Petersen 1984, 243–44). Or perhaps the object is a tin plate with a dedicatory inscription placed on a foundation stone or in a foundation deposit stone, and so analogous to the inscribed object of 3:9 (so Petersen 1984, 243–44). The KJV's "plummet," following the LXX, makes little sense for an object of tin, a lightweight metal; a plumb line ought to be made of a heavier metal, like lead. Such deposit-stone objects enhance the apparent value of a building, and thus, perhaps, provide an answer to those who "despise the day of small things" (4:10a; Petersen 1984, 244).

In the ancient Near East, temple-building was a function of kings, not governors. Zechariah's fifth vision report legitimates *this* temple as the work of *this* governor, under the benevolent gaze of the seven eyes of Yahweh (4:10).[26] Together, the twin central vision reports of Zech 3 and Zech 4 provide convincing evidence of Zechariah's role as a central authority prophet, aiding a perhaps doubt-prone leadership—Joshua and Zerubbabel—in the fledgling work of a Yehudean restoration badly in need of social, political and religious consolidation.

VISION REPORT #6, THE FLYING SCROLL, ZECH 5:1–4. With the end of the fifth report, about leaders, the literary movement of the visionary series again turns outward toward broader concerns. The sixth and seventh of Zechariah's night visions deal with negative aspects of life in Yehud. The visions fix the seer's attention upon the correction of corrupt elements in the life of the postexilic community. None of the preceding visions in the series is focused so thoroughly upon sinful aspects. Even in Zech 3:1–10, no accusation

---

was quickly, if not immediately, added to them. Petersen, similarly, sees the insertion as arising on a scroll of Zechariah's collected oracles (1984, 239).

[26] Boda, however, reminds us that Zechariah is not primarily a temple-building prophet. More central to his concerns are repentance and faithfulness to Yahweh, as highlighted in the book's opening oracle, by a number of the vision reports, and by the oracles of Zech 7–8 (2003).

was permitted against the dung-covered high priest. The previous tone has been one of sustained encouragement and deepening hope. But before the visions can rightly come to their resting-place, Yahweh must deal definitively with forces that threaten to corrupt the community. That burden comes to the fore in the sixth and seventh vision reports.

The sixth vision report (5:1–4) draws our attention to a fantasy image, an immense flying scroll, twenty cubit long and ten cubits wide,[27] apparently with writing on both of its sides, as in the woe-filled scroll of Ezek 2:10. This scroll flies into the house of a miscreant, imbeds itself into the architecture, and destroys the building completely, down to its very beams and masonry. In the Hebrew Bible flight is usually associated with speed. The wildly vivid image of the immense flying scroll seems designed to communicate the inexorable speed and power of the divine curse inscribed on the scroll—a curse directed against thieves and those who swear falsely by Yahweh's name. No sanctuary can hide them; no power can protect them from the divine curse written on the scroll.

The writing on the scroll is identified as הָאָלָה, "the oath," or more likely, "the curse," הַיּוֹצֵאת עַל־פְּנֵי כָל־הָאָרֶץ, "going out over the face of all the land," the land of Yehud. The curse functions to purge every thief and false swearer, and to destroy their houses. Theft and the use of Yahweh's name in false oaths are matters proscribed in the Ten Commandments. The text perhaps serves as evidence that postexilic Jews thought of the Ten Commandments as comprised of two tables: theft is proscribed in the so-called "second table" of the law, while the command against the misuse of the divine name is found in the so-called "first table." If so, then the two commandments on the scroll are perhaps meant to represent the entire set of ten, or more generally, the Torah itself. The text thus also witnesses to the importance attributed to written scripture in the early postexilic period.

The text finds a parallel in the case law of Lev 5:20–26 [MT; ET=6:1–7], where restitution is required of the thief (גֹּזֵל, not Zech 5:3–4's גֹּנֵב), and of the person who swears falsely (וְנִשְׁבַּע לַשֶּׁקֶר) in a case regarding lost, stolen or extorted property. The scroll is then also the Torah's covenant curse, wrecking its vengeance upon covenant breakers.

The threatened destruction of houses is reminiscent of the covenant curses in the Sefire Stele treaty inscription (1, C. 21–23; Fitzmyer 1967), and, more directly, the sanctions threatened by Darius the Great in the edict to Tat-

---

[27] Attempts to link the flying scroll to the portico of Solomon's temple because of their comparable dimensions (Meyers and Meyers 1987, 279–83; Kline 2001, 179; Sweeney 2000, 615–16; cf. 1 Kgs 6:3) do not seem to be exegetically supportable. Of such efforts and others Mitchell observes, "the most ingenious among them has not been able to furnish an interpretation that is sufficiently obvious to commend itself to any but the inventor" (1912, 169).

tanu/Tattenai, governor of Trans-Euphrates, regarding temple-building in Yehud, now found in the book of Ezra: "For this crime [altering the royal decree], his house is to be made a pile of rubble" (6:11).

The vision likely addresses the presumably unsettled state of Yehud before the recent arrival of Zerubbabel and Joshua. Perhaps the gubernatorial office had been vacated for some time after the presumed death of Sheshbazzar. In any case, Zech 8:11 reminds Yehudeans of the recently past time when "the one coming and the one going had no peace from [his] enemy." The unwalled condition of the city, no doubt, contributed to the lack of security from theft. As the earlier vision reports proclaimed, Yahweh has returned to Yehud. His return means peace and prosperity for the penitent, but desolation for the impenitent.

The vision report may also look forward to the time when, in 458 B.C., the Persian administration of Artaxerxes I would send Ezra the Scribe to Yehud to enforce Torah as the law of the land (Ezra 7). If so, Zechariah's vision of the flying scroll foresees the time in the near future when Torah, mentioned also in Zech 7:12, shall be vigorously enforced under divine sanction. In any case, the vision report indicates Zechariah's strong affirmation of ancient Israelite values; the prophet is thus a traditionalist, not a radical revolutionary. Such enforcement shall serve to purge sinners and to purify the land of Yehud.

VISION REPORT #7, THE WICKED WOMAN IN THE EPHAH, ZECH 5:5–11. Purging and purity is likewise the concern of the seventh of the eightfold vision reports. Like the preceding report, this one deals with another corrupting influence in the land of Yehud, idolatry. The report describes a woman tucked inside an ephah basket borne by two stork-winged women and carried off to Babylon, where she is placed on a pedestal in a temple of her own. The woman is identified by the name "wickedness" (זֹאת הָרִשְׁעָה, 5:8). If we accept the text-critical emendation in 5:6 of עֵינָם, "their eye," to עֲוֹנָם, "their iniquity," (Mitchell 1912, 92; Petersen 1984, 254), then the contents of the basket are twice described as pertaining to sinfulness. On the other hand, Zechariah exhibits a peculiar propensity toward mentioning the eye. Perhaps the word עֵינָם is meant to evoke a *double entendre*, both "their iniquity" and "their eye." In such a case the "eye" may denote evil desire.[28] The woman represents a female fertility cult-figurine associated with Canaanite or Babylonian forms of religion. The *ephah* is a standard dry measure in Israelite society, and probably held somewhat more or less than a bushel basket (Meyers and Meyers 1987, 296). Since the ephah is said to contain a woman, either the woman is unnaturally diminutive, or the flying basket, like the flying scroll before it, is unnaturally large.

---

[28] Prov 21:4 says, "Haughty eyes and a proud heart—the lamp of the wicked—are sin." Cf. 1 John 2:16's mention of "the lust of the eyes."

The vivid imagery suggests the dangerous character of the woman: when the basket's lid is removed, the woman struggles to get free, but she is thrown "back into the basket," and its heavy metal lid "slammed" back into place over its opening (וַיַּשְׁלֵךְ אֶת־אֶבֶן הָעֹפֶרֶת אֶל־פִּיהָ). Thus the basket is also a kind of prison (so Merrill 1994, 174–75).

The imagery perhaps achieves an unexpected gender balance: it is not as though womankind is wicked—for it is women themselves who fly the ephah-basket out of the land of Judah to its true home. The two stork-winged women of 5:10 are the Bible's only female angels. Alternatively, noting that the stork is listed among the unclean animals, those with unclean wings are chosen to take the unclean woman out of the land of Yehud.

The angelic stork-winged women fly the wicked woman in her secure lead-lidded basket-prison off to "the land of Shinar," "to build for her a temple" there (לִבְנוֹת־לָהּ בַיִת בְּאֶרֶץ שִׁנְעָר), a reference sure to evoke memory of the story of the Tower of Babel, built "in the land of Shinar" (Gen 11:2; cf. Gen 10:10; Dan 1:1; Isa 11:11). The place name שִׁנְעָר, "Shinar" is inextricably bound up with the hubris of the biblical world's first center of paganism, Babylon, a city whose name in popular etymology meant "the gate of god."

In the final act of purification of the eight-vision set, the idol-woman is shoved back into her basket to be flown to Babylonia, where a temple with pedestal shall be built for her. Thus the remnants of idolatry are removed from the land of Yehud so that the purity of life with Yahweh may thrive. The text need not be taken to mean that *returned Yehudeans* were actually committing acts of idolatry. Perhaps there was idolatry on the part of non-*golah* Yehudeans, or by foreigners in Yehud. Indeed, it is quite possible that the vision represents the removal of the uncleanness left behind by the disobedient generations or by the Babylonian invaders in 587 B.C.[29]

Regardless, with the removal of the woman, the wickedness of Yehud is removed as well. The purity of land, people, leaders and rebuilt temple is thus assured to the vision report's original readers and hearers. In short, the vision means that Yahweh wins. According, only one more vision-report follows: a vision of angelic charioteers that brings rest to the land.

VISION REPORT #8, YAHWEH'S CHARIOTS, ZECH 6:1–8. Once again the number four appears, reminding the reader of the universal scope of earlier vision reports—four horns (2:1; ET=1:18), four blacksmiths (2:3; ET=1:20), and perhaps four horses (1:8). The angelic horse theme of the first

---

[29] But see the discussion by Julia M. O'Brien (1990, 66–69), in regard to Mal 2:11, taking the phrase, "Judah has married the daughter of a foreign god," as a reference to idolatry in Yehud. Gordon P. Hugenberger offers a persuasive rebuttal of this interpretation (1994, 34–36).

vision report recurs as an *inclusio*, only now the horses are attached to four chariots. The four chariots with their horses are soon interpreted as "the four winds/spirits of heaven going out after presenting themselves before the Sovereign of all the earth" (אַרְבַּע רֻחוֹת הַשָּׁמַיִם יוֹצְאוֹת מֵהִתְיַצֵּב עַל־אֲדוֹן כָּל־הָאָרֶץ). As in 4:14 (אֲדוֹן כָּל־הָאָרֶץ), at the core of the vision reports, Yahweh's universal rule is emphasized at the conclusion of the vision reports.

In the vision, the chariots/winds/spirits have just come from appearing before Yahweh at the divine council. They have exited the heavenly realm—the gate of which is depicted as between two bronze mountains, the bronze evoking the two bronze pillars, Yachin and Boaz, flanking the portico of Solomon's temple. Just as the pillars mark the entry to Yahweh's earthly dwelling, so the mountains mark the entry to Yahweh's heavenly dwelling. The mountains also evoke the eastern Mediterranean imagery of sunrise/sunset, and the chariots of the sun (2 Kgs 23:11). But these are Yahweh's war chariots (Kline 2001, 210), apparently going forth either to make war on the enemies of his people, or to enforce the universal exercise of Yahweh's dominion over the earth. Merrill surmises that the red-horsed chariot is the *mal'ak yahweh*'s command chariot (1994, 186), which is probably correct. Hence, the red chariot is omitted from the list of those going forth to the various points of the compass.

The vision report focuses on the chariots' activity in אֶרֶץ צָפוֹן, "the land of the north" (6:8), a phrase seen elsewhere in the MT only in Zech 2:10, 6:6 and the book of Jeremiah. In Jeremiah it typically denotes the invasion route by which Babylonian destruction shall come, or, after destruction, the region from whence the exiles shall return to their land. Here in Zech 6 it denotes the anti-Yahweh forces of evil,[30] embodied in the same empires symbolized by the four horns of 2:1–4 (ET=1:18–21). In Yahweh's sovereign dominion over the earth, Persia has overcome Babylon, reversed its punitive policies, and has allowed the exiles to go home; the earth is now pacified under Persia's—and Yahweh's—dominion. The northbound horses' exercise of dominion is then described as follows: הֵנִיחוּ אֶת־רוּחִי בְּאֶרֶץ צָפוֹן, "they have appeased my Spirit in the land of the north" (6:8). That is, Yahweh's wrath against the enemy has been spent (cf. כָּלָה אַפִּי וַהֲנִחוֹתִי חֲמָתִי בָּם in Ezek 5:13); the threats to his universal sovereignty have been removed; and Yahweh's reign over all earth is commencing: all exiles should now return in peace (Petersen 1984, 272). Moreover, the hiphil הֵנִיחוּ verb evokes the usage of the same verbal root (in the hophal) found in the seventh vision report, where the woman from the ephah is "set down there on her pedestal" (הֻנִּיחָה שָּׁם עַל־מְכֻנָתָהּ) in her temple in the land of Shinar (5:11). Contrary to the corrupting power of the wicked woman enshrined in Shinar,

---

[30] Influence from Ezek 38–39 may also be present. Cf. Ezek 38:6, 15; 39:2, where God and Magog are vaguely "northern" diabolical powers arrayed against Israel.

Yahweh's Spirit moves to inhabit the land of the north, transforming it from a place of threat and curse to a place of cultic purity and beatific peace.

Redditt observes, "this vision reversed conditions in the first vision, where the nations were at rest, but God was jealous and angry with them. In this last vision, God was at rest, because the north country (Babylon) has been defeated (1:18–21), and the Holy Land cleansed" (1995, 75).

With this assurance of Yahweh's worldwide victory, like the scenes of the western hero riding off into the sunset, the vision reports come to an appropriate conclusion. The readers and hearers have been brought from the core of inner-Yehudean concerns in the fifth vision report back to the world-wide scope with which they started. However, one more oracle is attached to the series, addressing the issue of what the returned exiles should do in response to these remarkable vision reports.

CONCLUDING PROPHETIC SIGN ACTION: ZECH 6:9–15 AND THE CROWNS

The account of the episode in Zech 6:9–15, a concluding prophetic sign action involving crowns, is important for the social location analysis of the prophet.[31] It poses several difficulties for the interpreter, not least of which is the redaction-history of the passage, the number of crowns involved in the actions of 6:11 and 6:14, the question of who is being crowned in 6:11, and the number of thrones in 6:13. I will deal with these four difficulties in that order

Many suppose, following Wellhausen and others (Mitchell 1912, 185–86; Amsler 1981, 106; and Cook 1995, 134), that this passage was only later written and appended to the vision reports. Alternatively, Ackroyd regards the episode and composition as occurring before the night-visions, perhaps even in Babylonia, in recognition of Zerubbabel's new appointment as governor of Yehud (1968, 197). Redditt sees only 6:11b–13 as secondary, along with 4:6b–10a and 3:1–10. These were added by "quite possibly Zechariah himself" as part of a revised and expanded second edition of the book, addressed to the Jerusalem audience; the first edition, without these materials, he sees as addressed to the exiles still living in Babylonia (1995, 42). Meyers and Meyers likewise see added material in 3:8–10, 4:6b–10a, and 6:12b–13, but view it, like Redditt, as authentic Zechariah, and now "integral to the visionary sequence" (1992).

If these units were later compositions, they must have been composed very early, since 4:9 and 6:12 both pertain to the still-unfinished temple-building

---

[31] On the nature of prophetic sign actions in the Hebrew Bible, see Kevin G. Friebel (1999), who considers them as nonverbal rhetorical vehicles, designed to communicate "graphically specifiable message-contents" (466).

project. In any case, they should be viewed as authentic material from the prophet. Moreover, as Redditt points out, Zech 6:9–15 in its present location has the function of urging the people "to take action based on what Zechariah had reported" from the visions (1995, 76). It therefore fulfills an understandable and perhaps even necessary task in the overall plan of the series.

The text and translation of 6:11 is a *crux criticorum*. The MT reads,

וְלָקַחְתָּ כֶסֶף־וְזָהָב וְעָשִׂיתָ עֲטָרוֹת וְשַׂמְתָּ בְּרֹאשׁ יְהוֹשֻׁעַ בֶּן־יְהוֹצָדָק הַכֹּהֵן הַגָּדוֹל

The difficulty lies in the word עֲטָרוֹת, "crowns," and the fact that only Joshua the high priest is named as being crowned. Hence, many textual critics seek either to emend the עֲטָרוֹת to the singular form, עֲטֶרֶת (so *BHS*), or rewrite the text to introduce a second person to be crowned, namely Zerubbabel (so Hanson 1979, 256), or to replace Joshua's name with that of Zerubbabel (so Wellhausen 1898, 185; Mitchell 1912, 189; Ackroyd 1968, 196; and *BHS*). The latter suggestion need not depend upon Waterman's "messianic conspiracy" theory, that Zerubbabel's name, original to the text, was suppressed because of his execution by the Persians for fomenting revolt in Yehud (1954). Ackroyd more reasonably argues that, in the course of Second Temple history, as is well known, rulership in Yehud passed somehow from the Davidides to the high priests. Hence, the text was rewritten to reflect the later polity (1968, 196).

But this supposition overlooks a still better explanation, one in keeping with the exegetically warranted distinction between Zerubbabel and the *Zemah* that we observed in Zech 3.[32] Retaining the MT's עֲטָרוֹת, two crowns are to be made, perhaps one of silver and one of gold, since these two metals are named in 6:11a (so Meyers and Meyers 1987, 349). One crown, likely the first-mentioned silver one, is to be placed symbolically on Joshua's head, signifying the perhaps-expanded duties of the high priest in a time without a Yehudean monarch. Silver, however, is not the material for a royal crown. The other crown, the royal one of gold, is held in reserve: it is for the future *Zemah*. As Meyers and Meyers suggest, the second crown presupposes the "eschatological restoration of the monarchy" (1987, 353). "Joshua endorses a great hope for the future but eschews it for the present" (1987, 355). Perhaps Zerubbabel had already been invested by Persian authority and therefore needed no coronation. Following Meyers and Meyers, I suggest the following translation for 6:11:

Take silver and gold and make [two] crowns, and place [one] on the head of Joshua ben-Jehozadak, the high priest.

---

[32] Berquist notes, "There is no reason to read a rejection of Zerubbabel into this emphasis on Joshua" (1995, 73).

Once the understanding appears that the *Zemah* is not Zerubbabel, but a future Davidide, many of the difficulties in 6:9–15 vanish. Regarding the rewritten text theory Stephen L. Cook writes, "no textual support exists for the suggestion, often adopted since Wellhausen, that the crowning was originally of Zerubbabel but was changed to Joshua" (1995, 134).[33] Rose also concludes, "once one takes a closer look at the hypothesis of a rewritten text and thinks through its implications, it loses any attractiveness which it might have had at first sight" (2000, 172).[34]

The expected temple of 6:12–13 that the *Zemah* shall build, then, is not the Zerubbabel temple, or if so, it is a substantial enlargement or renovation of that temple, which is likely under the influence of the temple vision in Ezek 40–48. In keeping with royal functions in the ancient Near East, and the Solomonic tradition, the restored Davidide king will engage in temple construction or temple renovation activity.

The next crux to face is that of 6:13b, the matter of thrones. The NIV reads, "he [the *Zemah*] will be a priest upon his throne," an old understanding found also in the KJV that comports well with the priestly functions I noted for the *Zemah* in my discussion of Zech 3. In this case, the *Zemah* becomes a priest-king, a view also found in New Testament Christology. However, this view has difficulty with 6:13. The MT reads:

וְהוּא־יִשָּׂא הוֹד וְיָשַׁב וּמָשַׁל עַל־כִּסְאוֹ וְהָיָה כֹהֵן עַל־כִּסְאוֹ
וַעֲצַת שָׁלוֹם תִּהְיֶה בֵּין שְׁנֵיהֶם

He will bear royal insignia, and shall sit and reign upon his throne; and there will [also] be a priest upon his [own] throne, and peaceful counsel shall prevail between the two of them. (6:13)

Here the phrase עַל־כִּסְאוֹ, "upon his throne," appears twice, once for the Davidide *Zemah* and once for the high priest. This understanding of two thrones, *contra* the NIV's "he [the *Zemah*] will be a priest on his throne," is supported by עֲטָרוֹת, "[two] crowns" in 6:11, and by the phrase וַעֲצַת שָׁלוֹם תִּהְיֶה בֵּין שְׁנֵיהֶם, "peaceful counsel shall prevail between the two of them."[35] The main remaining

---

[33] Wellhausen wrote, "das Diadem ist von Zacharia für Zerubabel als künftigen König bestimmt, erst von einem späteren Diaskeuasten für den Hohenpriester Josua. Der Diaskeuast trug den Verhältnissen Rechnung, wie sie sich tatsächlich gestalteten: der Priester wurde das Haupt der Theokratie, nicht der Davidide" (1898, 185).

[34] For exegetical arguments that the *Zemah* is not Zerubbabel, see Rose (2003, 174–81).

[35] The NRSV's "There shall be a priest by his throne" (6:13) reflects the LXX's καὶ ἔσται ὁ ἱερεὺς ἐκ δεξιῶν αὐτοῦ. The NAB also follows this reading. The Qumran

textual problem, the word הָעֲטָרֹת in 6:14, is less crucial to the overall interpretation of the text. If we follow the MT, which presents a *defectio* spelling of the plural, then both crowns shall be placed, perhaps on display, in the temple. If we repoint it to the singular, then Joshua retains his (silver) crown, while the royal golden crown is held in reserve in the temple for the messianic age. In either case we still have a coherent reading of the text, with little or no emendation.

The unit ends with the promise that "those far away" (exiles or non-Israelites, or both; cf. Isa 60:4, 10) will come to build the temple, the eschatological temple associated with the restoration of Davidide rule. This action will confirm Zechariah as a true prophet.

The final line is theologically weighted:

וְהָיָה אִם־שָׁמוֹעַ תִּשְׁמְעוּן בְּקוֹל יְהוָה אֱלֹהֵיכֶם

This will happen if you diligently obey Yahweh your God. (6:15)

It promises fulfillment of the oracle—and perhaps of all the predictive elements in the oracles associated with the whole set of vision reports in Zech 1:7–6:15—*if* the Yehudeans obey their God. This conditionality matches the opening oracle of the book: "'Return to me ... and I will return to you,' says Yahweh of the heavenly armies" (1:3; so Moseman 2000, 490, 494). Thus, some elements in the series are firm: "I have returned to Jerusalem in mercy" (1:16), for example; others are rendered tentative, conditioned upon reverent obedience to the prophetic word of Zechariah, Yahweh's messenger. Among these conditional promises are the coming of the *Zemah*, the arrival of "those far away," and the building of the eschatological temple. However, elsewhere in the visions and oracles the coming of the *Zemah* is so central to the divine intention for Yehud that this conditionality can hardly be permanently prohibitive. For this reason, perhaps, Meyers and Meyers render the אִם of the last line, not as an "if," but as a "when": "This will be so when you truly listen to the voice of Yahweh your God" (1987, 336). This translation is theologically and contextually warranted, especially in light of the oracular announcement in 4:6:

לֹא בְחַיִל וְלֹא בְכֹחַ כִּי אִם־בְּרוּחִי
אָמַר יְהוָה צְבָאוֹת

"Not by might, and not by power, but surely by my Spirit,"
—says Yahweh of the heavenly armies.

---

expectation of two messiahs in the Rule of the Community (cf. 1QS IX, 11) is likely influenced by the tradition now preserved here in the MT.

Human failure shall not forever hinder the divine plan.

To summarize, in Zech 6:9–15 the prophet is told to enact a prophetic sign action, involving the making of two crowns, the non-royal crowning of the high priest Joshua, and the preparation for a future royal crowning of the Davidide *Zemah*. One or both crowns are to be held in reserve in the temple, in anticipation of that future event. The certainty of that event depends in part upon the faithfulness of the Yehudeans to Zechariah's prophetic message. We are not told whether the crowning of Joshua was ever carried out. Presumably, it was.

In social location analysis, Zechariah shows himself to be a loyal, but not an unconditional, supporter of the Yehudean restoration led by Zerubbabel and Joshua. He is also loyal to the Persian emperor, but is able to see beyond Persian domination to a time of Yehudean autonomy, when the *Zemah* will rule. Zerubbabel is not the *Zemah*; that role is given to a future figure. The high priest shall not bear royal responsibility, his is a lesser, though prominent, role. The closing exhortation implies a warning about the prospect of failure. Obedience to the prophetic message is in part the determining criterion for future fulfillment. Hence, the leaders are beholden to the prophet for Yahweh's directives. Hanson's claim that the visions and oracles, culminating in 6:9–15 constitute "a propagandistic message of the hierocracy" (1979, 256) is not sustained. The relationship of the prophet to the Yehudean leaders is not one of uncritical endorsement, but one of strong yet conditional acceptance, subject to future review. This conditionality frames the set, as evident in 1:3's שׁוּבוּ אֵלַי command and in 6:15's אִם clause.

PART ONE, UNIT THREE: 7:1–8:23
QUESTION AND ANSWER

That Zech 7–8 constitute a separate unit is readily seen by several features of the text: first, the date formula of 7:1, closely matching those at 1:1 and 1:7; second, the absence of visionary material; third, the pervasive presence of oracles announced by the set phrases, וַיְהִי דְבַר־יְהוָה צְבָאוֹת אֵלַי לֵאמֹר (found in 7:4, 8; 8:1 and 18, with some variations), and כֹּה אָמַר יְהוָה צְבָאוֹת לֵאמֹר (appearing with little variation in 7:9; and 8:1, 3, 4, 6, 7, 9, 11, 14, 19, 20 and 23).[36] It is also widely recognized that the new unit reprises themes, terms and phrases found earlier in the book. In particular, Zech 7–8 repeats themes in Zech 1:1–6 and in Haggai. It is therefore justified to see in Zech 7–8 the conclusion of the larger unity of Zech 1–8, but also the conclusion of the early composite unity of Haggai–Zech 1–8, as proposed by Meyers and Meyers (1987). The unit sustains

---

[36] See the structural analysis of Zech 7–8 offered by David J. Clark (1985), based on the pattern of these introductory formulae.

the sense of conditionality expressed in Zech 6:15 about the fulfillment of the predictions, and does so by evoking the language of earlier prophecy, especially Amos and Micah in the Book of the Twelve, but also Isaiah, Jeremiah, and Ezekiel, but with the closest ties to Jeremiah. Like Zech 1:4–5, it makes direct mention of הַנְּבִיאִים הָרִאשֹׁנִים, "the former prophets" and their ominous message to preexilic Judah (7:7).

The date form of 7:1, the fourth of Kislev in the fourth year of Darius, 518 B.C.,[37] introduces an incident in which priests and prophets at the still-incomplete temple are to be consulted by a delegation from Bethel about a question of fasting. We are not told if Haggai is still among the prophets, but there are more prophets present than simply Zechariah, and Zechariah is likely presented as a temple-based prophet.[38] The fasting question becomes the occasion for a series of oracles, which introduce many topics drawn from both ancient and more recent prophetic concerns.

The unit shows signs of literary integrity, structured as an *inclusio* of vocabulary and action. The text gives the words a public, oral setting, as temple preaching (Mason 1984). As in Jer 36:32, the message may have been augmented in its written form. In vocabulary, the key term is the piel verb, לְחַלּוֹת, "to entreat," which appears in identical form at the outset in 7:2, and at the conclusion in 8:21 and in 22. In both cases people are entreating Yahweh. In action, there is pilgrimage in 7:2–3 of Yehudeans from Bethel to Jerusalem, on a mission of divine inquiry; in 8:20–23 it is people "of all languages and nations" who come to Jerusalem on pilgrimage. This concluding unit on pilgrimage will likewise be matched thematically at the conclusion to the entire book of Zechariah, where in 14:16–21 the nations are portrayed as coming to Jerusalem on pilgrimage, this time for the Feast of Tabernacles. The theology of the whole of Zech 7–8 is contextualized by the *inclusio*, לְחַלּוֹת, a plea for divine mercy.

Following Chisholm with but minor revision, the reader may detect a near-chiasm for the unit (2002, 465), shown below in Chart 5.2. In his structural study of Zechariah, Mike Butterworth gives a similar proposal (1992, 163, adapted), shown further below in Chart 5.3.

As the chiastic analysis shows, the themes of meaningful fasting and joyous feasting, the priority of social justice, the history of Judean disobedience in the land and of divine wrath in the exile, Yahweh's decision to return to Zion and restore his people, and the eschatological pilgrimage of the nations dominate the prophetic rhetoric. At the core of Chisholm's virtual chiasm, as can be seen in

---

[37] December 7, 518 B.C.
[38] Note the plurality of prophets also in Neh 6:11, 14, and in Zech 8:9.
[39] Chisholm entitles the unit, "Yahweh will restore meaningful fasts" (2002, 465).

CHART 5.2 — CHISHOLM'S CHIASM

A. Messengers come from Bethel to entreat (לְחַלּוֹת) Yahweh	7:1–3
B. Yahweh denounces meaningless fasts	7:4–7
C. Yahweh's priority is social justice	7:8–12
D. Yahweh sent his people into exile	7:13–14
E. Yahweh will restore Jerusalem	8:1–3
F. Yahweh will bless the remnant	8:4–6
D'. Yahweh will bring back the remnant	8:7–8
F'. Yahweh will bless the remnant	8:9–13
E'. Yahweh will restore Jerusalem	8:14–15
C'. Yahweh's priority is social justice	8:16–17
B'. Yahweh will transform fasts into joyous feasts[39]	8:18–19
A'. Many nations will come to entreat (לְחַלּוֹת) Yahweh	8:20–23

CHART 5.3 — BUTTERWORTH'S CHIASM

A. Men of Bethel come to entreat the favor (לְחַלּוֹת) of Yahweh	7:2
B. Question about fasting	7:3
Off-putting reply	7:4–7
C. Former prophets said, Render true judgments Do not devise evil in your heart	7:8–10
D. Therefore great wrath (קֶצֶף) came Land became desolate	7:12b–14

E. I will dwell in the midst of Jerusalem
          Promise of blessing for the remnant
          Yahweh will save (מוֹשִׁיעַ) from east and west
          They will dwell in midst of Jerusalem
	8:2–8a

F. They will be my people and I will be their God	8:8b

E'. Let your hands be strong
          Promise of blessing for remnant
          Yahweh will save (אוֹשִׁיעַ)
	8:9–13

D'. As I purposed evil when provoked (קצף) So now I purpose to do good to Jerusalem	8:14–15
C'. So now: render true judgments Do not devise evil in your heart	8:16–17
B'. Fasts will become joyous feasts	8:18–19
A'. Many will come to entreat the favor (לְחַלּוֹת) of Yahweh	8:20–23

sections E, E', F, and F', is the divine intention to bring back and prosper the exiles. Zechariah 8:13 is characteristic of this proposed core:

וְהָיָה כַּאֲשֶׁר הֱיִיתֶם קְלָלָה בַּגּוֹיִם בֵּית יְהוּדָה וּבֵית יִשְׂרָאֵל
כֵּן אוֹשִׁיעַ אֶתְכֶם וִהְיִיתֶם בְּרָכָה

> Just as you were a curse among the nations,
> O house of Judah and house of Israel,
> so I will save you so that you will be a blessing.

The verse ends with the exhortation, so appropriate for Zech 1–8, "Do not fear! Let your hands be strong!" (אַל־תִּירָאוּ תֶּחֱזַקְנָה יְדֵיכֶם). The similar chiastic analysis of Butterworth has the covenant formulary at its core:

וְהָיוּ־לִי לְעָם וַאֲנִי אֶהְיֶה לָהֶם לֵאלֹהִים

> They will be my people and I will be their God. (8:8b)

Butterworth's proposal, with its focus on repeated vocabulary, may be the more persuasive. In either case, a good case for the literary unity and purposeful structuring of the unit can be made. Zechariah 7–8 is not simply a collection of miscellaneous prophetic sayings, and not a haphazardly augmented redactional unit.[40]

Despite the note of joy with which it concludes, a serious and sober tone controls the unit. The initial question asked by the delegation is,

הַאֶבְכֶּה בַּחֹדֶשׁ הַחֲמִשִׁי הִנָּזֵר כַּאֲשֶׁר עָשִׂיתִי זֶה כַּמֶּה שָׁנִים

> Should I mourn and fast in the fifth month, as I have been doing these many years? (7:3)

The question in turn evokes a flurry of counter-questions in oracular form, implicitly accusing "all the people of the land and the priests" (7:4) of hypocrisy.[41] The reported speech then declares, with what appears to be deliberate ambiguity as to its intended audience, a summary of the classic message of the preexilic prophets: "administer true justice, show mercy and compassion ... do not op-

---

[40] Again, see Clark for an alternative unitary structural analysis of Zech 7–8 (1985).
[41] Here the term עַם הָאָרֶץ, as in Hag 2:4 and Ezek 7:27, denotes the general population of land-holding citizens, and does not bear the negative connotations found in later texts like Ezra 4:4, or even later, Avot 2:5, where we read, "No unlearned person refrains from sin, and no עַם הָאָרֶץ is pious" (Grunneweg 1983, 437–40).

press the widow, the orphan or the resident alien" (7:9–10; cf. Jer 22:3)—words that, as v. 11 indicates, were spoken to no avail to the ancestors, but which, in *double entendre* style, are directed also at the present audience. The risk of doom, like that which overtook the ancestors, is implied for the postexilic audience, assembled from Bethel and Jerusalem.[42]

The prophet's rhetoric revisits some of the most vivid language of the earlier prophetic tradition: the ancestors "turned their backs" (7:11 cf. Jer 32:33) and made their hearts "as hard as flint" (7:12, cf. Ezek 3:8–9), so that Yahweh scattered them "with a whirlwind" (7:14, cf. Jer 23:19), leaving the "pleasant land" "desolate" (7:14, cf. Jer 3:19 and 7:34).

Nonetheless, Yahweh declares his "burning zeal" for Jerusalem (8:2) as said before in 1:14, and proclaims "I have returned to Zion and will dwell in the midst of Jerusalem" (8:3), evoking his earlier declaration in 1:16. Jerusalem will become "the City of Truth" (cf. Jer 33:16 and Mic 4:1); its streets filled with the sound of children at play and the sight of the elderly at well-deserved rest (8:4–5, cf. Jer 30:20). After further words about the "marvelous" (יִפָּלֵא) return of the remnant (8:6, cf. Jer 32:17), and the eschatological reassertion of the covenant formulary (8:8b), the prophetic text evokes the exhortation of Haggai—"let your hands be strong!" (תֶּחֱזַקְנָה יְדֵיכֶם)—for the work of temple building (8:9, cf. Hag 2:4). Again the text evokes Haggai's messages by citing both the barren economic conditions before the temple work recommenced (8:10, cf. Hag 1:6; 2:15–17), and the ensuing divine decision to change cursedness to blessing (8:11–15, cf. Hag 2:18–19).

The note of conditionality is sounded again in 8:16–17, where the command reiterates the duty to "render true justice in the courts." The text revisits the expurgation theme of Zech 5:1–4 in its exhortation to "speak the truth" and its prohibition against false swearing. After rhetorical delay, the answer to the Bethel delegation's question about fasting appears: mercy has triumphed over judgment; the fasts that have long commemorated the disaster of Jerusalem's destruction are to be transformed into "seasons of exultation and gladness, and joyous feasts" (לְשָׂשׂוֹן וּלְשִׂמְחָה וּלְמֹעֲדִים טוֹבִים, 8:19a).

---

[42] Blenkinsopp reconstructs the event as a delegation from Babylon going to Bethel, a reading supported by the LXX's ἐξαπέστειλεν εἰς Βαιθηλ, to inquire of priests and prophets there, to the consternation of Zechariah, who denounces both Bethel and the fasting that has taken place there (1998, 32–34). This interpretation is rendered unlikely by the reference to לְבֵית־יְהוָה צְבָאוֹת in 7:3, which Blenkinsopp takes to refer to an active temple of Yahweh in Bethel at the time of the return. Everywhere else in Haggai–Zech, בֵּית־יְהוָה means the Jerusalem temple, including, in this passage, Zech 8:9, which refers to the current Jerusalem temple-construction project. Why should 7:3 be different?

After one more exhortation, to "love truth and peace" (הָאֱמֶת וְהַשָּׁלוֹם אֱהָבוּ, 8:19b), the text turns to its closing *inclusio* theme: the eschatological pilgrimage of the nations to "entreat" (לְחַלּוֹת) Yahweh in Jerusalem. In a final, graphic image, the text presents ten gentiles grabbing one Yehudean (אִישׁ יְהוּדִי) by the garment with the plea, נֵלְכָה עִמָּכֶם כִּי שָׁמַעְנוּ אֱלֹהִים עִמָּכֶם, "let us go with you, for we have heard that God is with you!" Their plea evokes the message of Haggai one last time: the briefest oracle in all the Bible, אֲנִי אִתְּכֶם נְאֻם־יְהוָה, "'I am with you'—oracle of Yahweh" (Hag 1:13). The two messages, "I am with you!" and "God is with you!" make an appropriate framing device for the entire composite work of Haggai–Zech 1–8. Divine presence is the active force in Yehud's restoration.

In social location analysis, the unit's rhetoric balances between threat and assurance. Zechariah assures the people that Yahweh shall certainly act to bring about the eschatological promise, but Yehud is not exempt from the prophet's probing evaluation and searching criticism. The prophet thus shows his independence from the temple establishment. The exhortations contain the implication of conditionality previously seen in 1:3 and 6:15. Like Muhammad at Mecca in the first years of his preaching, the prophet is at risk of rejection. The prophet is thus sufficiently independent of the political powers and the *vox populi* to be their critic, even while he labors to consolidate the Yahwistic restoration of Yehud.

THE FUTURE FORTUNES OF THE PROPHET ZECHARIAH

In this balance did Zechariah continue to function as a central authority prophet in Yehud? His values are the ancient values of the people, as enshrined in the publicly sanctioned collections of the oracles of the earlier prophets and of the legal traditions of the Torah (7:12), but did he remain a publicly credited prophetic figure in Jerusalem? The narrative of Zech 7–8 does not tell us how this message in the fourth year of Darius was received by his audience society.

We might surmise from the book of Ezra (6:14) that Zechariah did continue to receive public accreditation at least until the time the temple was completed, in 515 B.C. But the author of Ezra 1–6, or his source for the narrative of 5:1–6:22, appears to know about Haggai and Zechariah solely from the prophetic record that we ourselves also possess in the biblical canon. No new and independent information about the two prophets appears in Ezra. Instead, we are told the following:

> The prophets, Haggai and Zechariah son of Iddo, prophesied to the Yehudeans who were in Yehud and Jerusalem, in the name of the God of Israel who was over them. Then Zerubbabel son of Shealtiel and Joshua son of

Jehozadak set out to rebuild the house of God in Jerusalem; and with them were the prophets of God, helping them. (Ezra 5:1–2)

And this as well:

So the elders of the Yehudeans built and prospered, through the prophesying of the prophet Haggai and Zechariah son of Iddo. They finished their building by command of the God of Israel and by decree of Cyrus, Darius, and King Artaxerxes of Persia. (Ezra 6:14)

Hence, it would be a mistake to interpret the text of Ezra as asserting that Zechariah (or Haggai, for that matter) still functioned as a publicly accredited prophet at the time of temple completion. Nonetheless, we are probably justified in assuming such accreditation for Zechariah, since temple completion would likely have been widely viewed as fulfillment of his predictive word in Zech 4:9:

יְדֵי זְרֻבָּבֶל יִסְּדוּ הַבַּיִת הַזֶּה וְיָדָיו תְּבַצַּעְנָה
וִידַעְתָּ כִּי־יְהוָה צְבָאוֹת שְׁלָחַנִי אֲלֵכֶם

The hands of Zerubbabel have laid the foundation of this house; his hands shall also complete it. Then you will know that Yahweh of the heavenly armies has sent me to you.

This supposition rests upon the further assumption that it was Zerubbabel who did indeed complete the rebuilding of the temple; unfortunately, there is no text that informs us of such completion under his administration. We are only told, in Ezra 6:14, that it was שָׂבֵי יְהוּדָיֵא, "the elders of the Yehudeans," who accomplished the task. However, it would be difficult to imagine the continued circulation of Haggai–Zech 1–8 if Zerubbabel had *not* overseen the completion of the work. We are left, then, with the probability that, though fully capable of independence, Zechariah remained a prophet in public accreditation at least as late as the third of Adar in the sixth year of Darius, March 12, 515 B.C., the time of temple completion (Ezra 6:15). But did Zechariah remain so accredited? This question shall be addressed in the discussion of Zech 9–14.

6

HISTORY, LITERATURE, AND SOCIAL LOCATION
PART TWO, UNIT ONE: ZECH 9–11, THE FIRST מַשָּׂא

*"Today the only poetry worthy of the name is eschatological,
that is, poetry which rejects the present inhuman world
in the name of a great change."*
—Czeslaw Milosz, *The Captive Mind* (1955, 226)

INTRODUCTION

Zechariah 9–14: the difficulties of interpretation that arose in Part One seem almost slight in comparison with those encountered in Part Two of this mysterious book. Petersen's important commentary on Zech 9–14 begins with the daunting declaration that these chapters "constitute arguably the most difficult texts for the interpreter of the Old Testament" (1995, 1). I have already quoted the words of Jerome about this *"obscurissimus liber."* Jerome further complains that in Zechariah, *"ab obscuris ad obscuriora transimus"* and *"abyssus abyssum invocat, in voce cataractarum Dei"* (quoted in Lamarche 1961, 7 n. 1).[1] In citing these words, Lamarche observes that Jerome wrote such lines, *"avec une insistance qui n'est pas exempte d'humour"* (1961, 7), no doubt an important attitude to adopt, lest we take our own interpretations of this difficult material too seriously.

Historical-critical interpretation made its mark upon the world of biblical study by insisting upon the careful determination of questions of authorship, original audience, time of composition, and the like; but all of these issues are open questions for Zech 9–14. Alluding to the few lines of latter Zechariah that might have seemed to give us historical data, Redditt says, "the attempt to date Zechariah 9–14 by interpreting historical allusions in 11:8 has been unsuccessful," and "the results of the effort to date Zechariah 9–14 on the basis of historical allusions in 9:1–8, 11:8, and 12:10 have been so discouraging that scholars have abandoned the project or else sought other methods" (1994, 668–69).

---

[1] Cf. Ps 42:7 (= Vulg. Ps 41:8), "Deep calls to deep in the roar of your waterfalls."

HANSON'S PROPOSAL

The most important proposal regarding the social location of prophecy and Zech 9–14 undoubtedly comes from the pen of Paul D. Hanson. His *Dawn of Apocalyptic: The Historical and Sociological Roots of Jewish Apocalyptic Eschatology* (1979 [1975]) stands as a pioneering work in the sociohistorical exegesis of prophetic and proto-apocalyptic texts. Hanson's proposals in *Dawn of Apocalyptic* are both widely influential and widely criticized. There is much to be learned in this sprawling and erudite work, but there are significant weaknesses. Here Hanson deals not only with Zech 9–14, but also with Isa 55–66, Ezekiel, Haggai and Zech 1–8, and the Chronicler. As is well known, Hanson, following in the footsteps of Otto Plöger's *Theocracy and Eschatology* (1968), posits a sharp break between the eschatologically oriented visionary disciples of Second Isaiah and the Zadokite priests who controlled the postexilic Jerusalem cult. Hanson's later work, *The People Called* (1986), moderates some of his more controversial points.

A sketch of Hanson's 1979 proposals regarding Zech 9–14 is in order. According to Hanson, Zech 9–14 is comprised of six compositions whose dates range from roughly 550 B.C. to perhaps as late as 425 B.C. It is the combination of literary, sociological, and theological analysis that provides the chief material for Hanson's creative exegesis of these texts. In his proposal, the compositions appear in roughly chronological order, and exhibit the progressive development of apocalyptic eschatology, a theological development defined for Hanson by its gradual disengagement with real history and present-worldly solutions, a hallmark of the visionary party in Yehud. Sociologically, they exhibit the increasingly bitter split between hierocrats and visionaries. Thirdly, the literary style of the compositions moves from classical poetical forms of "pure" type to post-classical forms of mixed type and chaotic meter, and prose texts.

According to Hanson, Zech 9:1–17 is a single composition, a prophetic adaptation of a "divine warrior hymn." The text announces the coming triumph of Yahweh, the divine warrior, over the nations, and the redemption of the exiled people of Judah. The dating is partly dependent upon the supposition that the hymn posits no inner-community conflict among Yehudeans, but rather the restoration of land and prosperity to them all. Strong divisions only arose among Yehudeans, Hanson thinks, early in the postexilic period. The poetry, moreover, is close in style to the exilic-era poems of Second Isaiah, bearing a purity of form before the postexilic breakdown of the classical standards of Hebrew poetry, but with a more advanced eschatology. Hanson therefore suggests a date around 550 B.C. (1979, 322–24).

In Zech 10:1–12 another divine warrior hymn appears, this one adapted to a situation of "inner-community polemic" involving a *rib*-lawsuit against Yehudean leaders. The hymn is similar to the poetry of Zech 9, but without the same purity of Second-Isaianic literary style. The combination of the *rib*-pattern with the divine warrior hymn, a mixed type, is reminiscent of Third Isaiah, says Hanson; he suggests a date between 550 and 525 B.C. (334).

Zechariah 11:1–3 is too brief to determine much about its dating; its form consists of a taunt against foreign nations, but the form is now ironically redirected against Yehudean leaders. It originated within the same community as that of Zech 11:4–17, Hanson suggests, and provides a fitting prelude to the following unit (334).

Zechariah 11:4–17 is, according to Hanson, "a commissioning narrative trans-formed into a prophecy of doom" against the leaders of the community, with the similar material in 13:7–9 constituting perhaps "an early addition" to the composition (337–38). The "worthless shepherd" of 11:15–16 is a governing member of the house of David (350). The text gives an account of "the rejection of the visionaries and their expulsion from positions of power in the community" (348). The poetical portions, as in 10:1–12, exhibit a "chaotic" meter (341) akin to the poems of Trito-Isaiah. The hopelessness of the passage, with its "flock doomed to slaughter" (11:7), suggests the time shortly after the completion of the temple, when, according to Hanson, the victory of the hierocratic party was complete. He suggests a date of about 500 B.C. (354).

Chapters 12–14, which comprise a new booklet, "fall at a more advanced point on the typology of Jewish eschatology" and are written with a narrow concern for Jewish salvation (355). There are two main compositions, both apocalypses, 12:1–13:6 and 14:1–21. Hanson treats 13:7–9, as we have seen, as an addition to 11:4–17. Zechariah 13:2–6 "may or may not be an original part of the composition" of 12:1–13:1 (367).

Zechariah 12:1–13:6, says Hanson, is "an apocalypse molded by the inner-community struggle" (354). In the text's conflict myth plot-structure, the nations come against Jerusalem for the great eschatological battle. The siege is against Jerusalem, and against Yehud as well—because the visionaries no longer live in the city. Both are delivered when Yahweh strikes the enemy. Yahweh directly battles the nameless foe, showing, Hanson suggests, the complete disengagement of the visionaries from real history. The text's prose character reflects the fifth century, says Hanson, an age of prose, but the late apocalyptic division between the righteous and the wicked within Israel is not yet in play. Hence, the composition is "middle apocalyptic" and dated to the first half of the fifth century (368).

Zechariah 14:1–21 is Hanson's last and most advanced apocalyptic composition in Zech 9–14. He makes the claim that with ch. 14, "one enters the period of full-blown apocalyptic literature" (369). In this unit, Hanson finds the combination of earlier genres. First, there is the salvation-judgment oracle, a form which replaced the classical oracle-of-salvation and oracle-of-judgment forms of preexilic times, and which sought to distinguish between the fate of the righteous in Israel and the fate of the wicked in Israel. Then there is the covenant-curse form: the *shalom* of final peace does not apply to all (14:12–13). The two forms are fused into a conflict myth of the eschatological battle-and-deliverance. Hanson writes:

> No longer could the whole community of Israel be addressed in a divine speech cast in one of the classical oracle forms, for the community was no longer viewed by the visionary group as a unified entity. Rather, a bitter conflict had torn a deep rift between hierocratic and visionary factions, implying that for the latter that there were henceforth *two* Israels. (373)

As in the previous apocalypse, a period of apocalyptic woes precedes the victory. Yahweh again is the divine warrior, only this time he fights by himself; no Yehudean joins him as he alone wins the victory (384). The victory includes salvation not only for the righteous in Israel, but also for the repentant survivors from among the nations. Thus salvation is no longer conceived in nationalist terms, but in ethical terms (386). Accordingly, the pilgrim Feast of Tabernacles shall be celebrated not only by Israelites, but by the nations as well (14:16). Hanson thus speaks of the "democratization" of religion—against the "narrow exclusiveness of the hierocratic party" (387). This future of the visionaries involves the sacralization of all, when not only Israel shall be "a kingdom of priests and a holy nation" (Exod 19:6), but the pagans also, worshiping Yahweh at a shared temple in Jerusalem (388). The curses on the Yehudean wicked in the devastation of Jerusalem in Zech 14 reveal "a feverish degree of polemical wrath on the part of the visionaries against their hierocratic opponents" (391–92).

In Zech 14, according to Hanson, the struggle within the community "reaches its most desperate level" (399). "One can hardly imagine a more desperate and vindictive vision of Yahweh's dealing with the opponents of the visionaries within the postexilic community" (400). With such literary, sociological, and theological considerations in mind, Hanson proposes a date not earlier than 475 B.C., his suggested date for Zech 12. Since Hanson discerns in the Chronicler a late fifth century cooling of the struggle between hierocrats and visionaries, a *terminus ad quem* of ca. 425 is suggested (400). Thus the community behind the literature of Zech 9–14 moves from an exilic-era unity, to an early postexilic schism, to a later hatred, to a middle Persian-period reconciliation; and the literature moves from divine warrior hymns to "full-blown" apocalyptic.

CRITIQUE OF HANSON'S PROPOSAL

How shall this fascinating proposal be critiqued? The chief weakness of Hanson's proposal is methodological. His chosen method attempts to correlate particular types of poetical and prose compositions to particular dates in exilic and postexilic history without a sufficient comparative base, and attempts to discern particular stages in the history of apocalyptic literature, again without a sufficient comparative base. He further links the history of the apocalyptic literature to a parallel history of a social group experiencing increasing disenfranchisement and alienation. But he fails to note that deprivation theory—based on his reading of Karl Mannheim (1936), Max Weber (1963), and Ernst Troeltsch (1968)—is a weak base for the consideration of apocalypticism. As Stephen L. Cook has demonstrated, social groups in power can also give rise to apocalyptic and millennialist eschatology, as he shows concerning nineteenth-century Britain's Irvingites, fifteenth-century Florence's Savonarola, and sixteenth-century Spanish Franciscans in the New World, among others (1995, 55–84).

For his genre history, Hanson attempts to construct a comparative base out of numerous passages from the Psalms and Deutero- and Trito-Isaiah, building a typology that reaches from ancient Canaanite conflict myth, to ancient Israelite conflict myth, to divine warrior hymn in Jerusalemite royal theology, to exilic prophecy, to proto-apocalyptic literature, to middle-apocalyptic, and at last to fully formed apocalypse. But dating the psalms is notoriously difficult, assigning firm dates to compositions in Isa 55–66 is much contested, and linking his typology to real history can hardly be done with the degree of specificity that his detailed proposal requires. And, the comparative base in "divine warrior hymns" is so dubious—a cluster of themes, rather than a literary form, that Floyd doubts the existence of such a genre at all (2000, 521). Genres are based on literary structure; the divine warrior is a literary motif, not a *structural* basis for a genre.

Moreover, we should note that Hanson's proposed historical sequence moves by quarter-centuries and half-centuries, spanning ca. 550 B.C. to 475–425 B.C. Does the social location of prophetic and apocalyptic groups move so slowly as this? As we have seen in the history of the prophetess Alice Lenshina's Lumpa Church, social location change can occur with great swiftness. Lenshina was baptized in 1953; she became the center of a movement in 1954; broke with the Scottish church mission in 1955; led her movement to its peak at 50,000 to 100,000 adherents in 1958; and completed the Lumpa Cathedral that same year, but swiftly lost membership. She then forbade membership in UNIP in 1962; adopted a radical, imminent millennialist message in about 1963; built illegal, armed villages in about that same year; refused to acknowledge governmental authority in 1964; and in July of that year led the now socially implosive Lumpa Church into massacre and disaster. This brief ten-year trajectory is a lesson for the *longue durée*. Hanson's hundred-year trajectory could have taken place in one-tenth of the time.

Further, the designation "apocalyptic" for passages such as Zech 12 and Zech 14 has come under widespread criticism. According to John J. Collins, a leading figure in apocalyptic studies, an apocalypse is

> a genre of revelatory literature with a narrative framework, in which a revelation is mediated by an otherworldly being to a human recipient,

disclosing a transcendent reality which is both temporal, in that it envisages eschatological salvation, and spatial, in that it involves another, supernatural world. (1984, 4, 105)

This definition, worked out at a colloquy sponsored by the experimental journal *Semeia* and promoted in the FOTL series, has received widespread support in the scholarly community. By this definition, the night visions of Zech 1–6 may have a better claim to the designation "apocalypse" than Zech 14. There are no angelic mediators of revelation in Zech 12–14. But Zech 14 is not an apocalypse. As Petersen has recognized (1995, 24 and n. 65) and as Floyd has maintained in his own FOTL volume (2000, 444–52, 499–508), the compositions contained in Zech 9–14 fall best into the genre categories of prophetic literature. Zechariah 12–14 does indeed contain what Collins calls "cosmic eschatology" (1987, 540), and cosmic eschatology may lay at the heart of truly apocalyptic literature, but it is a mistake to designate Zech 14 as an apocalypse, let alone "full-blown apocalyptic literature" (Hanson 1979, 369). As such, the ideological divide that Hanson posits between the prophetic literature of Zech 1–8 and the proto- and fully apocalyptic literature of Zech 9–14 must be rejected. Both portions are prophetic literature. There may indeed be an ideological difference between chs. 1–8 and chs. 9–14, but the difference is not as great as Hanson, or Childs for that matter, posits. Already in Haggai we find prediction about Yahweh's cosmic shaking of "the heavens and the earth, the sea and the dry land ... and the throne of kingdoms" (2:6, 22). The historical Zechariah was no stranger to such ideas.

One final criticism involves the assignment of divisions for the literary units. Mike Butterworth (1992), Katrina Larkin (1994), and Michael H. Floyd (2000) have all subjected Zech 9–14 to particularly close structural examination, none sustaining Hanson's text divisions (see for example, Butterworth's assessment of Hanson on Zech 9; 1992, 195–97). Instead of divine warrior hymns with a clear myth-and-ritual pattern, they find Hanson's designations arbitrary, forcing the texts to fit his thesis. So, in his methodology, his use of deprivation theory for the social sources of apocalyptic, his historical sequence, his designation of texts in Zech 9–14 as apocalyptic, and his text-divisions with their accompanying genre designations, Hanson's thesis is found wanting. Can elements in Hanson's theory be sustained? I shall discuss this prospect in the final chapter after my own review of Zech 9–14. What is Zech 9–14?

WHAT IS ZECH 9-14?

Zechariah 9–14 is an anthology of prophetic texts, linked thematically and progressively into a composite unit with its own literary integrity. Although overtly structured by the two *mas'ot*[2] headings at 9:1 and 12:1, these units are themselves interlaced by the so-called Shepherd Allegory, which is told first in 11:4–17 and continued in 13:7–9. The placement of 13:7–9, although treated by many commentators (starting apparently with Ewald) and the NEB translation as a misplaced oracle, to be restored to its due location after 11:17, is instead a key to the centrality of the Shepherd Allegory, as argued by Larkin (1994, 175–76; 2001). Redditt says, "it is sufficient to recognize behind 11:4–17 and 13:7–9 a common author" (1995, 136),[3] It is not possible to maintain certainty about the division of the materials in 9–14, and there is no scholarly consensus. Contributing to the difficulty is the lack of unanimity in the masoretic tradition's *petuhah* (פ) and *setumah* (ס) divisions. As Katrina Larkin found, BHS and its basis, the Leningrad Codex (L), are not adequate witnesses to the pluriform manuscript tradition regarding these markings (1994, 49–50). Nonetheless, the *petuhah* and *setumah* markings in BHS are still helpful, and represent one major tradition of divisions. I shall follow these in the main, with some variation based on Larkin's findings.

The structure that I shall adopt proceeds as follows: Zech 9:1–8 serves as a poetical introduction to the whole first *massa'*, as well as to the compound poetical unit of 9:9–10 + 9:11–17, divided by a *setumah* at the end of v. 8. Zechariah 10:1–2 is a brief unit of prophetic poetry,[4] marked by a change of topic and exhortation mode of address. Its final word, רֹעֶה, "shepherd," followed by *petuhah* (10:2), signals the next unit with its new topic, Yahweh's wrath at the shepherds as told in a judgment/salvation oracle (10:3–12), which closes with the divine signature, נְאֻם יְהוָה, and another *setumah*. The whole of chs. 9 and 10 is poetical.

Zechariah 11:1–3 contains another brief prophetic poetical linking unit, set off by *setumah* (v. 3), and its new address to personified Lebanon (v. 1), and the return of the shepherd theme: this time in the wailing of the shepherds (v. 2) over the devastation of trees and pastures. Chapter 11:1–3 appears to serve as the introduction to the next unit. A longer prose unit follows, 11:4–16, the so-called

---

[2] According to rabbinic texts, the plural form of *massa'* is *massa'ot*, not *mas'ot* (so Jastrow 1982, 848). However in Lam 2:14 the form appears as מַשְׂאוֹת (cf. Petersen 1995, 2 n. 1). Some singular nouns that feature the doubling of the second root letter, such as *kisse'*, "throne," drop the doubling in the plural, *kis'ot*. I shall follow this latter convention for *mas'ot*.

[3] Redditt sees this author as a redactor of the whole of Zech 9–14 (1995, 136).

[4] Or, as Meyers and Meyers would put it, "oracular prose" (1987, lxiv).

Shepherd Allegory. In actuality, the passage is a report of prophetic sign enactment (so Floyd 2000, 490; also Petersen 1995, 88), with allegorical aspects.[5] A *setumah* follows 11:16. Zechariah 11:17, "Woe to the worthless shepherd," offers a poetical climax to the prose report. Another *setumah* at the end of v. 17 sets off the whole unit. This concludes the first *massa'*. However, the reader is left dangling with the conclusion of 11:17, a worthless shepherd with wounded right arm and blinded right eye—what is the reader to do?

Following Ewald, many have supposed that 13:7–9, another brief shepherd-theme poem, originally concluded ch. 11. Its conclusion—an adaptation of the covenant formulary—may make for a more satisfactory ending. However, there is not a shred of manuscript evidence to support the supposition. Noting with Larkin that Zech 9–14 is characterized by longer units interspersed with brief connecting poetical units, Zech 13:7–9 can be recognized as fulfilling this linking function between the long eschatological narratives of 12:1–13:6 and 14:1–21. Removing 13:7–9 disrupts the pattern of long-short-long followed in the whole. The real conclusion to 11:17's disturbing text is the next *massa'*, Zech 12–14, with its declaration of eschatological victory. The presence of the shepherd-theme poem at 13:7–9 thus helps link the two *mas'ot* together as a compound unit. Hence, we should not speak of a Trito-Zechariah.

The whole of Zech 12:1 provides the title for the second *massa'*, elaborating on the opening מַשָּׂא דְבַר־יְהוָה עַל־יִשְׂרָאֵל with a doxology to the God who "stretches out heaven and establishes earth, and forms man's spirit within him." A *petuhah* follows the verse. Chapter 12:2 begins the first of two prophetic eschatological narratives with a forceful הִנֵּה! The *petuhah* at the end of 12:6 is nonetheless followed by a *vav*-consecutive at 12:7a, continuing the story of Jerusalem's future salvation. The *setumah* at the end of 12:14 is a mistake in *BHS*; it does not appear in L, nor in other codices examined by C. D. Ginsberg (so Larkin 1994, 50). Three בַּיּוֹם הַהוּא oracles follow Zech 12:14, at 13:1, 13:2, and 13:4, these three eschatological oracles link together as the conclusion to Zech 12. A concluding *setumah* appears at the end of 13:6.

One more brief linking poem appears, 13:7–9, once again addressing the shepherd theme that unifies so much of Zech 9–14. The second prophetic eschatological narrative begins in 14:1, again announced by a forceful הִנֵּה! No further *petuhah* or *setumah* divisions occur in ch. 14 in L. Instead the narrative is peppered with seven בַּיּוֹם הַהוּא clauses ("on that day"), keyed to the opening הִנֵּה יוֹם־בָּא לַיהוָה, "See! A day belonging to Yahweh is coming!" (14:1). In other medieval masoretic manuscripts, *setumah* appears before 14:6 and 14:12 (Larkin 1994, 50). These are but paragraph breaks in the long prose narrative. The first of these precedes the three closely spaced בַּיּוֹם הַהוּא clauses in 14:6, 8,

---

[5] On the other hand, both Hanson (1979) and Kline (2001) take it as a commissioning narrative.

and 9b. The second precedes the paragraph-long description of the plague on the warring nations in 14:12–15.

In summary, then, there are six major units, 9:1–8, 9:11–17, 10:3–12, 11:4–16, 12:1–13:6, and 14:1–21. These are interspersed by five brief thematic connecting poems, no less significant despite their brevity: 9:9–10, 10:1–2, 11:1–3, 11:17, and 13:7–9 (so also, Larkin 1994, 221; quite similarly Petersen 1988; 1995; similarly, but not identically, Meyers and Meyers 1993). Chart 6.1 below displays the organization of the anthology.

CHART 6.1
THE STRUCTURE OF ZECHARIAH 9–14

Text	Titles	Long Units	Short Linking Units
Zech 9:1a	Title, מַשָּׂא		
Zech 9:1b–8		First Judgment-Salvation Oracle	
Zech 9:9–10			Prophetic Call to Rejoicing
Zech 9:11–17		Judgment-Salvation Oracle (continued)	
Zech 10:1–2			Prophetic Exhortation
Zech 10:3–12		Second Judgment-Salvation Oracle	
Zech 11:1–3			Taunt Song against the Davidides
Zech 11:4–16		Shepherd Sign-Enactment Report	
Zech 11:17			Curse on the Foolish Shepherd
Zech 12:1	Title, מַשָּׂא		
Zech 12:2–13:6		First Eschatological Narrative	
Zech 13:7–9			Final Shepherd Oracle
Zech 14:1–21		Second Eschatological Narrative	

The major themes of the text, generally in the order in which they are found, are (1) the future restoration of the Davidic empire as the kingdom of Yahweh, (2) its concomitant victory over the nations, (3) the incorporation of the defeated nations as one people with Yehud, (4) the reunification and purification of Israel and Yehud, (5) in the meantime, a crisis of leadership in Yehud—ruthless sheep-merchants and wicked shepherds—to the detriment of the flock of the people of Yahweh, and (6) the slaying of a prominent figure, perhaps a Davidide, who is then deeply mourned, (7) the purification of Jerusalem from sin, (8) the banishment of idols and false prophets, (9) the eschatological battle against Jerusalem, followed by (10) the worship of Yahweh at Jerusalem by a restored Israel and converted survivors of the nations.

I shall now assess Zech 9–14 unit by unit for evidence regarding the genre, central ideas, historical setting, and social location of the prophet and his tradent community. For the present I shall leave open the question of the identity of the prophet in chs. 9–14, but shall return to this question later in the chapter.

PART TWO, UNIT ONE: ZECH 9:1–11:17, THE FIRST מַשָּׂא

The heading מַשָּׂא, *massa'*, "oracle," "pronouncement," appears frequently in oracles of judgment against foreign nations (Isa 13:1; 14:28; 15:1, for example), though in some texts (Ezek 12:10) it denotes judgment against Israel. The term is thought by Richard Weis to denote "prophetic exposition of divine revelation" (1992, 28). If so, it itself also partakes of the character of divine revelation. Floyd speaks of the *massa'* as a literary product of scribes who study earlier prophetic oracles and produce new revelatory texts based on their study (2000, 449, 632; 2002, 409–11). If so, then Zech 9, with its very low prose particle density, a sign of early composition, may well serve as an earlier prophetic text reused or reshaped within its Zech 9–14 context.[6] Discussion of Zech 9–11, unit by unit, with poetic delineation, follows.

ZECHARIAH 9:1–17
THE FIRST JUDGMENT-SALVATION ORACLE

ZECHARIAH 9:1–8, DELINEATED

poetic accent count	prose particle count		poetic delineation
			9:1 מַשָּׂא
2+2		וְדַמֶּשֶׂק מְנֻחָתוֹ	דְּבַר־יְהוָה בְּאֶרֶץ חַדְרָךְ
3+1		וְכֹל שִׁבְטֵי יִשְׂרָאֵל	כִּי לַיהוָה עֵין אָדָם
2+2+3		צֹר וְצִידוֹן	2 וְגַם־חֲמָת תִּגְבָּל־בָּהּ
			כִּי חָכְמָה מְאֹד
4+2+3		וַתִּצְבָּר־כֶּסֶף כֶּעָפָר	3 וַתִּבֶן צֹר מָצוֹר לָהּ
			וְחָרוּץ כְּטִיט חוּצוֹת
3+3+3		וְהִכָּה בַיָּם חֵילָהּ	4 הִנֵּה אֲדֹנָי יוֹרִשֶׁנָּה
			וְהִיא בָּאֵשׁ תֵּאָכֵל
	(continued)		

---

[6] Prose Particle Density analysis shall be explained later in this chapter

3+2	וְעַזָּה וְתָחִיל מְאֹד	5 תֵּרֶא אַשְׁקְלוֹן וְתִרָא
3+3+3	וְאָבַד מֶלֶךְ מֵעַזָּה	וְעֶקְרוֹן כִּי־הֹבִישׁ מֶבָּטָהּ
		וְאַשְׁקְלוֹן לֹא תֵשֵׁב
3+2	וְהִכְרַתִּי גְּאוֹן פְּלִשְׁתִּים	6 וְיָשַׁב מַמְזֵר בְּאַשְׁדּוֹד
3+3	וְשִׁקֻּצָיו מִבֵּין שִׁנָּיו	7 וַהֲסִרֹתִי דָמָיו מִפִּיו
3+3+2	וְהָיָה כְּאַלֻּף בִּיהוּדָה	וְנִשְׁאַר גַּם־הוּא לֵאלֹהֵינוּ
		וְעֶקְרוֹן כִּיבוּסִי
3+2	מֵעֹבֵר וּמִשָּׁב	8 וְחָנִיתִי לְבֵיתִי מִצָּבָה
4+4	כִּי עַתָּה רָאִיתִי בְעֵינָי ס	וְלֹא־יַעֲבֹר עֲלֵיהֶם עוֹד נֹגֵשׂ

Prose Particle Count = 0/93 words = 0% Prose Particle Density (PPD)

ZECHARIAH 9:1–8 IN TRANSLATION

1 An Oracle.
   Yahweh's word [is] against the land of Hadrach
      and Damascus [is] its resting place;
  —for to Yahweh belong/are turned the eye[s] of the human race,
      as well as [the eyes] of all the tribes of Israel—
2 even Hamath which borders on it [i.e., Hadrach] [is included],
      Tyre and Sidon too, even though they are very wise.
3 Even though Tyre has built herself a fortress,
      and amassed silver like dust,
      gold like the mire of the streets,
4 watch!—the Sovereign One will dispossess her!
      Upon the sea he will strike her wealth,[7]
      and by fire she will be consumed!
5 Ashkelon will see—and seize up in fear;
      Gaza [will gaze on it]—and agonize,[8]
      and Ekron, too—for her hope he humiliates.
   Then a king will perish from Gaza,
      Ashkelon will have no throne-sitter,
        6 while a bastard sits enthroned in Ashdod![9]
      "Thus I shall cut off the pride of the Philistines.

---

[7] Or "He will defeat her force at sea" (NJPS).

[8] lit: "and Gaza, and she will writhe greatly." Or, to maintain the sense of paronomasia, "Gaza will gaze agape."

[9] One is tempted to try to reproduce the word-play tactics of the overall text by rendering it, "an ass will sit enthroned in Ashdod."

7 But I will wipe away the [unclean] blood from his mouth,
    and remove the idolatrous meat from between his teeth."
  He indeed will become a remnant for our God,
    and become like a war-clan in Judah;
      thus Ekron will be [adopted] like the Jebusite[s].
8 "Then I will encamp at my House like a garrisoned force
    against the marching and counter-marching [enemy] troops.
  No oppressor shall invade them ever again,
    for now my eyes are on the watch!"

ZECHARIAH 9:1-8. The text of 9:1-8 appears to be a unit, bound as an *inclusio* by the occurrence of the word עֵין/עֵינֵי, "eye"/ "eyes" in vv. 1c and 8d. It is clearly a poetical unit as the measured brevity of the lines and the regularity of the accent count indicates. The length of the title is in doubt, and it may be that there is no clear boundary between title and text. The *massa'* term apparently pertains to all of chs. 9–11. The text begins as a poetical prophetic judgment speech against Aramaean, Phoenician, and Philistine cities and regions. The oracle is not, however, in the classic form identified by Claus Westermann (1967, 174–75) — no explicit reason for the judgment is stated except for 9:6's "pride" of the Philistines. Moreover, the text appears to require a written, rather than a spoken, origin. Yahweh's interests are declared to extend far beyond Israel, to include not only extensive northern and southern territory, but also the whole of humanity. Hence, soon judgment is turned to salvation, as the collective Philistines of v. 6d are transformed by v. 7a into an individual who shall be cleansed of abominations and reclaimed by Yahweh. Yahweh is now the main speaker of this half of the text (vv. 6b–8). Like the Jebusites, the Philistine remnant shall be absorbed into Yehud and join the people of God.

The expression in 9:1 regarding the מְנֻחָתוֹ ("resting place") of the divine word at Damascus is striking. The uncommon term seems to bear an intertextual relationship with both Zech 5:11, where the idol-woman "Wickedness" has her pedestal where she is "placed" (וְהֻנִּיחָה שָּׁם עַל־מְכֻנָתָהּ) in her Shinar temple, and Zech 6:8, where Yahweh's wrathful spirit has been "given rest in the land of the north" (הֵנִיחוּ אֶת־רוּחִי בְּאֶרֶץ צָפוֹן). Elsewhere the מְנֻחָה term is used of the resting place of Yahweh's ark of the covenant (Num 10:33), and Israel's resting place represented by the Promised Land (Deut 12:9). Here in Zech 9:1 the term connotes the sacralization of Damascus as the dwelling place of the divine word in the north.

The unit ends at 9:8 with Yahweh's declaration of defense for his "House" (לְבֵיתִי) — either Jerusalem's temple, or Yahweh's Yehudean "estate." Hanson correctly noted that the literary form combines judgment and salvation into one oracle.

Zechariah 9:1–8 has generated much exegetical attention, especially since it has been widely viewed as providing evidence for a Hellenistic date for this section of the book. A major argument for Hellenistic dating depends upon the view that the names of the cities in 9:1–6 represent the itinerary of Alexander the Great's march through Syro-Palestine. We do know that two of the cities in the text, Tyre (9:2) and Gaza (9:5), offered Alexander resistance, and were eventually reduced by siege to surrender, Tyre after seven months, and Gaza after two. But this Alexandrian view overlooks the fact that after the battle of Issus in 333 B.C., located in the narrow strip of land between the coast and the mountains at the extreme northeast corner of the Mediterranean (Tcherikover 1972, 10–11), Alexander did not go to Damascus (9:1), but proceeded due south along the coastline toward Sidon and Tyre (9:2). Alexander did send a separate force under the capable commander Parmenion to subdue Damascus, which surrendered without a struggle, but he did not come to Damascus until after his successful campaign in Egypt. Moreover, the Zechariah text names Tyre before naming Sidon, even though Alexander certainly reached the more northerly Sidon first. Zechariah 9:1–8, then, does not represent Alexander's itinerary, nor, as far as I am aware, the itinerary of any other Hellenistic conqueror, and therefore does not provide evidential value for a Hellenistic date. The list of cities is not a travel itinerary at all. It is instead a listing in a general but not invariable north-to-south regional pattern. Not only is Sidon north of Tyre, but Gaza, mentioned after Ashkelon, is north of that city, as are also Ekron and Ashdod, though these last two are the final members of the listing. In short, the cities named are prominent spots that anyone at nearly any time in Israel's history could have named, when thinking of traditional enemies. With one interesting exception—Hadrach. Hadrach in Zech 9:1 is a *hapax legomenon*, and thus appears in no other prophetic texts of oracles against the nations, such as Amos 1–2, Isa 13–23, Jer 46–51, or Ezek 25–32, each of which likely bears some degree of intertextuality with Zech 9:1–8. Hadrach appears in Neo-Assyrian texts, and on the strength of these parallels, some have tried to date Zech 9:1–8 to the Neo-Assyrian period (Kraeling 1924; Malamat 1950–51). The latest clear attestation of the region's name, according to Petersen (1995, 43) is in an eponym text dated to 689 B.C., named with its governor, Gihilu. But we probably should not think that Hadrach (Akkadian, *Hatarika*) then ceased to exist. Place names possess a peculiar longevity, as one can see from any gazetteer of Arabic toponyms in Syro-Palestine today. The presence of the name Hadrach is thus not good evidence of a Neo-Assyrian date for Zech 9:1–8.

I have a new proposal to help explain the role of these northern toponyms. Admittedly, the identification of Damascus with the more northerly territory of Hadrach is strange. Petersen says outright that "the author, though mistaken geographically, views Damascus as the capital of Hadrak" (1995, 40). My proposal takes another path. The identification of Damascus with the land of Hadrach seems to be dependent upon an earlier tradition or narrative about David's northern campaigns, now found in 2 Sam 8:3–12 (closely paralleled in 1 Chr 18:3–11), in which Damascus becomes David's administrative center for several northerly territories.¹⁰ 2 Sam 8 and its Chronicles parallel are the two texts in the Bible's historical narratives that most clearly display the claim of a multinational Davidic empire. In both versions the narration contains this sequence (using the versification of 2 Sam 8):

> 8:3b: King David and his troops march north toward the upper Euphrates, perhaps to restore an Israelite monument.¹¹
> 8:3a–4: David's forces decisively defeat local defensive troops under the command of King Hadadezer of Zobah, a kingdom likely located in the Beka'a Valley, directly north of Israel.
> 8:5a: Neighboring Aramean forces march west to Hadadezer's relief, but they arrive too late.
> 8:5b: David's forces decisively defeat the Arameans.
> 8:6–8: David incorporates "Aram of Damascus" into his domain, garrisoning troops there, receiving local tribute, including the golden shields of the defeated Hadadezer's officers, and taking much more tribute, especially in bronze metal; the city of Damascus (8.6) now serves as David's garrison city and administrative center for the northern cities and territories.
> 8:9–10: King Toi of Hamath, ruler of a large territory north north-west of Damascus and adjacent to Hadrach, sends his son Joram in diplomatic embassy, offering yet more tribute in metals—"articles of silver, gold, and bronze," in apparent gratitude for delivering his region from his militaristic neighbor, Hadadezer of Zobah.
> 8:11–12: David dedicates the vast northern tribute to Yahweh; he adds to the gift further tribute from the western and southern territories of, respectively, Moab, Ammon, Philistia, and Amalek.

My suggestion is that Zech 9:1's identification of the city of Damascus with "the land of Hadrach" serves as a midrash-like inner-biblical interpretation dependent on the material now in 2 Sam 8. David, in exerting his military power

---

¹⁰ I assume that the Samuel scroll, as part of the Deuteronomistic History, was available in substantial form to postexilic Yehudeans.

¹¹ The MT of 2 Sam 8:3 has לְהָשִׁיב יָדוֹ בִּנְהַר־, "to restore his monument on the river," followed by an unusual masoretic feature: the supplied *qere* reading, פְּרָת, 'Euphrates," has no accompanying *ketiv* in the main text. The name of the river may have fallen out in the Samuel account, or else the word נָהָר, "river," denotes the Euphrates. The masoretic pointing may also be in error, construing the consonantal text as an indefinite *binehar* instead of the definite *bannahar*. 1 Chr 18:3 has instead לְהַצִּיב יָדוֹ בִּנְהַר־פְּרָת, and no Q–K annotation. הַנָּהָר by itself often refers to the Euphrates, and in poetical texts the ה is routinely dropped. The reference to the "monument," a secondary meaning for יָד, "hand" (here יָדוֹ, "his monument"), as in 1 Sam 15:12, is sometimes taken instead to mean "power," that is, military domination.

in the far north of Syro-Palestine, makes Damascus his "resting place," i.e., his tribute center, hence, Yahweh makes Damascus his "resting place" in the reassertion of Yahwistic empire in Zech 9. It was likely at this administrative center that representatives from Hamath and other northern territories are said to deliver their tribute, just as Pharaoh Neco and later Nebuchadnezzar used Riblah as their administrative center for their Syro-Palestinian territories (2 Kgs 23:33; 25:6, 21; Jer 39:5–6; 52:9–10, 26–27). The claims of 2 Sam 8 may thus lie behind Zech 9. In Zech 9:1–2 Yahweh reasserts Davidic empire for the postexilic context. The boundaries of this empire are to conform to those in the tradition found in Gen 15:18, demarcating the territory in rather aggrandized terms: "from the River of Egypt [Wadi Besor] to the Great River, the River Euphrates" (מִנְּהַר מִצְרַיִם עַד־הַנָּהָר הַגָּדֹל נְהַר־פְּרָת). Yohanan Aharoni and Michael Avi-Yonah locate Hadrach north of Hamath, and lying between the northern bend of the Orontes River and the upper Euphrates (1977, 96, map 150). By including Hamath and the land of Hadrach, the author of Zech 9:1–8 asserts Davidic empire to the fullest northerly extent exhibited by the ancient traditions, and perhaps beyond.[12]

Strikingly, the text also lists Tyre and Sidon, cities that were never said to be under tribute to David or Solomon. However, in Ezekiel's idealized borders of the eschatological land of Israel, Tyre falls into the territory of Manasseh, and Sidon falls into Naphtali's (Ezek 48:3–4; so Zimmerli 1983, 2:537; and Lamar E. Cooper 1994, 428). In Zech 9:1–8 the Yahwistic empire is perhaps seen through the lens of Ezekiel's expansive boundaries.

Tyre and Sidon hold a regular place in the prophets' oracles against the nations, and they are named together elsewhere in oracles of judgment in Jer 25:22, 27:3, 47:4, and Joel 3:4. Unlike most other Persian period cities, Tyre and Sidon were administered by semi-autonomous kings (Briant 2002, 489), a political privilege no doubt linked to their unusual wealth, and in Tyre's case at least, extensive fortifications — both noted in Zech 9:3.

Any reassertion of Davidic/Yahwistic empire would likely show interest in Philistia. I note the mention of the Philistines in 2 Sam 8:12 and the listing of the Philistine cities in Zech 9:5–6. In the Persian period there was no longer any trace of the distinctive Philistine culture so evident, for example, in the pottery of Iron Age I. But the oracle is dealing with traditional enemies, and even Ezekiel (25:15–16) and Joel (3:4) can name the Philistines in words of judgment. Zechariah 9:1–8's city list, then, involves an appeal to ancient tradition, and does not provide evidential value for a specific time setting for its origin. It suits the Persian period as well as any other in the mid-first millennium B.C. The text

---

[12] Hamath and Damascus are also named together in the idealization of Israelite territory found in Ezekiel's eschatological temple vision in 47:16–17 and 48:1.

does, however provide evidence regarding the ideology of its postexilic promulgators, whether Zechariah or his post-Zecharian circle of tradents.

The core theology of Zech 9:1–8 is the assertion that Yahweh will rule the nations. Some may acquiesce to his claims, perhaps Damascus in this list; others, like Tyre, will go up in flames. Yahweh's interest is keenly upon his ancient people, yet it also extends to the unclean Philistines, some of whom shall be converted and adopted into Yehud, and thus gain a place of honor among Yahweh's people. The goal of the historical process is international Yahwistic empire, centered in Jerusalem and the restored temple. The writer of such a text could be a good candidate for a central authority prophet. Or, the text could be written by a marginalized Yehudean traditionalist with a restorationist ideology. Discussion of Zech 9:9-17 follows the boxed text and translation, below.

ZECHARIAH 9:9–17, DELINEATED

poetic accent count	prose particle count		poetic delineation	
3+2		הָרִיעִי בַּת יְרוּשָׁלָם	גִּילִי מְאֹד בַּת־צִיּוֹן	9:9
4+3		צַדִּיק וְנוֹשָׁע הוּא	הִנֵּה מַלְכֵּךְ יָבוֹא לָךְ	
2+2+2		וְסוּס מִירוּשָׁלָם	וְהִכְרַתִּי־רֶכֶב מֵאֶפְרַיִם	10
			וְנִכְרְתָה קֶשֶׁת מִלְחָמָה	
3+3+2		וּמָשְׁלוֹ מַיִם עַד־יָם	וְדִבֶּר שָׁלוֹם לַגּוֹיִם	
			וּמִנָּהָר עַד־אַפְסֵי־אָרֶץ	
2+6		שִׁלַּחְתִּי אֲסִירַיִךְ מִבּוֹר אֵין מַיִם בּוֹ	גַּם־אַתְּ בְּדַם־בְּרִיתֵךְ	11
3+5	ה =2	גַּם־הַיּוֹם מַגִּיד מִשְׁנֶה אָשִׁיב לָךְ	שׁוּבוּ לְבִצָּרוֹן אֲסִירֵי הַתִּקְוָה	12
4+2		מִלֵּאתִי אֶפְרַיִם	כִּי־דָרַכְתִּי לִי יְהוּדָה קֶשֶׁת	13
3+2+2		עַל־בָּנַיִךְ יָוָן	וְעוֹרַרְתִּי בָנַיִךְ צִיּוֹן	
			וְשַׂמְתִּיךְ כְּחֶרֶב גִּבּוֹר	
3+3		וְיָצָא כַבָּרָק חִצּוֹ	וַיהוָה עֲלֵיהֶם יֵרָאֶה	14
4+2		וְהָלַךְ בְּסַעֲרוֹת תֵּימָן	וַאדֹנָי יְהוִה בַּשּׁוֹפָר יִתְקָע	
4+3		וְאָכְלוּ וְכָבְשׁוּ אַבְנֵי־קֶלַע	יְהוָה צְבָאוֹת יָגֵן עֲלֵיהֶם	15
3+3		וּמָלְאוּ כַּמִּזְרָק כְּזָוִיּוֹת מִזְבֵּחַ	וְשָׁתוּ הָמוּ כְּמוֹ־יָיִן	
3+3+4	ה =1	בַּיּוֹם הַהוּא כְּצֹאן עַמּוֹ	וְהוֹשִׁיעָם יְהוָה אֱלֹהֵיהֶם	16
		עַל־אַדְמָתוֹ	כִּי אַבְנֵי־נֵזֶר מִתְנוֹסְסוֹת	
3+2+3			כִּי מַה־טּוּבוֹ וּמַה־יָפְיוֹ	17
		וְתִירוֹשׁ יְנוֹבֵב בְּתֻלוֹת	דָּגָן בַּחוּרִים	

Prose Particle Count = 3/129 words = 2.3% PPD

ZECHARIAH 9:9–17 IN TRANSLATION

9   Rejoice greatly, Zion-Daughter!
    Raise the triumph-call, Jerusalem-Daughter!
    Look—your king will come to you!
        Righteous and endowed with victory is he,
        humble and riding on a donkey,
            upon a young donkey, the foal of she-asses.
10 "Thus I will cut off the chariot from Ephraim,
        and the war-steed from Jerusalem
        and the battle-bow will be cut off."
    Thus he will proclaim peace to the nations:
        his dominion from sea to sea,
        from the River to the ends of the earth.

11 "As for you, [Zion-Daughter],
        because of the blood of your covenant,
        I have released your prisoners from the waterless pit.
12 —Return to [your home-]fortresses,[13]
        you prisoners of the hope!
    And as for today, I announce
        [that] I will restore to you double [what you had lost].
13 For I have strung Judah like my battle-bow,
        and I have fitted [it] with Ephraim [my arrow].
    Thus I shall arouse your sons, [Mother] Zion,
        against your sons, [Mother] Greece,
        and I will make you like a warrior's sword!"
14 Then Yahweh will appear above them!
        His arrow will speed forth like lightning!
    —Then Lord Yahweh shall blow the trumpet-blast
        and march in the storms of the southern deserts!
15 Yahweh of the heavenly armies shall shield them from above.
        They will consume and conquer with sling-stones.
    They will drink and carouse, as with wine.
        They will be filled like the basin,
        like [the basins at the] corners of an altar.
16 Yahweh their God will save them on that day,
        his people will be like a flock;

---

[13] NJPS suggests that *bitstsaron* is a rhymed word play on Samaria, *shomeron* (1988, 1092, note j). Koehler and Baumgartner suggest an emendation based upon a presumed metathesis from an original *letsibbaron*, "in throngs" (1994, 1:149a). Better than either of these, I think, is my proposal that *bitstsaron* is meant to play in assonance with the *bat-ziyyon* of 9:9. The *bitstsaron* is the masculine-counterpart fortress to *bat-ziyyon*'s feminine city.

for like precious stones of a crown,
    they will sparkle over his land.
17 How good and how lovely it is!
    Grain [will make] the young men [flourish],
    and new wine the young women!

ZECHARIAH 9:9–17. Zechariah 9:9–17 appears to be a compound unit. The delimitation is signaled by the *inclusio* of the feminine figures of fair Daughter-Zion in 9:9 and the lovely young women of 9:17. The strophe break at v. 11, signaled by the unusually long line and the change of topic is compensated for by the continuation of the second-person feminine singular address, begun in 9:9's הָרִיעִי and גִּילִי, continued in 9:11's גַּם־אַתְּ, in its feminine pronominal objects (בְּרִיתֵךְ, אֲסִירַיִךְ), and the reference to Zion's "sons" in 9:13. It may be that all of 9:9–17 is meant to serve as the continuation of the judgment-salvation oracle that begins in 9:1–8, in a compound form.

The בַּת־צִיּוֹן phrase appears to be original to Isaiah, and is attested almost exclusively in the latter prophets and Lamentations. It appears in the opening line of Isaiah's oracle of Sennacherib's fall, reportedly spoken to King Hezekiah in Isa 37:22 (par. 2 Kgs 19:21). The phrase בַּת־צִיּוֹן should be translated "Daughter-Zion" or perhaps "Fair Zion" (so NJPS), and not "daughter of Zion," because the daughter is Zion herself.[14] Cities may have metaphorical "daughters," but these are the outlying villages, not the main settlement (cf. Num 21:25, חֶשְׁבּוֹן וּבְכָל־בְּנֹתֶיהָ, "Heshbon and all of her daughters"). As in Zeph 3:14–20, and probably Zech 2:14, two passages with which Zech 9:9–17 shares much in common, the address to בַּת־צִיּוֹן comes at the beginning of the rhetorical unit.

The reason for Zion's rejoicing is the coming of her king. The king's description evokes the Davidic tradition of the righteous, victorious ruler. This ruler is both peaceable and warlike: he is humble and donkey-mounted; yet he *declares* peace (וְדִבֶּר שָׁלוֹם) to the warring nations and (or is it Yahweh alone who does this?) violently cuts off their chariots, warhorses and battle bows. As in Ps 72, another passage in the Davidic tradition, his reign is universal: וְיֵרְדְּ מִיָּם עַד־יָם וּמִנָּהָר עַד־אַפְסֵי־אָרֶץ, "May he rule from sea to sea, and from the River to the ends of the earth" (Ps 72:8).[15] The passage accordingly well suits its present location after Zech 9:1–8: both anticipate Yahwistic empire over the nations.

---

[14] If so, it is a case of the "genitive of association." See Waltke and O'Connor 1990, §9.5.3h.
[15] Hence, Petersen's attempt at a collective interpretation of the king is rejected (1995, 59 and n. 50).

Zechariah 9:9–10 need not be taken as a postexilic text; even in the days of King Zedekiah the prophet Jeremiah could announce the coming of a just king, whose name is יְהוָה צִדְקֵנוּ, *yahweh-tsidqenu*, "Yahweh-is-our-Righteousness" (23:5–6). But the postexilic setting of Zech 9 likewise is suitable. The prediction of the coming king, then, is not a secure foundation for a postexilic date.

Better evidence of a postexilic date for the text comes with 9:11–12, with its declaration of the release of prisoners, the return of hope, and the double restoration (מִשְׁנֶה אָשִׁיב לָךְ), which intertextually evokes Isa 40:2. If Zech 9 is an exilic or preexilic text, prosodic analysis suggests that Zech 9:11–12 is perhaps a postexilic interpretive addition. These two verses alone bear clauses of five or six accents each, the longest clauses of the poem, and, as we shall see below, they also bear the definite article ה twice (9:12), a sign of late origin in Hebrew poetry. Perhaps, then, vv. 11–12 reflect an early postexilic adaptation of an older text, for use in the book of Zechariah.

STADE AND THE בָּנֶיךָ יָוָן OF ZECH 9:13. Zechariah 9:13, with its mention of בָּנֶיךָ יָוָן, "your sons, O Yavan," stood as Bernhard Stade's chief evidence of the Hellenistic origin of Zech 9. Yavan is cognate to Ionia, and for the MT denotes the Aegean islands and the Greek mainland. The phrase בְּנֵי יָוָן, "sons of Yavan," denotes all the native Greek-speaking peoples of the Aegean world. The form appears in the genealogies of Gen 10 and 1 Chr 1, and the plural form הַיְּוָנִים, "the Yavanim," appears in Joel 4:6. The term יָוָן, "Yavan," also appears in Isa 66:19, Ezek 27:13 and 19 as well as in apocalyptic passages in Daniel (8:21; 10:20; 11:2).

Stade held that the reference to the sons of Yavan in 9:13 "is alone a compelling basis" ("allein ein zwingender Grund") to show that these oracles arose in Hellenistic times (1882b, 290). He believed that the בְּנֵי יָוָן had to denote the dominant world power at the time ("Weltmacht," 1882b, 275). Aelred Cody adds, "the sons of *Yawan* [sic] … could hardly be pitched against Zion … before the arrival of the armies of Alexander the Great in the Near East in 333" (1990, 353). However, while the text if taken alone permits a Hellenistic dating, a Hellenistic date is far from required. Nor is it compelling. Nonetheless, Nogalski writes in support of Stade's view:

> The reference to the Greeks as a world power (Zech 9:13) makes this [Hellenistic] date the most acceptable starting point (1993b, 216). Those such as Hanson and Otzen, who argue for an earlier date create real problems by trying to explain away the reference to the Greeks as the chief adversary of chapter 9. While there were long-standing relationships between Greece and Palestine, Zech 9:13 clearly pits Judah, Ephraim and Jerusalem against Greece using military imagery implying Greece as the chief threat, i.e., political power of the time. This is difficult to harmonize with any known events prior to the time of Alexander. (216, n. 24)

Nogalski then mentions Otzen who tries to explain the Greeks as a reference to Greek mercenaries in Egypt in the seventh century, and Hanson, who deletes the reference to the Greeks in 9:13 as a dittographic error (1979, 298).[16]

I think a strong argument can be made against Stade, Cody, and Nogalski's position, without recourse to textual emendation or much dependence on the mercenary-in-Egypt argument of Otzen. Stade underestimated the geopolitical significance of Greece in the early Persian period, and wrongly believed that the phrase בְּנֵי יָוָן had to denote the *dominant* world power. He also did not pay sufficient regard for Yehud's political commitment to the Persian Empire. In all these respects he was mistaken, as I shall now attempt to show.

PERSIAN-GREEK CONFLICT IN THE EASTERN MEDITERRANEAN WORLD. Historians John H. Hayes and Sara Mandell (1998) list a litany of Greek presence in Syro-Palestine starting as early as 738 B.C., when an Assyrian official in Phoenicia wrote to Tiglath-Pileser III with the complaint that Ionian Greeks were staging raids on his coastal cities. Greek settlements on the northern Syrian coastline at Al Mina and Tell Sukas also hail from the eighth century, probably. The Egyptian army under Pharaoh Psammetichus I (664–610 B.C.) had a strong presence of Greek mercenaries, and Greek mercenaries probably fought on both the Egyptian and Babylonian sides at the Battle of Carchemish in 605 B.C. (1998, 19). "From the seventh century B.C.E. on, Greek mercenaries, traders and even tourists became significant in eastern Mediterranean life" (20). The Egyptian military forces that passed through and encamped in Palestine in the seventh century, and the Persian forces that did the same in the sixth and fifth centuries, certainly enlisted Greeks within their ranks. In the late fifth century Jews and Greeks certainly served together at the Persian military colony at Elephantine. Greek pottery is attested at pre-Hellenistic sites too numerous to mention, and Greek coinage decidedly influenced the design of the fourth-century Yehud coins, issued in obvious imitation of the Greek drachma (20).

The Persian Empire first came into significant conflict with Greeks in the aftermath of Cyrus's successful campaign against King Croesus of Lydia, located near the western rim of Asia Minor, in 546 B.C. Cyrus's victory at Sardis brought his empire to the very edge of the Aegean world of the Greeks. The Spartans immediately sent envoys to Cyrus to forbid him from making war on Greek territory—on either side of the Aegean. Cyrus is reported to have replied something like, "Who are the Spartans?" (Herodotus *Hist.* 1:153). The Persians would soon find out.

The Lydians soon revolted under Pactyes, with Greek assistance, and laid siege to Persian Sardis, but in vain. In about four years' time the Greek-speaking cities of the east Aegean coastline all fell to Cyrus's power (Briant 2002,

---

[16] The last three letters of צִיּוֹן, Zion, spell יָוָן, Yavan.

36–38), including Caria in the coastal southwest, whence Herodotus of Halicarnassus (ca. 484 B.C.–420 B.C.), the chronicler of all things Persian, came.

The Egypt of Amasis (r. 570–525 B.C.) and Psammetichus III (r. 525 B.C.), who opposed Cambyses's invasion, was defended to a substantial degree by Greek mercenary troops from Ionia and Caria. From 540 B.C. until his death in 522 B.C. Polycrates, the tyrant of Samos, aspired to dominion over Ionia and the islands. He was perceived as a major threat to the Persians—until they succeeded in murdering him at a pretended parlay and impaling his body. He had maintained a navy of one hundred fifty-oared galleys and forty triremes, a considerable force, which he held with the support of Pharaoh Amasis (Briant 2002, 52). Herodotus says that it was Polycrates who made the first attempt to control the whole Aegean (*Hist.* 3.124). Darius had to subdue the Egyptian revolt in 519–518 B.C., but soon was compelled to leave Egypt in order to pay attention to the northwestern fringe of his empire. By about 516 B.C. Darius and his generals succeeded in subjecting the Greeks of Samos, the Hellespont, and the Thracians to Persian rule (Briant 2002, 141–46). After an unsuccessful campaign against the Scythians in about 513 B.C., Darius returned to Sardis. J. M. Cook reflects that by this time, he "must have been aware that the free Greeks across the Aegean constituted a problem which, with the intervening sea, was more intractable than any which had confronted his predecessors" (1983, 64).

His failure against the Scythians did much to encourage Ionian unrest. In 500 B.C. the great Ionian Revolt began, with Athenian support, surely one of the most difficult military campaigns of Darius's long career. The revolt may have been provoked by an unsuccessful Persian strike at Naxos in the Cyclades. In any case, Ionia refused to be ruled by Persians any longer, and went to war. In 498 B.C. an Athenian-led force including Ionians and Eretrians captured and burned Sardis, the satrapic capital. The cities of Cyprus soon joined in the revolt (Sealey 1976, 177). The revolt was not put down until about 493 B.C. after a long and bloody campaign, requiring substantial—and expensive—help from the Phoenician fleet.

After the burning of Sardis, Herodotus entertainingly reports that Darius ordered one of his servants to say to him three times every day at dinner, "Master, remember the Athenians" (*Hist.* 5.105; cf. Sealey 1976, 179). He would, soon enough. In 492 B.C., Mardonius, Darius's son-in-law, led a Persian land force across the Hellespont, while the Persian fleet made its way around the cape at Mt. Athos for the invasion of Greece. The targets were apparently Athens and Eretria. Mardonius met with mixed success on land, but the fleet encountered a disastrous storm and the alleged loss of 300 ships and 20,000 men (so Herodotus, *Hist.* 6.47). Nonetheless he did succeed in consolidating Persian power in the northern Aegean coastlands (Sealey 1976, 178).

Darius was not to be put off. In 490 B.C. he launched another campaign against Greece. This time his force of some 20,000 men and some 800 cavalry crossed the Aegean, burned Naxos along the way, and landed on Euboea, where they besieged and conquered Eretria, one of their main targets. They then proceeded to the Attic mainland, where they disembarked on the lowland beaches at the Bay of Marathon. At Marathon they faced a force of some 10,000 Athenians and allies,[17] smaller in number, but better armed and better trained. There the Persians were famously defeated (Sealey, 1976, 187–92).

However, the Persian dream of revenge against Athens and the subjugation of Greece did not die on the battlefield of Marathon. After the succession of Darius's son Xerxes (r. 486 B.C.–465 B.C.) and the quelling of a second Egyptian revolt (486 B.C.–485 B.C.), plans were again laid to conquer Greece, this time by a massive joint land-and-sea campaign. The invasion was launched in 480 B.C., with the Great King himself at the helm of vast forces. There he faced the armies of a newly formed Hellenic league. The Spartans under Leonidas held the narrow pass at Thermopylae, to their enduring fame. But their position was betrayed and they were taken by Xerxes's "Immortals," the Persians' most elite troops, who trekked a goat-herd path all night long to overwhelm them from the rear. Athens was evacuated; Xerxes's forces arrived and set fire to the city. Then in September came the great sea battle at Salamis, a surprising and massive defeat for Xerxes (220–21). Xerxes withdrew to Sardis, leaving another Persian force under Mardonius wintering in Thessaly. Spring of 479 B.C. saw more action as Mardonius advanced south. Athens again evacuated. Attica was sacked. The two armies met at Plataea. After days of indecisive fighting, the Spartan and Tigean right flank overwhelmed the Persian wing and actually killed Mardonius. Thus the battle was decided for the Greeks (224).

The Persians then sailed for Samos, followed closely by a Greek force led by the Spartan king Leotychides. They met in battle on the Ionian mainland opposite Samos, at Mycale, where the Persians were again defeated, but the Greek commanders wisely saw that they could not hold the Asia Minor mainland against the Persians reinforcements sure to arrive. They admitted the Ionian islanders to their Hellenic league, and abandoned the mainland to Persia (226–28). Persian-Greek skirmishes in the Aegean world were not over, but in their war of defense the Greeks had won. Persia would not again attempt to take the Greek mainland.

Both Byzantium and Cyprus (temporarily) fell to the Greeks in 478 B.C. (242–43). That year also saw the Athenians' founding of the Delian League, whose express purpose according to Thucydides (1.96) was "to compensate themselves for their losses by ravaging the territory of the King of Persia." In about 469 B.C. a major confrontation took place at the Eurymedon River, on the southern coast of Asia Minor. There the Greek commander Cimon crushed both the Persian land and sea forces, with the loss of about 200 Phoenician triremes, a humiliating defeat. Kenneth G. Hoglund observes, "The destruction of the Per-

---

[17] The Spartans arrived for the battle one day too late.

sian fleet at Eurymedon left the empire incapable of checking Athenian penetration into the eastern Mediterranean" (1992, 146). By the mid-fifth century cities such as Dor on the Palestinian coast were tributary to the Delian League (153–54). By 431 B.C. the league had also recaptured all the Aegean islands except Melos and Thera (Sealey 1976, 251).

Meanwhile, Egypt saw yet a third revolt, this time under the Libyan king, Inaros, with massive Athenian support. The Inaros Revolt almost succeeded in freeing Egypt from the Persians. In about 464 B.C. Inaros's forces met those of Achaemenes, satrap of Egypt, brother to Xerxes, and uncle to Artaxerxes I, probably in the western Delta. The death of Achaemenes and victory of Inaros in battle must have been a great shock to the Persians (Hoglund 1992, 142–43). Inaros and his newly arrived Athenian allies then had the Persian forces besieged at the satrapal capital, Memphis, in its "White Fortress" (Sealey 1976, 269; Briant 2002, 575). Control of the rest of Egypt was within Inaros's grasp, although Briant points out that he did not exercise this control beyond the region of Memphis and the Delta (2002, 575). Athens contributed no less than 200 triremes to Inaros's war effort. Meanwhile the Persians attempted to induce the Spartans to attack the Delian League, unsuccessfully (Hoglund 1992, 150). A massive Persian force eventually arrived, broke the long siege of Memphis, and put Inaros and his Greek allies to flight. They took refuge on the Nile island of Prosopitis, where they were besieged by the Persians for 18 months, ending in 454 B.C. with the capture and execution of Inaros and great loss to the Greek forces, as well as the near total destruction of fifty more ships sent in relief from Greece (Sealey 1976, 272; Hoglund 1992, 155; Briant 2002, 573–76).

In nearly a hundred years of warfare, both sides had suffered enormous losses. The Peace of Callias, ca. 449 B.C., apparently brought an end to active hostilities between the two parties. The Greeks left Egypt and Cyprus; the Persians were to leave the Delian League's tributary cities inviolate. Other provisions of the treaty are disputed, and some, like Sealey (1976, 478–82), doubt such a treaty was ever negotiated. In any case, an uneasy truce settled over the eastern Mediterranean world, with the Great King, Artaxerxes I, mainly on his side of the water, and the Greeks on theirs.

This survey of the period from 546 B.C. to 449 B.C. demonstrates, *contra* Stade, that the Greeks rose to the status of a world power late in the sixth century or early in the fifth century B.C., successfully opposing the greatest empire of the world, the Persians, and fighting it to a stalemate (so also Robinson 1965, 195–97). By 513 B.C. the Greeks were indeed, as J. M. Cook had noted, an "intractable" problem. By 479 B.C. they were no longer on the defensive, but taking the war into Asia Minor and Cyprus. By about 469 B.C. they showed that they could beat the Persians on their own imperial soil, at Eurymedon. Despite the setback at Prosopitis in 454 B.C. they were still a formidable foe to the Persians. Hoglund has argued that it was the Inaros Revolt and the Greek threat that led Artaxerxes I to send Nehemiah to fortify Jerusalem in 445 B.C.—the Persian king needed a secure and loyal ally on his Egyptian frontier. Hoglund's major thesis is that the work of Ezra and Nehemiah ought to be understood as expressions of the strategically important Persian policy of securing the Syro-Palestinian frontier against Greek incursions (1992; Curtis 1996).

ZECHARIAH 9:13, THE GREEKS, AND YEHUDEAN LOYALTY TO PERSIA. As we have seen, then, already in 520–518 B.C., the time of the oracles of Zech 1–8, the Greeks were a major source of conflict for the Persians. If, as we have seen, the historical Zechariah was a young man in 520–518 B.C., as his presence in the priestly list in Neh 12:12–21 (v. 16), naming the heads of priestly families in the generation of Joiakim, Joshua's son (ca. 500 B.C.), indicates, then he witnessed the rise of Greece to the world-power status that my historical survey indicates.

Stade held, however, that the בְּנֵי יָוָן, the "sons of Yavan," of Zech 9:13 denoted the *dominant* world power at the time of its composition. This conclusion is not textually warranted. First, the Greeks are only named once in Zech 9–14, not repeatedly. Second, very little is actually asserted about the Greeks in 9:13. The text announces conflict between the sons of Zion and of Yavan. It predicts the victory of the sons of Zion, but tells us nothing further of the historical conditions. We are left in the dark. I conclude, then, that Zech 9:13 does not require the בְּנֵי יָוָן to be the *dominant* world power, only a *significant* world power, one that shall threaten Zion. This is entirely in keeping with an early Persian period date for Zech 9:13.

A parallel issue to the Greek question rises in regard to Yehudean support for Persian aims in the geo-politics of the late sixth century and early fifth century B.C. Given Greek-Persian conflict, would Yehudeans care? Would Yehudeans be loyal supporters of Persian interests in this period? Stade does not discuss this question. Most of the evidence that we possess indicates a favorable answer. I shall consider six lines of argument.

First there is the role of Cyrus and the Persians in Isa 44:24–45:7, a text that would very likely have been known and accredited in the era of Darius in Yehud, since it predicts the Persian-sponsored restoration of Yehud and the rebuilding of the temple, the major program of the era. As is well known, there Yahweh is said to call Cyrus, the empire's founder, רֹעִי, "my shepherd" (44:28), to whom he gives "the treasures of darkness" (נָתַתִּי לְךָ אוֹצְרוֹת חֹשֶׁךְ). There also Cyrus is called מְשִׁיחוֹ, "his [Yahweh's] anointed one" (45:1), who shall "carry out" all of the divine "purpose" (כָּל־חֶפְצִי יַשְׁלִם, 44:28), despite that fact that he "does not know" Yahweh (לֹא יְדַעְתָּנִי, 45:4). This passage is quoted so frequently that its shocking character is no longer felt. Terminology once associated exclusively with the royal Davidic line is here attributed not only to a non-Davidide, but to a non-Israelite king. Followers of the Isaiah tradition would thus feel duty-bound to Persian loyalty, at least in the days of Cyrus, and probably for long afterward.

Second, as I have demonstrated in the section on date forms in the latter prophets, formulae that date biblical texts to the reigns of non-Israelite kings begin with Jer 25:1, which names the first year of Nebuchadnezzar, who quite remarkably is described later in the chapter as Yahweh's "servant" (נְבוּכַדְרֶאצַּר מֶלֶךְ־בָּבֶל עַבְדִּי, 25:9), a royal title in Judah. In this regard Isa 44–45 and Jer 25 are parallel texts. In this dated oracle (605 B.C.), Jeremiah reports Yahweh's oracle of judgment against Judah, giving it over to the power of Nebuchadnezzar and his Babylonian successors for seventy years (25:11). The novel Nebuchadnezzar date formula reflects the theo-political loyalty of scribal practice in the book of Jeremiah. Nebuchadnezzar was now the Yahweh-appointed legitimate monarch of the province of Judah. We should read the Persian-era date formula of Haggai and Zech 1–8 in a similar manner: the framers of the composite book were Persian loyalists, under theological obligation. The Isaiah text transfers power from one "servant," Nebuchadnezzar and his successors, to another "servant," Cyrus. Darius is now the heir to that theological transfer of power.

Next we must consider Zerubbabel, Joshua, and the geopolitics of 521–518 B.C. If the reconstruction is correct that Zerubbabel and Joshua arrived in about 521 B.C., the newly enthroned Darius would have been especially keen to ascertain the loyalty of these two leaders, and of the colonists who would accompany them (Berquist 1995, 63–65). After all, according to the Behistun Inscription, he had just succeeded in putting down multiple revolts. Yehudean loyalty was necessary. Briant also suggests that in 521 B.C. there may have been a minor Egyptian revolt, headed by a certain Petubastis, that was soon put down by the local satrap, Aryandes (2002, 115). In any case, Egypt was still a newly conquered territory, unstable, and would soon engage in a massive revolt, not unanticipated, requiring Darius's personal attention in 519–518 B.C. Darius needed a loyal Yehud on his western frontier. It seems reasonable to think that he got it. His 519–518 B.C. marches through Syro-Palestine would surely guarantee local loyalty as well (Berquist 1995, 63–65).

Fourth, Ezra 6:14–15 shows that Persian loyalty in Yehud was not a matter that lasted only one generation. This remarkable mid- or late fifth-century text is said to be the only verse in the Hebrew Bible where both Yahweh and human beings are brought together as the agents of the same action. The Aramaic reads:

וּבְנוֹ וְשַׁכְלִלוּ מִן־טַעַם אֱלָהּ יִשְׂרָאֵל וּמִטְּעֵם כּוֹרֶשׁ וְדָרְיָוֶשׁ
וְאַרְתַּחְשַׁשְׂתְּא מֶלֶךְ פָּרָס

They built and completed [the temple] according to the decree of the God of Israel and according to the decree[18] of Cyrus, Darius, and Artaxerxes,[19] kings of Persia. (Ezra 6:14)

The text continues:

וְשֵׁיצִיא בַּיְתָה דְנָה עַד יוֹם תְּלָתָה לִירַח אֲדָר דִּי־הִיא
שְׁנַת־שֵׁת לְמַלְכוּת דָּרְיָוֶשׁ מַלְכָּא

This temple was finished on the third[20] day of the month of Adar, which was in the sixth year of the reign of Darius the King. (6:15)

The theology of the Aramaic text is striking: The decree of the Persian kings matches the decree of the God of heaven; "The king's heart is in Yahweh's hand; he directs it like a watercourse wherever he pleases" (Prov 21:1). The text presupposes not only the legitimacy of the Persian kings, but their instrumentality in bringing about the divine intention for Yehud. For the community reflected in Ezra–Nehemiah, Persian loyalty was a given.

Fifth, we know of the Yehudean perception of Greece as a hostile power from other exilic and postexilic texts. Ezekiel 27, an exilic text, says in judgment of Tyre:

יָוָן תֻּבַל וָמֶשֶׁךְ הֵמָּה רֹכְלָיִךְ בְּנֶפֶשׁ אָדָם וּכְלֵי נְחֹשֶׁת נָתְנוּ מַעֲרָבֵךְ

Yavan, Tubal, and Meshach traded with you; slaves and articles of bronze they exchanged for your merchandise. (27:13)[21]

Verse 19 adds:

Danites and Greeks[22] from Uzal bought your merchandise; they exchanged wrought iron, cassia and calamus for your wares. (NIV)

---

[18] Williamson suggests that the two different forms of the word "decree" may reflect a theological desire to distinguish the divine decree from the human one (1985, 72).

[19] The presence of the name of Artaxerxes I on the list probably reflects an Ezra-era composition, when it could be reported that Artaxerxes I had benefitted the temple, as recorded in the decree in Ezra 7:12–24. Hence 6:15 anticipates 7:12–24.

[20] Williamson and Blenkinsopp both suggest the restoration of the number to "twenty-third" based on the parallel account in 1 Esdr 7:5 (1985, 72; 1988, 129). If we follow this plausible emendation, temple completion took place April 1, 515 B.C.

[21] Zimmerli treats Ezek 27:12–25a, as a later prose expansion in a sixth-century poetical text (1983, 54–56). The unit is certainly prose, and it may be a later expansion by the prophet, but there is no reason to suppose that it, too, is not a sixth century text.

Joel 4, a postexilic text, says in judgment of Tyre and Sidon:

וּבְנֵי יְהוּדָה וּבְנֵי יְרוּשָׁלִַם מְכַרְתֶּם לִבְנֵי הַיְּוָנִים לְמַעַן הַרְחִיקָם מֵעַל גְּבוּלָם

The sons of Yehud and the sons of Jerusalem you sold to the sons of the Greeks (*yavanim*), in order to send them far from their own homeland. (4:6)

Yavan, then, was ill-reputed as a slave master over Judean slaves, already in the early Persian period.

Sixth and last, Yehudean men would certainly have served in the Persian military, leading their families back home in Yehud to hope for their victory in battle. Although Herodotus does not specifically mention Yehudeans in his listings of ethnic units in the Persian military, regarding the 480 B.C. invasion force he does assert, "There was not a nation in all Asia that [Xerxes] did not take with him against Greece" (*Hist.* 7.22). Despite the unusual magnitude of the Xerxes invasion force, we should not think that Yehudean conscription or Jewish military service was unique to the time of Xerxes. Later in the Persian period Jewish soldiers guarded the Persian Empire's African frontier at their garrison on the far-distant island of Yeb, as we know from the Elephantine Papyri.[23] Throughout Persian history the empire relied on levies[24] of young men for service in its armies or navies. The prediction of Zech 9:13 might denote the Persian campaigns of 516 B.C. against the Greeks of Samos and the Hellespont, when, conceivably, Yehudeans could have made victorious war against Greeks.

I conclude, then, against Stade, Cody, and Nogalski, that Zech 9:13 makes good sense within the early Persian period. Ultimately, however, the sons of Yavan represent the powers of evil, whom Yahweh will defeat on the great eschatological day, the Day of Yahweh (בַּיּוֹם הַהוּא, 9:16). In Zech 9:11–17 Yahweh wages war against the eschatological enemy; his bow is Yehud, and his arrow is Ephraim. He marches to the blast of the trumpet.

---

[22] The MT's וְדָן וְיָוָן מְאוּזָל בְּעִזְבוֹנַיִךְ נָתָנּוּ in 27:19 is uncertain. LXX reads καὶ οἶνον εἰς τὴν ἀγοράν σου ἔδωκαν. Zimmerli, based on LXX, suggests the first two words are a dittography for an original יָיִן (1983, 49). The NRSV transliterates the first word as a place name, Vedan. However, in defense of the MT, I note that Homer uses *Danae* (Danites) as a name for Greeks. Dan and Yavan make good sense as a pair of ethnic terms in Ezekiel's prose.

[23] For Aramaic texts and translations, see Bezalel Porten and Jonas C. Greenfield (1974), and James M. Lindenberger (1994).

[24] Herodotus, *Hist.* 7.96, says that "every nation had as many officers as it had towns.... These native officers were not really commanders; like the rest of the troops, they merely served under compulsion."

THE CONCLUSION OF ZECH 9:9–17.

Near the end of the unit a new key word is introduced, צֹאן, "flock":

וְהוֹשִׁיעָם יְהוָה אֱלֹהֵיהֶם בַּיּוֹם הַהוּא כְּצֹאן עַמּוֹ
כִּי אַבְנֵי־נֵזֶר מִתְנוֹסְסוֹת עַל־אַדְמָתוֹ

> Yahweh their God will save them on that day,
>   His people will be like a flock;
> for like precious stones of a crown,
>   they will sparkle over his land. (9:16)

This text brims over with inner-biblical references, not least of which is the pairing of "people" with "flock" in multiple texts. The significant reference to "his [i.e., Yahweh's] land," though a *dislegomenon* with Deut 32:43, nonetheless evokes the אַדְמַת הַקֹּדֶשׁ ("holy land") of Zech 2:16, a *hapax legomenon*. The flock imagery (צֹאן) will appear eight times in Zechariah, all in chs. 9–14, and it shall be accompanied by another key term in chs. 9–14, רֹעֶה, *shepherd*, ten times, with the verb ר.ע.ה four more times. All three terms are significant for social location analysis, but must await further development later in this chapter. The unit ends with another reference to stones (cf. 3:9; 4:10) and crowns (cf. 3:5; 6:11, 14), this time the sparkling gemstones of a crown (9:16), an appropriate simile for the thriving young men and women of the final verse (9:17).

If Zech 9 represents an early Persian period adaptation or expansion of an exilic or preexilic text, then we should consider vv. 11–13, with its longer line length (v. 11), its exhortation for the exiles to return (v. 12), its use of the definite article in otherwise anarthrous poetry (v. 12, אֲסִירֵי הַתִּקְוָה and גַּם־הַיּוֹם), and its promise of victory over Greeks (v. 13) as the early postexilic level of the text. If a *massa'* is indeed a revelatory reflection upon earlier revelation, the *Urtext* of Zech 9 is a possible candidate for the earlier revelatory text. On the other hand, some anarthrous poetry seems to be postexilic. Hence, on these grounds Zech 9 could be entirely a postexilic composition, and from one hand. There is nothing in the text that forbids Zech 9 from being assigned to the historical prophet Zechariah.

In conclusion, then, Zech 9:9–17 is a prophetic call to rejoicing (9:9–10) joined to a subunit of mixed type (9:11–17), combining elements of the prophetic exhortation ("Return to your fortresses, you prisoners of hope!" 9:11), of the war oracle ("His arrow will speed forth like lightning!" 9:14), and of the prophetic salvation oracle ("Yahweh their God will save them on that day"). With the exception of the statement about the sons of Yavan, the elements are all quite traditional, and could be spoken or written by a central authority prophet, or by an estranged Zion traditionalist. As Petersen observes, "The text offers hope set within standard Israelite traditions" (1995, 67). The innovative element is the setting in which they are spoken. Hence, Petersen adds, "[the text] addresses a situation radically different from that during which those traditions originally came to expression" (67).

HISTORICAL LINGUISTICS AND THE DATE OF ZECH 9

The best evidence for the date of Zech 9, though not without its limitations, may lie in historical linguistics. The method of prose particle analysis, though still in some respects experimental, produces significant results in distinguishing Hebrew poetry from Hebrew prose. This method was developed around 1980 by Francis I. Andersen, A. D. Forbes, and David Noel Freedman, based on massive computerized analyses of the Hebrew text (Andersen and Forbes, 1983, 165–83). The prose particles are the relative particle אֲשֶׁר, the definite direct object marker אֵת, and the definite article ה. It has long been noted that these particles are common in prose, but rare in poetry. The method measures the frequency of these three prose particles within any given text, and yields a percentage figure that represents the prose particle density (PPD) of the selected text.

Freedman concludes after a close comparison of the statistics with passages generally accepted as poetry and those generally accepted as prose, that "practically everything with a reading of 5% or less will be poetry," and "practically everything with a reading above 15% will be prose" (1997, 215). My own testing of the data confirms this thesis sufficiently to sustain the proposal as a good working hypothesis in adjudicating disputed texts and in discerning more precisely the boundaries between poetry and prose. I note that Andrew E. Hill, who analyzed the historical linguistics of the book of Malachi, made rich use of this method in determining the literary genre of that book in his Anchor Bible commentary (1998; cf. Hill 1981; 1982; 1983; cf. Cross 1995, 308 and Forbes 1995).

Most oracular material happens to fall between these two limits, between 5% and 15%, into a category many now call "oracular prose," a form of exalted prose speech that owes much to the line structure and ornamentation techniques employed in poetry. Meyers and Meyers consider much of Zech 1–8 to be oracular prose (1987, lxiv). More recently, Hill identified Malachi as mainly oracular prose also (1998, 26). On the other hand, M. O'Connor considers the book of Zephaniah to exemplify what he calls "prophetic verse," a style that Adele Berlin calls "not formally metrical," but containing many poetic rhythms and tropes, enough for the book to qualify. Thus for O'Connor (1980, 240–62) and Berlin (1994, 11), Zephaniah *is* verse, but of the prophetic variety. Parts of Zech 9–14 can also be considered "prophetic verse."

I shall not attempt to resolve the apparent incongruity between the two positions and their preferred terms, "oracular prose" and "prophetic verse." It is sufficient simply to note that regardless of the term, prophetic speech is dissimilar in some important respects from both the Hebrew of prose narrative, and the

Hebrew of the books universally recognized as poetry such as the Psalms, Job, and Lamentations.

Freedman also suggests that prose particle counts (PPCs) may help us distinguish earlier poetry from later poetry. He writes: "There is some evidence to show that the so-called prose particles are almost entirely absent from the earliest poetry, while they increase in number in late poetry" (1997, 214). This tool has limits, however: while no early poetry features high PPCs, some late poems have low PPCs.

According to Meyers and Meyers, Zech 9–14 has a total of 1383 words in the MT, of which 16 are אֲשֶׁר, 48 are אֵת, and 133 are ה, totaling 195, and yielding a PPD of 13.4%, approaching the borderline of prose. These totals, however, conceal the deeper picture. Zechariah 9:1–17 has only 3 prose particles in 222 words of the MT, yielding a PPD of 1.4%, remarkably low for a text in a postexilic literary context. Chart 6.2 below reproduces their data (1993, 30), with some corrections.

As can be clearly seen from Chart 6.2, Zech 9 is remarkably low in PPD at 1.4%, with Zech 10 following at a close second at 6.6%. The remainder of the section is much higher, near 14% or above, and reaching an upper limit of 21.3% in Zech 11. These latter numbers are quite close to the overall statistics for Zech 1–8, where the average PPD, according to Meyers and Meyers, is 15.8%, with no unit below 13.2% (Zech 2) and no unit above 20% (Zech 5).

CHART 6.2
PROSE PARTICLE DENSITY BY CHAPTER IN ZECH 9–14

Chapter	Words	אֲשֶׁר	אֵת	ה	Totals	Percentage
9:1–17	222	0	0	3	3	1.4%
10:1–12	166	1	5	5	11	6.6%
11:1–17	254	4	18	32	54	21.3%
12:1–14	227	1	8	22	31	13.7%
13:1–9	152	1	8	19	28	18.4%
14:1–21	372	9	6	53	68	18.3%
Totals	1393	16	47	134	197	14.2%

These numbers suggest that Zech 9:1–17 and Zech 10:1–12 may be early texts reused by the postexilic prophet or his prophet-tradent community. Again, if Anderson and Freedman are correct, no high PPD text is early, but some low PPD texts *may* be late, so caution is in order. These two chapters may still be entirely postexilic.

If we refine our method further, testing not whole chapters (which may not conform to the divisions of the literary units), but testing discrete sections, we discover the following for Zech 11:1–3 plus 11:17, and for the prose unit in 11:4–16, according to Chart 6.3:

CHART 6.3
PROSE PARTICLE DENSITY BY UNIT IN ZECH 11

Chapter	Words	אשר	את	ה	Totals	Percentage
11:1–3	34	1	0	3	4	11.8%
11:4–16	202	3	18	27	48	23.8%
11:17	18	0	0	2	2	11.1%

Contrast those numbers with these from Zech 9 in Chart 6.4:

CHART 6.4
PROSE PARTICLE DENSITY BY UNIT IN ZECH 9

Chapter	Words	אשר	את	ה	Totals	Percentage
9:1–8	93	0	0	0	0	0%
9:9–10	41	0	0	0	0	0%
9:11–17	88	0	0	3	3	3.4%
Total	222	0	0	3	3	1.4%

If Weis (1992) and Floyd (2000; 2002) are correct about the *massa'* genre involving reflection upon earlier prophetic texts, then Zech 9 is a good candidate for such a text. The data confirm Hanson's suggestion that Zech 9 may be the earliest text in the collection of Zech 9–14. While not necessarily indicating his proposed date of ca. 550 B.C., the data suggest that Hanson's date is possible. I suggest then that the function of Zech 9 is to serve as a declaration of the overall theology of the Zechariah tradent group, and to act as a springboard for the remainder of the book, Zech 10–14. Zechariah 10:1–12 may then have been composed in a quasi-poetical style in imitation of Zech 9, as were the oracles of 11:1–3 and 11:17.

Returning briefly to Zech 1–8, I note that the בַּת־צִיּוֹן oracle of 2:14–17 likewise has a low PPD of 6%, as in Chart 6.5 below:

CHART 6.5
PROSE PARTICLE DENSITY BY UNIT IN ZECH 2:1–17

Chapter	Words	אשר	את	ה	Totals	Percentage
2:1–13	171	2	10	14	26	15.2%
2:14–17	49	0	1	2	3	6.0%

The בַּת־צִיּוֹן oracles of Zech 2 and Zech 9, both prophetic calls to rejoicing, may play a peculiar role in the overall shaping of the material in Zech 1–14. I developed this idea in an earlier paper (Curtis 2000), where I argued that the בַּת־צִיּוֹן oracles of Zeph 3:14–18,[25] which also has a low PPD of 1.8% (2000, 176) and Zech 9, with its low PPD of 1.4%, ought to be seen as a pair. These oracles stand at major "seams" in the formative Book of the Twelve, may serve as significant markers for the tradent-scribe redactors who assembled the book in its latter stages into something like its final twelve-book form. If so, the Zion-Daughter oracles herald something of the Zion-restoration ideology of this tradent community, the theology of the community responsible for the Book of the Twelve. We now move on to consider Zech 10:1–2.

ZECHARIAH 10:1–2
PROPHETIC EXHORTATION

ZECHARIAH 10:1–2 DELINEATED

poetic accent count	prose particle count		poetic delineation	
3+1		בְּעֵת מַלְקוֹשׁ	שַׁאֲלוּ מֵיהוָה מָטָר	10:1
3+1		וּמְטַר־גֶּשֶׁם	יְהוָה עֹשֶׂה חֲזִיזִים	
3+2		עֵשֶׂב בַּשָּׂדֶה	יִתֵּן לָהֶם לְאִישׁ	
3+3	ה =2	וְהַקּוֹסְמִים חָזוּ שֶׁקֶר	כִּי הַתְּרָפִים דִּבְּרוּ־אָוֶן	2
3+2	ה =1	הֶבֶל יְנַחֵמוּן	וַחֲלֹמוֹת הַשָּׁוְא יְדַבֵּרוּ	
3+3		יַעֲנוּ כִּי־אֵין רֹעֶה פ	עַל־כֵּן נָסְעוּ כְמוֹ־צֹאן	

Prose Particle Count total = 3/36 words = 8.3% PPD

ZECHARIAH 10:1–2 IN TRANSLATION

1 Ask for rain from Yahweh
    at the time of the late rains.
Yahweh makes stormy winds
    and heavy rainfall.
He gives to them—to the human race—
    the greenery of the field.

---

[25] Zeph 3:19–20, with its high PPD of 30.8% is likely a prose expansion appended to the poetical oracle (so Curtis 2000, 176–80).

2 But the idols speak iniquity,
>   the diviners envision falsehood;
> worthless dreams they declare,
>   and offer empty comfort.
> Therefore [the people] stray like a flock,
>   and suffer for they have no shepherd.

As suggested above, Zech 10 consists of two units, 10:1–2, a short linking poem, and 10:3–12. The connective unit binds the two surrounding units together, but the closer relationship seems to be to 10:3–12, with its opening עַל־הָרֹעִים, "against the shepherds." The prophetic poetry is crisp, each line commencing with three accents followed by half lines of one, two, or three accents. There are only three prose particles. The content of 10:1–2 appears to be traditional prophetic exhortation against idolaters and soothsayers, and prophetic exhortation urging the proper invocation of Yahweh for rain and fertility. It is Yahweh who sees to the greening of the earth; not the idols. His prophets speak the true word; not the diviners.

The poem ends with a statement of the consequences of idolatry and divination: עַל־כֵּן נָסְעוּ כְמוֹ־צֹאן יַעֲנוּ כִּי־אֵין רֹעֶה, "Therefore [the people] stray like a flock, and suffer for they have no shepherd" (10:2). This line evokes perhaps three passages: Lev 27:16–17, Moses's request to Yahweh for a successor:

> "Let Yahweh, the God of the spirits of all flesh, appoint someone over the assembly who shall go out before them and come in before them, who shall lead them out and bring them in, so that Yahweh's assembly may not be like sheep without a shepherd" (וְלֹא תִהְיֶה עֲדַת יְהוָה כַּצֹּאן אֲשֶׁר אֵין־לָהֶם רֹעֶה).

1 Kings 22:17 — Micaiah's oracle to King Ahab:

> "I saw all Israel scattered on the mountains, like sheep without a shepherd (כַּצֹּאן אֲשֶׁר אֵין־לָהֶם רֹעֶה); and Yahweh said, 'These have no master; let each one go home in peace.'"

And Ezek 34:8 — Ezekiel's oracle against the "shepherds of Israel":

> "As I live," says the Lord Yahweh, "because my sheep have become a prey, and my sheep have become food for all the wild animals, since there was no shepherd (מֵאֵין רֹעֶה); and because my shepherds have not searched for my sheep, but the shepherds have fed themselves, and have not fed my sheep."

At least one of these texts, Ezek 34, appears to be crucial to the inner-biblical exegesis carried out in Zech 9–14, because of the several repetitions of phrases and key ideas. Perhaps all three texts are involved in some way.[26] In evoking these texts, it is clear that the author is either estranged from central authority of some kind, or challenging improper central authority from his own central authority position. The Micaiah oracle was aimed against King Ahab, and the Ezekiel passage was directed, at least in part, against evil kings. But it is not immediately clear what kind of bad leaders are in mind in Zech 10:2. The Ezekiel oracle undoubtedly included reference to the Judean nobility, and it probably also included public officials, priestly authority figures, and false prophets, all of whom are targeted one by one in Ezek 22. But we have no such direct information in Zech 10:1–2. Instead we must infer from context: perhaps the reference to diviners means that the shepherds are false prophets. This proposal has merit, and I shall return to it later in this chapter. However, the most one can say with strong confidence from the prophetic exhortation speech in 10:1–12 alone is that Yehud is in a crisis of leadership: there is no true רֹעֶה. Hence, the people suffer. Other texts besides 10:1–2 must fill in the gap, if possible.

THE SECOND JUDGMENT-SALVATION ORACLE

ZECHARIAH 10:3–12, DELINEATED

poetic accent count	prose particle count		poetic delineation
3+2	ה= 2	וְעַל־הָעַתּוּדִים אֶפְקוֹד	10:3 עַל־הָרֹעִים חָרָה אַפִּי
3+2	את= 3	אֶת־עֶדְרוֹ אֶת־בֵּית יְהוּדָה	כִּי־פָקַד יְהוָה צְבָאוֹת
2+2		כְּסוּס הוֹדוֹ בַּמִּלְחָמָה	וְשָׂם אוֹתָם
2+2		מִמֶּנּוּ יָתֵד	4 מִמֶּנּוּ פִנָּה
2+4		מִמֶּנּוּ יֵצֵא כָל־נוֹגֵשׂ יַחְדָּו	מִמֶּנּוּ קֶשֶׁת מִלְחָמָה
2+3		בּוֹסִים בְּטִיט חוּצוֹת בַּמִּלְחָמָה	5 וְהָיוּ כְגִבֹּרִים
4+2		וְהֹבִישׁוּ רֹכְבֵי סוּסִים	וְנִלְחֲמוּ כִּי יְהוָה עִמָּם
2+2	את= 2	וְאֶת־בֵּית יוֹסֵף אוֹשִׁיעַ	6 וְגִבַּרְתִּי אֶת־בֵּית יְהוּדָה
3+3	אשר= 1	וְהָיוּ כַּאֲשֶׁר לֹא־זְנַחְתִּים	וְהוֹשְׁבוֹתִים כִּי רִחַמְתִּים
4+1		וַאֲנֵנֵם	כִּי אֲנִי יְהוָה אֱלֹהֵיהֶם
3+3		וְשָׂמַח לִבָּם כְּמוֹ־יָיִן	7 וְהָיוּ כְגִבּוֹר אֶפְרַיִם
3+3		וְגֵל לִבָּם בַּיהוָה	וּבְנֵיהֶם יִרְאוּ וְשָׂמֵחוּ
3+2+3		כִּי פְדִיתִים	8 אֶשְׁרְקָה לָהֶם וַאֲקַבְּצֵם
			וְרָבוּ כְּמוֹ רָבוּ
2+2		וּבַמֶּרְחַקִּים יִזְכְּרוּנִי	9 וְאֶזְרָעֵם בָּעַמִּים
2+1		וְשָׁבוּ	וְחָיוּ אֶת־בְּנֵיהֶם
		(continued)	

---

[26] Zechariah 10:1–2 also seems to show repeated dependence upon Jer 14:1–22.

2+2	וּמֵאַשּׁוּר אֲקַבְּצֵם	10 וַהֲשִׁיבוֹתִים מֵאֶרֶץ מִצְרַיִם
3+3	וְלֹא יִמָּצֵא לָהֶם	וְאֶל־אֶרֶץ גִּלְעָד וּלְבָנוֹן אֲבִיאֵם
2+3+2	וְהִכָּה בַיָּם גַּלִּים	11 וְעָבַר בַּיָּם צָרָה
		וְהֹבִישׁוּ כֹּל מְצוּלוֹת יְאֹר
2+2	וְשֵׁבֶט מִצְרַיִם יָסוּר	וְהוּרַד גְּאוֹן אַשּׁוּר
2+2+1	וּבִשְׁמוֹ יִתְהַלָּכוּ	12 וְגִבַּרְתִּים בַּיהוָה
		נְאֻם יְהוָה ס

Prose Particle Count for 10:3–12 = 8/130 words = 6.2% PPD
Prose Particle Count for 10:1–12 = 11/166 words = 6.6% PPD

ZECHARIAH 10:3–12 IN TRANSLATION

3 "Against the shepherds my anger burns,
    and against the he-goats I will wreak punishment,"
  for Yahweh of the heavenly armies will visit
    his herd, the House of Judah,
  and he will make them
    like his majestic steed[27] in the battle.
4 From them[28] will come[29] the cornerstone;
  from them the tent-peg;
  from them the battle-bow;
    from them every commander together.
5 They will be like heroes
    trampling the mire of the streets in the battle.
  They will fight, for Yahweh is with them,
    and they will put to shame the horsemen.
6 "I will make the House of Judah superior
    and the House of Joseph I will save,
  and I will bring them back, for I will have compassion on them,
    and it will be as if I had not rejected them,
  for I am Yahweh their God,
    and I will answer them."

---

[27] "Steed," סוּס, could be collective, of Yahweh's warhorses (so Petersen 1995, 69). However, it likely evokes the opening and closing visions of Zech 1:8–6:15. In 1:8, 11 it was probably the *mal'ak yahweh* who sat astride the red horse. Nowhere in the Hebrew Bible except in Zechariah does a divine figure ride on a horse.

[28] The Hebrew is singular, but it refers to the house of Judah in v. 3.

[29] The Hebrew verb יֵצֵא appears only in the last clause of the verse, but it applies to all four clauses (Meyers and Meyers 1993, 199).

> 7 Ephraim will be like a warrior
>   and their heart will rejoice as with wine,
>   and their children will see and rejoice,
>   their heart will be glad in Yahweh.
> 8 "I will whistle for them and I will gather them
>   for I have redeemed them,
>   and they will be as numerous and they were before.
> 9 Although I scattered them among the peoples
>   yet in distant places they will remember me.
>   They will cause their children to live,[30]
>   and they shall return.
> 10 I will lead them back from the Land of Egypt
>   and from Assyria I will gather them,
>   and to the Land of Gilead and to Lebanon I will bring them,
>   and [even those lands] will not be enough for them."
> 11 He will cross over the sea of distress;
>   he will smite the sea-waves.
>   All the depths of the Nile will dry up.
>   The pride of Assyria will be overturned;
>   the scepter of Egypt will depart.
> 12 "But I will make them mighty in Yahweh
>   and in his name shall they stride forth."
>   —oracle of Yahweh.

Zechariah 10:3–12 resumes the theme of judgment upon the evil shepherds, but soon breaks into the language of a salvation oracle. As Hanson suggests, the late mixed form joins judgment and salvation into the same oracle. The passage alternates between divine first-person oracular speech (vv. 3a–b, 6, 8–10, 12) and prophetic third-person speech (vv. 3c–5, 7, 11). The motif of the divine warrior is present, perhaps on horseback (10:3), as perhaps in Zech 1:8. But here it is Israel who shall do the fighting, not Yahweh as in Zech 9:11–17, though Yahweh will be with them, strengthening them (10:5). The oracle promises victory not only to the house of Judah, but to the house of Joseph (10:6), which, like Ephraim (10:7), is a designation for northern Israelites. The exiles shall return from the formerly oppressive powers, Egypt and Assyria; they shall be so numerous that the land of Israel cannot hold them all, not even when expanded to include all Gilead and Lebanon (10:10). The return shall be like the events of the Exodus at the Sea of Reeds and the parting of the waters: Yahweh is victor not only over the nations but over the cosmic power of the sea (10:11).

Meyers and Meyers grant that 10:4, with its imagery of cornerstone and tent-peg (cf. Isa 33:20; 54:2), refers to a messianic Davidide, who comes from the tribe of Judah. Regarding the פִּנָּה of 10:4 they rightly comment:

---

[30] Reading חָיוּ as a piel form, חִיּוּ, following *BHS*.

Its figurative meaning, representing a chief or leader—probably the royal leader, an eschatological Davidide—is appropriate not only to the immediate context of this verse, where "House of Judah" (10:3) is the source of the cornerstone/leader (king?), but also to the expectation of a future royal ruler that appears in Zech 9:9 ... and at several points in First Zechariah. (1993, 200)[31]

It is not possible to exegete Zechariah correctly without granting a prominent role to a future Davidic figure. In Zech 1–8 he is the *Zemah*. In Zech 9–14 he appears first as the humble-triumphant king (9:9), and now as the cornerstone and tent peg (10:4). Zechariah 9–14 will have more to say about the future of the house of David.

The double reference to Egypt and Assyria in 10:10–11 is a notable *crux* in the history of interpretation:

> [10] I will lead them back from the Land of Egypt
>   and from Assyria I will gather them....
> [11] He will cross over the sea of distress;
>   he will smite the sea-waves.
>   All the depths of the Nile will dry up.
>   The pride of Assyria will be overturned;
>   the scepter of Egypt will depart.

Just as Zech 9:11 evoked the blood-ceremony at the Sinai covenant, so Zech 10:11 evokes the memory of the Exodus, only now it is not only the "sea of distress" that Yahweh will "smite"; the Nile too shall dry up. Stade and many others have taken the Egypt-Assyria pairing as evidence of a Hellenistic date for the passage. He wrote, "Dass mit Aegypten das Reich der Ptolemäer bezeichnet werden kann, ist selbstverständlich" (1882b, 291). "Ein Kampf mit der Weltmacht Javan ist für einen Palästinenser weitans die grösste Zeit nothwendig ein Kampf mit Syrien oder Aegypte oder mit beiden" (291). As Stade noted, the word אַשּׁוּר, Ashur, sometimes is used in the Hebrew Bible to denote later Mesopotamian kingdoms. Accordingly, the "King of Ashur" (מֶלֶךְ־אַשּׁוּר) in Ezra 6:22 is Darius, and the "King of Babylon" (מַלְכָּא דִּי בָבֶל) in Ezra 5:13 is Cyrus. In ancient Near Eastern political propaganda, the title "King of Assyria" had durability, long after the fall of the empires that held the best claim to that usage. Hence, it is not beyond reach that the Seleucid Empire could be designated "Ashur."

Regarding Egypt and the Ptolemaic Empire, it is well known that Ptolemy I and his successors reigned as pharaohs, taking on the garb, titles, and traditions

---

[31] In Judg 20:2 (פִּנּוֹת כָּל־הָעָם כֹּל שִׁבְטֵי יִשְׂרָאֵל) and 1 Sam 14:38 (כֹּל פִּנּוֹת הָעָם), the פִּנּוֹת refers to military leaders.

of the ancient Egyptian court. Hence, the ancient and long-standing name "Egypt" could designate the Ptolemaic Empire. But as we have seen, our writer is a traditionalist. He names Hadrach and Philistia, two antique names, among the territories to be conquered in Yahweh's empire in Zech 9:1–8. The naming of Egypt and Assyria, two long-standing politico-geographic terms in the world surrounding Palestine, does not provide any historical evidence whatsoever in favor of a Hellenistic date. Isaiah 19:23–25 likewise pairs Egypt and Assyria in a prophetic oracle, yet no one, to my knowledge, attempts to date Isa 19 to the Hellenistic period on that basis. There are thirteen texts in the latter prophets and Lamentations that name both Egypt and Assyria together.[32] The pairing is deeply embedded in prophetic diction. These are traditional names of traditional enemies, and little more could or should be made of them. That Assyria is not forgotten in the early Persian period in Palestine is plain from the reference to the horns in Zech 2:2: "These are the horns that have scattered Judah, *Israel*, and Jerusalem" (emphasis mine). Assyria was the power that scattered Israel, and so from Assyria must come the exiles of Zech 10:10—"from Ashur I will gather them" (מֵאַשּׁוּר אֲקַבְּצֵם), a text that probably is meant to evoke Hos 11:11—

יֶחֶרְדוּ כְצִפּוֹר מִמִּצְרַיִם וּכְיוֹנָה מֵאֶרֶץ אַשּׁוּר
וְהוֹשַׁבְתִּים עַל־בָּתֵּיהֶם נְאֻם־יְהוָה

"They shall come trembling like birds from Egypt,
and like doves from the land of Assyria;
and I will return them to their homes," says Yahweh.

Two important problems remain: What is the date of 10:3–12, and who are the shepherds of 10:3? Regarding the date, Hanson suggests on stylistic grounds that the composition is slightly later than Zech 9; he dates it to the late sixth century B.C. (1979, 334). The piece bears several marks of similarity to the poem of Zech 9. If Zech 9 represents a late preexilic or exilic text reused by Zechariah or by his tradent community, then Zech 10:3–12 may be written in imitation of the earlier work. In prose particle analysis, the poem stands at 6.2% PPD, slightly higher than the PPD for standard Hebrew poetry, but far below the 15% PPD bottom-level for standard Hebrew prose.[33] On these grounds, Hanson's suggestion that Zech 10 is slightly later than Zech 9 may be correct. Hill's date for Zech 10–14, between 515 B.C. to 475 B.C., also places it within the early Persian period (1982, 105).

---

[32] Isa 7:18; 11:11, 16; 19:23, 24, 25; 20:4; 27:13; Jer 2:18, 36; Lam 5:6; Hos 7:11; 9:3; 11:5, 11; 12:1; Mic 7:12; and Zech 10:11, 12.
[33] I note that the prose particles are contained exclusively in two verses: 10:3 and 10:6.

Who are the shepherds? Again Zech 10:3–12 offers us few clues. Here the plural term הָרֹעִים, "shepherds," is paired with הָעַתּוּדִים, "he-goats" (10:3), but the metaphorical use of this term for leaders is not specific enough to tell us what kind of leaders are involved. In Isa 14:9 the term is parallel to "kings," but in Jer 50:8, it appears to refer to community leaders of any sort who lead the way out of Babylon. Sweeney, on the strength of the passage's dependence upon Isaiah and Jer 23, concludes that the shepherds are the Persian kings (cf. Cyrus as shepherd in Isa 44:28) who have failed in their divine mandate to see to the full restoration of Jerusalem (2000, 668–71). This proposal has much to commend it: it suits the context, with 10:11's naming of the imperial powers Egypt and Assyria as objects of Yahweh's wrath, and the evoking of cornerstone and tent peg in 10:4 as symbols of royal Davidic leadership. However, the text is unclear against whom the house of Judah and the house of Joseph will fight in ch. 10, and it does not seem to be against Egypt and Assyria. If the battle is against the evil shepherds and he-goats of 10:3, we are not specifically told who that foe might be, unless it is the diviners of the preceding linking unit, 10:1–2.[34] Again, we shall have to let the question rest momentarily until the discussion of Zech 11, where we get the most information about the shepherds in Zech 9–14.

ZECHARIAH 11:1–3
TAUNT SONG AGAINST THE DAVIDIDES

ZECHARIAH 11:1–3 DELINEATED

poetic accent count	prose particle count		poetic delineation	
3+3		וְתֹאכַל אֵשׁ בַּאֲרָזֶיךָ	פְּתַח לְבָנוֹן דְּלָתֶיךָ	11:1
2+2+3		כִּי־נָפַל אֶרֶז	הֵילֵל בְּרוֹשׁ	2
	אֲשֶׁר= 1		אֲשֶׁר אַדִּרִים שֻׁדָּדוּ	
2+3	ה= 1	כִּי יָרַד יַעַר הַבָּצוּר [הַ][בָּצִיר]	הֵילִילוּ אַלּוֹנֵי בָשָׁן	
1+3	ה= 1	כִּי שֻׁדְּדָה אַדַּרְתָּם	קוֹל יִלְלַת הָרֹעִים	3
1+3	ה= 1	כִּי שֻׁדַּד גְּאוֹן הַיַּרְדֵּן	קוֹל שַׁאֲגַת כְּפִירִים	

Prose Particle Count = 4/34 words = 11.8% PPD

---

[34] Mitchell, with his late date, understandably sees the evil shepherds as the Hellenistic kings of the Ptolemaic and Seleucid empires (1912, 288).

ZECHARIAH 11:1–3 IN TRANSLATION

1 Open your doors, O Lebanon,
　　so that fire may consume your cedars!
2 Howl, O cypress,
　　for the cedar has fallen!
　　—for the mighty [trees] are destroyed!
　Howl, you terebinths of Bashan,
　　for the impenetrable forest has come down!
3 [Listen!—] the sound of the shepherds' howling,
　　for their splendor is destroyed.
　[Listen!—] the sound of the lions' roaring,
　　for the pride of the Jordan is destroyed!

The unit in 11:1–3 appears to be an example of the genre of the taunt-song against foreign nations. Here the taunt is ironically redirected to Yehud, rather than the nations. "Lebanon" with its mighty cedars represents the political leaders of Yehud. Reasons for this identification are as follows: (1) although both the kingdom-period palace and temple were built of Lebanese cedar-timber, the palace became known as בֵּית יַעַר הַלְּבָנוֹן, "the Palace of the Lebanon Forest" (1 Kgs 7:2; cf. יַעַר in Zech 11:2e), noted so because of its quadruple rows of cedar pillars in the main hall, upholding forty-five cedar rafters, symbolizing a great forest (Webb 2003, 145). Here in Zech 11:1 the forest-palace is exhorted to throw wide its doors—not in reception of its triumphant king, but for a procession of destructive fire (so Hanson 1979, 335–36). (2) In Jer 22:20–23, another "Lebanon" oracle with which Zech 11:1–3 shares much in common, "You who live in Lebanon" is paralleled by "you who are nestled in cedar buildings" (22:23), persons who are identified in context as Jehoiakim (22:18) and Jehoiachin (22:24). Here in Jeremiah "Lebanon" denotes the Jerusalem palace. (3) The Yehudean identification of the symbolism's meaning is signaled by the final line of the poem: it is the destruction of "the pride of the Jordan" (11:3d), not Lebanese territory at all. (4) Elsewhere in Zechariah גָּאוֹן, "pride," denotes a royal figure, whether of Philistia (9:6) or of Assyria (10:11). (5) The shepherds' wailing (11:3a) is the wailing of the Yehudean leaders, later denoted as "lions" (11:3c) traditional symbol of Judah/Yehud (Gen 49:9), and of the house of David (Ezek 19:1–9). Trees also serve as a common motif for political leaders (Ezek 17:1–10; Dan 4:10–12).

In social function, then, Zech 11:1–3 is a prophetic denunciation of the house of David or other civil leaders, predicting their ruination at the hands of unnamed forces. No reason is given for the ruination, but the reader may assume sufficient reason was known by the prophet. If taken with Zech 11:4–17, a rich indictment is forthcoming. Regarding the question of social location, the author of such an arcane and ironic composition as 11:1–3 is likely to be an alienated member of the Yehudean literati, strongly opposed to the political leadership, and well-versed in knowledge of earlier prophecy, especially the book of Jeremiah.[35] Discussion of Zech 11:4–17 follows the boxed text below.

ZECHARIAH 11:4–16+17, THE SHEPHERD SIGN-ENACTMENT REPORT, WITH CURSE

ZECHARIAH 11:4–17 IN TRANSLATION[36]

4 This is what Yahweh my God said: "Shepherd the flock doomed to slaughter, 5 whose buyers slaughter them and are held guiltless. They say, 'Blessed be Yahweh, for I have become rich!' Their shepherds show them no pity; 6 therefore I shall no longer pity the inhabitants of the earth"—Yahweh's oracle.

"See—I will make each man fall by the hand of his companion, and by the hand of his king. They will crush the earth and I will not deliver [it] from their power."

7 So, on behalf of the sheep-merchants[37] I became the shepherd of the flock doomed to slaughter. I took for myself two rods. The one I named "Favor," and the other I named "Bonds," and thus I shepherded the flock.

8 I got rid of three shepherds in one month. Now I lost patience with them, and they detested me. 9 So I said, "I will not be your shepherd! Let the dying die, let the wandering be lost,[38] and let the rest devour each other's flesh!"

10 Then I took my staff called Favor and I broke it in two, to revoke my covenant[39] which I had cut with all the peoples. 11 And so it was broken on

---

[35] Note the multiple vocabulary connections between Zech 11:1–13 and Jer 25:34–38. The case for inner-biblical exegesis here is strong. The opening line in Jer is sufficient to show the tendency: הֵילִילוּ הָרֹעִים וְזַעֲקוּ וְהִתְפַּלְּשׁוּ אַדִּירֵי הַצֹּאן, "Howl, you shepherds and cry out! Roll in the dust, you leaders/nobles of the flock!" (Jer 25:35).

[36] I do not display the Hebrew text here, because it is not susceptible to poetical delineation. Note Zech 11's high PPD in the chart following the translation. Text-critical decisions that affect the translation are footnoted.

[37] I construe כֵן עֲנִיֵּי as one word, כִּנְעֲנֵיֵי, "merchants," following LXX, Χαναανίτιν. So Stade (1881, 26, n. 2), Petersen (1995, 87) and many others. Without emendation, the MT translates as, "particularly the oppressed of the flock."

[38] Following LXX, καὶ τὸ ἐκλεῖπον ἐκλειπέτω. Cf. VanGemeren 1997, 2:631.

[39] Petersen, based on a targum reading, emends אֶת־בְּרִיתִי אֲשֶׁר כָּרַתִּי to read in the third-person singular, "the covenant of Yahweh, which he had made" (1995, 87). This proposal smooths out the unexpected first-person forms, but does away with the *lectio difficilior*. What if the prophet is called upon to enact Yahweh's role?

that day. Thus the sheep-merchants[40] who were watching me knew that it was a message from Yahweh.

12 Then I said to them, "If it seems good to you, give me my wages, but if not, don't." So they weighed out my wages—thirty [sheqels] of silver. 13 Then Yahweh said to me, "Throw it to the potter"[41]—the splendid price at which I was valued by them. So I took the thirty [sheqels] of silver and threw it in the House of Yahweh to the potter. 14 Then I broke in two my second rod, Bonds, to revoke the brotherhood between Judah and Israel.

15 Yahweh said to me again, "Take for yourself the gear of a foolish shepherd. 16 For I am raising up a shepherd in the land who will not care for the lost, nor seek for the young, nor heal the broken, nor provide for the exhausted. Instead, the flesh of the choice ones he will devour, and even their hooves he will tear off!"

17 "Woe to my worthless shepherd,
 who abandons[42] the flock.
May a sword strike his arm and his right eye!
May his arm be completely withered,
 his right eye utterly blind!"

CHART 6.6
PROSE PARTICLE DENSITY BY UNIT IN ZECH 11

Chapter	Words	אשׁר	את	ה	Totals	Percentage
11:1–3	34	1	0	3	4	11.8%
11:4–16	202	3	18	27	48	23.8%
11:17	18	0	0	2	2	11.1%

The ironic taunt song of Zech 11:1–3 serves as a suitable introduction to the pericope known as the "Shepherd Allegory." The term allegory, however, is

---

[40] See note on v. 7.

[41] Many emend יוֹצֵר, "potter," to אוֹצָר, "treasury," following the Syriac, a proposal that has some merit. Others see יוֹצֵר as an Aramaized spelling of אוֹצָר. See the erudite discussion in Mitchell (1912, 313–14). Mitchell mentions one medieval manuscript, Kennicott 530, which does read אוֹצָר.

[42] The final *yod* of 11:17's עֹזְבִי appears to be a case of *yod-campaginis*. So GKC §90.3(a); Mitchell (1912, 319); Waltke and O'Connor (1990, §8.2e); and Meyers and Meyers (1993, 290). The final *yod* of 11:17's רֹעִי may also be as well, but is uncertain. In defense of the translation "my shepherd," I note that the text of Zechariah exhibits a tendency toward unexpected uses of first-person singular object pronouns and possessive pronouns (2:12; 7:4; 11:4; 11:10). The fact that two of these occurrences appear in Zech 11:4–16 strengthens the case for it in 11:17. Cf. also Zech 13:7.

problematic, for it appears that the prophet acts out his orders publicly. Hence, many interpreters now see the text as a report of a prophetic sign action (Floyd 2000, 490; Petersen 1995, 89; Sweeney 2000, 678), and this genre designation is preferable.[43] In actuality it is a double sign enactment report. Hanson and Kline both see the text as a commissioning narrative, but this is unpersuasive: the prophet is meant temporarily to act out certain roles. Allegorical elements occur in the narrative. The prophet himself acts out a symbolic role as a "shepherd," and apparently later as a "foolish shepherd." Zech 11:4–17 is crucially important for understanding the social location of the prophet and his tradent community, and therefore requires careful analysis.

The text of Zech 11 is readily distinguished between ordinary prose narrative (vv. 4–16) and prophetic poetry (or "oracular prose," vv. 1–3, 17). I have treated 11:1–3 as a semi-independent unit; Zech 11:4–17, however, appears to be a literary unit with a poetical conclusion. Zechariah 11:17 is not a free-standing piece; its meaning depends upon the meaning of Zech 11:4–16. The text also exhibits strong intertextuality with the well-known shepherd passages in Jer 23:1–4, and Ezek 34, and upon Ezek 37's prophetic symbolic action involving the union of two sticks.

In the narrative there is a flock of sheep (צֹאן), sheep-merchants—buyers and sellers—who own the flock, and hired shepherds who tend the flock.[44] There are two shepherd's staffs or crooks, given symbolical names. There is also mention of thirty sheqels' worth of silver, the temple of Yahweh (בֵּית יְהוָה), and some mysterious role for a יוֹצֵר, a "potter," in the temple, unless this term is to be read as אוֹצָר, "treasury." Most of these elements require some kind of allegorical interpretation, but we should not lose sight of the prospect that the prophet is assigned to act out his message in public, presumably in Jerusalem. Twice divine speeches intervene in the action (vv. 6 and 16), once for each of the two primary sign-acts, both introduced by the interjection הִנֵּה, providing an applicative word regarding their meaning.

In the first sign action, Yahweh commands the prophet to "shepherd the flock doomed to slaughter" (רְעֵה אֶת־צֹאן הַהֲרֵגָה). Petersen points out that, of course, every flock is in some sense "doomed to slaughter"—destined to be used as human food. But shepherds ordinarily act to conserve the flock, sparing the ewes who bear young, breeding to increase the flock, slaughtering only a select portion. The disturbing feature in 11:4–17 is that there is no such conservancy here: the whole flock is marked for death, even the ewes, a fact noted in the text by the frequency of feminine possessive pronouns not easily represented in translation (קֹנֵיהֶן ... וּמֹכְרֵיהֶן, 11:4 and elsewhere; so Baldwin 1972, 180). The buyers "slaughter them," and the ... shepherds "show no pity" (11:5). Accordingly

---

[43] For a detailed study of prophetic sign actions, see Friebel (1999).
[44] Redditt's review of the issues regarding Zech 11:4–17 is helpful (1993).

Yahweh will show no pity for the flock—either the Yehudeans, or the human race, if we take v. 6's יֹשְׁבֵי הָאָרֶץ as "inhabitants," not "of the land," but "of the earth," as seems probable. Yahweh has determined no longer to restrain the worldly powers, but to permit them free rein to tyrannize the earth (Sweeney 2000, 679).

The prophetic sign action continues in v. 7: the prophet-shepherd takes two shepherd's staffs, the appropriate equipment for his role-enactment. The staffs' names, "Favor" (נֹעַם) and "Bonds" (חֹבְלִים), signify, first, the graciousness of Yahweh's intended governance of the flock, and second, the covenanted union of the people of God, Israel and Judah, symbolized in Ezek 37:16–22 by two sticks joined as one. Thus equipped—perhaps, with two staffs, excessively so—the prophet pastures the flock.

He is not the only shepherd to do so, but the other shepherds are hostile to him. In the allegory he has the authority to fire these shepherds, and does so "in one month" (v. 8). It is unclear who these "three shepherds in one month" are, and no attempt to identify them has proved persuasive. The "one month" is also difficult: does it mean a literal month?—or a relatively brief period of time?—or a symbolic month of years, such as thirty years? Most commentators now take it as non-literal and referring to a relatively brief period. But this does little to solve the problem of the identity of the three shepherds.

The last two clauses of 11:8 are ambiguous: with whom does the prophet-shepherd lose patience, and who detests him? Is it the fired shepherds of 11:8a, or is it the flock of 11:9a? A case can be made for both referents, and it may be that the text is multivalent. In any case, it seems that the prophet-shepherd's act of deposing the three worthless shepherds causes the flock to disdain him. This disdain is ironic, for the act of deposing served the flock's welfare. Tensions have risen to a high level. In deep disgust the prophet-shepherd refuses to tend to the flock any more: "let the dying die!" (11:9b).

Symbolizing the break in relationship is the breaking of the first staff, "Favor" (11:10). Not only is the prophet-to-flock relationship broken, but Yahweh's covenant "with all the peoples" is also broken. It is difficult to know to what covenant v. 10 refers. Both the Noahic covenant and the Abrahamic covenant have reference to non-Israelites. Isaiah 24 speaks of an "everlasting covenant" (בְּרִית עוֹלָם, 24:5) involving the whole world, broken by human disobedience, leading to world-wide destruction. The Isaiah text may refer to the Noahic covenant, although in Gen 8–9 that covenant is unconditional. Redditt simply speaks of the arrangement between the shepherd and his flock, the agreement undertaken as terms of employment (1993). In any case, a covenant involving Yahweh's "favor" (נֹעַם) is revoked, and the outcome can only be wrath and violence. According to 11:11, the sheep-merchants[45] watching the prophetic sign enactment recognize it as divine revelation (דְבַר־יְהוָה).

The next episode in the first sign-enactment involves the sheep-merchants themselves, who pay off the now-unemployed prophet-shepherd with thirty sheqels' weight of silver—either back pay or severance pay. The amount is usually taken, rightly so, to be an insultingly pitiful sum. Yahweh then directs the prophet to throw it to the יוֹצֵר, perhaps "potter," or perhaps אוֹצָר, "treasury," another difficulty in interpretation. In either case, it is clear that the prophet despises the sum and disposes of it in an act of contempt both for it and—remarkably—the temple of Yahweh (בֵּית יְהוָה). This act of contempt implicates the temple in the crisis depicted in Zech 11.

Having so disposed of his pay-off, the prophet enacts another prophetic sign of breaking: his second staff, "Bonds" (now definite, הַחֹבְלִים, v. 14). Having broken the divine relationship between Yahweh and human beings, now the prophet breaks the relationship between Israel and Judah, dissolving the human community of God's people.

Both acts of breaking are part of the first sign-enactment report. The second sign enactment report comes with 11:15, the second divine command to the prophet: "Take for yourself the gear of a foolish shepherd." Perhaps this foolish shepherd gear includes the broken staves of the first sign enactment, now rendered ineffective. No report of the prophet actually enacting the second sign is given. Instead we are given the divine interpretation of the sign, the second occurrence of divine interpretation in the narrative: The foolish shepherd shall be overcome by another "shepherd"—a ruthless power—who shall destroy and devour the flock, consuming them even down to the marrow of the hooves (11:16).

The second sign report ends with a curse (11:17) invoked upon the current or perhaps future worthless shepherd of the flock, who has abandoned or shall abandon the flock. The destructive power threatened in 11:16 is coming, and with terrible results: "May a sword strike him!" The opening line of the curse-poem echoes Jer 23:1, הוֹי רֹעִים מְאַבְּדִים וּמְפִצִים אֶת־צֹאן מַרְעִיתִי, "Woe to the shepherds who are destroying and scattering the sheep of my pasturage!" Again in 11:17 there is a reference to the key word "eye" (עַיִן). In contrast to the all-knowing, beneficent eyes of Yahweh in Zech 3:9, 4:10, and 9:8, the eye of this worthless shepherd shall be totally blind. The blinded eye of 11:17 may reflect contemporary Persian-era punishments. Regarding the Sagartian rebel, Ciçantakhma, Darius records that "I cut off both his nose and ears and put out one eye" (DB §33; Briant 2002, 123). Regarding Fravartis the Mede, "I cut off his nose, ears and tongue, and plucked out an eye" (DB Bab. §125; Briant 2002, 123). With

---

[45] Alternatively, following MT, it is "the afflicted of the flock" who recognize it; but if so, then the אֲלֵיהֶם of v. 12 has no conveniently nearby antecedent.

blinded eye and withered arm, such a person could no longer serve as a shepherd. With this curse upon the worthless shepherd the first *massa'* disturbingly ends.

INTERPRETATION OF THE SHEPHERD SIGN-ENACTMENT REPORT. There are few points about Zech 11:4–17 that are beyond dispute, but one of them is that the text is about leadership (Baldwin 1972, 179). I take it that the text is an autobiographical report on the part of the prophet and that there is a crisis in leadership in the prophet's own time in Yehud. The text has some reference to the foreign nations in 11:10's "covenant with all the peoples," and probably also in 11:6's "inhabitants of the land/earth." Nonetheless, the main interest is in the fate of the people of Yehud, the "flock," and the conduct of Yehudean leaders, whether "buyers and sellers" or "shepherds."

If the textual reconstruction in 11:7's כְּנַעֲנֵי, "merchants," is correct, the prophet becomes a shepherd "on behalf of" (לְ) the merchants. That is, his role enactment is in some respects dependent upon these merchants, and it is these merchants who shall weigh out to him his thirty sheqels' worth of silver at the end of his employment. This action seems to mean that the prophet actually took on some professionally paid role in the community, a role that could be designated metaphorically as a "shepherd," and one in which he had some authority over other "shepherds," whom he could depose, or a public role of persuasiveness in which he could induce others to depose them. How this role is to be reconciled with the also-apparently literal taking and breaking of shepherds' crooks is difficult to say. Sweeney takes it that the prophet is also a priest who has been hired to oversee the temple flock of sacrificial sheep (2000, 680), but this interpretation seems excessively literal. Nonetheless, just as the temple and the potter/treasury are real, both the silver and the staves seem to be real as well.

If this very general scenario is accepted, then the owners would seem to be the political rulers of Yehud, corrupt, ready for unjust gain, and neglectful of the people's needs. The shepherds, accordingly, are the religious leaders of Yehud, whether prophets or priests, or both, is not clear. If the text is to be associated with the historical Zechariah, as Sweeney's view permits, perhaps we need not distinguish between them. As the reader will recall, Zech 7:3 presented Zechariah as one of a number of prophets and priests at the temple in Jerusalem, receiving a delegation of inquirers from Bethel.

Since the prophet implicates the temple in the crimes of the leadership, the high priest should be listed either among the merchants or the shepherds. In light of the dyarchic polity of early Persian period Yehud, the high priest is likely one of the merchants in charge, rather than an underling shepherd.

As we have seen, Zech 10:2's reference to a shepherd, with its diviner context, suggests that the shepherds were false prophets. This prospect may be strengthened by recourse to Zech 13:2–6, where prophets who speak "in order to deceive" (13:4) are treated negatively. In Neh 6:10–14, another Persian period text, Tobiah and Sanballat hire false prophets to intimidate Nehemiah. Two of them are named, Shemaiah (6:10) and the prophetess Noadiah (6:14), and there are unnamed others in the incident. Nehemiah himself is accused of hiring prophets to announce his kingship (6:7). Hence, we see that false prophecy remained an unsolved problem in Yehudean history. Meyers and Meyers, accordingly, emphasize false prophecy in their interpretation of Zech 11 (1993, 257; 1995, 218).

On the other hand, we saw in Zech 11:1–3 that the shepherds in that text were members of the house of David, symbolized as "Lebanon," a symbol of the preexilic royal palace, and as "lions." It would seem that these evil shepherds are the equivalent of the merchants, the ruthless buyers and sellers of 11:5. Finally, the shepherd of 11:16 seems to represent a powerful political or military leader who shall wreak destruction upon Yehud and its leadership.

The shepherd image in Zech 9–14, then, is multivalent, as Petersen suggests (1995, 73). In 11:5 the shepherds seem to represent false prophets and perhaps impious priests in Yehud. In the first sign-enactment, the prophet is the good shepherd. This good shepherd ultimately represents Yahweh himself, as we see in 11:10's first-person pronoun phrase, "my covenant which I cut with all the peoples" (אֶת־בְּרִיתִי אֲשֶׁר כָּרַתִּי אֶת־כָּל־הָעַמִּים), a phrase otherwise inexplicable on the prophet's lips. The prophet, acting for Yahweh, succeeds in deposing (three?) worthless Yehudean leaders for the benefit of the people, but the people despise him for this benevolent action. In judgment, then, Yahweh ceases to shepherd the disobedient people of Yehud any longer. Instead, according to the second sign-enactment, a "foolish" (v. 15) and "worthless" (v. 17) shepherd comes into place—now a corrupt political figure it seems—on whom the prophet invokes a curse. It is not clear if the second sign-enactment involves one or two figures. If two, then in 11:16 a final shepherd, neither worthless nor foolish, whom Yahweh "raise[s] up over the land" is a royal figure, a future tyrannical power, who shall destroy the flock and enact the curse against its current "shepherd." With the description of this figure we are well on the way toward the antichrist texts of the full-blooded apocalypses.

SOCIAL LOCATION IN ZECH 11:4–17

The social location analysis of Zech 11:4–17 is, fortunately, one of the clearer aspects of the text. The prophet once enjoyed official recognition for his role as a divine spokesperson. He is accepted as a "shepherd," a religious leader. The "merchants" of 11:11, political leaders, see the sign enactment of breaking the first staff and understand it to be divine revelation, unwelcome though it is. The prophet's wise and benevolent shepherding leads to a power conflict with other figures like him. Though he at first succeeds against them, even deposing some, the people reject him (11:8b). He then refuses to play the public, influential role he once enjoyed as an accredited prophet. Estranged from both the people and its worthless leadership, the prophet pronounces doom upon the community and invokes a curse upon its leader. The prophet is now counted among the marginalized, bereft of power, except the power of words. With this doom the narrative dramatically ends. Zechariah 11:4–17, then, tells the story of a social location trajectory for a prophetic individual in Persian period Yehud, a trajectory that leads from somewhere near the centers of power to the periphery. The prophet is now rejected.

In social location, Zech 11:4–17 then begins where Zech 7–8 ends, with a recognized, publicly accredited prophet whose words are sought by inquirers, but who is also capable of sharp criticism of the way things are in Yehud (7:5–7). Given the review of the data of Persian period history, of the historical linguistics of Zech 9–11, and of the swiftly changing possibilities in the social location of prophecy in our case studies, there seems to be no barrier left to prevent us from assigning the historical Zechariah as the author, or principal author, of the text of the first *massa'*. I shall return to this point in chapter eight.

A POSSIBLE HISTORICAL FULFILLMENT OF ZECH 11:15–17

Regarding Zech 9–14, André Lacocque reminds us, "La question du *Sitz im Leben* du II Zacharie est la plus difficile de toutes à résoudre" (1981, 139). Hence, my proposals can only be put forth tentatively, with a goodly measure of interpretive humility. If my supposition is correct that at least some of the merchants of Zech 11:4–17 are the civil leaders of Yehud, then the evidence of the book of Nehemiah may be relevant to their identification. A clue may be found in Neh 5:14–15.

> Moreover from the time that I was appointed to be their governor in the land of Judah, from the twentieth year to the thirty-second year of King Artaxerxes, twelve years, neither I nor my brothers ate the food allowance of the governor. The former governors (וְהַפַּחוֹת הָרִאשֹׁנִים) who were before me laid heavy burdens on the people, and took food and wine from them, besides forty shekels of silver. Even their servants lorded it over the people. But I did not do so, because of the fear of God. (Neh 5:14–15 NRSV)

According to the book of Nehemiah, then, assuming that פַּחוֹת refers to the same office, at least two and possibly more of his gubernatorial predecessors were oppressors, laying "heavy burdens on the people." We now may possess some of the names of these prior governors because of evidence obtained from Yehud coins and bullae. Eric M. Meyers proposed a tentative reconstruction, presented in Chart 6.7 below (1987, 518 n. 8; cf. 1995, 208).

CHART 6.7
GOVERNORS OF YEHUD, 538 B.C.–433 B.C.

1) Sheshbazzar	538–520 B.C. (פֶּחָה, Ezr 5:14; הַנָּשִׂיא יְהוּדָה, Ezr 1:8)	
2) Zerubbabel	520–510? B.C. (פַּחַת יְהוּדָה, Hag 1:1, 1:14)	
3) Elnathan	510?–490? B.C. (פח bulla and seal)	
	Cf. Shelomith, "אמה of Elnathan" (seal),	
	daughter of Zerubbabel (1 Chr 3:19), born ca. 545 B.C.	
4) Yeho'ezer	490?–470? B.C. (פחוא, jar impression)	
5) Ahzai	470? B.C. (פחוא, jar impression)	
6) [gap?]		
7) Nehemiah	445–433 B.C. (פֶּחָם בְּאֶרֶץ יְהוּדָה, Neh 5:14; 12:26)	

At least two of these names in Chart 6.7 are Davidides: Zerubbabel and his daughter Shelomith; perhaps Sheshbazzar was a Davidide as well. It is unlikely that Elnathan was a Davidide, but he was perhaps married to one, Shelomith, who perhaps ruled as co-regent (= אָמָה?). We know that Persian policy fostered the stability of local leadership in subprovinces like Yehud, and that dynastic-like succession was enjoyed by many local ruling families. Perhaps Yeho'ezer and Ahzai, whose names may not be in the correct historical order or position, were descended from the Elnathan-Shelomith pair, continuing the line of David through their mother's and grandmother's side. On the other hand, the seals that bear these two names, found in a refuse dump at Ramat Rahel, cannot inform us if they preceded Nehemiah or followed him as governor (Williamson 1992). We do know that the house of David faced some sort of crisis and demotion in the early Persian period. Nehemiah (r. 445 B.C.–433 B.C.; and 432 B.C.–? B.C.) is certainly not of the line of David, and Zech 12–14 seems to suggest a troubled history for the Davidide line (Meyers and Meyers 1995). In 408 B.C. Yehud is governed by a certain Bagohi, as we see from the Elephantine papyrii, and perhaps from Josephus (*A.J.* 11.7.1). This Persian name need not be viewed as a mark of Persian ethnicity: in this period such names were also used by some Jews. In any case, Elnathan, via his אָמָה Shelomith, is the last governor of Yehud we know about who had Davidide connections.

We also know that Jerusalem experienced some kind of military defeat or setback in the time before Nehemiah's arrival in 445 B.C. Nehemiah 1:3 presents the city walls as "broken down" and the gates as "burned with fire." This troubling condition of the city is related to recent events, not to Babylonian-era destruction. Perhaps this destruction was the work of Sanballat and his allies, or the result of the decree against the refortification of Jerusalem issued by Artaxerxes I (465–425 B.C.), as told in Ezra 4:7–23. There the story tells us that when Artaxerxes I issued his decree, a high official named Rehum came "in haste" to Jerusalem and stopped the refortification "by force" (בְּאֶדְרָע וְחָיִל, 4:23),

a description that may imply acts of destruction. Perhaps the loss of Davidic governorship and the failure of refortification can be tied to the same set of events, but this cannot be asserted with confidence. Some interpreters suggest that these events in Judah should be linked with the Inaros revolt in Egypt (464 B.C.–454 B.C.), or to the alleged revolt of the Persian aristocrat Megabyzus in Syria, which seems to have taken place shortly after the revolt of Inaros (Meyers 1987, 515). But we have no confirmation of such a connection (Briant 2002, 578–79).

I suggest as a hypothesis that it is to the generation of Elnathan and Shelomith, or perhaps to the subsequent generation, that we must look for the era of Zech 11:4–17's ruthless "sheep-merchants" and "worthless shepherds." If we assume twenty-year governorships, then Nehemiah's cutthroat predecessors, minimally two in number and perhaps more, take us back at least to ca. 485 B.C., and perhaps as far as ca. 505 B.C., the presumed time of Elnathan and Shelomith. If Zechariah is a young man in 520 B.C., as I have shown to be likely, then we are within his probable lifetime with the first of these dates and within quite plausible reach with the second. If he was born ca. 545 B.C. ± five, as our evidence shows, Zechariah would have been about forty ± five years old in 505 B.C., about sixty ± five years old in 485 B.C., assuming he lived so long.

The high priest of the generation of Elnathan and Shelomith is Joiakim ben-Joshua, according to the generational list in Neh 12:10–11. The list names six postexilic generations: Joshua, Joiakim, Eliashib, Joiada, Jonathan, and Jaddua, and presumably takes us a generation or so past the time of Nehemiah, since he appears as a figure of the past at the end of the genealogical unit, in Neh 12:26. As we have seen, the lists in Neh 12 also report the names of the priestly heads of families of Joiakim's generation, including Zechariah, head of the family once led by Iddo (12:16; see the detailed discussion of Persian period priestly lists in Ezra–Nehemiah in Scolnic 1999, 185–205; 235–44). The "Eliashib the priest" (אֶלְיָשִׁיב הַכֹּהֵן) who was "put in charge" (by whom?) of certain rooms in the temple precinct and whom the book of Nehemiah accuses of "evil" deeds (13:4–9) can hardly be the same individual as "Eliashib the high priest" (יָשִׁיב הַכֹּהֵן הַגָּדוֹל אֶל), who assisted Nehemiah in the building of the wall (3:1; cf. 3:20–21). Even though the identification requires some long life-spans, the latter is apparently the one named in Neh 12:10 as grandson of Joshua and son of Joiakim, unless we assume a gap in the Neh 12 list and invoke the principle of high-priestly papponymy as suggested by Cross (1975), and as assumed by Meyers and Meyers (1993, 19).[46]

---

[46] For evaluations of Cross's papponymy theory, see Scolnic (1999:1–26) and VanderKam (2004, 85–99). VanderKam concludes that the present six-member list of high priests in Neh 12 should be retained without revision (97–99).

Perhaps other Davidides from the descendents of Zerubbabel or his brother should also be on the list of candidates for the ruthless "sheep-merchants" of Zech 11:4–17. According to 1 Chr 3:19 Zerubbabel had a brother named Shimei, who may be the same Shimei named as progenitor of a clan in Zech 12:13, unless the Levitical clan of Num 3:17 is in mind, or the Benjamite clan of David's opponent in 2 Sam 16:5. First Chronicles 3:19–20 apparently names Zerubbabel's seven sons: Meshullam, Hananiah, Hashubah, Ohel, Berekiah, Hasadiah, and Jushab-Hesed. Curiously, only the first two on this list are expressly called "the sons of Zerubbabel"; [47] the rest are simply said to be "five others."[48] Perhaps that fact reflects a special prominence (or notoriety?) in history for Meshullam and Hananiah. But we know nothing more of these persons. Zechariah 12:12 also names the clan of the house of Nathan, which might refer to descendents of Solomon's full-brother, Nathan, named in the Davidide genealogy in 1 Chr 3:5, or perhaps to the clan of the prophet Nathan, otherwise unattested, or to some other Nathan; the MT names at least five different Nathans.

One other set of events may be relevant to the identification of the ruthless "sheep-merchants." In tantalizingly brief reportage Ezra 4 mentions that "at the beginning of the reign of Xerxes, they [i.e., "the enemies of Judah and Benjamin" (4:1)] lodged an accusation against the people of Judah and Jerusalem" (4:6). We know nothing more of this accusation or the nature of the events that instigated it, but it is significant to note that just prior to the death of Darius and the accession of Xerxes in 486 B.C., Egypt revolted against Persia. Herodotus tells us that Darius was in the midst of preparations for a military campaign to quell the rebellion when he was seized by an illness and died (*Hist.* 7.3–7; Briant 2002, 161). What was the nature of the accusation against Yehud in ca. 486 B.C.? The text does not tell us, but it is tempting to think that this event may be linked to the fall from gubernatorial power of the house of David in Yehud.[49]

Where does this evidence lead? Nowhere that is conclusive. We have lists of Yehudean names for the historical period, and we seem to have real events in Zech 11:4–17 and Ezra 4, but we cannot link these names to these events. Nor can we connect the Ezra 4 events to the apparent Zech 11 events. However, it is suggestive that the generation of Elnathan the governor and Joiakim the high priest—the generation after Zerubbabel and Joshua, and the generation before Eliashib—may be the time of Zech 11:4–17's political and religious declension, and that these two, Elnathan and Joiakim, are, or are among, the ruthless "sheep-merchants" of our mysterious text. That is the period of Zechariah's prime of

---

[47] The MT reads, וּבְנֵי פְדָיָה זְרֻבָּבֶל וְשִׁמְעִי וּבֶן־זְרֻבָּבֶל מְשֻׁלָּם וַחֲנַנְיָה וּשְׁלֹמִית אֲחוֹתָם (1 Chr 3:19).

[48] The MT reads, וַחֲשֻׁבָה וָאֹהֶל וּבֶרֶכְיָה וַחֲסַדְיָה יוּשַׁב חֶסֶד חָמֵשׁ (1 Chr 3:20).

[49] See the elaborate but implausible reconstruction of a Yehudean disaster in 485 B.C. offered by Julius Morgenstern (1956; 1957).

life. My reconstruction does not require him to have reached extreme old age for this period, merely adult maturity.

It is now necessary to take up the task of interpreting Part Two, Unit Two, the second *massa'*, Zech 12–14. To this task we turn in the next chapter.

7

HISTORY, LITERATURE, AND SOCIAL LOCATION PART TWO, UNIT TWO: ZECH 12–14 THE SECOND מַשָּׂא

The first *massa'* of Part Two of Zechariah ended on the dire note of a wicked shepherd in control of Yehud, and the threat of a tyrannical shepherd who shall come with the sword. That dire conclusion leaves important points in the first *massa'* unresolved. How shall the earnestly desired massive return of the scattered exiles be achieved, as Zech 10:10 asserts? How shall both Yehud and the house of Joseph be saved and restored, as 10:6 promises, if a tyrannical shepherd is coming? How shall it happen that the flock doomed to slaughter shall become "the sparkling crown" in Yahweh's land, as 9:16 indicates? How shall the future Davidide come to his benevolent rule over Yehud and the nations, as 9:9 predicts? How shall the Philistines enter into adoptive status as honored Yehudeans, as 9:7 declares? Not only is the dire conclusion in need of grace, but the unresolved issues require that there be a further text to clarify them. What is the future of Yehud? That is the apparent purpose of the second *massa'*, Zech 12–14. In the second *massa'*, we see something of how Yahweh shall bring about the "death and transfiguration of the holy city" (Leithart 1995).

Moreover, the first *massa'* left unsolved important issues in Part One of the book, Zech 1–8. How shall Jerusalem become "Yahweh's portion in the Holy Land" (2:16)? How shall "the iniquity of the land" be removed "in a single day" (3:9)? How shall "many nations be joined to Yahweh" in "that day" (2:15)? What are the future fortunes of the house of David (6:12)? How shall unjust Jerusalem become "the City of Truth," and Zion the "Holy Mountain" (8:3)? Finally, how shall the future pilgrimage of the nations to Jerusalem be effected (8:20–23)?

In light of these two sets of unanswered questions, Zech 12–14 may be seen as a *massa'* that takes Zech 1–8 and Zech 9–11 as base texts in need of further interpretation (so Floyd 2000, 508). The textual organization of the second *massa'* appears to be as shown in Chart 7.1 below.

As we see from Chart 7.1, Zech 12–14 consists of two relatively lengthy eschatological narratives joined by a brief connecting poem, the last of the shepherd-theme oracles. In Chart 7.2, further below, showing the Prose Particle Densities for Zech 12–14, the PPD of the eschatological narratives, 13.7% for Zech 12:1–14, and 18.3% for Zech 14:1–21, is unsurprising. However, the PPD figures for 13:1–6 and 13:7–9 are unexpected. The first, because of the length and irregularity of its clauses, appears to be a prose narrative, despite its low 6.3% PPD. The second, Zech 13:7–9, with its strong parallelism and rhythmic structure, appears to be poetical, despite its very high 22.8% PPD. I shall return to this feature later in the chapter.

CHART 7.1
THE STRUCTURE OF ZECH 12–14

Text	Titles	Long Units	Short Linking Unit
Zech 12:1	title, מַשָּׂא		
Zech 12:2–13:6		first eschatological narrative	
Zech 13:7–9			final shepherd oracle
Zech 14:1–21		second eschatological narrative	

CHART 7.2
PROSE PARTICLE DENSITY BY UNIT IN ZECH 12–14

Chapter	Words	אשר	את	ה	Totals	Percentage
12:1–14	227	1	8	22	31	13.7%
13:1–6	95	1	3	11	15	6.3%
13:7–9	57	0	5	8	13	22.8%
14:1–21	372	9	6	53	68	18.3%

The whole of Zech 12:1 provides the title for the second *massa'*, and a suitable introduction for the long unit in 12:2–13:6. Whereas the first דְּבַר־יְהוָה was "in" or "against" (בְּ) the northern land of Hadrach (9:1) and other foreign regions, this second דְּבַר־יְהוָה is "concerning (עַל) Israel" (12:1), but the unnamed nations remain significant in this second *massa'* as well. The hymnic participial phrases of 12:1, נֹטֶה שָׁמַיִם וְיֹסֵד אֶרֶץ וְיֹצֵר רוּחַ־אָדָם בְּקִרְבּוֹ ("who stretches out heaven, who founds earth, who forms the inner spirit of a person"), emphasize at the outset Yahweh's creative power. There are no prose particles in the balanced hymnic lines, representing good classical poetical style. The burden of the ensuing narrative, dominated by nine בַּיּוֹם הַהוּא ("on that day") phrases, is eschatological. Hence, the unit links creation and future destiny, *Urzeit und Endzeit*. Yahweh the omnipotent is more than able to bring about his intended goal for Israel and the nations.

The interjection הִנֵּה ("lo!") appears at the outset of both narratives, at 12:2 and 14:1, and nowhere else in this second *massa'*. This arrangement is similar to the first *massa'*, where we saw in Zech 11 only two uses of הִנֵּה, each used to introduce one of the two divine speeches of the shepherd narrative (11:6; 11:16). Elsewhere in Zech 9–14 the הִנֵּה appears only at 9:4's "Lo, the Sovereign One will dispossess her [Tyre]," and at 9:9's "Lo, your king comes to you!" The rhetorical mirroring of paired הִנֵּה clauses in 11:4–17 and 12–14, and perhaps 9:1–17, is another indication of the literary unity of Zech 9–14.

APOCALYPTIC, ESCHATOLOGY, AND SOCIAL LOCATION

The most germane question to address for my purposes is the question of the social location of the narratives and poetry found in Zech 12–14. Under the influence of Hanson and others these chapters are frequently described as apocalyptic or proto-apocalyptic, and therefore as from a marginalized community. However, as we have seen, no composition in chs 12–14 can be accurately described as an apocalypse (cf. Collins 1984).

Hanson, however, has distinguished between apocalypse as a literary genre, apocalyptic as a type of religious thinking, and apocalyptic as a kind of believing community (1976). Does Zech 12–14 qualify as an example of apocalyptic thought? My answers are, for 12:1–13:6, no; for 13:7–9, not clearly so; and for Zech 14:1–21, perhaps. Hanson saw the key to apocalyptic thought in the notion that during the early Persian period, despair over pervasive evil and the human inability to effect the coming of the righteous rule of Yahweh became so profound, that the only hope lay in some great and radical act of Yahweh to remake the world. He thus distinguished between prophetic eschatology, where human actions of justice, mercy, and community (Hanson 1986) were seen to bring about positive changes in Yahweh's world; and apocalyptic eschatology, where no human action could. Hanson calls the first "real politics," a world of "plain history" and of "human instrumentality" (1979, 11). The second is largely devoid of all three, because of the "bleak post-exilic conditions" of life under the apparently indomitable rule or foreigners, which bred "a pessimistic view of reality" (11). And so Hanson's postexilic community divided itself between compromised "hierocrats" wedded to *Realpolitik*, and "visionaries," unbounded by the mundane. Prophets and visionaries did share an important core value according to Hanson: an "essential vision of restoration," "the vision of Yahweh's people restored as a holy community in a glorified Zion" (12). The visionaries, however, "increasingly abdicate the other dimensions of the prophetic office, the translation into historical events." At such a point of abandonment, "we enter the period of the transition from prophetic eschatology into apocalyptic eschatology" (16).

Katrina Larkin has effectively raised the point of whether we should castigate apocalyptic eschatology as a form of despair. "There seems to be no theoretical reason why a supra-historical eschatology, which looks to a God who is hope ... should be pessimistic" (1994, 11). This point is an important one.

Those who believe in the God of hope shall not likely be pessimists. Moreover, when examining the various recognized apocalypses, we see that there are multiple forms of eschatology, not one kind (Larkin 1994, 16).

Eschatology is often a form of theodicy, the "justification" of the ways of God. It need not arise among the despairing. Ordinary people of all sorts recognize the existence of some kind of evil in the world. Bryan R. Wilson assesses religions as embodying various "responses to the world," the thaumaturgical, the revolutionist, the conversionist, the reformist, and others, each involving a judgment regarding the nature of the evil and a means of overcoming it (1973, 21–26). Each of these social models is thus also a theodicy of sorts, a way of dealing with evil in light of the divine. Eschatology, too, is a response to the perceived evil in the world, and makes the claim that the divine order shall overcome evil and banish it from the world, or shall remake the world in some way that excludes evil forever. Eschatology, then, is an assertion of hope.

Questions arise about the nature of the continuity between the present order and the future. Hanson proposes a demarcation between the prophetic eschatology and the apocalyptic, but it will have to be admitted that even the most radical alleged "apocalypticist" will usually still insist upon the eschatological salvation of something from the present world: namely, the believer and the believing community. There is thus a personal continuity between the old past and the new future. Visions of the future that involve *recreatio ex nihilo in toto* are quite rare, and absent from the Bible.

I am not convinced that such a firm divide can be drawn to distinguish between a prophetic and an apocalyptic eschatology. Haggai, a prophet deeply interested in the historical fortunes of the high priest Joshua and the governor Zerubbabel, twice announced the cosmic shaking of heaven and earth (2:6, 22). The account of the people's revolt in Num 14 represents God as saying, חַי־אָנִי וְיִמָּלֵא כְבוֹד־יְהוָה אֶת־כָּל־הָאָרֶץ, "as I live, all the earth shall be filled with Yahweh's glory" (14:21); this is a priestly text with a cosmic eschatology. In chs. 1–8 Zechariah foresees the eschatological time when Yahweh "will remove the iniquity of this land in a single day" (3:9), and when "ten men from all languages and nations will take grasp of one Yehudean by the hem of his robe, and say, 'Let us go with you, for we have heard that God is with you!'" (8:23). These two texts together witness to Zechariah's priestly concerns regarding atonement and his eschatological hope.

All of this is to underscore the point that the creation of eschatological texts, or, if we grant the term, apocalyptic eschatological texts, does not require the creators of such texts to inhabit a certain social location. One cannot say that all, or even most, eschatologists are marginalized outcasts. Muhammad, too, at the center of his young empire, had an eschatology. Hanson grants the distinction between apocalyptic texts and apocalyptic communities. But in the end he seems to forget the distinction, at least as regards the community at the alleged "dawn" of apocalyptic. The presence of apocalyptic texts, or belief in a cosmic eschatology, is not necessarily accompanied by social marginalization, or to be explained by deprivation theory, as Stephen L. Cook has shown (1995, 35–52).

On the other hand, some eschatological communities have been social outcasts. The scenario that I think I see in the texts of Zech 12–14 is a marginalized community of prophetic eschatologists, in strong continuity with the eschatology of Zech 1–8. Consider Donald Gowan's description of Zech 8's eschatology, as found in his book, *Eschatology in the Old Testament:*

1) God's people shall be restored to the promised land (8:7–8).
2) No king is mentioned, but that is not to be wondered at, given the infrequent appearances of the "messianic figure" in the OT.
3) The nations will no longer mock and scorn (8:13), but will instead come voluntarily to Jerusalem to "entreat the favor of the Lord, and to seek the Lord of hosts" (8:20–23).
4) The people of Zion will make it possible to characterize Jerusalem as "the faithful city" (8:3). The possibility that as in the past they will be unable to obey the *torah* which he recites (8:16–17) is not considered an option for the people of the city of the future.
5) Peace and security will be enjoyed by all: old men and old women, boys and girls. No one will be left out (8:4–5).... There will be no reason for fasting, and the fasts for Jerusalem will be turned into seasons of joy and cheerful feasts (8:19).
6) The curse on nature had resulted in fruitless work in the past (8:10a), but the day is coming when "the vine shall yield its fruit ... and I will cause the remnant of this people to possess all these things" (8:12). (1986, 5)

Gowan's description is accurate in the main; I would modify his comments about the messianic figure, especially in light of Zech 1–8's future *Zemah*. Gowan does admit later in the discussion that the eschatological figure of a "righteous king" "plays an important though limited role in many pictures of the ideal future, but there are a good many texts in which he does not appear at all" (1986, 37). Here Gowan more accurately describes the OT texts about such a figure. With this added proviso, we must ask how different from Gowan's six summary expectations from Zech 8 are those of Zech 12–14? Not much, we shall see. Let us examine the texts.

ZECHARIAH 12:1–13:6
THE FIRST ESCHATOLOGICAL NARRATIVE

As I have mentioned, Zech 12:1–13:6 is largely organized around nine "on that day" phrases. The text resembles a collection of eschatological sayings, but there is a narrational unity in the whole. It is not merely an anthology of diverse sayings. Petersen adopts the artistic term "montage" to describe the unit, a fair description (1995, 109), given that montages are intentionally constructed pieces that thus exhibit composition. It is not an apocalypse, failing to meet the agreed-upon criteria for that genre designation. I therefore prefer to call it, for lack of a better term, an eschatological narrative.[50] Much of the narration, but not all, is told by way of first-person divine speech, in oracular form. The alternation of first-person divine speech (12:2–4; 6, 9, 10a: 13:2) and third-person prophetic speech (12:1, 5, 7–8, 10b, 11–14; 13:1, 3–6) complicates the interpretation, and has given rise to many proposed textual emendations, mostly unwarranted. The fate of Jerusalem dominates the unit; Yehud or the house of Judah also gets prominent attention. There is also great interest in the role of the nations. The Zion tradition figures prominently, as does the holy war tradition. The David tradition also appears (109), but in a startling, innovative manner.

The narration begins with the striking metaphor that Yahweh will make Jerusalem "a cup of staggering for all the surrounding peoples" (12:2). This is shortly followed by the similar metaphor that Yahweh will make Jerusalem "a heavy stone for all the peoples" (12:3). This work of Yahweh will take place "on the day when all the nations of the earth are gathered against" Jerusalem (12:3). The theme is a familiar one from Ezekiel, and includes important reminiscences from Isaiah: Jerusalem besieged. The prophet foresees the time of the nations' eschatological attempt to destroy the city and people of Yahweh. In the first image, Jerusalem, like a cup of wine, will cause the nations to stagger with drunkenness. In the second image, Jerusalem, like a sharp and heavy stone, will lacerate those who try to move it. These are promises of divine protection. Those who try to harm Jerusalem will themselves be harmed. The text implicates Yehud in the siege as well, though with a lack of grammatical clarity: shall Yehud be besieged with Jerusalem, or shall Yehud join with the besiegers (וְגַם עַל־יְהוּדָה יִהְיֶה בַמָּצוֹר עַל־יְרוּשָׁלָ͏ִם, 12:2)? Although the siege idea is awkward for the countryside setting of Yehud, the prepositional phrase עַל־יְהוּדָה, "against Yehud," most likely means that Yehud shall also be attacked by the nations that attack Jerusalem.

Then, in a text that evokes both Exod 15:1 and Deut 28:28–29, Yahweh threatens enemy horses and riders with "panic and madness" (12:4). Again the text employs the unifying motif of the eye: this time it is the eyes of the horses that shall be "struck with blindness," while Yahweh "opens" his eyes (אֶפְקַח אֶת־עֵינַי) upon the "house of Judah"—another motif of protection, denoting watchful care (12:4; cf. 9:8). The next line in the Masoretic Text is difficult: אָמְצָה לִּי יֹשְׁבֵי יְרוּשָׁלַ͏ִם בַּיהוָה צְבָאוֹת אֱלֹהֵיהֶם. Probably the *yod* of the לִי should be deleted as a dittography (so Mitchell 1912, 328), to read לְיֹשְׁבֵי יְרוּשָׁלַ͏ִם, and the line translated as, "Then the leaders of Yehud will say in their hearts,

---

[50] Floyd designates the genre as "a prophecy of punishment against a foreign nation" (2000, 521–23).

'The strength of the residents of Jerusalem [is] in Yahweh of the heavenly armies, their God!'" (12:5). This reading confirms my prior decision to read Yehud as besieged alongside Jerusalem.

Now the leaders of Yehud are treated to two striking similes of their own: they shall become "like a firepot on the woodpile, like a torch among sheaves, devouring right and left all the besieging peoples" (12:6). The great result of their remarkable heroism is that "Jerusalem shall still dwell [intact] in her place—in Jerusalem" (וְיָשְׁבָה יְרוּשָׁלַם עוֹד תַּחְתֶּיהָ בִּירוּשָׁלָ͏ם, 12:6). That is, despite the siege, Jerusalem shall endure as before. In the next line a democratizing element has been noticed by the commentators: Yahweh will so conduct himself in the battle that the battle-honors of Judah shall equal the battle-honors of the house of David (12:7). Moreover, in this war, even the feeblest Jerusalemites shall fight as valiantly as David, and the house of David like a deity, like the *mal'ak yahweh* (12:8). The *mal'ak yahweh* as warrior evokes Zech 1:8's rider on the red horse, who is also, it seems, the *mal'ak yahweh*. The battle scenario ends at 12:9 with Yahweh's declared intention to destroy (אֲבַקֵּשׁ לְהַשְׁמִיד) all the nations that attack Jerusalem, thus reinforcing the main message of the text. The special attention given to the non-urban countryside in 13:2, 5, 6, and 7 may indicate that the rural Yehudeans are viewed more favorably than their urban counterparts.

"THE ONE WHOM THEY PIERCED/STABBED"

The following topical unit, 12:10–14, concerns the well-known and perplexing reference to Jerusalem's mourning for "the one whom they pierced/stabbed" (אֵת אֲשֶׁר־דָּקָרוּ, 12:10). The MT of 12:10 is difficult and numerous emendations have been proposed. Nonetheless it may be best to keep emendation of the MT to a minimum here, following the *lectio difficilior*. The MT reads

וְשָׁפַכְתִּי עַל־בֵּית דָּוִיד וְעַל יוֹשֵׁב יְרוּשָׁלַם רוּחַ חֵן וְתַחֲנוּנִים
וְהִבִּיטוּ אֵלַי אֵת אֲשֶׁר־דָּקָרוּ וְסָפְדוּ עָלָיו כְּמִסְפֵּד עַל־הַיָּחִיד
וְהָמֵר עָלָיו כְּהָמֵר עַל־הַבְּכוֹר

I shall pour out upon the house of David and upon the inhabitants[51] of Jerusalem a spirit of compassion and supplication. They shall look upon me whom they pierced/stabbed, and they shall lament over him as one laments an only child, and grieve for him as one grieves for a firstborn son. (12:10)

The text singles out "the house of David" for special attention. It is not just Jerusalem upon whom Yahweh pours out a "spirit of compassion and supplica-

---

[51] Emend יוֹשֵׁב יְרוּשָׁלַם to read יוֹשְׁבֵי יְרוּשָׁלַם, due to haplography of the final *yod*.

tion" (רוּחַ חֵן וְתַחֲנוּנִים, 12:10), so that they mourn deeply; it is "the house of David" in particular. The peculiar attention to "the house of David" suggests that the Davidides were in particular need of such a spirit, perhaps having committed certain crimes alienating them from Yahweh and from the prophet's tradent community. We saw in Zech 11:4–17 the ruthless merchants and the pitiless shepherds who did not spare the flock. If my identification of the merchants as Davidide leaders is correct, then Zech 12 points to the future rehabilitation of the Davidides, but only after they commit some act of atrocity involving piercing or stabbing. Such theological rehabilitation need not be accompanied by restoration of Davidide rule.

The line that reads, וְהִבִּיטוּ אֵלַי אֵת אֲשֶׁר־דָּקָרוּ וְסָפְדוּ עָלָיו, appears incongruous, with its mixed pronouns in first and third person. Hence, many emend the אֵלַי to read אֵלָיו, "to him," or defectively, אֵלָו, to match the pronoun עָלָיו. However, I have noted the text's peculiar affinity for the first person pronoun in unexpected places (2:12; 7:3; 7:4; 8:18; 9:11; 11:4; 11:10; 11:17; 13:7; note especially 11:10). Meyers and Meyers also cite, against Mitchell's emendation (1912, 334–35), the massive support of the ancient versions (1993, 336–37). They translate the Hebrew, "they will look to me concerning the one they have stabbed" (307). However, this rendering of the אֵת אֲשֶׁר seems unnatural, and it is probably better to translate, with the tradition, "They shall look to me, the one they pierced/stabbed, and they shall mourn for him."

The notion of the "pierced/stabbed" one has drawn out many conjectures: Absalom, pierced by Joab's spears (so Ackroyd 1953, 130–31 n. 4); Josiah, pierced by Pharaoh Neco's arrows, a view made attractive by the reference to Megiddo in 12:11 (so Sweeney 2000, 689); the murder of a certain Jesus by his brother, the high priest Johannes, ca. 400 B.C., as mentioned by Josephus (*Ant.* 11.7.1; so Plöger 1968, 86); visionaries, persecuted by hierocrats (so Hanson 1979, 366); prophets, persecuted by "shepherds"/leaders (so Meyers and Meyers 1993, 340); Onias III, martyred in 170 B.C.; Simon Maccabee,[52] assassinated in 134 B.C. (both mentioned by Mitchell 1912, 330–31; and by Baldwin 1972, 191); Zerubbabel, mysteriously absent from the text after Zech 4 (mentioned by Sweeney 2000, 689–90; and by the messianic conspiracy theorists); and so on.[53]

Christian interpretation traditionally viewed the pierced one as Jesus. Zechariah 12:10 is cited in John 19:37 and Rev 1:7 in regard to the crucified Christ. Lamarche related Zech 12:10 to the Suffering Servant of Isaiah, and saw Zech 12:10, with 13:1's "fountain" for cleansing "sin and impurity" (לְחַטַּאת וּלְנִדָּה), as dependent upon the combination of Isa 53's slain servant, Isa 44:3's outpouring

---

[52] As Hanson rightly points out, the proposals of both Onias III and Simon Maccabee are rendered implausible by the evidence from the Qumran scrolls (1979, 358).

[53] Lacocque provides a useful excursus on the numerous exegetical problems (1981, 190–92).

of water/Spirit upon Jacob's offspring, and Ezek 36:25-26's cleansing/new spirit texts (1961, 136-37). A good case can be made for the intertextual relationship. McComiskey (1998, 1214-15) relates the "pierced/stabbed" one to the good-but-rejected shepherd of 11:4-14, tied mysteriously to the *mal'ak yahweh* of 12:8; the latter connection seems dubious, while the shepherd connection is plausible.

In any case, it is not possible to construct out of Zech 12:10/13:1 alone a doctrine of vicarious suffering for sin. The plot structure of 12:10-13:6 suggests otherwise. The implicit order of events in the narrative seems to be as follows: (1) the house of David perpetrates an atrocity involving the stabbing/piercing of someone, probably in Jerusalem; (2) Yahweh pours out on the house of David and the Jerusalemites a changed spirit of contrition and compassion, reversing the prior hostility; (3) the various leading houses of Jerusalem mourn: Davidides, Nathanites, Levites, and Shimeites, and the rest of the clans, men and women separately; (4) Yahweh responds to the grief and penitence by opening up a fountain for cleansing sin and impurity for the house of David and Jerusalem. (5) Accompanying the outpouring of the cleansing fountain shall be the eradication of religious impurity such as idolatry (13:2) and false prophecy (13:3-6) from the land.

The text refers to members of the royal houses, taking Nathan as a reference to David's son by that name (1 Chr 3:5), and the priestly houses, taking Shimei as a reference to Levi's grandson by Gershon (Exod 6:17; 1 Chr 23:7). Alternatively, Zerubbabel had a brother named Shimei (1 Chr 3:19). However, the naming of Davidides and Levite families together is likely a sign of the dyarchic rule of the postexilic era already witnessed in Haggai–Zech 1-8, or at least the after-effects of dyarchic rule. These are the prominent families of Jerusalem in the prophet's time, and in some way complicit in the atrocity committed against the "pierced/stabbed" one.

Resuming the discussion of Zech 12:1-13:6, I note that 13:1-6 features the final three "on that day" sub-units of the nine occasions of that key structural phrase. All three follow the *setumah* mark after 12:14, and are closely related thematically. The first of these I have already discussed, as providing for the cleansing of sin and impurity for the guilty house of David and the residents of Jerusalem (13:1). The final two of these sub-units Zech 13:2-3 and Zech 13:4-6 are closely related, pertaining to the end of false prophecy in the community. The eradication of religious impurities, the idolatry and false prophecy of 13:2-6, again underscores the adversarial relationship between the prophet and other community leaders. The reference to idolatry is a traditional element in prophetic rhetoric and need not be taken literally. However, the false prophets represent a real threat to the prophet and his tradent community, since he views himself and his associates as representatives of true prophecy.

Returning to the problem of Zech 12:10, it is fortunately not necessary for me to solve all the exegetical problems of this difficult pericope. A minimalist approach suffices. To do so, I take recourse to a text not yet discussed, Zech

13:7–9, the last of the shepherd passages, a passage that links Zech 12–14 with Zech 9–11, and one that, with Zech 11:17, frames 12:1–13:6 with poems of the shepherd motif.

ZECHARIAH 13:7–9
THE FINAL SHEPHERD ORACLE

ZECHARIAH 13:7–9 DELINEATED

poetic accent count	prose particle count		poetic delineation
3+1+1		וְעַל־גֶּבֶר עֲמִיתִי	13:7 חֶרֶב עוּרִי עַל־רֹעִי
2+2+3	את =1 ה =3	וּתְפוּצֶיןָ הַצֹּאן	נְאֻם יְהוָה צְבָאוֹת הַךְ אֶת־הָרֹעֶה
3+4+3	ה =2	פִּי־שְׁנַיִם בָּהּ יִכָּרְתוּ יִגְוָעוּ	וַהֲשִׁבֹתִי יָדִי עַל־הַצֹּעֲרִים 8 וְהָיָה בְכָל־הָאָרֶץ נְאֻם־יְהוָה וְהַשְּׁלִשִׁית יִוָּתֶר בָּהּ
3+3+3	את =3 ה =3	וּצְרַפְתִּים כִּצְרֹף אֶת־הַכֶּסֶף	9 וְהֵבֵאתִי אֶת־הַשְּׁלִשִׁית בָּאֵשׁ וּבְחַנְתִּים כִּבְחֹן אֶת־הַזָּהָב
3+3	את =1	וַאֲנִי אֶעֱנֶה אֹתוֹ	הוּא יִקְרָא בִשְׁמִי
3+4		וְהוּא יֹאמַר יְהוָה אֱלֹהָי	אָמַרְתִּי עַמִּי הוּא

Prose Particle Count = 13/57 words = 22.8% PPD

ZECHARIAH 13:7–9 IN TRANSLATION

7 "O sword, rouse yourself against my shepherd,
    against my intimate friend"
      —oracle of Yahweh of the heavenly armies.
"Strike the shepherd
    so that the flock will be scattered,
    and then I will turn my hand against the little ones."
8 "It will be in all the land"—oracle of Yahweh—
    "that two-thirds in it will be cut off and will die,
    and one-third will be left in it.
9 Then I will bring the one-third into the fire,
    and I will smelt them as one smelts silver,
    and I will test them as one tests gold.

> They[54] will call upon my name,
> and I will answer them.
> I will say, 'they are my people,'
> and they will say, 'Yahweh is my God.'"

The text of 13:7–9 is an example of late prophetic poetry, marked by strong semantic and syntactical parallelism, with four tricola followed climactically by two bicola. The text is also marked by the unusually high PPD of 22.8%. The unit exhibits the highest PPD of any poetical unit in the book of Zechariah, comparable to the PPD of the most prosaic books of the MT, even those that do not feature much poetry of any sort, such as Leviticus. It is also comparable to the PPD of the highly prosaic narrative unit in Zech 11:4–16, at 23.8%. Accordingly, Zech 13:7–9 perhaps represents the latest composition in the set of prophetic poems found in the book of Zechariah.

The shepherd of 13:7 is not the one last seen in 11:17, the worthless shepherd who abandons the flock, Yehud's current or future ruler. Instead, he appears to be a good shepherd, perhaps the one personified by the prophet in his first sign-enactment report in 11:4–14. That shepherd also represented Yahweh in some way, if my interpretation of the first-person pronoun in 11:10 is correct. There the prophet-shepherd broke his staff, "Favor," revoking his/Yahweh's covenant with the peoples. In 12:10 the "pierced/stabbed" one is also mysteriously related to Yahweh.[55] Resisting the proposed textual emendations both in 11:10 and 12:10, I retain the first-person pronouns, and translate 12:10 as "they shall look to me, whom they pierced/stabbed, and shall mourn for him." Accordingly, in Zech 11:4–14 the good shepherd represents Yahweh; in Zech 12:10 the "pierced/stabbed" one in some mysterious manner *is* Yahweh, i.e., it is "me" they have "pierced," yet a Davidide is mourned; and in Zech 13:7 the good shepherd is Yahweh's intimate friend struck down by the sword, probably also a Davidide. The imagery is multivalent and shifting.

Although the shepherd in 13:7 is Yahweh's close associate, his intimate friend (עֲמִיתִי), Yahweh nonetheless invokes the sword against him. The "piercing/stabbing" (דְּקָרוּ) of 12:10 is reprised in 13:7—"Awake, O sword, against my shepherd, against my close associate" (חֶרֶב עוּרִי עַל־רֹעִי וְעַל־גֶּבֶר עֲמִיתִי). The ד.ק.ר verb in the Hebrew Bible, used in 12:10, typically denotes stabbing by a sword, usually with lethal effect. Zechariah 13:7 also employs a sword.

---

[54] In formal equivalence, "He will call ... I will answer him." So also the next two clauses.

[55] Hanson interprets the figure corporately, as of the suffering visionary community (1979, 366). Sweeney (2000, 689) also supports a corporate identification—for the slain of the nations in the eschatological battle.

Unlike the sword that comes in judgment against the worthless shepherd of 11:17, the sword of 13:17 strikes Yahweh's friend. Aside from the unremarkable reference to sheep in both Isa 53:6 and Zech 13:7, the vocabulary of Isa 53 is absent from Zech 13:7–9. Nonetheless, in both texts we have the slaying of Yahweh's intimate associate. Accordingly, in Zech 13:7–9, the influence of the earlier Isa 53 is likely. In Zech 13:7–9 the slaying of the shepherd results in both judgment and salvation for the sheep, the people of Yehud. First they are scattered, and even the little ones suffer. Then there is a winnowing and refining process—a process of destruction followed by purification. Two-thirds perish; one-third survives, and these, the remnant, come forth from the crucible of testing as precious metals, as silver and gold. The narrowing in the Hebrew text is more dramatic than the English versions show. The "they" who call upon Yahweh's name in vs. 9 are represented by the masculine singular subject pronoun, הוּא, "he," an individual. Israel, symbolized by this individual, calls out to Yahweh, and Yahweh answers, in fulfillment of the promise of 10:6.[56] Then Yahweh calls out to him, "He is my people" (עַמִּי הוּא), with a word ('ammi) drawn from the new names given to the children in Hos 2:1. As in Hos 2:25,[57] Israel likewise answers, "Yahweh is my God!" (יְהוָה אֱלֹהָי, 13:9). The covenant formula of 13:9 stands in blessed contrast to the curse that ends the prior shepherd unit in 11:17. The striking of the good shepherd in 13:7 is the catalyst that brings about both this massive judgment and this reconciliation of the wandering people to their God.

In the overall narratology of the second *massa'*, Zech 13:7–9 introduces the notion of fractional destruction, a motif found also in Isa 6:13 and Ezek 5:2–4, 12. The prophet follows the Ezekiel fraction: two-thirds of the land shall perish. This fractional destruction gives specificity to the theme already more generally broached in 11:4–17's "flock doomed to slaughter," but adds also a fractional deliverance. One-third survives. The surviving third, emerging through testing, shall call upon the divine name. The fractional destruction/deliverance provides an appropriate thematic link to the final eschatological unit in 14:1–21, where half the city is exiled while the other half remains in place (14:2). Accordingly, Ewald's proposal, followed by Mitchell, Hanson, and the NEB, among others, relocating 13:7–9 to a position following 11:17 is to be rejected.[58]

---

[56] אֲנִי יְהוָה אֱלֹהֵיהֶם וְאֶעֱנֵם (10:6). Cf. וַאֲנִי אֶעֱנֶה אֹתוֹ (13:9).
[57] וְאָמַרְתִּי לְלֹא־עַמִּי עַמִּי־אַתָּה וְהוּא יֹאמַר אֱלֹהָי (Hos 2:25).
[58] On the placement of the pericope, see further the useful discussion in Nogalski (2003, 292–304).

SOCIAL LOCATION AND ESCHATOLOGY

In social location analysis, Zech 13:7–9 implies a prophet who is estranged from his community, deeply convinced that his own people harbor massive evil and stand in need of real purification. Only a minority of the people shall be delivered, and even they only after a searching process akin to refining and assaying precious metals. In this respect, the social location analysis agrees with the analysis of other texts in Zech 9–14, especially Zech 11:1–3 which excoriated the Davidides, and Zech 11:4–17 which implicitly denounced the sheep-merchants and worthless shepherds, Jerusalem's civil and religious leaders. The analysis also agrees with the assessment of Zech 12:1–13:6, where we saw both the house of David and the house of Levi as complicit, along with other Jerusalemites, in some atrocity, while the ruralists were not. Also, in 13:2–6, the end of the first eschatological narrative, we saw the prophet and his tradent group in competition against false prophets for the loyalty of the community. Elsewhere in chs. 9–14 it becomes clear that the Zechariah group has lost such loyalty. The split is not so much between visionaries and hierocrats, as Hanson would have it. Rather it is between true prophets and the civil and religious leadership, and between true prophets and false prophets. The picture in part in Zech 9–13 pits visionary against visionary.

Regarding the eschatology of Zech 12:1–13:6, in relation to Gowan's eschatological description for Zech 8, I shall consider the issues in the order in which there were discussed by Gowan, one by one:

1) In both texts Jerusalem is the central focus and the problem of exile has been definitively solved.
2) In both texts (in total context) there is a real but limited role for a future Davidide. In Zech 1–8 he is the future *Zemah* who shall come and rule righteously. In Zech 12–13:6 the Davidide is the "pierced/stabbed" one who is mourned, and at whose mourning purification comes from Yahweh.
3) In Zech 8 the nations come to Jerusalem for eschatological pilgrimage; in Zech 12 no mention of a pilgrimage is made; instead the nations come for battle and are defeated.
4) In Zech 8 the problem of Jerusalem's injustice has been definitively solved: it is "the faithful city," and Zion "the holy mountain" (8:3); in Zech 13:1 the city has been definitively cleansed of sin and impurity. Return to the old way of religious rebellion is out of the question altogether in both texts.
5) In Zech 8 peace and security are enjoyed by all Yehudeans, young and old alike. In Zech 12:1–13:6, Israel is afterwards forever safe from foreign attack. The nations are defeated.
6) In Zech 8 the curse on nature has been lifted and the fields and vineyards are abundantly productive. In Zech 12:1–13:6 no mention is made of

this provision. Perhaps on this ground one could conclude that Zech 8's eschatology is more advanced than Zech 12:1–13:6's.

The main eschatological features of Zech 12:1–13:6 not expressly present in Zech 8 include the end of idolatry and false prophecy (although one would assume that "the faithful city" would have no idols or false prophets); and the final victorious battle against the nations. But none of these is remarkably more supernaturalist or divine-interventionist or anti-historical than elements already present in Zech 8. In sum, the eschatology of Zech 12:1–13:6 cannot be said to be definitively different from that of Zech 8 so as to warrant the label "apocalyptic." If Zech 8's eschatology is "prophetic," then so is that of Zech 12:1–13:6.

Finally, regarding Zech 12:1–13:6, I have placed the social location of the prophet and tradent group behind this eschatological narrative at the social margins of Yehudean life, not because I think that eschatologists (or millennialists and apocalypticists, for that matter) are necessarily marginal figures, but because independent evidence from the text indicates the social margin. As Stephen L. Cook has shown (1995), some millennial groups operate from the social center. His insights correlate well with my own view—pursued in chapters 1, 2, and 3—that prophecy can inhabit any number of social locations and occupy multiple social roles. Those at the center of a society, even a good society, may perceive the need for the kind of theodicy that eschatology provides, hope in a final solution to evil. Yehudean society in the restoration era needed an eschatological theodicy. The prophet-tradent community begun by the historical Haggai and Zechariah might have remained in its place as a central authority group in Yehud. Unfortunately, our texts tell us it did not. "The course of true love never did run smooth."

A SPECULATION ON ZECH 12:10 AND 1 CHR 3:19–21

In 1 Chr 3:19 the genealogy of the Davidides lists in first position two sons of Zerubbabel, Meshullam and Hananiah, and then names Shelomith, their sister, before listing five other sons. Presumably Meshullam was the firstborn son. The next generational textual unit (3:21a) lists Hananiah as the next progenitor, and omits Meshullam. This generational unit then lists two sons of Hananiah, namely Pelatiah and Jeshaiah. No further members of the line of Zerubbabel appear in the genealogical text. The subsequent lines of text, though often taken as listing further members of the line of Zerubbabel, instead mention unnamed sons of different Davidide families, not descended from Zerubbabel: "the sons of Rephaiah, the sons of Arnan, the sons of Obadiah, and the sons of Shecaniah"

(3:21b).⁵⁹ The next genealogical units (3:22–24) then list the descendents of Shecaniah for four more generations—according to the MT these are not from Zerubbabel's line. Meshullam, then, appears to be a firstborn son of Zerubbabel who had no sons himself. Did Meshullam die untimely? Is Meshullam the firstborn son mourned over in Zech 12:10–14? Since Hananiah lived to have sons of his own, why is he not known as a Davidide governor in the generation after Zerubbabel? Why does this privilege go to Elnathan, presumed husband of the sister of Meshullam and Hananiah, Shelomith? If the house of David is complicit in an atrocity involving a stabbing in Jerusalem, and if a Davidide is the one "pierced/stabbed," is Meshullam the "pierced/stabbed" one, and Hananiah his murderer? Did the prophet-tradent community of Zechariah place its hopes in a righteous Davidide, Meshullam, only to have them dashed by an act of murder? Finally, did the prophet-tradent community see in the death of a Davidide the catalyst that would lead to yet another episode of dire judgment and deliverance for Yehud?

The speculation is an attractive one, but cannot be confirmed by our present evidence. Against it possibly lies the fact that Zech 12:10 does not denote the mourned one as a literal "firstborn son," but that the clans shall grieve "as one grieves for a firstborn son." This objection may be quibbling.

ZECHARIAH 14:1–21
THE SECOND ESCHATOLOGICAL NARRATIVE

The final and climactic unit of the book of Zechariah, Zech 14:1–21 narrates a retelling of the eschatological battle already reviewed in Zech 12:1–9. The story contains perplexing differences, adds crucial details and brings the reader to a theological climax, completing the revelatory program of the second *massa'* begun in 12:1, which in turn is the continuation of the first *massa'*. The unit also exhibits strong intertextuality with Zech 8, and thus makes a fitting conclusion to the entire book of Zechariah.

The text is not an apocalypse, but an eschatological narrative. Despite Meyers and Meyers setting out vv. 1–2 and 9 as poetical (1993, 407–08), the majority take the text as wholly prose; a high PPD (averaging 18.3%) characterizes the entire text, as shown in Chart 7.3 below.

---

⁵⁹ Several of the ancient and modern versions construe the whole list as descendents of Zerubbabel. Williamson rightly defends the MT over against the ancient versions, as the *lectio difficilior* (1982, 58).

CHART 7.3
PROSE PARTICLE DENSITY IN ZECH 14

Chapter	Words	אשר	את	ה	Totals	Percentage
14:1–21	372	9	6	53	68	18.3%

Like the earlier eschatological narrative, this second begins with a bold הִנֵּה, and is marked by multiple בַּיּוֹם הַהוּא, "on that day," introductory clauses, this time seven in number. Unlike 12:1–13:6, divine oracular speech is limited to the second saying, "I will gather all the nations to Jerusalem to fight against it" in 14:2, and perhaps the reference to "the valley of my mountains" in 14:5, which may reflect intertextuality with Ezek 38:21. In light of this circumstance, the whole unit 14:1–21 may reflect prophetic elaboration of an originally brief divine oracular saying. Petersen again terms this unit, like 12:1–13:6, a "montage," but notes some differences between the organization of the two units, in that Zech 14 is comprised of ten eschatological "vignettes" or "sayings" (1995, 138–39, 161). Sweeney correctly observes that the organization of the narrative is not so much by the בַּיּוֹם הַהוּא phrases, but by the disjunctive clause at 14:12, as well as by the shift in theme from Yahweh's actions concerning Jerusalem in vv. 1–11 to Yahweh's actions concerning the nations in vv. 12–21 (2000, 697).

In the first eschatological narrative, Jerusalem was presented as vigorously defended by Yahweh and by divinely energized Yehudeans, fighting "like David ... like a deity ... like the *mal'ak yahweh*" (12:8). Now instead we see Jerusalem momentarily defeated, captured, ransacked, and the women raped (14:2). The text brutally but realistically speaks the experience of real warfare. This is not the inviolable Jerusalem of Isaiah and Hezekiah; it is the Jerusalem that had seen defeat and destruction at the hand of the Babylonians. Accordingly, half the city goes into exile (14:2), repeating the experience memorialized in Zech 1–8. Floyd astutely comments,

> The plausibility of this reversal depends on its being at least partly comparable to something that Yahweh has achieved before. The story in 14:1–21, telling how Yahweh will allow Jerusalem to be destroyed so that it can be purified and restored, thus takes as its precedent the concept of exile and restoration described in chs. 1–8. (2000, 507)

Here we see some of the ideational unity that joins Zech 1–14 together.

Several important differences between the first and second eschatological narratives have been noted in the commentary literature. Lacocque presents a responsible listing:

Ch 12: L'attaque des nations s'oppose à la volonté de Die;
Ch 14: Dieu réunit les nations contre Jérusalem;
Ch 12: Jérusalem est imprenable;
Ch 14: La Ville est investie par YHWH lui-même;
Ch 12: Dieu intervient avant les ennemis ne constituent un reél danger;
Ch 14: Dieu intervient après the ennemis soient vainqueurs;
Ch 12: L'attaque des nations a pour conséquence la repentance des inhabitants de Jérusalem;
Ch 14: La prise de Jérusalem marque le tournant eschatologique conduisant "de la Jérusalem actuelle à la Jérusalem à venir." (1981, 198 n. 1)

The plot-line of the narrative begins with the announcement that a day belonging to Yahweh is imminent (הִנֵּה יוֹם־בָּא לַיהוָה), a day when "your plunder will be divided in your midst." The story thus begins *in media res*. The term שְׁלָלֵךְ, "your plunder" (14:1), with its second-person feminine singular possessive ending, has no antecedent within the narrative unit: the antecedent appears to be the name Jerusalem in Zech 12:1–13:6, or perhaps even the Zion-Daughter of Zech 9:9 (cf. 9:11), thus linking the entirety of Zech 9–14 as a macro-unit. The term "plunder" is ambiguous: is it Jerusalem who shall be plundered, or Jerusalem who shall do the plundering (Petersen 1995, 135)? The text apparently means that on the Day of Yahweh Jerusalem shall be plundered, but then shall plunder her plunderers. Thus Jerusalem is told "your plunder will be divided among you," rather than among the enemy forces (14:1; cf. v. 14).

As in the days of Zedekiah, Yahweh himself will rally the enemy to attack the city, an act of divine judgment. The city falls to the enemy. After the exile of half the city, Yahweh will then reverse his actions, turning to fight against the nations at Jerusalem (14:3). These actions compress into brief space themes from Jerusalem's history with the Babylonians, once used as Yahweh's means of judgment, but then divinely opposed and judged, as in Jer 25:12. The reader is not expressly told what shall happen to the half of the populace that is exiled. Apparently they remain under punishment, in keeping with the fractional salvation theme announced in 13:8–9 (cf. Ezek 5:2–4). Verse 2 contains the only negative saying for Jerusalem in the entire text.

Verse 4 introduces the first of the striking cosmic changes that shall accompany the new world order that is the focus of ch. 14. Yahweh the divine warrior himself takes his stand in theophanic form upon the Mount of Olives; the mountain heaves into two, forming a great east-west valley—the escape route for Jerusalem's survivors (14:5a). Their flight is reminiscent of the flight from the earthquake in the days of King Uzziah (Amos 1:1).

Another episode of theophanic encounter is narrated in Zech 14:5b: "Then Yahweh my God will come and all the holy ones with you" (וּבָא יְהוָה אֱלֹהַי כָּל־קְדֹשִׁים עִמָּךְ). Mitchell (1912, 229) emends אֱלֹהַי and קְדֹשִׁים and עִמָּךְ to read, "then Yahweh *your* God shall come, and *his* holy ones with him." Only the last of these is well supported by the ancient versions and is perhaps warranted. Petersen (1995, 136) nonetheless accepts all three emendations; Meyers and Meyers defend the reading אֱלֹהַי as a sign of the author's originality in altering the stock phrase (1993, 429). As I have noted previously, the book of Zechariah exhibits a peculiar tendency regarding the use of pronouns. The coming of Yahweh produces further cosmic changes:

1) no longer cold or frost (לֹא־יִהְיֶה אוֹר[61] יְקָרוֹת[60] יְקִפָּאוֹן‎ [וְקִפָּאוֹן], 14:6);
2) no longer day and night, but only perpetual light (לְעֵת־עֶרֶב יִהְיֶה־אוֹר, 14:7);
3) no longer times of drought, not even in summer, but a perpetual river of "living water" (מַיִם־חַיִּים, 14:8) shall stream from Jerusalem to both east and west, summer and winter, a development out of Ezek 47's altar-river.

These first three provisions, then, amend the created order described in Gen 8:22.

4) no longer shall the land be rugged with hills and valleys; "the whole land ... shall become like the Arabah" (יִסּוֹב כָּל־הָאָרֶץ כָּעֲרָבָה, 14:10a), a lowland plain, as in Isa 40:4;
5) in contrast, Jerusalem shall be exalted to its former heights, the cultic center of the whole earth (יְרוּשָׁלַם וְרָאֲמָה וְיָשְׁבָה תַחְתֶּיהָ, 14:10b), as Isa 2:2 promised.

The unit features two strategies of narrative climax. The first is based on seven בַּיּוֹם הַהוּא clauses; the second based on syntax and theme. Out of the seven בַּיּוֹם הַהוּא phrases, the fourth, the midpoint, announces Yahweh's kingship:

וְהָיָה יְהוָה לְמֶלֶךְ עַל־כָּל־הָאָרֶץ
בַּיּוֹם הַהוּא יִהְיֶה יְהוָה אֶחָד וּשְׁמוֹ אֶחָד

Yahweh will become king over the whole earth;
On that day Yahweh will be one, and his name one. (14:9)

Zechariah 14 thus contains elements of a final eschatology. The cosmos shall be transformed; and there shall be no more challenges to Yahweh's supreme authority. He shall be universally revered, his kingship everlasting. The lan-

---

[60] Read קָרוֹת for יְקָרוֹת. So Holladay (1988, 325).
[61] With Meyers and Meyers (1993, 407), read עוֹד for אוֹר.

guage of 14:9 is, of course, drawn from Deut 6:4;[62] the eschatology of divine kingship in Zion from the book of Isaiah and numerous Psalms. The oneness of Yahweh and of his name, as Meyers and Meyers point out, indicates a monotheistic claim in Zechariah. It is not merely that Yahweh shall be the only God for Israel; Yahweh shall be the only God for the nations, too (1993, 440). Monolatrous interpretation might be possible for Deut 6:4—Yahweh is "our God," i.e., Israel's (so Armstrong 1994, 52–53); but nothing short of monotheism suits Zech 14. The midpoint בַּיּוֹם הַהוּא, then, contains an appropriately climactic theological dictum for the postexilic age.

Verse 11 contains the other climax, signaled both by the following disjunctive syntax in v. 12 and by the change of theme. There the text asserts unequivocally,

וְיָשְׁבוּ בָהּ וְחֵרֶם לֹא יִהְיֶה־עוֹד וְיָשְׁבָה יְרוּשָׁלַ͏ִם לָבֶטַח

They [the Yehudeans] will dwell in her, and destruction shall be no more; Jerusalem shall dwell securely. (14:11)

The climactic line contains the goal not only of Zech 14, but also of Zech 12, where v. 6 announced,

וְיָשְׁבָה יְרוּשָׁלַ͏ִם עוֹד תַּחְתֶּיהָ בִּירוּשָׁלָ͏ִם

Jerusalem shall remain still in her place—in Jerusalem.

Thus the eschatological direction both of Zech 12:1–13:6 and of Zech 14:1–21 is shown to arrive at the same point: a secure Jerusalem, her inviolability restored, under the sole dominion of Yahweh. With this assurance the first half of the unit draws to a close (vv. 1–11).[63]

---

[62] Despite the Deuteronomic language of 14:9 and elsewhere, we need not suppose, with Raymond F. Person (1993, 202, and *passim*), that Zech 9–14 was redacted by the Deuteronomic school in the postexilic period. Postexilic Yehud had ample access to Deuteronomic literature. Tradents of prophetic literature, such as Zechariah and his tradent group, would have known this literature and have studied it intensively.

[63] According to Floyd, the first half of Zech 14 "carries the story forward, recounting what 9:1–17 seems finally to call for but does not actually describe: the emergence of a whole new world order in which international conflict is no longer the dominant force, so that Yahweh's people are no longer dominated by others, and their own leaders are no longer given any opportunity to misrule them. In order for this new world order to emerge, however, all must suffer the cataclysmic demise of the old world" (2000, 507).

The second half, Zech 14:12–21, addresses Yahweh's dealings with the nations. He shall strike man and beast with plague and panic (14:12–13, 15). In their divinely induced terror, the besieging nations will attack and slay each other. Yehud and Jerusalem, now presumably victorious, will plunder the foreign encampments of great wealth (14:14); thus the "wealth of nations" shall be carried into Jerusalem (Isa 60:11).

But just as only a portion of Jerusalem is marked for punishment, only a portion of the nations shall perish. The survivors of the nations shall worship Yahweh. As Isaiah foresaw and as Zech 8:20–23 (cf. 2:15; 6:15) predicted, the nations shall stream up to Jerusalem in pilgrimage (14:16). The autumn Feast of Tabernacles, the greatest of the postexilic feasts (so Harrelson 1968) shall become the annual occasion of the recognition of Yahweh's international dominion, the imperial rule foreseen in Zech 9:1–8.[64] The annual event shall be not the mere exercise of coercive power, but one of festivity; the nations come "to worship" and "to celebrate" this joyous yearly feast before "Yahweh the King" (לְהִשְׁתַּחֲוֺת לְמֶלֶךְ יְהוָה צְבָאוֹת וְלָחֹג אֶת־חַג הַסֻּכּוֹת, v. 16). Like the Philistine of Zech 9:7, adopted into Yehud with a place of honor, the nations will become Yahwists.

But Zech 14 only contains *elements* of a final eschatology. The prospect of rebellion persists. Human evil, diseases, and climatic ills remain possible. And so the text says that if any nation refuses pilgrimage, drought will be its punishment (14:17). Egypt is singled out for peculiar mention because rain is so rare there; instead, if the Egyptians refuse the call of Yahweh, plague shall befall them (14:18), evoking the plagues of the book of Exodus. We see, then, that Zech 14 is a strange mixture of ultimate and penultimate eschatology.

The text ends on a note of ultimate eschatology. The holiness of Yahweh shall be so pervasive that even the humblest objects—cooking bowls and bridle bells—shall be inscribed with the motto of the golden plate on the high priest's turban, קֹדֶשׁ לַיהוָה, "Sacred to Yahweh" (14:20; cf. Exod 28:36; 39:30). The text evokes the memory of Zech 3, with its high priest and priestly tiara (3:5), and with its divinely inscribed plate or stone with seven eyes/facets (3:9). Whereas in Zech 3:9 the inscribed object was probably some rare and precious object, gemstone, or precious metal, the objects of Zech 14:20 are common. The point is that the boundary between the sacred and the profane, the holy and the common, has been changed: the realm of the sacred is now vastly expanded: all of Yehud is sacred.

In another unifying motif, the final line of text evokes once again the ruthless sheep-merchants of Zech 11:4–17. In contrast to the corrupted leadership of the prophet-tradent group's present day, in the blessed future "there

---

[64] Does this element reflect a Yahweh-kingship enthronement as part of the Feast of Tabernacles? The evidence is scant, but see the discussion in Harrelson (1968).

shall no longer be a merchant (כְּנַעֲנִי) in the temple of Yahweh" (14:21). Thus the text ends with Yehud, Jerusalem, and its temple secure under Yahweh's protective power. The final words of the text involve an *inclusio* with its opening. Zechariah 14 began with "See!—a day belonging to Yahweh is coming," הִנֵּה יוֹם־בָּא לַיהוָה; it ends with the seventh and last occurrence of בַּיּוֹם הַהוּא, "on that day."

IS ZECH 14 APOCALYPTIC?

Is Zech 14 apocalyptic? It is not an apocalypse, but does it bear apocalyptic eschatology? Perhaps. Remembering Donald Gowan's six eschatological points drawn from Zech 8 (1986, 5) and revised above, I see strong elements of continuity, but also strong elements of discontinuity between the two texts.

1) God's people are restored—at least some of them in Zech 14. Zechariah 14 distinguishes between righteous Yehudeans and unrighteous Yehudeans in a way that Zech 8 does not.
2) The *Zemah* figure of Zech 1–8 receives no mention in Zech 14, but neither does the returning Davidide king of Zech 9:9–10, nor the cornerstone-tent peg of 10:4, nor the righteous, martyred Davidide perhaps implied in Zech 12–13. Yahweh is the king.
3) The nations will indeed make their pilgrimage to Zion to worship Yahweh, as both Zech 8:20–23 and Zech 14:16 indicate. Zechariah 14, however, contains an element of coercion not found in Zech 8.
4) Jerusalem is "the faithful city" (8:3), Zion "the holy mountain"— emphatically so in Zech 14, especially since Zion is the *only* mountain. Future disobedience by Yehudeans is not an option in either text.
5) In both texts, peace and security shall be enjoyed by all in Zion, but not necessarily by the nations in Zech 14: some may face drought and plague if they resist the call to worship.
6) In both texts the curse on nature has been lifted; fertility and fruitfulness are guaranteed (8:12; 14:6–8). In Zech 14, this is true to such an extent that elements of the old world order no longer obtain: no cold or killing frost, no night but perpetual light; no distinction between summer and winter; and a constant supply of "living water," refreshing the ground east and west. These elements, with their cancellation of the natural order decreed in Gen 8:22, are among the most trans-historical aspects of Zech 14.

In summary, some elements of Zech 8 indicate a more advanced eschatology than those of Zech 14, and *vice versa*. In Zech 8 the nations are uncoerced; on the other hand, in Zech 14 the nations do *celebrate* (לָחֹג). But Zech 14 shows several more trans-historical elements than seen in Zech 8. The whole geography of the world is altered; the climate dramatically changed. Nevertheless, in

Zech 14 there is still the prospect of human sin, disease, and climatic ills. Drought and plague threaten the nations. In light of these indications, I still must resist Hanson's claim that with Zech 14 "one enters the period of full-blown apocalyptic literature" (1979, 369). The best that can be said is that Zech 14 carries a proto-apocalyptic eschatology, but still stands in strong continuity with the eschatology of Zech 8. It is more advanced than Zech 8, but not so radically different that Zech 14 *must* come from a later hand than Zechariah's. A prophet-rhetor, once centralized, now marginalized, might well come to see his world in such a manner.[65]

SOCIAL LOCATION ANALYSIS OF ZECH 14:1-21

The social location analysis of the prophetic author of Zech 14:1–21 depends upon several lines of evidence in the text. First of all we see that he is a Zion traditionalist (cf. von Rad 1962, 46–48). As a Zion traditionalist, the author bears an intense concern for Yahweh. Here aspects of the tradition are intensified. Few texts in the Hebrew Bible witness so clearly to Yahwistic monotheism than Zech 14.[66] This is the first of his two main concerns. An inviolable Jerusalem is the second. Jerusalem must be restored and exalted above all other places on earth. Also, as a Zion traditionalist, the author anticipates Yahwistic empire, centered in Zion. Many texts speak of the pilgrimage of the nations; none develops the theme so concretely as Zech 14, with its annual Feast of Tabernacles celebration. Finally, as a Zion traditionalist, the prophet bears deep concern for the fate of the temple of Yahweh. The temple only receives two mentions in Zech 14, but they come at the climax of the whole, in 14:20–21, as the final sign of the integrity of the new order of the world, when temple-purity is guaranteed. Jerusalem's temple must become the cultic center of the world. We see, accordingly, the strong continuity between this text and the temple-laden thought-world of Zech 1–8.

Second, the prophetic author is convinced that his own people are in need of divine punishment of a nature similar to that merited by the wayward Jerusalem of Jeremiah's day. A significant number of the people deserve only capture and

---

[65] Reventlow observes, "In diesen Erwartungen sind die Propheten Sammler und Tradenten, deren Zeugnisse im zweiten Teil des Sacharjabuches vereint sind, treue Nachfolger des ersten Sacharja, dessen Visionen ebenfalls schon auf diese Heilzeit hinwiesen." He adds, "Zeitlich brauchen wir diese Kapitel nichte so erheblich, wie oft gefordet wird, vom ersten Sacharja abzurucken." Moreover, "sind wir von der Zeit der Chronik und Esra–Nehemias noch entfernt" (1993, 129).

[66] Isa 44–46; Deut 4:35–39; 1 Kgs 8:60; Joel 2:27 all contain the divine claim that there is "no other."

exile from Yahweh's city. Even the remainder must experience the devastation of earthquake and flight.

Third, the author bears concern not only for Jerusalem, but also for Yehud (v. 14). As in Zech 12, Yehud will demonstrate its valor in the battle.

Fourth comes the important reference, prosaic though it seems, that "there shall no longer be a merchant in the house of Yahweh of the heavenly armies." While some interpreters take the reference to כְּנַעֲנִי as to literal "merchants," declaring an end to commerce in the sacred precinct (so Mitchell 1912, 356–57; Harrelson 1968, 94), and others interpret the כְּנַעֲנִי as of literal Canaanites, i.e., unreconstructed pagans (so Meyers and Meyers 1993, 489–92; Sweeney 2000, 706; Webb 2003, 182), or perhaps Samaritans (so Elliger), it seems better to understand the reference in keeping with Zech 11:4–17. There the "Canaanites" were the merchants, the ruthless buyers and sellers of the flock, that is, the rulers of Yehud, probably including both members of the dyarchic pair, the governor and the high priest. Zechariah 14:21, it seems, means an end to ruthless rulers, especially in governance of the temple.

In social location, then, Zech 14 springs from a writer who is estranged from governing authorities in Jerusalem, and from a large proportion of its populace. As Rainer Albertz observes, he is in "deep dissent" (1994, 569). Some Jerusalemites are reckoned righteous, yet even these stand in need of purification through the trauma of earthquake and flight. Ruralists in Yehud (v. 14) apparently stand in better stead; they shall fight valiantly in the coming eschatological battle. The prophet, then, has but a limited validation by his intended audience. He rejects, and is probably rejected by, the leading authorities in temple and state. He stands closer to ruralists, and thus is marginal, probably in both the sociological and the geographical sense. It is important to note, however, that this assessment stands independently of the judgment that Zech 14 represents proto-apocalyptic eschatology. Separate lines of evidence support these two claims.

SOCIAL LOCATION IN ZECH 9–14

This analysis means that we have similar social locations for the series of texts in Zech 10–14, the series that began in the first *massa'* with 10:2's denunciation of false dreamers, diviners, and which bemoaned Yehud's "lack of a [true] shepherd." That series continues with 10:3's mention of Yahweh's wrath at the "shepherds" and "he-goats," code words perhaps for false prophets or other leaders; and comes to 11:1–3's calling for fire upon "Lebanon"—code word for the house of David. It continues with 11:4–17's sign-enactment report about ruthless sheep-merchants and worthless shepherds, code words, respectively, for rulers of the dyarchy, and for priests and false prophets. The series then resumes in the second *massa'* with 12:1–13:6's indictment of the house of David and the house of Levi (12:12–13) regarding the "pierced/stabbed" one (12:10), and its eager anticipation of the end of false prophecy (13:2–6). The line proceeds to 13:7–9's announcement of the striking of a shepherd and of fractional destruction/deliverance for Yehud.

In my reconstruction, Zech 11:4–17, the only autobiographical report in chs. 9–14, plays the key role, for it narrates the process by which a publicly accredited prophet came into rejection and social marginalization. On the other hand, the evidence regarding Zech 9's social location is ambivalent: it likely served as a statement of the Zechariah group's theology of Yahwistic empire in the Zion tradition, representing perhaps an earlier text reworked in the early postexilic era. Zechariah 14:1–21 brings the series to a close by foreseeing a siege and a well-deserved second exile for Jerusalem, but eschatological transformation as well, to make her the cultic center of the Yahwistic empire foreseen in Zech 1–8 and Zech 9.

In light of the exegesis presented here and the social location analysis of its origins, what can be said about the unity of the book of Zechariah? That is the next task at hand.

8

THE UNITY OF ZECHARIAH

As we have previously seen, Michael Floyd noted that "it is odd that no recent commentaries have attempted to grasp either the ideational concept or the sociohistorical context forming the matrix of the book [of Zechariah] as a whole." He then added, "For whatever reason, interpreters seem reluctant to confront the fact that the editors who put the prophetic corpus in its canonical form regarded all fourteen chapters of Zechariah as constituting a distinct prophetic book" (1999, 262). He further observed, "Historical as well as literary commentators must eventually ask what concept provided a basis for bringing 9–14 and 1–8 together as a single prophetic book named for Zechariah and what sociocultural circumstances made such a concept viable" (262). This dissertation is an attempt to achieve what Floyd called for in 1999, and which Floyd sought to achieve in a different way in his 2000 FOTL volume.

But first, a clarification: I do not think that unitary authorship for Zechariah is the only possible way to read these texts. There are other types of unity that may be sought in the book of Zechariah and found—among them, redactional unity and thematic unity. I have already discussed redactional unity for Haggai–Zech 1–8; hence, I am no opponent of the redactional construction of texts. Unitary authorship for Zechariah may be the wrong hypothesis, as the majority of scholarly interpreters have held since the time of Stade. Thus, I do not insist upon unitary authorship as a theological *a priori* in approaching the book, and I have argued elsewhere for plural authorship in Zeph 3:14–20, a text that I believe has import for the late redaction of the Book of the Twelve (Curtis 2000). But I have come to doubt the fitness of the plural authorship model for Zechariah. Is plural authorship exegetically warranted in this case? I do not think so.

Older defenders of authorial unity for Zechariah, as we have seen, include Ernst W. Hengstenberg (n.d. [1829–1835]), C. F. Keil (1884; 1975 [1853]), John Perowne (1875), C. H. H. Wright (1879), E. B. Pusey (1892), and George L. Robinson (1895–96). These argued in keeping with the ancient Christian and Jewish tradition that attributed the book to the historical Zechariah.[67] They

---

[67] Sometimes there was confusion among the ancient interpreters over which of the several biblical Zechariahs was the author of the book. Note "Zechariah ben-Jeberechiah" in Isa 8:2 and the discussion in Mitchell (1912, 82).

thought the ancient tradition of attribution was meaningful and not to be lightly cast aside.

Twentieth-century defenders of Zechariah's unity include, as we have seen, A. Van Hoonacker (1902), David Baron (1919), William F. Albright (1942b), E. J. Young (1949), H. C. Leupold (1971), Joyce Baldwin (1972), Eugene Merrill (1994), and Brian Tidiman (1996), among others. Its most recent defender may be Barry Webb (2003).

Albright held that Zech 9–14 contained oracles from the early restoration period, ca. 539–500 B.C., and, although Zecharian authorship could not be proved, he saw "no reason why most of [the oracles] cannot be credited to Zechariah himself" (1942b, 121). Joseph Klausner (1955, 197–200) put forth unitary authorship as a tentative suggestion. Having similarly placed the oracles and narratives of Zech 9–14 in the early Persian period, ca. 500–485 B.C., based on his assessment of Greco-Persian conflict, Klausner saw the prospect that this literature "perhaps" could be "by the very same Zechariah who composed Chapters 1–8 in his youth" (1955, 200). As Brian Tidiman asks, "Pourquoi refuser à Zacharie un ministère long et varié?" (1996, 43).

In 1965 J. Stafford Wright readily admitted that "it is not possible to prove the [authorial] unity of the book"; he then added, "but one should not too readily abandon it" (1356). I think these are words of wisdom. After presenting an argument for the authorial unity of the book, R. K. Harrison issued this cautionary word:

> If these phenomena do not actually constitute evidence for the close literary affinity of the two sections, they certainly indicate that the author of the second portion was careful to model his style and expression upon that which obtained in the first part, a fact that would hardly be surprising if the book is to be considered as a literary bifid. (1969, 954)

I present my argument for authorial unity in much the same spirit of tentativeness as William F. Albright, Joseph Klausner, J. Stafford Wright, and R. K. Harrison. But first, a consideration of the arguments against unitary authorship.

FIVE PILLARS FOR A POST-ZECHARIAN DATE

There are five pillars upholding the edifice of a post-Zecharian date for chs. 9–14. These are (1) the historical, (2) the sociological, (3) the theological, (4) the structural, and (5) the linguistic. I shall now summarize how my argument has answered each of the first four pillars, and then I shall develop my answer to the fifth pillar, the linguistic argument.

First, the historical argument depends mainly upon the analysis of Zech 9:1–8 as reflecting or anticipating the itinerary of Alexander the Great in 332 B.C., and of Zech 9:13's "sons of Yavan" and Zech 10:10–11's Egypt and

Assyria as referring to the Hellenistic kingdoms. Historical arguments based on identifications of 11:8's "three shepherds" and 12:10's "pierced one" have been abandoned (Redditt 1994). We saw that 9:1-8 is not a military itinerary, but a listing of traditionally hostile cities and regions named generally but not invariably from north to south. Given the long survivability of place names, even the antique reference to the land of Hadrach (9:1) cannot be taken as evidence of an Assyrian-era date, and nothing in the text fixes the date to any specific point in the mid-to-late first millennium B.C. Zechariah 9:1-8 is of no evidential value for this question. The geographic listing asserts the future expanse of Yahwistic empire. We also saw the mention of Zech 9:13's sons of Yavan would make little sense in the early first millennium B.C. However, given the long history of Persian-Greek hostilities in the aftermath of Cyrus's conquest of Lydia in 546 B.C., any date from the time of Darius, when Greece first rose to world-power status, to the Hellenistic era, when the Hellenistic kingdoms were the principal oppressors of Judaea, would suffice. Zechariah 9:13, then, cannot serve as evidence for an exclusively Hellenistic date.

As we have seen regarding the Egypt and Assyria references in 10:10-11, these are traditional names for traditionally hostile powers in the region, and thus have no evidential value for assigning a date in the Hellenistic era. Darius I is even called מֶלֶךְ־אַשּׁוּר, "King of Assyria," in Ezra 6:22. These three texts—Zech 9:1-8, 9:13, and 10:10-11—provide the main exegetical supports for the first pillar, the historical argument, and each one fails to deliver the goods.

As for the second pillar, the sociological argument rightly perceived social location difference between the historical Zechariah and his tradent community in Zech 1-8 and the prophet and tradent community in Zech 9-14. Difference in social location was taken to denote difference in authorship or tradent community. This argument was scuttled by our case study analysis of prophetic claimants and their associated movements. Alice Lenshina and her Lumpa Church climbed to the social center and back out again in social implosion and violent destruction, all in the brief span of ten years. Muhammad, in an opposite trajectory, moved from the social periphery in Mecca to the social center in Medina in about ten years; and then to the social center in Mecca, again in the brief span of about ten years. Thus we saw that prophetic claimant-led movements can quickly change social location. We also saw that prophetic speech frequently risks marginalization. Haggai took such risks in his first and fourth oracles. Zechariah took similar risks in his public speeches in Zech 1:2-6 and in Zech 7:4-8:23. In my scenario, he took a similar risk as reported in the shepherd sign-enactment narrative in ch. 11, and failed to sustain his audience accreditation as a prophet-speaker for the community. He was rejected. Social location change is no argument against Zecharian authorship for chs. 9-14. Rather, the known careers of prophetic claimants easily accommodate such social location changes. Finally, the actual passage in which we see the evidence of social location change is not Zech 9, but Zech 10-11, with its recurrent wicked shepherd theme, and its narrative of social marginalization in 11:4–16. Zechariah 9 could well stand in social location continuity with Zech 1–8. Hence, part of Zech 9–14 may be linked to the same social location as the historically known prophet Zechariah in chs. 1–8. This potential linkage would further undermine the Deutero-Zechariah hypothesis. Thus the sociological pillar does not supply proof of plural authorship.

For the third pillar, the theological argument claimed that Zech 1–8 featured prophetic speech and prophetic eschatology, while Zech 9–14 featured apocalyptic eschatology. I answered this argument by showing the strong lines of continuity between the eschatological expectation of Zech 1–8 and that of Zech 12:1–13:6 and 14:1–21. The work of Katrina J. A. Larkin on eschatology in Deutero-Zechariah (1994), and the work of Stephen L. Cook on millennial groups in power (1995) showed more continuity between prophecy and apocalyptic than is often detected. I note also that Petersen, who once thought differently, now treats Zech 9–14 as prophetic, rather than apocalyptic, literature (1995, 24; 2002, 208–09). My sociological argument also assists the theological issue. Social location change is often accompanied by rhetorical change and ideological shifts. As rhetorician Stephen D. O'Leary has shown (1994), millennialist and apocalyptic rhetors modify both their theological views and the way they express these views as their social location changes, or as they actively seek, for political purposes, to change their social location. Richard J. Coggins says,

> While it is indeed true that Zechariah 9–14 does not appear to come from the same setting as chapters 1–8, that is a very different thing from claiming that they are so different as to represent completely opposed viewpoints.... Each part has also been claimed to furnish vital clues as to the development from prophecy to the apocalypses. Indeed, the very fact that the two sections are now bound together as one book suggests very strongly that in some quarters at least they were not perceived as being in opposition to each other. (1989, 245)

Thus no firm theological line can be drawn between prophetic eschatology and apocalyptic eschatology in Zechariah.

Fourth, the structural pillar of the Deutero-Zechariah hypothesis proves to be weak. Zechariah 1–8, as we have seen, features date formulae, dating to the regnal years of Darius the various oracles, vision reports, and the sign action report now found in those chapters, reported mostly in prose. Zechariah 9–14 contains no date formulae and no vision reports; instead it consists of two *mas'ot*, with a substantial amount of prophetic poetry in the first. However, as we have seen, based on the analogy of date specificity in the Neo-Babylonian Chronicles, prophetic date formulae which bear specific dates, down to the day, appear to be keyed to acts of temple desecration and temple restoration. Since temple completion has presumably been achieved in Zech 9–14—witness the functioning temple in Zech 11:13 and 14:20–21—there was no further perceived need for date specificity. Sacred time had been restored with the restoration of sacred space, Jerusalem's temple of Yahweh. Moreover, out of the eighteen passages identified in the MT as *mas'ot*,[68] only one features a date formula, Isa 14:28–32. Hence, we should not think it strange that the two *mas'ot* in Zech 9–14 appear without date formulae. Such an absence is in keeping with the genre. The absence of date formulae in chs. 9–14 is thus no argument against Zecharian authorship.[69]

Fifth and finally, the linguistic pillar offers the most challenge to my thesis, for there are some important differences between Zech 1–8 and Zech 9–14 in word choice, phrasing, and stylistics. The list of words and phrases complied by Mitchell in his ICC Zechariah commentary (1912, 236) is apparently substantial. Both Ackroyd (1962, 651) and Coggins (1987, 62), among others, consider Mitchell's case against unitary authorship to be definitive. But closer examination shows a weaker case. Mitchell argues that various stylistic and lexical differences between Zech 1–8 and 9–14 point to different authors. In the section that follows I quote from or refer *seriatim* to Mitchell's list, and offer my replies.

MITCHELL'S LIST EXAMINED

Mitchell writes: "'The word of Yahweh came to me,' the formula by which the prophet regularly introduces his messages, does not occur in these [9–14] chapters. In 11:4 the corresponding formula is 'Thus said Yahweh to me.'" However, both of these formula are artificially made to conform to a set pattern through text-critical emendation. The frequent formula in Zech 1–8 is indeed כֹּה אָמַר יְהוָה צְבָאוֹת (seventeen times), a formula that does not appear at all in chs. 9–14, but Zech 11:4 has כֹּה אָמַר יְהוָה אֱלֹהָי, which should not be taken as so very different, and twice the formula appears in chs. 1–8 without צְבָאוֹת. Hence, כֹּה אָמַר יְהוָה is common to both parts of the book, an unremarkable phenomenon.

It is true that לֵאמֹר, "saying," is frequent in Zech 1–8 (twenty-eight times) but absent in chs. 9–14 (1912, 236). However, when we investigate all of the

---

[68] 2 Kgs 9:26a; Isa 13:2–14:23; 14:29–32; 15:1b–16:12; 17:1b–11; 19:1b–25; 21:1b–10, 11b–12, 13b–17; 22:1b–14; 23:1b–18; 30:6b–7; Ezek 12:11–16; Nah 1:2–3:19; Hab 1:2–2:20; Zech 9:1–11:17; 12:1–14:21; and Mal 1:2–3:24 [ET 1:2–4:6].

[69] Moreover, not all concur with the traditional delineation of the material between chs. 1–8 and 9–14. As we have seen, several recent dissenters are Floyd (2000), Sweeney (2000), Kline (2001), and Webb (2003). All treat the date formula at 7:1 as the literary heading for the remainder of the book.

eighteen passages marked as *mas'ot* in the MT, we find that לֵאמֹר is rare, appearing only three times in that entire corpus, in Isa 14:24, where it introduces a divine oath formula, in Isa 19:25, where it introduces a divine blessing formula, and in Isa 23:4, where the personified sea laments the slain children of Sidon. Hence, we should not readily expect the two *mas'ot* of Zech 9–14 to employ it.

Mitchell next says, "The appeal to the future, 'Then shall ye know,' etc., is used 4 t. in the first part of the book, but not at all in the second" (236). This is true enough, although 11:11, וַיֵּדְעוּ כֵן עֲנִיֵּי הַצֹּאן הַשֹּׁמְרִים אֹתִי כִּי דְבַר־יְהוָה הוּא, "and the sheep merchants, who were watching me, knew that it was Yahweh's word," reflects a similar usage and apparent knowledge of the formula.

"The Lord of the whole earth" [אֲדוֹן כָּל־הָאָרֶץ, 4:14; 6:5] is a title for God that would have suited the thought of these last chapters, but is not used, 'The King, Yahweh of Hosts,' being substituted for it" (236). This is a weak argument, based on an artificially confined view of language, as if a writer should be addicted to a single title for the deity. Moreover, in 14:9 it is said, "Yahweh will be king over all the earth," יְהוָה לְמֶלֶךְ עַל־כָּל־הָאָרֶץ, a close parallel to the earlier title.

"Zechariah makes large use of rhetorical questions, but there is only one question of any sort after the eighth chapter" (236). Again, this claim is true. Rhetorical questions are frequent in Haggai, Zech 1–8, and Malachi, but not Zech 9–14 (Pierce 1984a, 283–85), where the only question is found in 13:6 (Craig 1996, 244). However, Zech 1–8 has three social settings where interrogatives naturally could appear, the preaching encounter of 1:2–6, with its rhetorical questions, the interaction between the wise interpreting angel and the ignorant prophet in Zech 1:7–6:8, and the second preaching encounter in Zech 7–8, where Bethel's question about fasting sets the stage for the discourse. The only such personal encounter in Zech 9–14 is the brief shepherd narrative in 11:3–16. The nature of the material in 9–14 is accordingly not suited to the implicit give-and-take of rhetorical question and answer, as it is in Zech 1–8. Instead, we have a declarative genre, the *massa'*, based on the interpretation of earlier texts.[70]

"The use of the participle, with or without a preceding *behold* [*hinneh*], or in an adverbial sense, is frequent (29 t.) in chs. 1–8. Here [in 9–14] it is used in all only 12 t." (Mitchell 1912, 236). This is partly a correct observation, and also partly misleading. To begin with, it is somewhat unclear what Mitchell means by this description of participles. Does he mean to include all participles: those that are accompanied by an introductory *hinneh*/behold, those without the *hinneh*, as well as those that are used in what he calls an "adverbial" sense? A

---

[70] Malachi, however, also a *massa'*, contain numerous questions. Here the genre has been astonishingly transformed into disputation speech. Beth Glazier-McDonald classifies Malachi as "*Disputationsworte*" (1987, 21). Hill concurs (1998, 37).

close examination of Zechariah's participles clarifies what Mitchell likely intended.

Traditional Hebrew grammars classify participles according to their use as nominatives, as verbs, and as adjectives. By the term "adverbial," Mitchell seems to denote their use as verbs. This suggestion is confirmed by a rough count of the participles used in the book of Zechariah. I count about thirty verbal participles in Zech 1–8 and about twelve in Zech 9–14, close enough to Mitchell's numbers. A few ambiguous cases muddy the numbers a little. It would have been helpful if Mitchell had included a comparative base for considering this variety; in sorting out the participles, how do other prophetic books fare?

When one adds introductory *hinneh* to the participial mix, we find ten occurrences in Zech 1–8 and four more in Zech 9–14; but we should expect Zech 9–14's numbers to be somewhat fewer, since this is the shorter side of the book (2703 words to 2144 words, respectively[71]). Also, all but one of Zech 1–8's *hinneh*+participle combinations appear in the vision reports, a genre in which we expect *hinneh*. Moreover, two of the emphatic *hinneh* uses in Zech 9–14 are programmatic, serving as the grand introductions to the eschatological narratives in both ch. 12 and ch. 14. Hence, this alleged stylistic difference seems inconsequential.

Broadening our search, we find that there are in fact 139 participles in Zech 1–14: seventy-six in Zech 1–8, and sixty-three in Zech 9–14. When lexical densities for the participles are calculated for these two sections of the book, using a standard measure of "density per thousand words" (DPT), a procedure explained further below, one obtains a DPT of 28.12 for Zech 1–8 and a DPT of 29.38 for Zech 9–14, remarkably similar statistical profiles. The remarkable character of this congruence becomes clearer when one considers the DPT of participles throughout the MT. The following chart displays some of the data:

CHART 8.1
DISTRIBUTION OF PARTICIPLES (DPT) IN THE MT

	Torah	Former Prophets	Latter Prophets	The Twelve	Ketuvim
Participles	1507	1451	2604	573	3104
DPT	12.54	13.26	23.54	26.30	23.60

Chart 8.1 shows a low level of use of participles in the mainly narrative books of the Torah and the Former Prophets, and a much greater propensity toward participial use in the Latter Prophets; however, these larger numbers in the

---

[71] The figures are based on the count provided in Accordance, from Oak Tree Software.

Latter Prophets mask an important feature, shown more clearly in Chart 8.2 below.

CHART 8.2
DISTRIBUTION OF PARTICIPLES (DPT)
IN THE LATTER PROPHETS

	Isaiah	Jeremiah	Ezekiel	The Twelve
Participles	802	759	470	573
DPT	31.31	22.81	15.69	26.30

Notice the relative paucity of participles in Ezekiel, and virtually double that figure for Isaiah. But even this display conceals some wide and wild fluctuations in prophetic rhetoric, as seen in Chart 8.3, which focuses on the Book of the Twelve alone.

CHART 8.3
DISTRIBUTION OF PARTICIPLES (DPT)
IN THE BOOK OF THE TWELVE

	Hos	Joel	Amos	Obad	Jonah	Mic	Nah
Ptcs.	64	24	81	5	13	66	47
DPT	17.71	16.61	26.85	11.42	12.01	31.00	55.42

	Hab	Zeph	Hag	Zech 1–14	Zech 1–8	Zech 9–14	Mal
	29	38	10	139	76	63	57
	28.63	33.54	10.85	28.68	28.12	29.38	43.58

In Chart 8.3 we notice low DPTs such as the brief Haggai's 10.85, the lowest of the lot; the even briefer Obadiah's 11.42; the narrative-laden Jonah at 12.01; and the more representative paucity of Joel and Hosea at 16.61 and 17.71 respectively. At the opposite end of the scale lie Nahum at 55.42, nearly double the figures for Zechariah; Malachi at a very high 43.58; and Zephaniah at 33.54. Only Habakkuk and Amos are close to either side of Zechariah, at 28.63 and 26.85 respectively. Hence, the profile of Zech 1–8 is remarkably similar to that of Zech 9–14 in the number of participles employed, a feature of the language that would seem ordinarily to lie outside the conscious control of authors. To summarize, when we compare the use of participles as verbs, Zech 1–8 is denser than Zech 9–14, at 11.10 DPT to 5.60 DPT; but when we compare the use of all participles, the two portions are almost exactly equally dense, at 28.63 to 29.85 DPT, in a field (the Latter Prophets) where density varies greatly.

Mitchell's figures, which appear to favor a judgment of difference in style, are perhaps rather more than cancelled out by the larger figures for the use of all participles.

Mitchell then lists eleven words, drawn in part from R. Eckardt (1893, 104–5) that he says are characteristic of Proto-Zechariah, but not of Deutero-Zechariah:

"אֲנִי is used exclusively in the first, but only 2 out of 6 t. in the second, part of the book" (236). Here Mitchell is nearly right. While אֲנִי appears nine times in chs. 1–8 and twice in 9–14, אָנֹכִי appears only in chs. 9–14, five times, an interesting stylistic difference. Hill observed, "Hag and Zech 1–8 use *'ani* exclusively, while Zech 9–14 and Mal demonstrate alternation in using both *'ani*... and *'anoki*"; and "exclusive use of *'ani* ... is a mark of LBH" (1981, 87). In this respect, then, Zech 1–8 resembles the later use, and Zech 9–14 the earlier use.

Mitchell continues: "בחר, in the sense of *take pleasure*, is not found where it might be expected, even in ch. 14" (1912, 236). ב.ח.ר indeed appears only in Zech 1–8, three times (1:17; 2:16; 3:2), but Holladay does not list "take pleasure" as one of its meanings (1988, 37). Again, this is a weak argument, artificially requiring an author to use a certain word because he has used it before, on a few occasions.

"זעם, *purpose*, also, is wanting" (1912, 236). Here Mitchell undoubtedly intended to list ז.מ.ם, to "think, plan," which appears three times in Zech, in 1:6, 8:14, and 8:15. ז.ע.ם, to "curse, scold," does appear once, in 1:12. The previous objection about usage holds here as well.

"חלה, *appease*, might have been used in 14:16–18, but הִשְׁתַּחֲוָה was preferred" (236). Mitchell's objection here is futile, because ח.ל.ה (piel, "appease") is better suited to the context of Zech 8:20–23, where foreigners wish to gain access to Yahweh for the first time, becoming reconciled to him, whereas in Zech 14:16–18, לְהִשְׁתַּחֲוֹת denotes habitual acts of worship, year-by-year, at the Feast of Tabernacles, by the now-converted remnant of the nations.

"קרא is not found in the sense of *proclaim* in these chapters" (236). True. But in both 8:3 and in 11:7 it is used in the sense of "to name." Its only other use in Zech 9–14 is in the sense of "to invoke in prayer" in 13:9, which is matched by its use in 7:13. Also, Zech 9–14 features no occasion of public preaching, where Mitchell's favored sense would have been appropriate. Hence, the objection has no weight.

"שְׁאֵרִית, remnant, is wanting, יתר being used in 14:2 in its place" (236). But שְׁאֵרִית appears only in ch. 8 (8:6; 8:11 and 8:12). The two terms appear together in Zeph 2:9, and the two roots appear together in Isa 4:3, Jer 39:9, 44:7, and other texts. Hence, there is no reason why an author cannot employ the one term in ch. 8 and the other once (and only once) in ch. 14.

"שׁוּב, *return*, where it might be used adverbially in the sense of *again*, is replaced by עוד" (236). But עוד appears sixteen times in Zech, eight times in Zech 1–8 and eight more times in Zech 9–14. Moreover, the sense of "again" only appears twice in all of chs. 1–8, in 5:1 and 6:1, in the visionary formulaic וָאָשׁוּב וָאֶשָּׂא עֵינַי וָאֶרְאֶה, a usage not suited to the non-visionary material of chs. 9–14. Hence, it is difficult to see how this objection bears any force.

"שָׁכַן, *dwell*, is used like יָשַׁב, of both God and men in chs. 1–8. In chs. 9–14 only the latter occurs, and that 12 t." (236). This is true. However, the use of שׁ.כ.ן in Zech 1–8 occurs exclusively in the formula שׁ.כ.ן + בְּתוֹךְ/בְּתוֹכֵךְ (2:14, 15; 8:3, 8), usually regarding deity, an expression especially well-suited to the temple restoration specifically envisaged in those texts (cf. Exod 25:8 and 1 Kgs 6:13, where similar formulae pertain to the erection of Moses's tabernacle and Solomon's temple), a situation not found in Zech 9–14. Hence, the objection bears no weight.

"תוֹךְ, *midst*, very common in chs. 1–8, does not occur in 9–14, קֶרֶב being employed in its place" (236). True, תוֹךְ appears nine times, exclusively in chs. 1–8, while קֶרֶב appears twice, exclusively in chs. 9–14, at 12:1 and 14:1. However, in 12:1's phrase, וְיֹצֵר רוּחַ־אָדָם בְּקִרְבּוֹ, "and who forms the spirit of man within him," תוֹךְ is not to be expected, and the single remaining case in 14:1 is insubstantial.

This completes Mitchell's (and Eckardt's) list, and, as we have seen, few of the claims are both true and relevant: the observation about participles used in the so-called "adverbial" sense, and about the personal pronouns אֲנִי and אָנֹכִי—a weak set of linguistic evidences to go on. Now let us examine linguistic evidence for unity. My claim will be that authorial unity provides the better account of the linguistic features of Zech 1–14.

LEXICAL AND STYLISTIC EVIDENCE FOR UNITY

George L. Robinson suggested that "certain peculiarities of diction and style favor unity of authorship" (1895–96, 86). This claim, contrary to the consensus of scholarship, appears to be sustainable. To support his claim he listed a number of common words that cannot fairly be considered as positive evidence in the way he presents them, since common words may easily appear in both parts of a work of composite authorship.[72] He also failed to provide lexical density studies

---

[72] The rise of computers have made studies of frequent words (especially "function words") for testing authorship attribution much easier. See Fazli Can and Jon M. Patton (2004) for an explanation and example of the method. I shall not attempt this kind of analysis. Jeff Collins, *et al.* (2004), discuss the "function words" approach in the famous case of *The Federalist Papers*. Their study concludes that authorship attribution studies are more complicated than is usually thought, and that collaborative works, such as *The Federalist Papers*, may display a peculiar rhetorical strategy of authors accommodating each others' styles (27–29). If the book of Zechariah is a

of the terms he chose—a difficult task in his day—and so did not demonstrate that they bore either (1) any unusual character, or (2) any common statistical profile. However, it seems that a number of unusual terms and phrases do lend themselves toward a theory of unitary authorship. Lexical statistics do not prove the claim, but they do appear to assist this argument.

Lexical density has served as a significant measure in authorship attribution studies. Both Joseph Rudman (1998, 360) and David I. Holmes (1994, 96–97), authors of standard articles about statistical analysis in authorship attribution, acknowledge this point, while also exercising appropriate cautions. The analysis of lexical richness in authorship attribution is also supported by recent studies (A. Miranda-Garcia and J. Calle-Martin 2005, and the bibliography there). Yehoshua T. Radday and Dieter Wickmann (1975) further attest that vocabulary eccentricity is a useful measure in authorship attribution. I should note, however, that experts in the field of stylometry often insist that stylometrics alone is often insufficient to determine disputed authorship, and that other, more traditional methods should also be applied, as I have done in these chapters.

In my analyses of the vocabulary of the book of Zechariah, I have presupposed (1) that rare occurrences held in common, such as *hapax legomena* and *dislegomena*, count as evidence tending to favor literary unity, and (2) that unusually high densities of words held in common also count as evidence tending to favor literary unity. I have not attempted to prove these two suppositions. I have run lexical density analyses on Robinson's terms and others, measuring density based on occurrences per thousand Hebrew words.[73] This procedure removes the "skew" element created by short books, except for the shortest books, those with less than 1000 words, such as Obadiah, Habakkuk, or Haggai. In what follows *density per thousand words* (DPT) is the standard of measure for some of the terms. My procedure was to ascertain the DPT of a term in the MT, in the Latter Prophets, in the Book of the Twelve (=B12), in the Twelve *minus* Zechariah (=B11), and in the two main parts of Zechariah,[74] noting along the

---

composite work, how much did the deutero-author accommodate himself to the historical Zechariah's style?

[73] Density per thousand (DPT) is calculated by means of the database and program in Accordance, produced by OakTree Software, Altamonte, Florida, which uses the standard Groves-Wheeler Westminster Hebrew Morphology (3.5), based in turn upon the Michigan-Claremont-Westminster machine-readable text. For a description of the use of lexical statistics in Accordance, see Tyler F. Williams (1997).

[74] Zechariah 1–8 contains 2703 words, and Zech 9–14 has 2144 words (Accordance 7.0.1), well above the thousand-word minimum for density analysis using Accordance. Radday and Wickmann (1975, 31) give a different set of numbers, based on a different method of counting words, resulting in 1841 words for Zech 1–8 and 1381 words for Zech 9–14. The difference results mainly from the different answers given to the question of how attached attached particles are counted.

way unusual lexical and semantic features, such as *hapax legomena, dislegomena*, and other rare expressions. In my investigation, I have considered the most important comparative base to be the rhetoric of the Latter Prophets, especially the Book of the Twelve. Thus, words that may appear commonly in the Pentateuch, but only rarely in the Latter Prophets or in the Book of the Twelve, are treated as rare expressions. I also make some recourse to studies in Late Biblical Hebrew (LBH).

Given the current inconclusiveness of statistical studies in authorship attribution, I present my method and its results as tentative and experimental. My use of lexical density, *dislegomena*, and the like, should not be taken as definitive; it is deliberately polemical, provocative, and exploratory. There is not yet a large established body of published research using lexical statistics on Hebrew biblical texts. More work of this sort has been done in New Testament studies than in Hebrew Bible.[75] If the reader still regards Mitchell's list as determinative, as has the majority of scholars in the near-century since he wrote, it should be noted that my list below proceeds on similar grounds. If Mitchell's method is valid, then mine should be seen as valid, too. If my method is invalid, then so also is Mitchell's, and the question shall have to be settled on other, independent grounds.

The following list is based in part on lists found in Robinson (1895–96, 86–88), Eckardt (1893, 104), J. Stafford Wright (1965), and Harrison (1969, 954), to which I have added my own observations. In each case below, the distinctive word or phrase or usage appears in both parts of Zechariah.[76] The terms appear in alphabetical order. Chart 8.4 (below, after the list) summarizes findings involving high lexical densities, and Chart 8.5 (further below) summarizes findings involving rare words and expressions.

---

[75] For a discussion of lexical statistics in authorship attribution in New Testament studies, see H. W. Hoehner's stylometric discussion of the question of (non-)Pauline authorship for the Epistle to the Ephesians (2002, 24–29), and the extensive literature cited there. Hoehner concludes that "it is extremely difficult to determine authorship on the basis of language and style" (28–29). Using especially Galatians as a foil, his review shows that lexical statistical analysis of the undisputed Pauline letters indicates more diversity in language and style than is usually recognized; when this diversity is compared to the lexical diversity of Ephesians, the case against Pauline authorship appears seriously weakened. For more on New Testament stylometrics, see Anthony Kenny's monograph on the subject (1986). Kenny's chapter on the stylometrics of the Pauline epistles concludes that there is "no reason to reject the hypothesis that twelve of the Pauline epistles are the work of a single, unusually versatile author" (100). In Kenny's analysis, the Epistle to Titus is the odd man out (95–98). Is Zechariah, like Paul, an "unusually versatile" writer?

[76] Further research could be done to subject these observations to more rigorous statistical analysis, but I must leave that work to others.

LEXICAL EVIDENCE

אֶבֶן appears 278 times in the MT, and fifty-three times in the Latter Prophets, which makes it appear that the term is insignificant for authorship attribution studies. However, nine of the fifteen times it appears in the Book of the Twelve are in Zechariah (3:9 twice; 4:7, 10; 5:4, 8; 9:15, 16; and 12:3), giving Zechariah a higher density of its occurrences (1.86 DPT) than any book of the MT except for Haggai (2.17, with two occurrences) and Habakkuk (1.97, also with two occurrences). In both these latter cases the book's brevity skews the figures. The density for all of Zechariah is 1.86 DPT, compared to 0.55 for Isaiah, 0.21 for Jeremiah, 0.57 for Ezekiel, zero for all the books from Hosea through Jonah, Nahum, Zephaniah, and Malachi, and 0.94 for Micah. When we divide the book between its two main parts, the DPT for Zech 1–8 is 2.22, and for Zech 9–14 is 1.40, both higher than any other book of the MT except for the previously mentioned Habakkuk and Haggai. אֶבֶן is a significant term or subtheme in both sides of the book.

אֲדָמָה is common word, but it takes an unusual turn in Zechariah. In Zech 2:16 we see עַל אַדְמַת הַקֹּדֶשׁ, "upon the holy land," a *hapax legomenon*, and in Zech 9:16 we find עַל־אַדְמָתוֹ, "upon his [Yahweh's] land," both of which are perhaps dependent upon the usage in Isa 14:2 where we see עַל אַדְמַת יְהוָה, "upon Yahweh's land," or the phrase in Deut 32:43, where אַדְמָתוֹ refers to Yahweh's land. *There are no other cases of this usage.* Thus the parallel between 2:16 and 9:16 is strong.

אֶחָד/אַחַת and the use of numbers: The use of the number "one" is peculiar in Zechariah, bearing a much higher density than for any other book in the Twelve except for Haggai and Malachi, and surpassed only by Ezekiel, if we include the Former Prophets in the list. In Ezekiel, with a DPT of 3.60, the distribution is weighted heavily toward chs. 40–48, where numbers and measurements abound. In Zechariah, however, the distribution is weighted rather evenly between chs 1–8 (seven times), with a DPT of 2.59, and chs. 9–14 (six times), with a very similar DPT of 2.80. In contrast, Isaiah and Jeremiah, respectively, show DPTs of 0.82 and 0.42. Hosea, Joel, and Amos, typical examples, have densities of, respectively, 0.28, 0.00, and 1.66. Hence, the two parts of Zechariah are in strong accord on this point.

Both parts of Zechariah also exhibit a fondness for the number two or describing things in two parts or halves. שְׁנַיִם/שְׁתַּיִם appears twelve times in Zechariah, compared to twenty times in all of the Book of the Twelve. Aside from the number in date formulae, there are two olive trees (4:3, 12); two "sons of oil" (4:14); two stork-women (5:9); two mountains with a division between them (6:1); "the two of them" (the future priest and king, 6:13); two shepherd's staffs (11:7); two "third-parts" under judgment (13:8); two halves of the city

(14:2); the Mount of Olives split in halves, east and west (14:4); and the waters of life likewise split in halves, east and west (14:8).[77]

The cardinal numbers one through twenty appear in greater density in Zechariah than in other books in the Twelve, with the exception of Haggai, where brevity and many dates skew the figures. When calculated by DPT, Zechariah, with its thirty-one occurrences, has a density of 6.40, compared to Amos, the next highest, at 5.97, and then dropping to 3.06 in Malachi. Hosea, for example, has only two numbers, and the books of Joel, Nahum, and Habakkuk none at all. Hence, the twenty-three numbers in Zech 1–8, with its DPT of 8.51 compare favorably with the eight numbers that appear in the somewhat briefer Zech 9–14, with its DPT of 3.73, despite the apparent disparity. Both density figures are higher than any book in the Twelve except the brief Haggai with its frequent dates (yielding an artificially high DPT of 19.52) and Amos, with its numerical judgment oracles of chs. 1–2.

אִישׁ בְּרֵעֵהוּ: This expression appears only nine times in the MT, only five times in the Latter Prophets, and only twice in the Twelve, namely, Zech 8:10 and 11:6. Similar expressions appear in 8:16, 17; 11:9 (in feminine form); and 14:3, and thus appear an equal number of times in each part of the book.

ב.ק.שׁ (piel) followed by לְ with the infinitive construct is unusual in the MT, appearing only 12 times, and in the Latter Prophets only three times. Two of these are in Zechariah, in 6:7 and 12:9. The syntax appears nowhere else in the Twelve.

בַּת־צִיּוֹן appears thirty times in the MT, nineteen times in the latter prophets, and seven times in the Twelve. It would appear, then, that its double appearance in Zechariah (2:14 and 9:8) is not significant for stylistic studies. However, when we note its vocative use, preceded by an imperative verb, we only find six occurrences in the MT: Isa 52:2, Mic 4:10 and 13, Zeph 3:14, and notably both Zech 2:14 and 9:8.

חֵן is a relatively common word, appearing sixty-nine times in the MT, twenty-four times of the deity. But it is rare in the Latter Prophets, appearing only four times: Jer 32:2; Nah 3:4 (where it denotes not Yahweh's favor, but the allurements of Nineveh); and in Zech 4:7 and Zech 12:10.

יָד: The combination of יָד plus the verb ח.ז.ק is unusual in the Book of the Twelve. It appears twenty-six times in the Latter Prophets, but in the Twelve only in Zech 8:9, 13 and 14:13.

The י.ד.ע recognition formula, likely drawn from Ezekiel, or more remotely, Exodus, appears in 2:13, 2:15, 4:9, and 6:15. Zechariah 11:11, where the sheep-merchants "knew it [a prophetic sign-action] was Yahweh's word" seems dependent upon this earlier formula from Proto-Zechariah, although Ezekiel's influence cannot be ruled out.

---

[77] Some of these are listed in Robinson (1895–96, 86).

ירושלם: When we consider occurrences of the word Jerusalem, the DPT for each side of Zechariah is, respectively, 6.29 and 11.19, both numbers considerably higher than anything else in the MT except for Ezra's DPT of 7.94. The highest DPT elsewhere in the Latter Prophets is Obadiah's 4.57, but this is based on a mere 2 occurrences, a skewed figure. The next highest is Joel's 4.15. Isaiah yields but 1.91, Jeremiah, 3.22, and Ezekiel, a mere 0.87.

י.ש.ב in the intransitive sense is used of a land or city which "sits" or "abides in its place" (BDB 443a). Robinson mistakenly calls this sense "passive" (1895–96, 87). This intransitive use is unusual. It appears in the MT in this sense only fourteen times, in Isa 13:20; Jer 17:6, 25; 50:13, 39; Ezek 26:29; 29:11; 36:35;[78] and remarkably no less than six times in Zechariah: in 2:8; 7:7; 9:5; 12:6; and 14:10, 11.

When י.ש.ב appears in combination with ירושלם, we find 103 occasions in the MT; in the Latter Prophets we find high proportions only in Jeremiah and Zechariah. Of the forty-nine cases, twenty-six are in Jeremiah (DPT 1.77), and eleven are in Zechariah (DPT 3.09). If we consider the Twelve apart from Zechariah, we have but three cases, one each in Joel, Micah, and Zephaniah, with a combined DPT of 0.18 for the Eleven. The DPT for Zech 1–8 is 2.59, and for Zech 9–14 is 8.40, both figures higher than anything else in the entire MT.

מֵעֹבֵר וּמִשָּׁב appears nowhere else in the MT except in Zech 7:14 and 9:8, a phenomenon that Robinson rightly calls "very noteworthy" (87). Zechariah 7:14 says, in context, הָאָרֶץ נָשַׁמָּה אַחֲרֵיהֶם מֵעֹבֵר וּמִשָּׁב וַיָּשִׂימוּ אֶרֶץ־חֶמְדָּה לְשַׁמָּה, which reads, "The land became desolate after them so that no one went to and fro"; and Zech 9:8 says מֵעֹבֵר וּמִשָּׁב חָנִיתִי לְבֵיתִי מִצָּבָה, "Then I will encamp at my House like a garrisoned force against the marching and counter-marching [troops]." The only close comparison appears in Ezek 35:7 where we see the phrase הִכְרַתִּי מִמֶּנּוּ עֹבֵר וָשָׁב, "I will cut off from it all who come and go." The likely scenario is either the author of Zech 9:8 was acting in conscious imitation of Zech 7:14, or it was the same author who wrote both texts.

מְצוּלָה appears twelve times in the MT; but only four times in the Twelve: Jonah 2:4, Mic 7:19, and in Zech 1:8 and 10:11.

נ.ו.ח appears three times in Zechariah (5:11; 6:8; 9:1), twice in programmatic fashion. In 6:8 at the conclusion of the night vision reports it denotes the goal of the visions: Yahweh's spirit has "found rest" in the land of the north. In 9:1 it denotes the "resting place" that Yahweh's word has found in Damascus and the northern regions. The use in 9:1 seems dependent upon its use in 6:8, resuming the earlier theme.

נ.ח.ם in the piel appears in the MT fifty-one times, in the Latter Prophets twenty times, and in the Book of the Twelve only three times, Nah 3:7 and Zech 1:17 and 10:2.

---

[78] So BDB 443a.

סוּס appears fourteen times in Zechariah, seven times in each half. The DPT for this term in chs. 1–8 is 2.59, and in chs. 9–14 is 3.26, both far above the lexical density of the term for any other prophetic book except the brief book, Habakkuk, with its skewed DPT of 2.96. Jeremiah, the Hebrew Bible's longest book, mentions horses only sixteen times, with a low DPT of 0.48; Isaiah, Ezekiel, Hosea, Joel, and Micah all display similarly low densities.

ס.ו.ר (hiphil) appears in the Book of the Twelve only seven times, and twice in Zechariah, 3:4 and 9:7.

ס.פ.ד appears only thirty times in the MT, seventeen times in the Latter Prophets, but only five times in the Book of the Twelve, three of them in Zechariah: 7:5, where it denotes the ritual mourning of the traditional fasts of the exilic era; and 12:10, 12, where it denotes the ritual mourning over the mysterious "pierced/stabbed one."

ע.ב.ר (hiphil) appears in the Book of the Twelve only three times, and with the unusual sense of removing uncleanness only twice, in Zech 3:4 and 13:2. This unusual use of the hiphil appears elsewhere in the MT only in 2 Sam 12:13; 24:10 (=1 Chr 21:8) and Job 7:21.

עַיִן: This word is very common in the MT, appearing some 899 times. However, it displays an unusually high density in Zechariah, appearing nineteen times in its fourteen chapters, with a DPT of 3.92, the highest of any book except for Proverbs (4.82 DPT) and Lamentations (4.16 DPT). Compared to Isaiah (1.76), Jeremiah (1.65), Ezekiel (2.37), Hosea (0.55), Joel (0.69), and Amos (0.99), to take a fair sample, Zechariah's DPT is much higher. When we divide Zechariah into its two main parts we still see high densities for each part: a DPT of 4.44 with twelve occurrences for Zech 1–8, and a DPT of 3.26 with seven occurrences for Zech 9–14, both much higher than nearly all other books in the MT.

There is also the peculiar way in which the word for "eye" is used in both parts of Zechariah. Six times it refers, routinely, to Zechariah lifting his eyes in visionary state (וָאֶשָּׂא עֵינַי: 2:1, 5; 5:1, 5, 9; 6:1). However, five or perhaps six times it refers to Yahweh's eyes, a rare reference in the Latter Prophets. The stock phrase עֵינֵי יְהוָה, common elsewhere, appears only four times in the Latter Prophets; once each in Isaiah, Jeremiah, Zechariah, and Malachi. It is unusual in the Latter Prophets to find Yahweh's eyes referred to—as they are in Zech 2:12; 4:10; 8:6; 9:8; 12:4, and perhaps in 3:9. In three of these the sense is of Yahweh's protection of Yehud: 2:12; 9:8; and 12:4. The other occurrences of עַיִן in Zechariah are 5:6; 8:6; 9:1; 11:12; 11:17 (twice); and 14:2. Zechariah 11:17 and 12:4 both mention blindness. In 5:6 many textual critics suggest the emendation of עֵינָם "their eye," to עֲוֹנָם, "their iniquity," an attractive proposal until we perceive the thematic use of the "eye" in the book. In 11:17 the blinded foolish shepherd is an anti-Yahweh image, the antithesis of the all-seeing, beneficent deity, who "keeps a watchful eye over the house of Judah, but ... blinds the horses of the nations" (12:4). References to the eye in both parts of Zechariah thus far surpass the usage in the rest of the Twelve and the Latter Prophets. Larkin (2001, 612) calls the eye passages signs of redactional unity, but she presents no compelling reason against regarding them as signs of authorial unity.

עַל־יָמִין וְעַל־שְׂמֹאול: The combination of יָמִין followed by שְׂמֹאול is relatively common, appearing some eighty-four times in the MT in various syntactical configurations. However, Zechariah features a *unique* syntax, one appearing nowhere else in the MT: עַל־יָמִין וְעַל־שְׂמֹאול. This *dislegomenon*, using עַל ... וְעַל appears in both Zech 4:11 and 12:6.[79]

ר.ח.ם (piel) appears in the Book of the Twelve eight times, four in Hosea, where it takes on an important thematic role (Hos 1:6, 7; 2:6, 25), once each in Micah and Habakkuk, and once each in the two parts of Zechariah, 1:12 and 10:6.

שָׂכָר appears in the Book of the Twelve only five times, twice in succession in Zech 8:10, and again, strangely, twice in succession in Zech 11:12; it appears again in the Twelve only in Mal 3:5.

ש.ל.ל. appears in the Book of the Twelve in Zech 2:12, 13 and 14:1, and only elsewhere in the Twelve in Hab 2:8.

שֶׁקֶר appears in the Book of the Twelve nine times, two of them in Zech 1–8 (5:4 and 8:17), and two of them in Zech 9–14 (10:2 and 13:3). The other references are Hos 7:1; Mic 2:11; 6:12; Hab 2:18; and Mal 3:5. But when paired with the lexeme שֵׁם, referring to false oaths in Yahweh's name, it appears only eight times in the Latter Prophets: six in Jeremiah, where it is part of the polemic against false prophets, and nowhere else but in Zech 5:4 and 13:3. Its only other occurrence in the entire MT is in Lev 19:12.

תֵּימָן appears for the direction "south" in Zech 6:6 and 9:14, but not so elsewhere in the Book of the Twelve. Elsewhere in the Twelve it denotes the southerly region near the Wilderness of Zin, Teman (Amos 1:12; Obad 1:9; Hab 3:3). It is unusual also in that the word נֶגֶב also appears in Zech for "south" in 14:4, 10, and perhaps in this sense also in 7:7. Elsewhere in the Twelve נֶגֶב appears only in Obad 19 and 20, where it is taken in the regional sense.

Crown: the English word translates several terms in the MT, and appears some thirty-eight times in the NRSV, eight times in the Latter Prophets, but not at all in the Twelve except in Zech 6:11, 14 and 9:16.

Charts 8.4 and 8.5, shown below, summarize the lexical data given above. The charts show the occurrences of each item, first in the MT, then in the Latter prophets (LP), in the Book of the Twelve (B12), in the Eleven (B12 minus Zechariah), in Zechariah as a whole, and finally in both Zech 1–8 and Zech 9–14.

---

[79] In Zech 4:11 the final word appears with the possessive suffix: שְׂמֹאולָהּ.

CHART 8.4
SUMMARY OF LEXICAL DENSITIES

Word/Phrase	MT	LP	B12	B11	Zech 1–14	Zech 1–8	Zech 9–14
אָז	278	53	15	6	9	6	3
DPT	0.58	0.48	0.89	0.35	1.86	2.22	1.40
אֶחָד/אַחַת	960	172	29	16	13	7	6
DPT	2.01	1.55	1.33	0.94	2.68	2.59	2.80
שְׁנַיִם/שְׁתַּיִם	769	78	20	8	12	10	2
DPT	1.61	0.70	0.92	0.47	2.48	3.70	0.93
Numbers 1–20	2841	460	79	48[80]	31	23	8
DPT	5.96	4.16	3.62	2.83	6.40	8.51	3.73
ירושלם	655	247	65	24	41	17	24
DPT	1.37	2.23	2.98	1.41	8.46	6.29	11.19
י.ש.ב + ירושלם	103	49[81]	14	3	11	3	8
DPT	0.22	0.44	0.69	0.18	3.09	2.59	8.40
סוס	140	64	26	12	14	7	7
DPT	0.29	0.58	1.19	0.55	2.89	2.59	3.26
עַיִן	899	202	31	12	19	12	7
DPT	1.89	1.83	1.42	0.71	3.92	4.44	3.26

---

[80] Aside from Zechariah, two other books in the Twelve bear an unusually high number of these occurrence: Amos (18x; DPT 5.97) and Haggai (18x; DPT 19.52); this accounts for 75% of the numbers outside Zechariah in the Twelve.

[81] Twenty-six of these are in Jeremiah, yielding a DPT of 1.77.

CHART 8.5
SUMMARY OF UNUSUAL TERMS IN ZECHARIAH COMPARED TO MT, LATTER PROPHETS, AND THE TWELVE

Word/Phrase	MT	LP	B12	B11	Zech 1–14	Zech 1–8	Zech 9–14
אַדְמָה Yahweh's/his/holy	4	3	2	0	2	1	1
אִישׁ בְּרֵעֵהוּ	9	5	2	0	2	1	1
inf.+לְ+ב.ק.שׁ piel	12	3	2	0	2	1	1
imperative+בַּת־צִיּוֹן	6	6	5	3	2	1	1
הֵן	69	4	3	1	2	1	1
ח.ז.ק + יָד	29	10	3	0	3	2	1
י.ד.ע recog. form.	48	41[82]	7	2	5	4	1
י.שׁ.ב intransitive	14	14	6	0	6	2	4
מֵעֹבֵר וּמִשָּׁב	2	2	2	0	2	1	1
מְצוּלָה	12	4	4	2	2	1	1
נ.ח.ם piel	51	20	3	1	2	1	1
ס.ו.ר hiphil	132	32	7	5[83]	2	1	1
ס.פ.ד	30	17	5	2	3	1	2
ע.ב.ר hiphil, remove impurity	6	2	2	0	2	1	1
עַל־יָמִין וְעַל־שְׂמֹאול(ה)	2	2	2	0	2	1	1
ר.ח.ם piel	42	31	8	6[84]	2	1	1
שֵׂכָר	30	12	5	1	4	2	2
שׁ.ל.ל	92	35	5	2[85]	3	2	1
שֶׁקֶר	113	54	9	5[86]	4	2	2
שָׁקַר + שֵׁם	9	8[87]	2	0	2	1	1
תֵּימָן as *south* (NRSV)	23	7	2	0	2	1	1
crown (NRSV)	38	8	3	0	3	2	1

---

[82] The vast majority of these, thirty-two, are in Ezekiel.
[83] Two of these are in Hosea, one in Amos, and two in Zephaniah.
[84] Four are in Hosea, one in Micah, and one in Habakkuk.
[85] Both of these appear in Hab 2:8.
[86] One is in Hosea, two in Micah, one in Habakkuk, and one in Malachi.
[87] Six of these are in Jeremiah: 14:14; 23:25; 27:15; 29:9, 21, 23.

SYNTACTICAL AND STYLISTIC FEATURES

So far, then, the evidence of lexical density and of rare and unusual expressions suggests that a case for unitary authorship can be sustained. But there is more evidence for this claim.

Awkward syntax involving personal pronouns appears in both sections of the book, sometimes denoting deity. Thus in Zech 1–8 we find, in 2:12:

כִּי כֹה אָמַר יְהוָה צְבָאוֹת
אַחַר כָּבוֹד שְׁלָחַנִי אֶל־הַגּוֹיִם הַשֹּׁלְלִים אֶתְכֶם
כִּי הַנֹּגֵעַ בָּכֶם נֹגֵעַ בְּבָבַת עֵינוֹ

For this is what Yahweh of the heavenly armies says,
after glory has sent me to the nations who are plundering you,
for whoever touches you touches the pupil/ball of his eye.

Here both שְׁלָחַנִי and עֵינוֹ appear anomalous in a divine speech. Zechariah 6:15, at the conclusion of a divine speech, has this to say:

וּרְחוֹקִים יָבֹאוּ וּבָנוּ בְּהֵיכַל יְהוָה
וִידַעְתֶּם כִּי־יְהוָה צְבָאוֹת שְׁלָחַנִי אֲלֵיכֶם

Those far away will come and build Yahweh's temple,
Then you will know Yahweh of the heavenly armies has sent me to you.

Again the שְׁלָחַנִי appears anomalous, denoting the prophet. Again 7:3 has this anomaly:

הַאֶבְכֶּה בַּחֹדֶשׁ הַחֲמִשִׁי הִנָּזֵר כַּאֲשֶׁר עָשִׂיתִי זֶה כַּמֶּה שָׁנִים

Should I weep and fast in the fifth month, as I have done these many years?

There the two first person singular forms appear in the question posed by the people (plural) of Bethel (7:2). Two lines later, in a text introduced in the third person as a revelatory experience of Zechariah, we see these words in the first person singular (7:4):

וַיְהִי דְבַר־יְהוָה צְבָאוֹת אֵלַי לֵאמֹר

Then the word of Yahweh came to me . . .

Zechariah 7:13 reads:

Up the Steep and Stony Road: The Book of Zechariah   251

$$\text{וַיְהִי כַאֲשֶׁר־קָרָא וְלֹא שָׁמֵעוּ כֵּן יִקְרְאוּ וְלֹא אֶשְׁמָע}$$
$$\text{אָמַר יְהוָה צְבָאוֹת}$$

"Just as, when he [I] called, they would not hear, so, when they called, I would not hear," says Yahweh of the heavenly armies.

Here we expect קָרָאתִי in the first clause, but find the third masculine singular instead. In Zech 9–14 we find, in 9:11:

$$\text{גַּם־אַתְּ בְּדַם־בְּרִיתֵךְ שִׁלַּחְתִּי אֲסִירַיִךְ מִבּוֹר אֵין מַיִם בּוֹ}$$

As for you [Zion-Daughter], because of the blood of your covenant, I have released your prisoners from the waterless pit.

Here the expected form is בְּרִיתִי, not the second feminine singular suffix. Also 12:10:

$$\text{וְשָׁפַכְתִּי עַל־בֵּית דָּוִיד וְעַל יוֹשֵׁב יְרוּשָׁלַם רוּחַ חֵן וְתַחֲנוּנִים}$$
$$\text{וְהִבִּיטוּ אֵלַי אֵת אֲשֶׁר־דָּקָרוּ וְסָפְדוּ עָלָיו כְּמִסְפֵּד עַל־הַיָּחִיד}$$
$$\text{וְהָמֵר עָלָיו כְּהָמֵר עַל־הַבְּכוֹר}$$

Then I will pour out a spirit of compassion and supplication on the house of David and the inhabitants of Jerusalem, so that, when they look on me whom they have pierced, they shall mourn for him, as one mourns for an only child, and weep bitterly over him, as one weeps over a firstborn.

Here the אֵלַי fails to agree with the double occurrence of עָלָיו later in the text, and appears to denote Yahweh as the "pierced/stabbed one." Finally there is Zech 14:5:

$$\text{וְנַסְתֶּם גֵּיא־הָרַי כִּי־יַגִּיעַ גֵּי־הָרִים אֶל־אָצַל}$$
$$\text{וְנַסְתֶּם כַּאֲשֶׁר נַסְתֶּם מִפְּנֵי הָרַעַשׁ בִּימֵי עֻזִּיָּה מֶלֶךְ־יְהוּדָה}$$
$$\text{וּבָא יְהוָה אֱלֹהַי כָּל־קְדֹשִׁים עִמָּךְ}$$

Then you shall flee by the valley of my mountains, for the valley [between] the mountains [shall reach?] to Azal; and you shall flee as you fled from the earthquake in the days of King Uzziah of Judah. Then Yahweh my God will come, and all the holy ones with you.

Here the unexpected pronoun in "my mountain" again denotes deity. Then in the final clause, the meaning of the first person possessive pronoun changes to refer to the prophet in the divine name, "Yahweh my God." Finally, we see all the holy ones "with you," a strange feminine singular form which now seems to denote Zion. In considering this extensive list of pronoun incongruities, we might judge that some of these forms indeed involve textual errors. The overall pattern, however, leads me to prefer the *lectio difficilior* rule for the strange pronouns in the fourteen chapters of Zechariah, a pattern sustained in both parts of the book.

In his 1890's Leipzig dissertation, Robinson constructed a sizable list of commonalities as evidence of unitary authorship (1895–96, 84–89). Some of his arguments and evidences are weak, but others are telling. Among the weak arguments are such statements as "an unusually deep, spiritual tone pervades the entire book" (84); and "there is a similar attitude of hope and expectation in both parts" of the book (85). Such observations hardly advance his cause.

Robinson sometimes makes use of specious arguments. For example, he mentions "the habit of expanding one fundamental thought into the unusual number of five parallel clauses" (1895–96, 86); he then lists Zech 1:17, 3:8–9, 6:13, 9:5, 9:7, and 12:4 as examples. Such lines, call them pentacola if poetical, appear to be unusual. Samuel Terrien's strophic analysis of the book of Psalms yields an abundance of bicola and tricoloa, "and, exceptionally, a quadricolon," but no examples of pentacola (2003, 37). In the delineation of oracular poetry found in the NJPS version, the book of Hosea exhibits only two pentacola: Hos 9:16 and the concluding exhortation at 14:10. The book of Amos likewise exhibits only two pentacola in the NJPS: Amos 4:9 and 9:11b–12, although Amos 9:5–6 might contribute another pair of them. The NJPS version of Zephaniah contains none. Robinson (1895–96, 86) credits F. B. Köster, in a monograph published in 1818, with the discovery of Zechariah's pentacola. E. B. Pusey also makes something of Zechariah's pentacola (1892, 327), citing Köster. Mitchell tries to do away with some of them by text-critical rearrangement of the text (1912, 243), but unconvincingly.

Nevertheless, examining Robinson's list, we see that in Zech 1:17 there is at best a weak case for a pentacolon; as Mitchell points out, the first two clauses are introductory, followed by a tricolon (1912, 243). In 3:8–9, perhaps a better case appears. After the introductory lines about the high priest and his colleagues, the text breaks into a *hinneh* clause (3:8d), the first of three such clauses spread out over five lines of oracular poetry, about the coming of the *Zemah* figure and the future atonement for all the land. Still a better case appears in Zech 6:13, where five parallel lines delineate the future dyarchy of the *Zemah*-ruler and the high priest. So far the cases cited for all of Zech 1–8.

The cases for Zech 9–14 are apparently more numerous. A weak case is found in Zech 9:5, which indeed has five clauses, but is better scanned as a tricolon followed by a tetracolon through verse 6. Zechariah 9:7 is a strong case, five clauses all about the adoption into Judah of the once-abominable Philistine. Likewise one may list 9:13, 10:11, and possibly 9:15. Zechariah 12:4 is perhaps another strong case, contrasting the divine protection of Yehud against the blind panic of the enemy horses. Further prosaic examples apparently occur at 11:7, 11:9, and 14:8.

However, if we discern nothing unusual regarding the number of pentacola in Zech 1–8, finding only two good cases, quite like the situation we find in Hosea and in Amos, prophetic books of similar length to Zech 1–8, it matters little if we find many cases in Zech 9–14, and so the pentacola argument fades.

However, Robinson does make some interesting claims. Among the latter, he mentions these:

> The habit of dwelling on the same thought ... twice in rapid succession:
> "I will dwell in the midst of thee" (2:14 and 2:15)
> "the branch shall build the temple" (6:12 and 6:13)
> "the nations shall seek the Lord to pray to him" (8:21 and 8:22)
> "twice he pictures ... the streets of Jerusalem" (8:4 and 8:5)
> "And I fed the flock" (11:7, twice)
> "the father and mother who bore him" (13:3, twice)
> "and ye shall flee" (14:5, twice)
> "to keep the feast of Tabernacles" (14:16, 18, and 19) (1895–96, 85–86).[88]

And this:

> The resort made by the prophet to symbolic actions as a mode of instruction; e.g., the coronation scene in 6:9–15 and the breaking of the two staves in 11:4–14 (86).

The occurrence of prophetic sign enactment reports in a book purporting to be prophetic literature is not significant by itself. However, both sides of the book employ a prophetic sign action report at a literary climax: the crown-making scene in 6:9–15, which climaxes the vision reports, and the breaking of the two shepherds' staves which climaxes the first *massa'* (11:4–17).

Finally, several scholars including Robinson mention the frequent vocative address found in both chs. 1–8 and chs. 9–14 (1895–96, 87). We find the vocative with "Zion" (הוֹי צִיּוֹן, 2:11), "Zion-Daughter" (בַּת־צִיּוֹן, 2:14); "Accuser" (הַשָּׂטָן, 3:2), "Joshua the high priest" (שְׁמַע־נָא יְהוֹשֻׁעַ הַכֹּהֵן הַגָּדוֹל, 3:8), "mighty mountain" (מִי־אַתָּה הַר־הַגָּדוֹל, 4:7), "Zion-Daughter" again (גִּילִי מְאֹד בַּת־צִיּוֹן, 9:9), "Jerusalem-Daughter" (הָרִיעִי בַּת יְרוּשָׁלָם, 9:9), "Zion" again (בָּנַיִךְ צִיּוֹן, 9:13), "Yavan/Greece" (עַל־בָּנַיִךְ יָוָן, 9:13), "Lebanon" (פְּתַח לְבָנוֹן דְּלָתֶיךָ, 11:1), "cypress" (הֵילֵל בְּרוֹשׁ, 11:2), "you terebinths of Bashan" (הֵילִילוּ אַלּוֹנֵי בָשָׁן, 11:2), and "sword" (חֶרֶב עוּרִי, 13:7).[89] There are, accordingly, five vocatives in Zech 1–8 and eight in Zech 9–14, rather high numbers for each side of the book.

---

[88] We may add to this list Zech 6:10, וּבָאתָ ... וּבָאתָ; and 10:8, וְרָבוּ ... רָבוּ.
[89] Most of these are listed by J. Stafford Wright (1965, 1356) and Harrison (1969, 954); I have added others.

These linguistic, syntactical, and stylistic features, especially when taken together, and in light of the weakness of Mitchell's lexical data, constitute grounds for raising serious questions about the Deutero-Zechariah hypothesis, and entertaining once more the thesis of the authorial unity of Zechariah. At the least, they ought to move us to place the supposed author(s) of Deutero-Zechariah close to the original Zechariah of chs. 1–8. The reader must judge whether my explanations of the Mitchell's linguistic phenomena, and my own list of unifying commonalities and shared peculiarities is sufficient to sustain this plank of my argument, or, at least, to dislodge Mitchell's argument, and thus make the matter an open case once again.

STUHLMUELLER AND GOWAN

Carroll Stuhlmueller gives a list of differences between Zech 1–8 and 9–14 (1988, 113–14), four of which are seconded by Donald Gowan (1998, 169), and are taken as evidence of change in authorship for chs. 9–14. The four are (1) the lack of personal names in 9–14; (2) the lack of explicit mention of the temple; (3) the very negative assessment of the leaders; and (4) an ethos of strong militarism. Are these arguments impressive? I discuss the differences one by one.

1) In Zech 9–14 the lack of personal names is notable, given their prominence in Zech 1–8, but perhaps this difference can be overcome by other considerations. Could it be that Zechariah was eager to promote the names of priest and governor when they were favorable to his mission, but not inclined to mention such names when he was no longer in favor with central authority figures? In this case the reticence in the rhetoric of naming could be a function of social location change. Additionally, the lack of names may be attributed to genre considerations. Many other examples of the *massa'* genre lack personal names.

2) Regarding mention of the temple: Zech 9–14 *does* name the temple, and does so under the familiar phrase בֵּית יְהוָה in 11:13, 14:20 and 14:21, a form that also appears in 7:3 and 8:9. These deutero references may seem almost incidental, but if we suppose, according to the proposal, that in Zech 9–14 the temple has been completed and has been standing long enough for a change of leadership, or a falling out between the prophet and the existing leadership, there could well be no keen interest in naming the temple. On the other hand, two of the three deutero references are not so incidental as might be supposed. Zechariah 14:20–21, with a double naming of the temple, is the climax and conclusion of the book. There the prophet sees the consummation of his desires: Zion restored, and what's more, Zion made utterly holy, from the top of the scale of significance—the temple—all the way down to the least important, trivia such as cooking pots and bridle bells. In such a view of things, the temple is no small

matter: it stood near the center of the prophet's concern at the beginning of the book, and does so again at its conclusion.

3) The negative assessment of the leaders of Yehud is easily and obviously explained by my proposal: the prophet is no longer in favor. Either new leaders have arisen who oppose the prophet—perhaps in the generation of Elnathan, Shelomith, and the high priest Joiakim—or the present leaders have turned away from the prophetic word. In either case Zechariah is the rejected shepherd who has received his severance pay of thirty pieces of silver (11:13), and no longer shepherds the flock of Yehud. Again, the thesis of social location change readily accommodates itself to this objection. In many literatures, change of rhetoric regarding the leadership is a principal evidence of social location change.

4) Stuhlmueller's mention of the strong militarism of Zech 9–14 is harder to dismiss. After all, Yahweh's word proclaimed to Zerubbabel that the theocentric restoration of Yehud would take place לֹא בְחַיִל וְלֹא בְכֹחַ כִּי אִם־בְּרוּחִי, "not by power, not by might, but surely by my Spirit!" (4:6). The "power" and "might" of 4:6 are disavowals of military force. Coercion is refused. Yet it must be pointed out that the night visions open with a scene of angelic horsemen featuring probably the theophanic *mal'ak yahweh* himself mounted on the red horse,[90] a stallion of war (1:8). The night visions end with another scene of horses: Yahweh's war-chariots going forth to the land of the north, the land of the enemy. The contrast between quietism and militarism already exists within Zech 1–8. Meanwhile in Zech 12 even the feeblest of Jerusalemites fights "like David" (v. 8); but in Zech 14 only the divine Warrior can establish the kingdom of God; human military might cannot avail. After the city has been rampaged and ravaged by the enemy, וְיָצָא יְהוָה וְנִלְחַם בַּגּוֹיִם הָהֵם כְּיוֹם הִלָּחֲמוֹ בְּיוֹם קְרָב, "then Yahweh will go forth and fight against those nations as in his day of battle in time of war" (14:3), while the inhabitants flee to safety. Both sides of the book, then, participate in the tension between quietism and war. Moreover, both sides of the book mention the *mal'ak yahweh* in militant form: as the red-horsed "man" in Zech 1:8–11, and as a fighting theophanic angel in Zech 12:8. Accordingly, these objections carry little weight.

FIVE CONDITIONS FOR A NEW APPROACH TO UNITY

I have addressed the case against authorial unity. Now it is time to build more of the case in favor. Five conditions have emerged over the last thirty years that permit the question of the authorial unity of Zechariah to be pursued more fruitfully than before. The first of these that I shall consider is the warm recep-

---

[90] So Kline (2001, 1–3), perhaps influenced by the interpretation given by Hengstenberg (n.d., 963).

tion of the proposal about the book's thematic unity put forth by Rex Mason in 1976.[91] The second is Paul D. Hanson's against-the-tide dating of the Deutero-Zechariah material to the exilic and early Persian periods (1979 [1975]), a dating that is assisted by renewed appreciation among biblical scholars of Persian-Greek conflict in the early Persian period. The third is Andrew E. Hill's historical-linguistic analysis of Deutero-Zechariah, an analysis that confirmed an early Persian-period date for the material (1982). The fourth is the work of major commentators who accepted this new dating and exploited it in constructing an important new approach to the book, an approach that has met with much approbation by the scholarly community. The fifth new condition is the concept of social location trajectories for prophetic movements, a concept discussed in incipient form by Walter Brueggemann (1979; 1994), and which I have developed in this dissertation, using case studies of prophetic religions, mainly recent, and mainly in Africa. I shall now discuss these five conditions in the order given above.

REX MASON'S "CONTINUING LINES" OF ZECHARIAN TRADITION

In 1976 when Mason wrote, the standard view against the unity of Zechariah prevailed in such a way that not even thematic unity was countenanced by many in the scholarly community. As we have seen, J. Alberto Soggin could even say, "it [is] quite clear that chs. 9–14 have nothing at all to do with chs. 1–8 of the book in question"; and that the two units are "more or less independent of each other" (1976, 347). Mason, however, put forth an influential article that demonstrated five lines of thematic connections between the proto and deutero sections of the book. He referred to these themes as "continuing lines of tradition" (1976, 227). According to Mason, then, the deutero portion was written in conscious dependence upon Proto-Zechariah, and by a continuing circle of Zecharian tradents (238). He argued that thematic connections between Proto- and Deutero-Zechariah made it likely that those responsible for completing the book viewed the deutero material as an appropriate conclusion to Zech1–8. In my estimation, and in light of the linguistic arguments put forth above, more can perhaps be made of Mason's traditio-historical connections than Mason himself claims.

---

[91] Mason's dissertation, upon which his 1976 article was based, has only recently come into print (2003). The publication appears with response articles by Petersen, Floyd, Nogalski, Boda, and others, and is edited by Boda and Floyd.

THE ZION TRADITION. The first of Mason's connective lines was the prominence of the Zion tradition in both parts of the book. Mason considered the link between the Zion-Daughter units, with their command to "sing" or "rejoice" beginning in 2:14 and 9:9, to be perhaps the strongest sign of this theme's linkage, although in his view these two texts may be editorial rather than authorial in nature. Zion receives explicit mention eight times in the book, six times in chs. 1–8 (1:14; 1:17; 2:11, 14; 8:2, 3) and twice in chs. 9–14 (9:9, 13). But this number perhaps conceals the central importance of the Zion tradition in both parts of the book.

Gerhard von Rad well described the Zion tradition as carrying (1) the idea of Yahweh's election of Jerusalem and its mountain as the place for his special dwelling, and (2) the idea of divine protection for Jerusalem against attack by the nations; as well as certain mythico-cosmic themes presenting Zion as (3) a mountain "in the far north," and (4) the location of a refreshing river (1962, 46–47).

Zechariah 1–8 witnesses to the first two of these ideas. The election of Jerusalem and its divine protection are both forcefully attested in the first vision report, where Yahweh declares, קִנֵּאתִי לִירוּשָׁלַ͏ִם וּלְצִיּוֹן קִנְאָה גְדוֹלָה, "I am passionate for Jerusalem and for Zion with a great passion" (1:14), a text that can only be described as programmatic for Zech 1–8, devoted as it is to the restoration of Yahweh's presence and people to the city. Zechariah 1:17 expressly refers to the election of Mount Zion: וְנִחַם יְהוָה עוֹד אֶת־צִיּוֹן וּבָחַר עוֹד בִּירוּשָׁלָ͏ִם, "Yahweh shall again comfort Zion, again choose Jerusalem." Accordingly, referring once more to Jerusalem, the third vision report, evoking also the Exodus-Sinai tradition, says, וַאֲנִי אֶהְיֶה־לָּהּ נְאֻם־יְהוָה חוֹמַת אֵשׁ סָבִיב וּלְכָבוֹד אֶהְיֶה בְתוֹכָהּ, "I myself will be a wall of fire around her, and I will be glory in her midst" (2:9). One could multiply the references.

Likewise in the sermonic and oracular material in Zech 7–8, the Zion tradition sounds the theme. The question about fasting which controls the unit arises precisely because of the violation of the inviolable. Jerusalem had been destroyed; disasters had shaken their world. Should fasting in regard to these disasters continue? There Yahweh reiterates his passion for Zion: קִנֵּאתִי לְצִיּוֹן קִנְאָה גְדוֹלָה, "I am passionate for Zion with great passion" (8:2); and שַׁבְתִּי אֶל־צִיּוֹן וְשָׁכַנְתִּי בְּתוֹךְ יְרוּשָׁלָ͏ִם, "I have returned to Zion and I shall dwell in your midst, Jerusalem" (8:3). The unit ends with the pilgrimage of the nations to Jerusalem (8:22).

In Zech 9–14, explicit reference to Zion is limited to 9:9, where the Zion-Daughter is urged to "rejoice greatly" in the arrival of her king, and 9:13, where Yahweh wields Mother-Zion's sons as powerful weapons against the sons of Yavan. The feminine singular pronominal endings in Zech 14:1 and 14:5 may well have the Zion-Daughter of 9:9 as their antecedent, as do the feminine singular pronouns in 9:11. If my reading of Zech 9 as an early text reused as a kind of *testimonia* to the Zechariah group's theology is accepted, then the Zion theme may also be seen as programmatic to the deutero portion of the book.⁹² The first *massa'* with its reference to Damascus (9:1), Ephraim (9:13; 10:7), Joseph (10:6), Gilead, and Lebanon (10:10) certainly has a northern interest as well, but Zion's centrality is clearly visible in the second *massa'*, where both eschatological narratives are supremely devoted to the fate of Jerusalem. The questions pursued in these texts, of Jerusalem's inviolability (12:1–8), violation (14:1–2), and inviolability restored (14:11), are clearly a continuation of the Zion tradition in light of the events of exile and return. A strong argument can therefore be marshaled that the Zion tradition provides the overall program for the book of Zechariah. And, as we have seen, the name Jerusalem appears in both sides of the book with greater density than anywhere else in the MT except for Ezra. Barry Webb may overstate matters only slightly when he writes, "The book of Zechariah is about Jerusalem from beginning to end" (2003, 33).

CLEANSING. The second of Mason's connective themes was "the cleansing of the community," a point that he linked with repentance and conversion (1976, 231, 232). Harrison concurred that "the necessity for repentance and cleansing" is present in both parts of the book (1969, 953–54).⁹³ The most obvious texts pertaining to this important theme are Zech 3 with its vision of the cleansing of the filthy, dung-covered priest, and Zech 13:1 with its wondrous announcement of the eschatological fountain that shall be opened "for the house of David and the inhabitants of Jerusalem, to cleanse them from sin and impurity" (בַּיּוֹם הַהוּא יִהְיֶה מָקוֹר נִפְתָּח לְבֵית דָּוִיד וּלְיֹשְׁבֵי יְרוּשָׁלָם לְחַטַּאת וּלְנִדָּה). If, with Ackroyd (1968, 186), we take the vision of Zech 3 to refer not only to the cleansing of a priest but also to the cleansing of the community of Yehud for whom the priest would intercede, both texts refer to the community. The main difference is that the Proto-Zechariah text refers to the prophet's own day, while the Deutero-Zechariah text refers to the future, a difference appropriate to the social location trajectory I have proposed. The kind of impurity denoted in both texts is similar. In Zech 3:3 the high priest's robes are covered in human excrement (צוֹאִים), signifying the worst forms of ritual impurity. In Zech 13:1 the house of David and the residents of Jerusalem are to be cleansed from חַטָּאת, "sin," and from נִדָּה, a term that ordinarily denotes menstrual impurity. Mason fails to point out this linkage between צוֹאִים and נִדָּה, though he cites both these texts in his discussion.

Further, in another point regarding purity not noted by Mason, is the unusual reference to inscriptions relating to the high priest in Zech 3:9 and Zech

---

⁹² Mason considered that Zech 9–10, functioned as a kind of "eschatological hymnbook" for the Deutero-Zechariah tradent group (1976, 229; 2003, 204–05).
⁹³ Harrison listed the following texts under this theme: 1:4; 3:3, 4 9; 5:1ff.; 7:5ff.; 9:7; 12:10; and 13:1, 9. J. Stafford Wright offered a similar list (1965, 1356).

14:20–21. In the vision of Zech 3 the high priest Joshua receives an engraved stone with an inscription about the future purifying of the land of all iniquity (3:9). Similarly in 14:20–21, the actual inscription on the gold plate of the high priest's turban in Exod 28:36 and 39:30, קֹדֶשׁ לַיהוָה, "Holy to Yahweh," is said to appear on horse-bridle bells and possibly the cooking pots in future Jerusalem and Yehud, denoting the holiness of the whole land. In priestly legislation, holiness is the opposite of impurity. No other texts in all the Hebrew Bible outside of Exodus mention an engraved inscription pertaining to the high priest except Zech 3:9 and Zech 14:20–21. The correlation, with its application in both texts to the whole land of Yehud, hardly seems accidental.

Similar purging texts that Mason does point out include the sixth and seventh visions of Zech 5, where thieves, false swearers, and idolatry are removed from the community. He also links the cries of חֵן חֵן לָהּ, "Grace, grace to it" in Zech 4:7, with the spiritual renewal leading to the prayer of supplication noted in the eschatological narrative in 12:10. There "a spirit of grace and supplication," רוּחַ חֵן וְתַחֲנוּנִים, is poured out upon the families of the Jerusalemites. Since the shouts of Zech 4:7 occur in the context of Zech 4:6's appeal to the Spirit (לֹא בְחַיִל וְלֹא בְכֹחַ כִּי אִם־בְּרוּחִי), the continuing line of tradition to Zech 12 seems secure, despite the fact that in 4:6 the Spirit is Yahweh's while in 12:10 it is the human spirit. One link is that this new human spirit of 12:10 is "poured out" (שָׁפַכְתִּי) from Yahweh himself.

Mason remained uncertain if the deutero use of the cleansing theme in 12:10 lay in direct continuity with Proto-Zechariah, or if the Deutero-Zechariah author looked instead to Ezek 36, where the combination of cleansing (v. 25) followed by repentance (v. 31), is also accompanied by a reference to נִדָּה (v. 17), as in Zech 12:10 and 13:1 (1976, 232–33). Although influence from Ezekiel is likely, my treatment of the terms for impurity, צוֹאִים and נִדָּה, and the linking of חֵן and רוּחַ in both texts suggests continuity within the book of Zechariah itself.

UNIVERSALISM. Mason's third linking theme was "universalism," a term he used to denote the impressive internationalism fostered in the book's vision of eschatological salvation (1976, 233). Three striking texts come to mind, all treated by Mason: Zech 8:20–23; 9:7; and 14:16–21. In the first text, two eschatological sayings appear. The first of these sayings presents "the inhabitants of many cities" (8:20), and "many peoples and strong nations" (8:22) as going up to Jerusalem "to seek Yahweh" and "to entreat his favor." In the second saying (8:23), ten pagans "from every nation" lay hold of a single Yehudean by the robe, with the plea to be taken with him—presumably to Jerusalem to worship. These are remarkable oracular sayings.

Their striking character is sustained in Deutero-Zechariah. In Zech 9:7, as we have seen, the pagan Philistine with the abominably bloody meat in shreds between his teeth is cleansed and transformed by Yahweh to become "a remnant for our God," an honored member of the Yehudean worshiping community. Not to be outdone, the pagan-turned-remnant-for-our-God idea (נִשְׁאַר גַּם־הוּא לֵאלֹהֵינוּ) is turned to again at the conclusion of Deutero-Zechariah, in what might be considered an *inclusio* theme for chs. 9–14. Zechariah 9 begins with the pagan nations of the north. Zechariah 14 ends with the pilgrimage of the nations to Zion, a theme that reprises the concluding theme of Zech 8. Chapter 14's survivors (הַנּוֹתָר; cf. the close synonym נִשְׁאַר in 9:7)[94] of the no-longer-hostile nations stream up to Jerusalem "to worship King Yahweh of the heavenly armies" at the Feast of Tabernacles (14:16), and thus to receive the blessing of rain from heaven. The reference in 14:20 to cooking pots and horses' bridle bells as קֹדֶשׁ לַיהוָה, "holy to Yahweh," includes those used by the people of the once-pagan nations, some of whom have come on horseback from afar to sacrifice at Jerusalem's altar. In ch. 14, the tradition has somewhat heightened the internationalist theme in its last occurrence in the book, but only somewhat.

The importance of this internationalist theme in Zech 1–14, Mason noted, should not be underestimated, since it is by no means common in postexilic biblical texts. Its presence in both parts of the book is nothing less than "a striking phenomenon" (1976, 234), and a strong sign of the continuity of the Zecharian tradition. I suggest that Zech 14's account of the pilgrimage of the nations stands in such close connection to Zech 8's pilgrimage theme, that the former very probably stands in literary dependence upon the latter. The author of 14:16–19 knew the text of 8:20–23, and constructed 14:16–19 to match. Rolf Rendtorff put it this way: "Here we can see a deliberate combination of the two parts of the book" (1991, 241).[95]

APPEAL TO THE EARLIER PROPHETS. The fourth of Mason's tradent themes was "the appeal to the earlier prophets" (1976, 234). Explicit reference to the "earlier prophets" (הַנְּבִיאִים הָרִאשֹׁנִים) appears, as we saw, at the outset of Zech in ch. 1:2–6, in a text that reproduces no specific text in earlier oracles, but which resembles Jer 25:5. Explicit reference to the "earlier prophets" again appears in Zech 7:7 and again at 7:12, in texts that seem to evoke Jer 17:26, and other texts in both Jeremiah and Ezekiel. The summary of earlier preaching found in 7:9–10 evokes multiple texts, but Jer 22:3 most completely. This motif of the "earlier prophets," as we have seen, forms an *inclusio* envelope for

---

[94] These two synonymous verbs, similarly in the niphal, appear as a parallel pair in Isa 4:3, וְהָיָה הַנִּשְׁאָר בְּצִיּוֹן וְהַנּוֹתָר בִּירוּשָׁלַםִ קָדוֹשׁ יֵאָמֶר לוֹ, "Whoever is left in Zion and remains in Jerusalem will be called holy" (NRSV).

[95] Rendtorff (1991, 241) sees further intentional "cross-references" between the two parts of the book: "the undisturbed security of Jerusalem" (2:8; 9:8; 14:11); "the 'covenant formula'" (8:8; 13:9); "the return of the diaspora" (8:7; 10:9–12); "the outpouring of the spirit" (4:6; 12:10); "the removal of those who bear impurity" (5:4; 13:2); "the figure of the powerless Messiah" (4:6; 9:9–10).

Zech 1–8. Nor is reference in chs. 1–8 to earlier prophetic speech limited to the oracular speeches reported in 1:2–6 and 7:5–8:23. The night visions are replete with inner-biblical allusion.

Mason correctly notes that no such explicit reference appears in Zech 9–14. But as my exposition of chs. 9–14 has indicated, in keeping with earlier scholarship at least since Hengstenberg and Stade, the author of these chapters worked with a detailed knowledge of earlier prophecy, drawing especially upon Isaiah, Jeremiah, Ezekiel, but also other prophets in the Book of the Twelve. As Meyers and Meyers note, "there is some consensus that the three Major Prophets (Isaiah, Jeremiah, and Ezekiel) are particularly prominent in this regard" (1993, 38). It is this phenomenon that lies behind Katrina Larkin's attempt to discern in chs. 9–14 an anthology of "mantological" wisdom exegetical texts (1994, 248). The designation fails, but not because of any lack of epexegetical interests in Deutero-Zechariah. As Mason writes, "allusion to the words of the earlier prophets forms the warp and woof of these chapters." Moreover, "the same significance can only be seen in them as for proto-Zechariah" (1976, 235). In other words, the purported authors of Deutero-Zechariah were as steeped in prophetic literature, or as committed to its view of reality, as the historical Zechariah.

Now, it may be that many groups in postexilic Yehud were devoted to inscripturated and inscripturating traditions. Nogalski has argued that the book of Joel draws from other books within the Book of the Twelve at least nineteen times (1993b, 290–91). He makes Joel a "literary anchor" for the redaction of the Twelve, placing much of the redactional work at a "Joel-related layer" (275–76; cf. 2000, 92, 109). In Nogalski's work, Joel is nearly a mosaic of inner-biblical quotations and allusions. Sweeney similarly traces intertextuality in Joel to Exod 10, the Day of Yahweh tradition in the prophets, 2 Chr 20, Amos 1:2 and 9:13, Mic 4:1–5 (or Isa 2:2–4), and Obadiah (2003, 143–49). Yet, as Robinson argued, *"Zech. 1–8 shows familiarity with the same books of prophecy as those so often quoted by the author of chs. 9–14"* (1895–96, 88, italics original), with the greatest dependence upon Isaiah, Jeremiah, and Ezekiel (88–89). Childs agrees: "The same blocks of authoritative scripture—notably Isaiah, Jeremiah, Ezekiel—probably already in some written form were exercising an effect on the composition of both sections of Zechariah" (1979, 482). Clearly the two portions of Zechariah treasure the same part of the still-formative Hebrew canon above all other parts. It may even be said that no other two parts of the Hebrew Bible show the same kind of dependence upon these specific books of earlier prophecy.[96]

---

[96] Mitchell (1912, 239) tries to dethrone this argument by pointing out, unlike Zech 1–8, Zech 9–14's lack of dependence upon Haggai; but Haggai's temple-dominated themes may not have been pertinent to the prophet's probative agenda in chs. 9–14.

Moreover, we should not remark inordinately about the lack of explicit citation formulae in the inner-biblical material of chs. 9–14. The same lack of citation formulae characterizes the vision reports of Zech 1:7–6:15. It is only in the contexts where the book presents the prophet Zechariah as engaged in public preaching—ch. 1:2–6 and ch. 7:4–8:23—that we have the citation formulae. This affinity of citation formulae and public preaching suggests a rhetorical strategy appropriate to the public, oral context, a strategy that may not pertain to the more literary portions of this prophetic book. Hence, while Zech 7–8 resembles Zech 1:2–6 in its method of inner-biblical allusion, Zech 9–14 resembles Zech 1:7–6:8 in respect to its method of inner-biblical allusion.

LEADERSHIP AS A SIGN OF THE NEW AGE. Mason's fifth and final line of continuing tradition was "the provision of leadership as a sign of the new age" (1976, 235). In Proto-Zechariah, Joshua and Zerubbabel are signs of Yahweh's favor for a renewal of Yehudean life. Ackroyd calls them "mediators of divine power" (1968, 199), a line which Mason quotes favorably (1976, 235–36). Georg Sauer rightly suggests that Zerubbabel stood "im Mittelpunkt" of Zechariah's thought (1967, 199), and Joshua cannot linger far behind. The image of the two olive trees fueling the work of the Yehudean restoration and the return of Yahweh's presence in Zion is powerfully compelling. But Zerubbabel was not to wear the golden crown of 6:14. That royal crown was reserved for the future *Zemah* (so Rose 2000, 46–48). Hence, even in Zech 1–8 the vision of leadership bore with the limitations of ordinary mortals.

Leadership receives a different emphasis in chs. 9–14. As we have seen, the work of the interpreter of these texts is hindered by imposing problems. Mason names three:

> It is difficult always to be sure of the exact nature of the leadership envisaged, to be sure of the consistency of the oracles concerned, and certainly difficult to detect any of the enthusiasm for priestly and messianic leadership such as marks ch. 1–8. (1976, 236)

Mason leads off his discussion with Zech 9:9–10, the only *explicit* reference to a human king in Deutero-Zechariah. There the humble, victorious king enters Jerusalem, imposing peace upon the nations, and reigning (in terms borrowed from the tradition represented in the royal psalms) "from sea to sea, and from the River to the ends of the earth." This text, Mason suggests, is curiously "detached" from its context (236)—Katrina Larkin, it will be remembered, lists it as one of her brief connective units (1994, 77)—and it may at one time have been an independent unit. Hence, it is hard to know how it fits with its 9–14 context. But Larkin has made a good case that there is compositional unity to chs. 9–14, an overall plan linking long passages together by means of brief, imperatival, metrically balanced ones (77, 221). We should treat 9:9–10, therefore, as part of the plan, and not as an isolated unit. If the reading of Zech 9 as *testimonia* for the Zecharian tradent group is accepted, then 9:9–10's messianic image of the returning king need not be taken in so isolated a way as Mason suggests.[97] The clarity and power of the singular declaration—and it is a remarkable one—may stand in lieu of frequent reference. Wellhausen correctly notes this ruler-figure arises "nicht aus der in Jerusalem herrschenden Partei der Gottlosen, sondern aus der unterdrückten der Frommen." He then adds, "Was für ein Contrast zwischen diesem künftigen König von Sion und einem alten Könige von Israel!" (1898, 189).

My interpretive decision against seeing Zech 9:9–10 as isolated finds confirmation in the soon reappearing theme of royal Davidide leadership, expressed not explicitly, but nonetheless unmistakably, in 10:4's "cornerstone," "tent peg," and "battle-bow" imagery. This hoped-for future leadership stands in radical disparity against the current leadership excoriated so impressively in the next linking unit, 11:1–3, with its threat of fire against a metaphorical "Lebanon"—the prophet's code name for the Davidides of his own day. The following unit is the shepherd sign-enactment narrative, the text that plays the central role in Zech 9–14, wherein the Davidides are perhaps again featured as among the ruthless sheep-merchants of the flock "doomed to slaughter" (11:4–17). The narrative climaxes with the prophet's curse upon "the worthless shepherd who deserts the flock" (v. 17), perhaps the current or future political leader of Yehud.

In Zech 9–11, then, there is likely a programmatic reference to the future returning king near the beginning of the unit, 9:9–10, and again in 10:4, texts that stand in contrast with the negative view of the present-day leadership in 11:1–3 and 11:4–17. Here the answer to Yehud's political and religious crisis is nothing less than the Davidic messiah.

Leadership is more ambiguous in Zech 12–14. Although prominent as a family in Jerusalem (12:12), in these texts the house of David is not clearly in charge. Some interpreters even speak of a democratization or demotion in evidence in Zech 12:7–8, where in the eschatological war the battle-honors of the house of David shall not be greater than those of common Yehudeans. Or perhaps this expectation merely reflects the negative judgment of the prophet or his tradent group about current Davidide leadership. The "stabbed/pierced" one of 12:10 and the smitten good shepherd of 13:7 may also be Davidides (perhaps the same individual?), but their (his?) role remains mysterious in Zechariah. In 13:1 the house of David receives specific mention as in radical need of cleansing. In Zech 14, it is decidedly Yahweh alone who is "king over the whole earth" (וְהָיָה יְהוָה לְמֶלֶךְ עַל־כָּל־הָאָרֶץ, 14:9), and the nations "bow down before the king,

---

[97] Mason writes, "Either we have to say that this is so detached an oracle that it is unrelated to anything else at all in these chapters ... or judgment on its significance must depend on the attitude to leadership expressed elsewhere" (1976, 236).

Yahweh of the heavenly armies" (לְהִשְׁתַּחֲוֹת לְמֶלֶךְ יְהוָה צְבָאוֹת, 14:16, 17). No human figure is singled out as Yahweh's royal representative on earth. Mason observes, "[the] emphasis in these chapters seems to swing more and more to direct divine leadership, with the human figure fading more and more into the background" (1976, 237). This seems to be the right reading of chs. 9–14. Hence, it seems unwise to posit a homologous character regarding leadership between chs. 1–8 and chs. 9–14 — except on the point that, despite differences, both sides of the book indeed portray a future Davidide in authority in Jerusalem. The absence of the future Davidide from explicit mention in Zech 14 ought not to be allowed to silence his very real appearance in Zech 9 and 10. As Meyers and Meyers write, "the difference [regarding 'the restored human king' and 'Yahweh as king'] between the two chapters [9 and 14] may be one of emphasis rather than contradiction" (1995, 221).

Mason suggests that these latter chapters stem from a time of "self-seeking, compromising, oppressive and false leadership" (1976, 238; 2003, 206–07), when hopes regarding Joshua and Zerubbabel had long faded away. But as we have seen, it is unnecessary to posit long periods of time for such a change. My supposition that Zechariah or his immediate tradent group experienced radical marginalization well accounts for the data of the exegesis. If we take Zech 9–14 as literary evidence of a social location change for the prophet or his tradent group, then we may be dealing with the next phase or generation of Yehudean state and temple leadership in these texts, the generation of Elnathan, Shelomith, and the high priest Joiakim, leadership no longer sanctioned by the prophetic community, and a prophetic community no longer sanctioned by the leadership.[98]

To summarize the perspective adopted here, in Zech 1–8 the author writes in order to bolster a nascent leader and to anticipate a messianic leadership. In Zech 9–11 the author writes to condemn a tyrannical leadership and to anticipate a messianic leadership. In Zech 12–14 the author writes to rebuke the house of David and to anticipate a divine leadership. Thus, in respect to the leadership theme, chs. 9–14 stand partly in continuity with chs. 1–8, and partly in discontinuity.

WHAT OF MASON'S FIVE LINES OF TRADITION?

What, then, of Mason's five lines of continuing tradition? The first theme, Zion/Jerusalem, provides the overall program for the book. Mason's second theme, cleansing, stands in strong continuity from the proto to deutero sections

---

[98] Mason surmised that Zech 1–8 came into finished form ca. 300 B.C. and that Zech 9–14 should not be dated earlier than ca. 250 B.C. (2003, 206).

of the book. The third internationalist theme may exhibit the strongest line of continuity in the set, marked by the twin conclusions of repentant-pagan pilgrimage to Jerusalem in 8:20–23 and 14:16–21, which Rendtorff saw as "deliberate combination" (1991, 241). The fourth theme, the appeal to earlier prophecy, points to the similar use of the same books, especially Isaiah, Jeremiah, and Ezekiel. The fifth theme, leadership and the new age, is partly homologous—both sides of the book foresee a future Davidide—and the differences can be accounted for by the hypothesis of a social location trajectory over a brief period of time. Hence, four out of five of Mason's traditio-historical themes favor at least a unitary *thematic* reading of Zech 1–14. The fifth theme is no evidence against it, and stands partly in favor as well. Moreover, these themes are not peripheral to the overall message of either portion of the book. On the contrary, these five themes highlight arguably several of the most important aspects of the message, suggesting strong continuity of ideology from Zech 1–8 to Zech 9–14. Mason's list, then, helps us construe Zech 1–14 as one complete book, rather than two or more separate books. This construal, in turn, helps us further explore the prospect of unitary authorship.

OTHER "ELEMENTS OF CONGRUITY"

Other scholars have garnered lists of common themes, but none has proven to be as influential as Mason's. Childs names eleven "elements of congruity" (1979, 482–83). The connections arise, he suggests, from two different Jewish communities in two different times reflecting upon the same body of authoritative scriptures and religious traditions (482). Among his elements are: Jerusalem under "the special protection of Yahweh" (2:5 and 9:8; 14:11); the "return of paradisal fertility" (8:12 and 14:8); the "covenant formula reiterated as a promise" (8:8 and 13:9); a curse goes out upon the land in 5:3, whereas in 14:11 the curse will be removed; "divine judgment upon the nations," but also "their ultimate conversion" (2:15; 8:22; and 14:6) "and worship of Yahweh" (8:20 and 14:16); the "collection of the exiles" (8:7 and 10:9–12); "a change in the cultic rites" in the coming new age (8:18–19 and 14:20); the "outpouring of the spirit" which brings "transformation" (4:6 and 12:10); the purging of those who swear falsely in Yahweh's name, cf. הַנִּשְׁבָּע בִּשְׁמִי לַשָּׁקֶר (5:4) and שֶׁקֶר דִּבַּרְתָּ בְּשֵׁם יְהוָה (13:3); and finally, "the messianic figure who triumphs, not by might, but in humility" (3:8; 4:6; and 9:9). Several of these are dependent upon Mason and need not occupy us further, but four of these merit comment, and may advance the main thesis.

PARADISAL FERTILITY. The "return of paradisal fertility" may well describe conditions in Zech 14:6–8, in which the ecology of the world is wonderfully overturned and miraculous rivers of life flow forth from Zion, east and west. But this description seems forced for Zech 8:12's somewhat perplexing statement, which reads, כִּי־זֶרַע הַשָּׁלוֹם הַגֶּפֶן תִּתֵּן פִּרְיָהּ וְהָאָרֶץ תִּתֵּן אֶת־יְבוּלָהּ וְהַשָּׁמַיִם יִתְּנוּ טַלָּם. Perhaps if we accept one of the text-critical emendations proposed for the elliptical phrase כִּי־זֶרַע הַשָּׁלוֹם, a different picture might emerge. LXX reads ἀλλ' ἢ δείξω εἰρήνην, "but surely I shall sow peace," which suggests אֶזְרְעָה שָׁלוֹם, with the "I" referring to Yahweh. If the divine giver in the text is himself the sower, perhaps there is a stronger link to 14:8's preternaturalism. Amsler, however, proposes to read זַרְעָהּ שָׁלוֹם, "its seed shall be peace," which retains the consonants of the text, a reading which he rightly calls "moins conjectural" (1981, 120 n. 4), and which well accounts for the present MT reading. On the other hand, we may simply have here a genuine example of Hebrew ellipsis (so Merrill 1994, 227). It seems that 8:12, then, is about a bountiful, though natural, fertility: "There shall be peaceful sowing; the vine will yield its fruit, the earth will yield its produce, and the sky will yield its dew." In this case, the deutero example may be a preternatural heightening of the proto material, in a line of traditional development.

THE COVENANT FORMULA. The link between Zech 8:8 and 13:9 in the use of the covenant formula has been noticed by several scholars. Childs rightly describes both uses as promissory. Zechariah 8:8 evokes multiple texts, especially passages in Jeremiah and Ezekiel, where the exact terms of the formula appear (הָיוּ־לִי לְעָם וַאֲנִי אֶהְיֶה לָהֶם לֵאלֹהִים, Jer 32:38; Ezek 11:20; 14:11; 37:23; cf. Jer 24:7; 31:33 and Ezek 37:27). Zechariah 13:9 evokes Hos 2:23, 25 both in its use of "I will answer" (אֶעֱנֶה) and its third-person, masculine singular variation of the covenant formula (וַאֲנִי אֶעֱנֶה אֹתוֹ אָמַרְתִּי עַמִּי הוּא וְהוּא יֹאמַר יְהוָה אֱלֹהָי).[99] Significantly, no books in the Book of the Twelve use the covenant formula except Hosea (1:9; 2:25) and Zechariah (8:8; 13:9). Also, Zech 2:15 quotes half the formula and applies it to "many nations": הָיוּ לִי לְעָם: "They shall be my people." The formula is thus nearly an *inclusio* for the Twelve. In light of its absence elsewhere in the Twelve, its presence in both Zech 8:8 and 13:9 is all the more meaningful, and, *contra* Childs, likely marks a line of continuous tradition.

CULTIC RITES CHANGED. Childs notes the "change in the cultic rites" at the coming of the new age, as seen in Zech 8:18–19 and 14:20. As argued above, these two texts truly seem to stand in a line of continuous tradition. Zechariah 14 tells how the nations shall indeed come to worship Yahweh as foreseen in the pilgrimage of Zech 8, and tells when they shall do so—at the

---

[99] See Rendtorff (1998, 93–94) for a classification of the variations of the covenant formula in the MT. He mistakenly omits the singular form in Zech 13:9. For discussion of the formula in the prophets, see Rendtorff (1998, 14 n. 20, and 31–37).

pilgrim Feast of Tabernacles. Childs has simply noted one more way in which these two parallel texts are congruent. The first text involves the anticipated future ritual change from fasting to feasting, told in answer to the Bethel delegation's inquiry to the prophets and priests in Zech 7:1–3. The second text involves a change in who shall participate in the ritual feast—the converted survivors of the pagan nations, as already anticipated in Zech 8:20–23. This congruency strengthens my aforementioned argument.

THE CLEANSING THEME. Mason has already called attention to the purging/cleansing theme of both the proto and deutero sections of the book. Childs, however, points out a further congruency on this point, the purging of those who swear falsely by Yahweh's name, comparing הַנִּשְׁבָּע בִּשְׁמִי לַשָּׁקֶר in 5:4 with שֶׁקֶר דִּבַּרְתָּ בְּשֵׁם יְהוָה in 13:3. As we have seen, the verbal combination of the term שֵׁם, "name," and the term שֶׁקֶר, "false"/"falsely," appears only nine times in the MT, eight times in the Latter Prophets, six of these in Jeremiah, and nowhere else in the Prophets except in Zech 5:4 and 13:3. It is perhaps another mark of continuous tradition in Zechariah, or perhaps a mark of the influence of Jeremiah upon both sides of the book of Zechariah.

SUMMATION. What then of Childs's "elements of congruity"? I have found probable signs of a continuous tradition in the distinctively promissory use of the covenant formula; and in the foreseen change in cultic rites. A more tenuous connection may exist in the "return to paradisal fertility" theme, and in the judgment against those who speak falsely in Yahweh's name. The case for at least a thematic and redactional unity is somewhat advanced by these considerations.[100] But in light of my social location trajectory analysis and my lexical studies, these elements can also be seen as signs of authorial unity.

A PERSIAN PERIOD DATE FOR ZECH 9–14

The second of the new conditions conducive to exploring the question of the authorial unity of the book of Zechariah is the exilic and early Persian period dating assigned the texts of chs. 9–14 by Paul D. Hanson (1979). Rightly eschewing theories of late Zoroastrian influence for the rise of apocalyptic, Hanson sought to describe a continuum between the prophetic texts of the preexilic and exilic periods and the apocalyptic texts of the postexilic period. Such a continuum did not readily permit the centuries-long division traditionally assumed between canonical prophets of the Hebrew Bible and apocalyptic texts allegedly

---

[100] Lists similar to Mason's and Childs's can be found in J. Stafford Wright (1965, 1356) and in Harrison (1969, 953–54).

from the Hellenistic age. Hanson's line of development favored a much closer historical connection between the two, making the early Persian period the eastern horizon for his dawning apocalyptic.

This bold date was rendered more acceptable by the renewed appreciation among biblical scholars for the history of early Persian-Greek conflict. I note in passing Kenneth G. Hoglund (1992), and Meyers and Meyers (1993, 18–22), and their use of A. T. Olmstead's *History of the Persian Empire* (1948) and J. M. Cook's *Persian Empire* (1983) in their work, respectively, on Ezra–Nehemiah and on Zechariah. The early Persian period began to look a more hospitable home for Zech 9–14.[101] The enthusiastic response among biblical scholars to the appearance of Pierre Briant's *From Cyrus to Alexander* (2002; French original 1996) only reinforced this appreciation.

THE HISTORICAL LINGUISTICS OF ZECH 9–14

The third of our new conditions is the rise of historical-linguistic work on the biblical Hebrew text. Though Hanson's genre-historical and history-of-religions methods were widely disputed, Hanson's results for the dating of Zech 10–14 were independently confirmed by Andrew E. Hill (1982), who used a historical-linguistic method derived in part from Robert Polzin's study of Late Biblical Hebrew (LBH; 1976).[102] As we saw, Hill discerned the probable time of origin for this material to be between 515 B.C. and 475 B.C.

Hill's 1981 dissertation on the historical linguistic investigation of Malachi provides further help in the argument regarding Zechariah. Polzin's typology of LBH (1976) included a preliminary list of possible and probable LBH terms, based on postexilic prose texts drawn from Chronicles and Ezra–Nehemiah. His list featured some eighty-four words. Hill, using Polzin's list, did a frequency search on these terms in postexilic prophetic texts, with results relevant for the present study (1981, 86–103). Of the eighty-four terms, few indeed make their appearance either in Haggai–Zech 1–8 or in Zech 9–14, and none are found in Malachi. Malachi instead tends to agree with "earlier usage rather than LBH usage" (103). Hill used this data to conclude that Malachi likely arose before the work of the Chronicler and the authorship of Ezra–Nehemiah. He found that only

---

[101] But John J. S. Perowne could observe already in 1875 that "the mention of the 'sons of Javan' ... is suitable to the Persian period ... as it was then that the Jews were first brought into any close contact with the Greeks. It was in fact the fierce struggle between Greece and Persia which gave a peculiar meaning to his words when the prophet promised his own people victory over the Greeks" (3608).

[102] For further published research on LBH, see Avi Hurvitz (1968), Gary Rendsburg (1980; 2002), Andrew E. Hill (1981; 1983; 1998) Stanley Gevirtz (1986) and Mark F. Rooker (1994). Ian Young has published a collection of such studies (2003).

two of the eighty-four terms appear in Haggai, only five appear in Zech 1–8, and only two appear in Zech 9–14 (103).

If we assume that Polzin's list is indeed indicative of LBH, then we likely should assign both Malachi and Zech 9–14 to an era before the Chronicler. If we date the Chronicler on the basis of the latest historical notices present in the book, the Chronicler may be as early as ca. 450 B.C. This date is a suggestive *terminus a quo*.

One reason for this early *terminus a quo* for the Chronicler is that the latest generation in his genealogies is not five generations after Zerubbabel (1 Chr 3:19–24, so the NRSV, based on a textual emendation), but only two generations, if we follow the MT. Martin Noth, of course, dated the Chronicler much later, to perhaps well after 300 B.C., but it will be remembered that he based his dates not on the genealogies of Chronicles, which he considered to be hopelessly supplemented by later hands, but upon details in the accounts in Ezra–Nehemiah (1987, 69–73; 165–67 [1943 original]). Now, however, the once-assumed linkage in authorship between Chronicles and Ezra–Nehemiah has been gravely in doubt for more than twenty years, if not longer (Williamson 1982, 5–11; De Vries 1989, 8–10). Dates for the Chronicler should therefore avail themselves of the data in Chronicles itself, not data from Ezra–Nehemiah. Williamson suggested that the evidence, "requires a date at least two generations later than Zerubbabel and possibly more" (1982, 16). He tentatively settled on a date somewhere around the middle of the fourth century. De Vries also listed reasons to push the date into the fourth century (1989, 16–17), but these are inconclusive. If the Chronicler worked several generations after Zerubbabel, why did he not update his genealogical lists?

Williamson's exegetical argument for a later date for Chronicles, based in large part on the alleged quotation of Zech 4:10 in 2 Chr 16:9 fails, if we accept the Meyers and Meyers thesis that Haggai–Zech 1–8 was officially promulgated by or before temple completion in 515 B.C. Williamson wrote that significant time must have passed before the book of Zechariah could be cited by the Chronicler as authoritative scripture (1982, 274–75). But as I have argued, Zechariah himself was validated as a true prophet early in his career. The completion of the temple in 515 B.C. further validated him to his Yehudean audience as a true divine spokesman (וִידַעְתָּ כִּי־יְהוָה צְבָאוֹת שְׁלָחַנִי אֲלֵכֶם, Zech 4:9). Quotation of validated oracles therefore need not be a late phenomenon. Further, it remains uncertain if 2 Chr 16:9 is indeed a quotation from Zech 4:10. One notes the interesting differences in wording and grammatical forms between the two parallel texts:

עֵינֵי יְהוָה הֵמָּה מְשׁוֹטְטִים בְּכָל־הָאָרֶץ (Zech 4:10)

יְהוָה עֵינָיו מְשֹׁטְטוֹת בְּכָל־הָאָרֶץ (2 Chr 16:9)

Both versions may be translated as, "The eyes of Yahweh range throughout the whole earth," but the English masks differences. Among the differences, the eyes of Yahweh are construed as masculine gender in the first text, but as feminine in the second. Moreover, the first one employs a construct phrase plus the resumptive pronoun, while the second does not. The two texts may both reflect some common source, perhaps a prophetic motto, otherwise unattested. Alternatively, Zech 4 could even reflect an earlier source used also by the Chronicler in constructing his account of preexilic events occurring during the reign of Asa in 2 Chr 16:7–10.

Hill's 1981 vocabulary evidence, then, places Zech 9–14 in the period before the Chronicler, with the Chronicler perhaps as early as ca. 450 B.C. Hill directly addressed the date of the deutero portion of Zechariah in a 1982 article, using different criteria, grammatical and syntactical in nature, criteria again derived from Polzin (1976). The shift to grammatical and syntactical features strengthened Hill's analysis. Factoring out the poetical ch. 9, and assessing the remainder as prose, Hill concluded that chs. 10–14 "are linguistically similar" to Haggai–Zech 1–8, stand "in contrast" to Chronicles, Ezra, and Nehemiah, and therefore "must be dated between ca. 515 and 450 b.c. [sic], a date of 515–475 b.c. [sic] being preferred" (105). He adds, "in view of the diagnostic grammatical and syntactical homogeneity of the post-Exilic [sic] prophets, there seems to be little room for recourse to other alternatives" (130). The *terminus ad quem* of ca. 475 B.C. he based on the assumed sociolinguistic dominance of exilic Hebrew among the *golah*-returnees, who would have dominated the restoration community for a maximum period of fifty or sixty years after the first returns (132).

RADDAY AND WICKMANN. The linguistic analysis of Zechariah takes a more technical turn in the hands of Yehuda T. Radday and Dieter Wickmann, in a 1975 article that appeared in *ZAW*. There the co-authors examined the question of the authorial unity of Zechariah "in the light of statistical linguistics" (30). They considered criteria such as sentence length, syllable entropy, number of phonemes per word, frequency of particles, frequency of nouns and verbs, types of nouns and verbs, transitions from one part of speech to another, vocabulary richness, vocabulary concentration, and vocabulary eccentricity.

Meyers and Meyers incorrectly assert that Radday and Wickmann argued for the authorial unity of Zechariah (1993, 30, 53). Not so. Radday and Wickmann indeed argued that "there is not sufficient evidence to postulate a change" of authorship between Zech 8 and Zech 9 (1975, 54). However, they also argued that their evidence strongly supported a break in authorship between Zech 11 and Zech 12. Based on their evidence, they also warned that one may not conclude that unitary authorship for Zech 1–11 "has indeed been proved" (54). More criteria could perhaps be discovered in support of diversity of authorship. Moreover, in their view the authorial unity of Zech 1–11 and 12–14, while "not impossible," was "highly improbable" (54).

Unfortunately, Radday and Wickmann's study is marred by several weaknesses. Frequently, it is not chs. 12–14 that stand out as distinctive in their data sets, but chs. 9–11. Such is the case with statistics for the following criteria: syllable entropy, scarcity of particles, scarcity of nonfinite verbs, vocabulary richness, vocabulary concentration, and vocabulary eccentricity. Most of these findings are not surprising, since chs. 9–11 contain the texts that are the most poetical, or the closest to poetry, in the book: 9:1–8, 9:9–10; 9:11–17, 10:1–2, 10:3–12, 11:1–3, and 11:17. Strangely, Radday and Wickmann decided to ignore the genre differences between prose and poetical units when constructing their statistical analysis, even though it was already known in 1975 that Hebrew poetry often exhibits distinctive traits in regard to several of these criteria.

Some objection could also be raised about the size of the samples in question. According to Radday and Wickmann's count, their samples are respectively 843 words for Zech 1–4, their "Section IA"; 898 words for Zech 5–8, their "Section IB"; 642 words for Zech 9–11, their "Section II"; and 739 words for Zech 12–14, their "Section III" (1975, 31). These numbers may be too small for the kinds of statistical manipulation the co-authors attempt. This problem becomes apparent when they test for vocabulary richness using a test developed by P. Guiraud that ordinarily requires a sample size greater than 15,000 words (40). As Portnoy and Petersen asserted in criticism of Radday and Wickmann, "the book of Zechariah almost surely represents too small and too heterogeneous a body of literature for statistical methods alone" (1984, 12), a statement that also applies to the lexical statistical analyses I have attempted above. Later Portnoy and Petersen rightly state that statistical studies of authorship exhibit "the necessity of having a reasonably large body of works known to be written by a specific author" (15). This we lack for Zechariah.

Portnoy and Petersen also fault Radday and Wickmann for failing to account for genre differences, especially the differences between poetry and prose. "The basic point is this: even a highly statistically significant difference in the distribution of measures ... may not indicate different authorship" in works comprised of units of poetry alongside units of prose (15). Moreover, Portnoy and Petersen identify at least five mathematical and procedural errors in Radday and Wickmann's work, errors that call their conclusions into serious question. In their own conclusions, Portnoy and Petersen affirm the traditional historical-critical distinctions between Proto-, Deutero-, and Trito-Zechariah. However, they base these conclusions more on standard literary criteria such as content, form criticism, and tradition history, which provide "warrant for discerning three distinct sections" (20), rather than on statistical grounds. Their own statistical analysis proceeds on what they themselves are willing to call "a somewhat rash statistical assumption" (16). We would do well, then, to judge the statistical results —whether those of Radday and Wickmann, or those of Portnoy and Petersen—inconclusive, and perhaps my own as well. Few doubt that there are real differences between Zech 1–8, Zech 9–11, and Zech 12–14. It is the nature of those differences that is in question. Statistics have not established the authorial unity of the book; nor have they established authorial plurality. Finally, neither study provides firm grounds for rejecting Hill's proposed dating of the deutero material.

In 1994 David I. Holmes assessed computerized author-attribution studies, and found that such studies were, so far, ill-equipped to detect changes in a single author's style over time. Genre change also adversely influences such studies. He writes:

> When works which are of various literary genres are compared (or works written during different eras), the differences observed are likely to exceed greatly any distinguishing characteristics which may reliably identify authors.... Because authors are influenced by subject matter and because their powers develop with maturity and experience, attribution methods are likely to be most reliable when texts of known authorship are of the same date and genre as the anonymous work. (88, 104).

More recently, Fazli Can and Jon M. Patton found, while comparing the early and late works of two Turkish novelists, that "there is a significant difference between the old and new works of these authors.... The change can be attributed to a natural theme shift in the new and old works or a conscious style choice made by the writers" (2004, 62). The resulting statistical profiles—involving various works published between twenty-seven years and thirty-nine years apart—resemble in many respects the profiles of works by different authors, rather than works by the same author. For reasons like these and others, Joseph Rudman concluded in 1998 that "there is more wrong with [computerized] attribution studies than there is right" (351). In view of my hypothesis of an older Zechariah authoring chs. 9–14, uncritical acceptance of either Radday and Wickmann's statistical results, or Portnoy and Petersen's, seems unwarranted. My own statistical analyses are to be taken likewise as tentative.

ACCEPTANCE OF THE NEW DATE AMONG THE COMMENTATORS

The next condition that allows for the reemergence of the question of unitary authorship for Zechariah is the friendly reception of Hanson's and Hill's dating of the allegedly deutero texts. Though still disputed by some, the new date was picked up by major commentators—Carol L. Meyers and Eric M. Meyers in the Anchor Bible (1993), David L. Petersen in the Old Testament Library (1995), and Marvin A. Sweeney in Berit Olam (2000) in the United States, and Henning Graf Reventlow in Das Alte Testament Deutsch (1993) in Germany, among others, lending the authority of prestigious historical-critical and literary-critical commentary series to the discussion. Other scholars also chimed in, voicing their general agreement—Ralph Smith: at the end of the sixth century or at the beginning of the fifth century (1984, 170); Carroll Stuhlmueller: ca. 470–460 B.C. (1988, 117); Eugene H. Merrill: "possibly into the reign of the Persian king Artaxerxes I" (1994, 63); and Paul L, Redditt: "much material from the first half of the Persian period" (1995, 99–100). Andre Lacocque, based partly on Hanson, had already agreed with this general approach for the date of 9–14: "dans le première moitié du 5e siècle" (1981, 144). David Noel Freedman also came out in favor of an early date for Zech 9–14, perhaps as early as the end of the sixth century (1976; 1991, 60).

Although all the major historical-critical and literary-critical commentators follow the Deutero-Zechariah hypothesis, this openness to an early Persian period date helps render the case for Zecharian unity arguable once more, in a way that has not been true for a hundred years, Hence, this openness among the commentators to an early Persian period date is the fourth of our five conditions.

SOCIAL LOCATION TRAJECTORY ANALYSIS

The fifth of our conditions is the social location trajectory analysis of prophets and prophetic movements that I have developed in this work. My trajectories demonstrate that prophetic claimants and prophet-led movements do indeed change social location, sometimes radically, and sometimes with relative swiftness.

Difference in social location is one of the main marks leading scholars to suppose difference in authorship from Proto- to Deutero-Zechariah. But we saw how Alice Lenshina moved to become the social center of a mass movement, the Lumpa Church, and how that movement, contending for social control, lost its bid for fledgling Zambia and in social implosion brought about its own destruction; all this in the short span of ten years. We also saw how Muhammad in about ten years moved from periphery to center, in his *hajira*-flight from Mecca to Yathrib/Medina; and in about another ten years to social center again in Mecca. We saw, too, how Kimbanguism in a forty-year trajectory moved from periphery to center in the Congo, and how Shembism moved from center to periphery in Zulu society in South Africa. Similarly in some ways, we saw how Tomo Nyirenda, the *Mwana Lesa*, despite his central-authority status among the Nyasa, was criminalized and executed along with his chief, Shaiwila. Difference in social location can no longer be viewed as firm evidence of change in authorship; instead, biblical scholars must now consider social location trajectory analysis as an important new tool in the workshop of the guild. The same Zechariah who spoke out in risky challenge in Zech 1 and again in Zech 7–8, may well be the same prophet who experienced massive rejection by his Yehudean audience in Zech 11.

Future research on this question should now assess how social location trajectories affect language. Rhetorician Stephen O'Leary has studied American apocalyptic and millennial rhetoric (1994), and observed how changes in rhetoric accompany changes in the social location of the rhetors. He has also observed how some rhetors apparently consciously change their rhetoric in order to effect a social location change, especially from the periphery to the center (183). He has suggested the term "rhetorical trajectory" to describe such rhetorical movement (185),[103] a concept akin to the social location trajectory idea.

There are real stylistic differences between Zech 1–8 and Zech 9–14. Regarding these remaining differences, I argue that social location change is accompanied by rhetorical change, and rhetorical change can serve to produce social location change. The preaching of Alice Lenshina, already thaumaturgical, became more millennialist, more militant, and more supernaturalist in the final few years of her Lumpa Church prophet-movement. Although we do not possess transcripts of her preaching, her shift in topic from mainly moral themes to millennialist themes would likely have entailed significant vocabulary changes and altered speech forms. Also, as O'Leary has shown (1994, 183, 193), the pattern of change flows the opposite direction as well. His millennialist rhetors changed their rhetoric as they sought greater political influence in mainstream North America in the 1980s.

This area of rhetorical change, and its linkage to social location trajectories, stands in need of further study. Perhaps more work like that of O'Leary, but carried out at the sociolinguistic level, can clarify for us the nature of such changes in the rhetors and rhetoric of prophetic religions.

Such study could assist in strengthening my thesis, in modifying it, or in falsifying it. Since we now possess much reportage of the preaching of Isaiah Shembe (Hexham and Oosthuizen 1996–2002), perhaps future study could examine the preaching genres and content employed by Shembe at specific points in his social location trajectory. No doubt there are other prophet-rhetors or prophet-like rhetors whose careers are susceptible to similar study.[104]

Strangely for a study of authorship in Zechariah, my research means that authorship is perhaps a less significant category for interpretation than is traditionally understood. If an author's habits can change dramatically over time, then, ironically, unitary authorship is less significant for the interpretation of texts. Authors whom we think we know can achieve the truly surprising; they can jump out of their ruts and prove to be more innovative than we had sup-

---

[103] O'Leary writes, "The tragic apocalyptic vision remains a tragic presence at the fringes of our culture, and sometimes succeeds in moving closer to its center" (1994, 193).

[104] The rhetorical trajectories of Malcom X, Martin Luther King, Billy Graham, and John Paul II come to mind as likely material.

posed. Zechariah, I suggest, is one such author. In any case, the five pillars for a late, post-Zecharian date are shown to be far less substantial than previously thought, and the hypothesis of a Zecharian origin for Zech 1–14 now becomes sustainable, plausible, perhaps even probable.

THE BOOK OF ZECHARIAH
AND THE REDACTION OF THE BOOK OF THE TWELVE

If there once were three little booklets of anonymous prophecy—the three *mas'ot* of Zech 9–11, 12–14, and Mal 1–3—on what basis were they assigned to their present positions within the formative Book of the Twelve? Why invent a name, Malachi, to apply to the anonymous third booklet, when such a name could have covered all three little booklets? The most reasonable answer seems to be that there was a tradition of attribution for two of the little booklets, Zech 9–11 and Zech 12–14, a tradition that attributed these materials to the historical Zechariah, while there was no tradition of attribution for Mal 1–3, or a tradition that the redactors wished to suppress—perhaps a humble latter disciple who did not wish his name to be put on a par with such luminous visionaries as Amos and Zechariah.

Gene Tucker has rightly observed that, in the emerging Hebrew canon, editorial identification of prophetic authors played an important role in ancient Israel in validating written prophecy as divine revelation (1977, 67). Building on Tucker's observation, Hill suggested that "understanding Zech 9–11 and 12–14 as anonymous oracles is ... suspect." "Their canonical arrangement with Zechariah 1–8 legitimately connect[s] them with a divinely commissioned prophetic figure—Zechariah son of Berechiah" (1998, 138). If this hypothesis is rejected, then we still have to construct a genuinely satisfying way of accounting for the present fourteen-chaptered form of the book, and the social matrix that created it.

Since there are no clear historical markers within Zech 9–14, I suggest that the best guide to its origin and date is its redactional location within the Book of the Twelve. What can account for its present location as comprising two of three concluding *mas'ot* for the Book of the Twelve? If the three *mas'ot* once circulated together, or were brought together independently by a redactor, what can explain the curious book-demarcating break between Zech 14 and Mal 1? I suggest that the tradents of the prophetic movement founded by Haggai and continued by Zechariah well knew the authorial origins of the three *mas'ot*. This tradent-group had brought the three units together, perhaps on one brief scroll. Then they divided the three according to the remembered tradition of authorship: two *mas'ot* were attached to the older Zech 1–8, already proto-canonical in 515 B.C. This move left one remaining *massa'*, which became the anonymous Malachi. In joining together the two parts of Zechariah, the tradents also made Haggai a separate book. The three books together then became the concluding trilogy of the Book of the Twelve: Haggai, Zechariah, and Malachi.

This redactional scenario suggests a relative dating method for Zech 9–14: canonical placement. The date of Zech 1–8, 520–515 B.C., provides the *terminus a quo* and the date of Malachi, which Hill places before 475 B.C. (1998, 83), provides the *terminus ad quem*.

Redditt suggests an interesting alternative. Malachi, minus the double appendix of 3:22–24, was originally attached to the growing scroll of the formative Book of the Twelve after Zech 8, in order to account for the lack of fulfillment of the expectations found in Haggai–Zech 1–8. This act set the number of the books as twelve, an ideal number that could not be conveniently changed. The appendices to Mal 3 were then added as a canon-closer. Then Zech 9–14, which postdated Malachi, had to be tucked into a preexisting book. Placing this Persian-period literature between Haggai and Zech 1–8 was not an option, Redditt, suggests, because of the close thematic and redactional connections between Hag and Zech 1–8; hence, they were placed after Zech 1–8 (Redditt 1996, 258–61).

However, Redditt's proposed redactor had other, perhaps more attractive, options. He could have retained Haggai–Zech 1–8 as a single book, as would happen with Ezra–Nehemiah, thus making room for a book between Zech 8 and Malachi while retaining the number twelve. Alternatively, he could have made a single concluding book of the three *mas'ot* he had received, Malachi, already in the scroll, plus the two similarly proportioned *mas'ot*. This is an attractive option especially if the name Malachi is taken as a title, rather than as a proper name. But, if all three *mas'ot* were truly anonymous, why divide them in the strange manner in which they now appear?

It seems best, then, to take the three *mas'ot* as redacted together, as literary remains of the same circle of prophets and tradents. In such a case, the tradent-redactors, based on the remembered tradition of Zecharian attribution, assigned the first two *mas'ot*, to become Zech 9–11 and 12–14, and the final *massa'* to become the book of Malachi, the anonymous divine messenger.

9

CONCLUSION: UP THE STEEP AND STONY ROAD

I have argued above, following recent commentators and historical-linguistic investigation, for the probability—or at least the plausibility—that Zech 9–14 originated in the early Persian period, ca. 515–475 B.C. I have also argued, *contra* the consensus of scholarship, for the probability, or again the plausibility, that the historical Zechariah was the author of the allegedly deutero material. If Zechariah was about twenty-five ± five years old in 520 B.C., a likely age given his grandfather Iddo's active status in the chief priesthood at that time (Neh 12:4), then he would have been born ca. 545 B.C. ± five years, and he would have been about sixty ± five years old in 485 B.C., within the range of a healthy human lifetime to accommodate most of Hill's prospective date-range. All the biblical literature that now bears Zechariah's name could well have been written within this time frame. If we consider the swift social location trajectories of Alice Lenshina, Tomo Nyirenda, and Muhammad, all of the Zechariah material in its trajectory could have been produced in as little as ten years, from 520 to ca. 510 B.C.

As I have tried to demonstrate in these chapters, prophetic claimants, and prophet-led movements change social location, sometimes swiftly. They move from center to periphery, as did Alice Lenshina and her Lumpa Church, or Shembism in its second and third generations, or Tomo Nyirenda and his chief Shaiwila; or from periphery to center, as did Muhammad and his nascent Islamic *umma*, or Kimbanguism in the Congo. A social location trajectory for the prophet Zechariah ably explains the present shape of the book, fulfilling what Michael H. Floyd called for in 1999, the search for "the sociohistorical context forming the matrix for the book as a whole" (262). Such a trajectory readily accounts for the lack of names, the negative assessment of Yehud's leadership, the reduced role of the house of David (in chs. 12–14), the putative absence of focus on the temple, and the attitude of divine judgment toward the leaders and populace found in Zech 9–14. Such a trajectory accounts for the sociohistorical differences and may perhaps also account for the linguistic, stylistic, and rhetorical differences that indeed distinguish Zech 1–8 from Zech 9–14.

I have also argued that Hanson was in error about "the ignominious path upon which the prophetic office was sent by Haggai and Zechariah" (1979, 247). Theirs was not a servile and uncritical service of a specific political system. Hanson's position is easier to sustain when Zech 9–14 is shorn from chs. 1–8.

But even so, Haggai began his prophetic experience with risky, accusative speech (1:1–11); and Zechariah likewise began his prophetic career with risky, accusative speech (1:2–6) and sustained more such speech later in his career (7:4–13). Even taken alone, Zech 1–8 is not uncritical. If my reconstruction is correct, Zechariah continued this risky prophetic behavior, as attested in the texts that also bear his name, in Zech 9–14. Zechariah 11:4–17 is a record of prophet-rejection and marginalization; Sweeney even thought that this narrative may have derived from the historical Zechariah (2000, 566).

Hanson rightly saw that much of the message of Zechariah sought to bolster fledgling Yehud socially, politically, and theologically. Such was indeed the case in chs. 1–8, and, I would claim, these broad concerns continued to occupy the prophet in chs. 9–14. Zechariah's early prophetic work in support of Yehud was socially and politically necessary and theologically justified. Yehud needed to be consolidated as Yahweh's domain in the world. The fledgling work of reconstruction—sapped as it was by self-interest early in 520 B.C., and later by the "buyers" and "sellers" and "worthless shepherds" of ch. 11—needed divine guidance and support if it was to survive and thrive.

It is sometimes said that the preacher's work is "to comfort the afflicted and to afflict the comfortable." That saying is descriptive of the work of Zechariah. Zechariah withdrew his support when Yehud's leaders no longer sought justice or heeded the prophetic word. We may admire Hanson's rhetoric when he says that a "revolutionary element" is "always an essential ingredient in genuine prophecy" (247). But if one means by "revolutionary" that prophecy must *always* stand at the sidelines, at the social margins, in radical critique of human insufficiency, then a misunderstanding cripples work that would take the Hebrew prophets as its models. Prophecy is meant to be lived. The prophetic and the practical are not necessarily at odds one with another. Obedience is possible by grace. Zechariah 1–8 testifies to the achievability of obedience; Zech 9–14 testifies to its fragility.

Sociologist Theodore E. Long argued that prophetic charisma operates at the social periphery, or arises at the social center, or appears anywhere along the social spectrum (1986; 1988). I offer, then, a three-fold typology. There are prophets of reform, standing at some critical distance from social institutions and central authority figures, addressing areas of critical need, while remaining unalienated from society. Haggai and Zechariah both began their careers as such prophets of reform. Perhaps Malachi is another.

There are also prophets of the center, as Haggai and Zechariah came to be when their messages were embraced by their audience society and by its central authority figures. Such prophets provide a sacred core (Shils 1961; 1965), a foundation upon which to build a social world. But this status is always subject to critical reevaluation and redirection. Such prophets must maintain the freedom of God who always transcends human society. Zechariah demonstrated his critical freedom in the shepherd sign-enactment of 11:4–17, when he and his insistent message were rejected by his community and its central authority figures.

Hence, there are also prophets of the periphery, prophets who speak messages of radical judgment such as we see in Zech 10–14. These messages perhaps are no longer heard by society at large, but only by small tradent groups who preserve the tradition of deep dissent.

Finally, we see that a single prophet may occupy all three of these social locations in the course of his or her career. Such was the career of Zechariah, if my hypothesis is accepted.

The main observation I have put forth in these chapters is, at root, a simple one. It is that prophetic religions can change swiftly. In the book of Zechariah we see an example of a text about prophetic religion in social location change. That change may have been centuries long, as Stade thought in 1881; it may have been about a century long, as Hanson thought in 1979. My claim is that it may have been only a few decades long, or even a single decade, and perhaps all within the experience of a single mind, the mind of Zechariah ben-Berechiah ben-Iddo. I have argued that the unity of Zechariah is congruent with the data of the text and with the data of the sociology and cultural anthropology of prophetic religions. That unity may exist at the redactional level: a single group of tradents in a community established by the historical Haggai and Zechariah may be responsible for the whole book over one or two generations of time. My empirical evidence can perhaps be read in that manner. Or that unity may exist at an authorial level, over a lifetime of a single prophet. The best explanation for the current shape of the book, with the first two *mas'ot* assigned to the Zechariah portion and the third *massa'* assigned to an independent place in the Book of the Twelve as the concluding book of Malachi, is the latter of these two views. Unitary authorship for the book of Zechariah cannot be positively proved. Yet my social location trajectory for the authorial unity of Zechariah makes for a plausible, perhaps even probable, scenario.

Zechariah was no crony of politicos, sold out to a hieratic or Davidide establishment. He began his prophetic career as a critic of his culture (Zech 1:2–6), engaging in risky denunciation and exhortation. With his warnings embraced by his society, he along with his predecessor Haggai became its prophetic guides, providing divine sanction for its nascent leadership, Zerubbabel the Davidide governor and Joshua the high priest, and assisting in the refounding of the institutions of temple-based religion in Persian period Yehud (Ezra 5:1–2 and 6:14). The fledgling subprovince needed solid footing if its people were to survive and thrive as the people of Yahweh. Tradition maintenance is a legitimate prophetic calling, especially in weak societies. But, *contra* Hanson, this divine sanction was not in the uncritical service of an establishment, not even a temple establishment. Zechariah 9–10 indeed sets out a hope for a future Davidic king. But Zech 10–13 shows the prophet capable of scathing denunciation of Yehud's leaders, with its call for the fires of judgment upon metaphorical "Lebanon"—the house of the Davidides (11:1–3) — and with its tale of denunciation and renunciation in the Shepherd Allegory of 11:4–17. In the latter, Zechariah the prophet-shepherd tells the story of his radical rejection of, and by, his flock, the people of Yehud and their misguided leaders. Jerusalem thus must undergo divine judgment and purging once again (13:8–9; 14:1–2).

Yet again in Judean history a remnant must be purified and saved (13:1; 14:3–5). Only now the purified remnant shall be joined by the remnant of the nations in worshiping Yahweh (14:16), in a land purged of all evil, holy through and through. "Hard it is, very hard," to travel up that steep and stony road of prophetic calling, of prophetic obedience. Yet Zechariah the prophet trod that steep and stony road, toward a better hope for his world, and perhaps for our world as well.

WORKS CITED

Aberle, David. 1972 [1962]. A Note on Relative Deprivation Theory as Applied to Millenarian and Other Cult Movements. Pages 527–531 in *Reader in Comparative Religion: An Anthropological Approach*. Edited by W. A. Lessa and E. Z. Vogt. 3d ed. New York: Harper and Row.
Abrams, P. 1982. *Historical Sociology*. Ithaca, N.Y.: Cornell University Press.
Ackroyd, Peter R. 1951. Studies in the Book of Haggai, Part 1. *JJS* 2:163–76.
———. 1952. Studies in the Book of Haggai, Part 2. *JJS* 3:1–13.
———. 1953. Criteria for the Maccabean Dating of the Old Testament Literature. *VT* 3:113–32.
———. 1956. Some Interpretive Glosses in the Book of Haggai. *JJS* 7:163–7.
———. 1958. Two Old Testament Historical Problems in the Early Persian Period. *JNES* 17:13–27.
———. 1962. Zechariah. Pages 646–55 in *Peake's Commentary on the Bible*. Edited by Matthew Black. London: Nelson.
———. 1968. *Exile and Restoration: A Study of Hebrew Thought of the Sixth Century B.C.* OTL. Philadelphia: Westminster Press.
Adams, James Luther, and Thomas Mikelson. 1987. Legitimation. Pages 499–509 in vol. 8 of *The Encyclopedia of Religion*. Edited by Mircea Eliade. 16 vols. New York: Macmillan.
Aelred, Cody. 1990. *Haggai, Zechariah, Malachi*. Pages 349–61 in *The New Jerome Biblical Commentary*. Edited by Raymond E. Brown, Joseph A. Fitzmyer, and Roland E. Murphy. Englewood Cliffs, N.J.: Prentice Hall.
Aharoni, Yohanan, and Michael Avi-Yonah. 1977. *The Macmillan Bible Atlas*. New York: Macmillan.
Ahlström, Gösta W. 1968. Solomon, the Chosen One. *History of Religions* 8:93–110.
Albertz, Rainer. 1994. *A History of Israelite Religion in the Old Testament Period*. 2 vols. Translated by John Bowden. OTL. Louisville: Westminster John Knox.
———. 2003. *Israel in Exile: The History and Literature of the Sixth Century B.C.E.* Translated by David Green. Studies in Biblical Literature 3. Atlanta: Society of Biblical Literature.
Albright, William F. 1942a. King Joiakim in Exile. *BA* 5:49–55.
———. 1942b. Review of Robert H. Pfeiffer, *Introduction to the Old Testament*. *JBL* 61:111–26.
Alexander, Fran, Alan Isaacs, Jonathan Law, and Peter Lewis, editors. 1998. *Encyclopedia of World History*. Oxford: Oxford University Press.
Alter, Robert. 1981. *The Art of Biblical Narrative*. New York: Basic Books.
———. 1990. *The World of Biblical Literature*. New York: Basic Books.

Amsler, Samuel. 1981. *Aggée, Zacharie 1–8.* Pages 11–125 in *Aggée, Zacharie, Malachie.* Vol. 11c of *Commentaire de L'ancien Testament.* By Samuel Amsler, André Lacocque and René Vuilleumier. Neuchatel: Delachaux et Niestlé.

Andersen, Francis I. and A. D. Forbes. 1983. "Prose Particle" Counts of the Hebrew Bible. Pages 165–83 in *The Word of the Lord Shall Go Forth.* Edited by Carol L. Meyers and M. O'Connor. Winona Lake, Ind.: Eisenbrauns.

Andersson, Efraim. 1958. *Messianic Popular Movements in the Lower Congo.* Uppsala: Almquist and Wiksells Boktryckeri.

Armstrong, Karen. 1992. *Muhammad: A Biography of the Prophet.* San Francisco: HarperSanFrancisco.

———. 1994. *A History of God. The 4,000-Year Quest of Judaism, Christianity and Islam.* New York: Knopf.

Baker, David W. 1999. Israelite Prophets and Prophecy. Pages 266–94 in *The Face of Old Testament Studies: A Survey of Contemporary Approaches.* Edited by David W. Baker and Bill T. Arnold. Grand Rapids: Baker.

Baldwin, Joyce G. 1972. *Haggai, Zechariah, Malachi.* TOTC 24. Downers Grove: InterVarsity Press.

Barnes, D. F. 1978. Charisma and Religious Leadership: An Historical Analysis. *JSSR* 17:1–18.

Baron, David. 1972. *The Vision and Prophecies of Zechariah.* 2d ed. London: Hebrew Christian Testimony to Israel, 1919. Repr. Grand Rapids: Kregel.

Barratt, Brian. 1987. The Alice Lenshina Story: A Personal Account, pages 1–7. Cited March 20, 2003. Online: http://www.nrz.connectfree.co.uk/Brian Barratt/ LenshinaLHSbot.html

Barrett, David B. 1968. *Schism and Renewal in Africa: An Analysis of Six Thousand Contemporary Religious Movements.* International African Institute. Nairobi: Oxford University Press.

Barrett, David B., ed. 1982. *World Christian Encyclopedia: A Comparative Survey of Churches and Religions in the Modern World, A.D. 1900–2000.* Nairobi: Oxford University Press.

Barrett, David B., George T. Kurian and Todd M. Johnson, eds. 2001. *World Christian Encyclopedia.* Vol. 1 of *World Christian Encyclopedia.* 2d ed. New York: Oxford University Press.

Bedford, Peter R. 2001. *Temple Restoration in Early Achaemenid Judah.* Leiden: Brill.

Bellah, Robert N., et al. 1985. *Habits of the Heart: Individualism and Commitment in American Life.* Berkeley: University of California Press.

Bendix, R. 1960. *Max Weber: An Intellectual Portrait.* Garden City, N.Y.: Doubleday.

Ben Zvi, Ehud 1996. Twelve Prophetic Books or "The Twelve": A Few Preliminary Considerations. Pages 125–56 in *Forming Prophetic Literature: Essays on Isaiah and the Twelve in Honor of John D. W. Watts.* Edited by James W. Watts and Paul R. House. JSOTSup 235. Sheffield: Sheffield Academic Press.

Berger, Peter. 1963. Charisma and Religious Innovation: The Social Location of Israelite Prophecy. *ASR* 28: 940–50.

Berlin, Adele. 1994. *Zephaniah.* AB 25D. Edited by David Noel Freedman. Garden City, N.Y.: Doubleday.

Berquist, Jon L. 1995. *Judaism in Persia's Shadow: A Social and Historical Approach.* Minneapolis: Fortress.
Betlyon, John W. 1986. The Provincial Government of Persian Period Judah and the Yehud Coins. *JBL* 105:633–42.
———. 2006. A People Transformed: Palestine in the Persian Period. *NEA* 68.4–58.
Beuken, W. A. F. 1967. *Haggai–Sacharja 1–8: Studien zur Überlieferungsgeschichte der Frühnachexilischen Prophetie.* Assen: Van Gorcum.
Beyer, Bryan E. 1992. Zerubbabel. Pages 1084–86 in vol. 6 of *The Anchor Bible Dictionary.* Edited by David Noel Freedman. New York: Doubleday.
Biblia Hebraica Stuttgartensia. 1983. Edited by K. Elliger and W. Rudolph. Stuttgart: Deutsche Bibelgesellschaft.
Bickerman, Elias J. 1980. *Chronology of the Ancient World.* Ithaca, N.Y.: Cornell University Press.
———. 1984. Calendars and Chronology. Pages 60–69 in *Introduction: The Persian Period.* Volume 1 of *The Cambridge History of Judaism.* 3 vols. Edited by W. D. Davies and Louis Finkelstein. Cambridge: Cambridge University Press.
Blenkinsopp, Joseph. 1983. *A History of Prophecy in Israel; From the Settlement in the Land to the Hellenistic Period.* Philadelphia: Westminster Press.
———. 1988. *Ezra–Nehemiah.* OTL. Philadelphia: Westminster.
———. 1991. Temple and Society in Achaemenid Judah. Pages 22–53 in *The Persian Period.* Edited by Philip R. Davies. Second Temple Studies 1. JSOTSup 117. Sheffield: JSOT Press.
———. 1995. *Sage, Prophet, Priest: Religious and Intellectual Leadership in Ancient Israel.* Library of Ancient Israel. Louisville, Ky: Westminster John Knox.
———. 1996. *A History of Prophecy in Israel.* Rev. ed. Louisville, Ky: Westminster John Knox.
———. 1998. The Judaean Priesthood during the Neo-Babylonian and Achaemenid Periods: A Hypothetical Reconstruction. *CBQ* 60:25–43.
Bloomhardt, Paul F. 1928. The Poems of Haggai. *HUCA* 5:153–95.
Boda, Mark J. 2000. Haggai: Master Rhetorician. *Tyndale Bulletin* 51:295–304.
———. 2001. Oil, Crowns and Thrones: Prophet, Priest and King in Zechariah 1:7–6:15. *Journal of the Hebrew Scriptures* 3. N.p. Cited 30 December 2004. Online: http://www.arts.ualberta.ca/JHS/Articles/article_22. htm
———. 2003. Zechariah: Master Mason or Penitential Prophet? In *Yahwism after the Exile: Perspectives on Israelite Religion in the Persian Era.* Edited by Rainer Albertz and Bob Becking. Studies in Theology and Religion 5. Assen: Van Gorcum.
———. 2005. Terrifying the Horns: Persia and Babylon in Zechariah 1:7–6:15. *CBQ* 67:22–41.
Boda, Mark J. and Michael H. Floyd, eds. 2003. *Bringing out the Treasure: Inner Biblical Allusion in Zechariah 9–14.* JSOTSup 370. London: Sheffield Academic Press.
Bodley, R. 1946. *The Messenger: The Life of Muhammed.* New York: Greenwood.
Bond, George C. 1979. A Prophecy that Failed: The Lumpa Church of Uyombe, Zambia. Pages 137–160 in *African Christianity: Patterns of Religious Continuity.* Edited by George C. Bond, Walton Johnson and Sheila S. Walker. New York: Academic Press.

Bond, George C. 1987. Lenshina, Alice. Pages 513–14 in vol. 8 of *The Encyclopedia of Religion*. Edited by Mircea Eliade. 16 volumes. New York: Macmillan.

Bond, George C., Walton Johnson and Sheila S. Walker, eds. 1979. *African Christianity: Patterns of Religious Continuity*. New York: Academic Press.

Bormann, Ernest G. 1972. Fantasy and Rhetorical Vision: The Rhetorical Criticism of Social Reality. *Quarterly Journal of Speech* 58:396–407.

Bowen, John R. 2005. *Religions in Practice: An Approach to the Anthropology of Religion*. 3d ed. Boston: Allyn and Bacon.

Briant, Pierre. 1992. Persian Empire. Pages 236–44 in vol. 5 of *The Anchor Bible Dictionary*. Edited by David Noel Freedman. New York: Doubleday.

———. 2002. *From Cyrus to Alexander: A History of the Persian Empire*. Translated by Peter T. Daniels. Winona Lake, Ind: Eisenbrauns.

Brockman, Norbert C., ed. 1994. Lenshina Mulenga Mubisha, Alice. *An African Biographical Dictionary*. Santa Barbara, California: ABC-CLIO. Cited March 20, 2003. Online: http://www.gospelcom.net/dacb/stories/zambia/lenshina1_alice.html

Brown, F., S. R. Driver, and C. A. Briggs, eds., 1907. *Hebrew and English Lexicon of the Old Testament*. Oxford: Clarendon Press.

Brown, J. P. 1983. Men of the Land and the God of Justice in Greece and Israel. *ZAW* 95:376–402.

Brueggemann, Walter. 1978. *The Prophetic Imagination*. Philadelphia: Fortress.

———. 1979. Trajectories in Old Testament Literature and the Sociology of Ancient Israel. *JBL* 98: 161–85.

———. 1989. Prophetic Ministry: A Sustainable Alternative Community. *Horizons in Biblical Theology*. 11:1–33.

———. 1994. *A Social Reading of the Old Testament: Prophetic Approaches to Israel's Communal Life*. Edited by Patrick D. Miller. Minneapolis: Fortress.

Buthelezi, Mangosutho. 2001. Unveiling of the Plaque of the Shembe House Museum: Remarks by Mangosutho Bethelezi, MP, Minister of Home Affairs and President, Inkatha Freedom Party, December 21, 2001. Cited March 18, 2003. http://www.ifp .org.za/speeches/211201sp.htm.

Butterworth, Mike. 1992. *Structure and the Book of Zechariah*. Sheffield: JSOT Press.

Calvin, John. n.d. *The Minor Prophets*. Vol. 6 of *Calvin's Commentaries*. 6 volumes. Grand Rapids: Associated Publishers and Authors.

Can, Fazli, and Jon M. Patton. 2004. Change of Writing Style over Time. *Computers and the Humanities* 38:61–82.

Carroll Robert P. 1979. *When Prophecy Failed: Cognitive Dissonance in the Prophetic Traditions of the Old Testament*. New York: Seabury Press.

———. 1990. Whose Prophet? Whose History? Whose Social Reality? Troubling the Interpretive Community Again: Notes Toward a Response to Thomas W. Overholt's Critique. *JSOT* 48:33–49.

Carter, Charles E. 1994. The Province of Yehud in the Post-exilic Period: Soundings in Site Distribution and Demography. Pages 106–45 in *Temple and Community in the Persian Period*. Edited by Tamara C. Eshkenazi and Kent H. Richards. Second Temple Studies 2. JSOTSup 175. Sheffield: JSOT Press.

———. 1999. *The Emergence of Yehud in the Persian Period: A Social and Demographic Study*. JSOTSup 294. Sheffield: Sheffield Academic Press.

Works Cited

Carter, Charles E., and Carol L. Meyers. 1996. *Community, Identity and Ideology: Social Science Approaches to the Hebrew Bible*. Sources for Biblical and Theological Study 6. Winona Lake, Ind.: Eisenbrauns.
Chary, T. 1955. *Les Prophètes et le Cult à Partir de L'exil*. Tournai, Belgium: Desclée.
Childs, Brevard S. 1979. *Introduction to the Old Testament as Scripture*. Philadelphia: Fortress.
———. 2001. *Isaiah: A Commentary*. OTL. Louisville: Westminster John Knox.
Chisholm, Robert B. 2002. *Handbook on the Prophets*. Grand Rapids: Baker Academic.
Clark, David J. 1985. Discourse Structure in Zechariah 7.1–8.23. *The Bible Translator* 36:328–35.
Clarke, David L. 1978. *Analytical Archaeology*. 2d ed. New York: Columbia University Press.
Cody, Aelred. 1990. Zechariah. Pages 352–59 in *The New Jerome Biblical Commentary*. Edited by Raymond E. Brown, Joseph A. Fitzmyer and Roland E. Murphy. Englewood Cliffs, NJ: Prentice-Hall.
Coggins, Richard J. 1987. *Haggai, Zechariah, Malachi*. Old Testament Guides. Sheffield: JSOT Press.
———. 1989. After the Exile. Pages 227–49 in *Creating the Old Testament: The Emergence of the Hebrew Bible*. Edited by Stephen Bigger. Oxford: Basil Blackwell.
Collins, Jeff, et al. 2004. Detecting Collaboration in Text: Comparing the Authors' Rhetorical Language Choices in *The Federalist Papers*. *Computers and the Humanities* 38:15–36.
Collins, John J. 1984. *Daniel, with an Introduction to Apocalyptic Literature*. FOTL 20. Grand Rapids: Eerdmans.
Conrad, Edgar W. 1999. *Zechariah*. Sheffield: Sheffield Academic Press.
Cook, John Manuel. 1983. *The Persian Empire*. New York: Schocken.
Cook, Stephen L. 1995. *Prophecy and Apocalypticism: The Postexilic Setting*. Minneapolis: Fortress.
Cooper, Lamar E. *Ezekiel*. NAC 17. Edited by E. Ray Clendenen. N.p.: Broadman & Holman.
Coote, Robert. 1981. *Amos Among the Prophets: Composition and Theology*. Philadelphia: Fortress.
Craig, Kenneth M. 1996. Interrogatives in Haggai–Zechariah: A Literary Thread? Pages 224–44 in *Forming Prophetic Literature: Essays on Isaiah and the Twelve in Honor of John D. W. Watts*. Edited by James W. Watts and Paul R. House. JSOTSup 235. Sheffield: Sheffield Academic Press.
Cross, Frank Moore. 1975. A Reconstruction of the Judean Restoration. *JBL* 94:4–18.
———. 1995. Toward a History of Hebrew Prosody. Pages 298–309 in *Fortunate the Eyes that See: Essays in Honor of David Noel Freedman in Celebration of his Seventieth Birthday*. Edited by Astrid B. Beck, et al. Grand Rapids: Eerdmans.
Culley, Robert C. and Thomas W. Overholt, eds. 1982. *Anthropological Perspectives on the Old Testament*. Semeia 21.

Curtis, Byron G. 1996. Review of Kenneth G. Hoglund, *Achaemenid Imperial Administration in Syria-Palestine and the Missions of Ezra and Nehemiah*. *JETS* 39:649–50.

———. 2000. The Zion-Daughter Oracles: Evidence on the Identity and Ideology of the Late Redactors of the Book of the Twelve. Pages 166–84 in *Reading and Hearing the Book of the Twelve*. Edited by James D. Nogalski and Marvin A. Sweeney. SBL Symposium Series 15. Atlanta: Society of Biblical Literature.

———. 2003. After the Exile: Haggai and History. Pages 300–20 in *Giving the Sense: Understanding and Using Old Testament Historical Texts*. Edited by David M. Howard and Michael A. Grisanti. Grand Rapids: Kregel Academic.

Cutter, Charles H. 2004. *Africa 2004*. Harpers Ferry, W.Va.: Stryker-Post.

Davenport, T. R. H. 1977. *South Africa: A Modern History*. Toronto: University of Toronto Press.

Davies, Philip R. 1991. *Persian Period*. Second Temple Studies 1. JSOTSup 117. Sheffield: JSOT Press.

Davies, Philip R., and John M. Halligan. 2002. *Studies in Politics, Class and Material Culture*. Second Temple Studies 3. JSOTSup 340. Sheffield: Sheffield Academic Press.

Davies, W. D., and Louis Finkelstein, eds. 1984. *Introduction: The Persian Period*. Vol. 1 of *The Cambridge History of Judaism*. Cambridge, Mass.: Cambridge University Press.

Davis, Ellen F. 1989. *Swallowing the Scroll. Textuality and the Dynamics of Discourse in Ezekiel's Prophecy*. JSOTSup 78. Bible and Literature Series 21. Sheffield: Almond Press.

De Vries, Simon J. 1989. *1 and 2 Chronicles*. FOTL 11. Grand Rapids: Eerdmans.

Dearman, J. Andrew. 1992. *Religion and Culture in Ancient Israel*. Peabody, Mass.: Hendrikson.

Delcor, M. 1952. Les Sources du Deutéro-Zacharie et ses Procédés d'Emprunt. *RB* 59:385–411.

Denny, Frederick M. 1987. *Islam and the Muslim Community*. The Religious Traditions of the World. Edited by H. Byron Earhart. San Francisco: HarperCollins.

Didymus the Blind. 2006. *Commentary on Zechariah*. Translated by Robert C. Hill. Fathers of the Church 111. Washington, D. C.: Catholic University of America Press.

Donovan, James M. 2003. Defining Religion. Pages 61–98 in *Selected Readings in the Anthropology of Religion: Theoretical and Methodological Essays*. Contributions to the Study of Anthroplogy 9. Edited by Stephen D. Glazier and Charles A. Flowerday. Westport, Conn.: Praeger.

Dube, J. L. 1936. *uShembe*. Durban. [Zulu language; not seen].

Durkheim, Emile. 1947. *The Elementary Forms of the Religious Life*. New York: Free Press.

Eckardt, R. 1893. Der Sprachgebrauch von Zach. 9–14. *ZAW* 13:76–109.

Edgerton, Robert B. 2002. *The Troubled Heart of Africa: A History of the Congo*. New York: St. Martin's Press.

Eichrodt, Walther. 1961. *Theology of the Old Testament.* Translated by J. A. Baker. The OTL. Philadelphia: Westminster. Translation of *Theologie des Alten Testaments.* 6th ed. Stuttgart: Ehrenfried Klotz, 1959.
Eisenstadt, S. N. 1968. Introduction. Pages ix–lvi in *Max Weber on Charisma and Institution Building: Selected Papers.* Edited by S. N. Eisenstadt. Chicago: University of Chicago Press.
Eissfeldt, Otto. 1965. *The Old Testament: An Introduction.* Translated by Peter R. Ackroyd. New York: Harper and Row.
Eliade, Mircea. 1964. *Shamanism: Archaic Techniques of Ecstasy.* Translated by Willard R. Trask. Princeton: Princeton University Press.
Ellis, Richard S. 1968. *Foundation Deposits in Ancient Mesopotamia.* New Haven: Yale.
Emmerson, Grace. 1984. *Hosea: An Israelite Prophet in Judean Perspective.* JSOTSup 28. Sheffield: JSOT Press.
Emmet, Dorothy. 1956. Prophets and Their Societies. *Journal of the Royal Anthropological Institute* 86:13–23.
Eshkenazi, Tamara C., and Kent H. Richards. 1994. *Temple and Community in the Persian Period.* Second Temple Studies 2. JSOTSup 175. Sheffield: JSOT Press.
Esposito, John. 1988. *Islam: The Straight Path.* Oxford: Oxford University Press.
Evans-Pritchard, E. E. 1949. *The Sanusi of Cyrenaica.* Oxford: Clarendon.
Ewald, H. G. A. 1867. *Die Propheten des Alten Bundes.* 2d ed. Göttingen: Vandenhoeck & Ruprecht.
Farganis, James. 1996. *Readings in Social Theory: The Classic Tradition to Post-Modernism.* 2d ed. New York: McGraw-Hill.
Fasholé-Luke, Edward, Richard Gray, Adrian Hastings, and Godwin Tasie, eds. 1978. *Christianity in Independent Africa.* Bloomington: Indiana University Press.
Fernandez, James W. 1964. African Religious Movements: Types and Dynamics. *Journal of Modern African Studies* 2.4: 531–49.
Ferriero, Alberto, ed. 2003. *The Twelve Prophets.* The Ancient Christian Commentary on Scripture 14. Downers Grove: InterVarsity.
Fiensy, David. Using the Nuer Culture of Africa in Understanding the Old Testament. *JSOT* 38:73–83.
Finegan, Jack. 1964. *Handbook of Biblical Chronology: Principles of Time Reckoning in the Ancient World and Problems of Chronology in the Bible.* Princeton, N.J.: Princeton University Press.
Fitzmyer, Joseph A. 1967. *The Aramaic Inscriptions of Sefire.* Biblica et Orientalia 19. Rome: Biblical Institute Press.
Floyd, Michael H. 1999. Zechariah and Changing Views of Second Temple Judaism in Recent Commentaries. *RelSRev* 25.3:257–63.
———. 2000. *Minor Prophets: Part 2.* FOTL 22. Edited by Rolf P. Knierim, Gene M. Tucker and Marvin A. Sweeney. Grand Rapids: Eerdmans.
———. 2002. The מַשָּׂא (*Massa'*) as a Type of Prophetic Book. *JBL* 121:401–22.
Forbes, A. Dean. 1995. Sards, Strophes and Stats. Pages 310–21 in *Fortunate the Eyes that See: Essays in Honor of David Noel Freedman in Celebration of his Seventieth Birthday.* Edited by Astrid B. Beck et al. Grand Rapids: Eerdmans.

Freedman, David Noel. 1975. The Babylonian Chronicle. Pages 113–27 in *The Biblical Archaeologist Reader*. Vol. 1 of *The Biblical Archaeologist Reader*. Edited by G. Ernest Wright and David Noel Freedman. Missoula, MT: Scholars Press.

———. 1976. The Canon of the Old Testament. Pages 130–36 *The Interpreter's Dictionary of the Bible Supplemental Volume*. Edited by Keith Crim. Nashville: Abingdon.

———. 1991. *The Unity of the Hebrew Bible*. Ann Arbor: University of Michigan Press.

———. 1997. Another Look at Biblical Hebrew Poetry. Pages 213–26 in *Poetry and Orthography*. Vol. 2 of *Divine Commitment and Human Obligation: Selected Writing of David Noel Freedman*. Edited by J. R. Huddlestun. Grand Rapids: Eerdmans.

Freedy, K. S. and Redford, Donald B. 1970. The Dates in Ezekiel in Relation to Biblical, Babylonian, and Egyptian Sources. *JAOS* 90: 462–85.

Friebel, Kevin G. 1999. *Jeremiah's and Ezekiel's Sign-Acts: Rhetorical Nonverbal Communication*. JSOTSup 283. Sheffield: Sheffield Academic Press.

Fried, Lisbeth S. 2004. *The Priest and the Great King: Temple-Palace Relations in the Persian Empire*. Winona Lake, Ind.: Eisenbrauns.

Geertz, Clifford. 2002 [1973]. Religion as a Cultural System. Pages 62–82 in *A Reader in the Anthropology of Religion*. Edited by Michael Lambek. Oxford: Blackwell.

Gellner, Ernest. 1969. A Pendulum Swing Theory of Islam. Pages 127–138 in *Sociology of Religion*. Edited by Roland Robertson. Harmondsworth: Penguin.

Gerth, H. H. and C. Wright Mills. 1946. Introduction. Pages 1–74 in *From Max Weber: Essays in Sociology*. Edited and translated by H. H. Gerth and C. Wright Mills. New York: Oxford University Press.

Gesenius, Wilhelm. 1910. *Gesenius's Hebrew Grammar*. Edited by E. Kautzsch. Translated by A. E. Cowley. 2d ed. Oxford: Clarendon.

Gevirtz, Stanley. 1986. Of Syntax and Style in the "Late Biblical Hebrew"–"Old Canaanite" Connection. *JNES* 18:25–29.

Githieya, Francis K. 1997. *The Freedom of the Spirit: African Indigenous Churches in Kenya*. American Academy of Religion Academy Series 94. Edited by Susan B. Thistlethwaite. Atlanta: Scholars Press.

Glassner, Jean-Jacques. 2004. *Mesopotamian Chronicles*. Edited by Benjamin R. Foster. Writings from the Ancient World 19. Atlanta: Society of Biblical Literature.

Glazier-McDonald, Beth. 1987. *Malachi: The Divine Messenger*. SBLDS 98. Atlanta: Scholars Press.

Gordon, Robert P. 1995. *The Place is Too Small for Us: The Israelite Prophets in Recent Scholarship*. Sources for Biblical and Theological Scholarship 5. Winona Lake, Ind.: Eisenbrauns.

Gottwald, Norman K. 1979. *The Tribes of Yahweh: A Sociology of the Religion of Liberated Israel, 1250–1050 B.C.E.* Maryknoll, N.Y.: Orbis Press.

———. 1985. *The Hebrew Bible: A Socio-Literary Introduction*. Philadelphia: Fortress.

Gould, Stephen J. 1982. The Meaning of Punctuated Equilibrium and Its Role in Validating a Hierarchical Approach to Macroevolution. Pages 83–104 in *Perspectives in Evolution*. Edited by R. Milkman. Sunderland, Mass.: Sinauer.
Gowan, Donald E. 1986. *Eschatology in the Old Testament*. Philadelphia: Fortress.
———. 1998. *Theology of the Prophetic Books: The Death and Resurrection of Israel*. Louisville: Westminster John Knox.
Grabbe, Lester L. 1995. *Priests, Prophets, Diviners, Sages: A Study of Religious Specialists in Ancient Israel*. Valley Forge, PA.: Trinity Press International.
Greenberg, Moshe. 1983. *Ezekiel 1–20*. AB 22. Edited by David Noel Freedman. Garden City, N.Y.: Doubleday.
Grayson, A. K. 1975. *Assyrian and Babylonian Chronicles*. Texts from Cunieform Sources 5. Locust Valley, N. Y.: J. J. Augustin.
Grunneweg, A. H. J. 1983. עַם הָאָרֶץ–A Semantic Revolution. *ZAW* 95:437–40.
Hadden, Jeffery K. and Anson Shupe, eds. 1986. *Prophetic Religions and Politics*. Vol. 1 of *Religion and the Political Order*. New York: Paragon.
———. 1988. *The Politics of Religion and Social Change*. Vol. 2 of *Religion and the Political Order*. New York: Paragon.
———. 1999. Cult Group Controversies: Conceptualizing "Cult" and "Sect." Cited July 17, 2003. Online: http://religiousmovements.lib.virginia.edu/cult sect/concult.htm#scholar_v_public.
———. 2000. Religious Movements. Pages 2364–76 in vol. 4 *of Encyclopedia of Sociology*. 2d ed. Edited by Edgar F. Borgatta and Rhonda Montgomery. New York: Macmillan.
Haldar, A. 1945. *Associations of Cult Prophets Among the Ancient Semites*. Uppsala: Almqvist and Wiksells.
Haliburton, Gordon MacKay. 1971. *The Prophet Harris: A Study of an African Prophet and His Mass-Movement in the Ivory Coast and the Gold Coast 1913–1915*. London: Longman Group.
Hallo, William W. and William Kelly Simpson. 1971. *The Ancient Near East: A History*. New York: Harcourt Brace Jovanovich.
Hallo, William W. and K. Lawson Younger, editors. 2003. *The Context of Scripture*. 3 vols. Leiden: Brill.
Hanson, Paul D. 1976. Apocalypticism. Pages 28–34 in *Interpreters Dictionary of the Bible Supplement*. Nashville: Abingdon.
———. 1979. *The Dawn of Apocalyptic: The Historical and Sociological Roots of Jewish Apocalyptic Eschatology*. Rev. ed. Philadelphia: Fortress.
———. 1986. *The People Called: The Growth of Community in the Bible*. San Francisco: Harper and Row
———. 1987. Israelite Religion in the Early Postexilic Period. Pages 485–508 in *Ancient Israelite Religion: Essays in Honor of Frank Moore Cross*. Edited by Patrick D. Miller, Paul D. Hanson and S. Dean McBride. Philadelphia: Fortress.
Harrelson, Walter. 1968. The Celebration of the Feast of Booths According to Zech 14:16–21. Pages 88–96 in *Religions in Antiquity*. Studies in the History of Religions 14. Leiden: Brill.

Harrison, Roland K. 1969. *Introduction to the Old Testament.* Grand Rapids: Eerdmans.
Hayes, John H. 1988. *Amos, The Eighth Century Prophet: His Times and His Preaching.* Nashville: Abingdon.
Hayes, John H., and Sara R. Mandell. 1998. *The Jewish People in Classical Antiquity: From Alexander to Bar Kochba.* Louisville: Westminster John Knox.
Hayes, John H. and J. Maxwell Miller. 1977. *Israelite and Judean History.* London: SCM Press.
Hengstenberg, Ernst W. n.d. *Christology of the Old Testament.* 2 vols. Mac Dill AFB, Fla.: MacDonald. Repr. of 1854 translation of the four volume 1829–35 *Christologie des Alten Testaments.*
Herodotus. 1965. *The Histories.* Translated by Aubrey de Sélincourt. Baltimore: Penguin.
Heschel, Abraham. 1962. *The Prophets.* 2 vols. New York: Harper Torchbooks.
Hexham, Irving and Gerhardus C. Oosthuizen, eds. 1996–2002. *The Story of Isaiah Shembe.* 3 vols. Lewiston, N.Y.: Edwin Mellen.
Hill, Andrew E. 1981. "The Book of Malachi: Its Place in Post-Exilic Chronology Linguistically Reconsidered." Ph.D. diss. The University of Michigan.
———. 1982. Dating Second Zechariah: A Linguistic Examination. *HAR* 6: 105–34.
———. 1983. Dating the Book of Malachi: A Linguistic Reexamination. Pages 77–89 in *The Word of the Lord Shall Go Forth: Essays in Honor of David Noel Freedman in Celebration of His Sixtieth Birthday.* Edited by Carol. L. Meyers and M. O'Connor. Winona Lake, Ind.: Eisenbrauns.
———. 1998. *Malachi.* AB 25D. Edited by David Noel Freedman. Garden City, N.Y.: Doubleday.
Hill, Robert C. 2006. Introduction. Pages 1–24 of *Dydimus the Blind: Commentary on Zechariah.* Translated by Robert C. Hill. Fathers of the Church 111. Washington, D. C.: Catholic University of America Press.
Hoehner, Harold W. 2002. *Ephesians: An Exegetical Commentary.* Grand Rapids: Baker.
Hoglund, Kenneth G. 1992. *Achaemenid Imperial Administration in Syria-Palestine and the Missions of Ezra and Nehemiah.* SBLDS 125. Atlanta: Scholars Press.
Holladay, William L. 1988. *A Concise Hebrew and Aramaic Lexicon of the Old Testament.* Grand Rapids: Eerdmans.
———. 1989. *Jeremiah 2.* Hermeneia. Minneapolis: Fortress.
Holmes, David I. 1994. Authorship Attribution. *Computers and the Humanities* 28: 87–106.
Hölscher, G. 1914. *Die Profeten. Untersuchungen zur Religionsgeschichte Israels.* Leipzig: J. Hinrichs.
Holt, P. M., Ann K. S. Lambton, and Bernard Lewis, eds. 1970. *The Central Islamic Lands.* Vol. I of *The Cambridge History of Islam.* Cambridge: Cambridge University Press.
Hooper, Richard. 1922. Henry Hammond. Pages 1126–30 in vol. 8 of *The Dictionary of National Biography.* Edited by Leslie Smith and Sidney Lee. Oxford: Oxford University Press.

Houghton, D. H. 1964. *The South African Economy*. Capetown: Oxford University Press.
Hugenberger, Gordon P. 1994. *Marriage as a Covenant: Biblical Law and Ethics as Developed from Malachi*. Biblical Studies Library. Grand Rapids: Baker Books.
Hurvitz, Avi. 1968. The Chronological Significance of Aramaisms in Biblical Hebrew. *IEJ* 18:234–40.
Hutton, Rodney R. 1994. *Charisma and Authority in Israelite Society*. Minneapolis: Fortress.
Ipenburg, At. 1992. *"All Good Men": The Development of the Lubwa Mission, Chinsali, Zambia, 1905–1967*. Studies in the Intellectual History of Christianity 83. Frankfurt: Peter Lang.
Jastrow, Marcus. 1982. *A Dictionary of the Targumim, the Talmud Babli and Yerushalmi, and the Midrashic Literature*. New York: Judaica Press.
Jepsen, A. 1934. *Nabi: Soziologische Studien zur alttestamentlichen Literatur und Religionsgeschichte*. Munich: C. H. Beck.
Johnson, A. R. 1962 [1944]. *The Cultic Prophet in Ancient Israel*. 2d ed. Cardiff: University of Wales.
Johnson, M. P. 1983. Called to Be: Isangoma or Prophet? Pages 165–79 in *Afro-Christianity at the Crossroads: Its Dynamics and Strategies*. Edited by G. C. Oosthuizen, et al. Leiden: E. J. Brill.
Johnson, Walton. 1979. The Africanization of a Mission Church. Pages 89–107 in *African Christianity: Patterns of Religious Continuity*. Edited by George Bond, Walton Johnson and Sheila S. Walker. Studies in Anthropology. New York: Academic Press.
Jones, Douglas R. 1962a. A Fresh Interpretation of Zechariah 9–11. *VT* 12:241–59.
———. 1962b. *Haggai, Zechariah and Malachi*. Torch Bible Commentaries. London.
Jules-Rosette, Bennetta. 1979a. Symbols of Power and Change: An Introduction to New Perspectives on Contemporary African Religion. Pages 1–21 in *The New Religions of Africa*. Edited by Bennetta Jules-Rosette. Norwood, N.J.: Ablex Publishing Company.
———. 1979b. Conclusions: The Arcadian Wish: Toward a Theory of Contemporary African Religion. Pages 219–29 in *The New Religions of Africa*. Edited by Bennetta Jules-Rosette. Norwood, N.J.: Ablex Publishing Company.
———. 1987. African Religion: Modern Movements. Pages 82–89 in vol. 1 of *The Encyclopedia of Religion*. Edited by Mircea Eliade. New York: Macmillan.
Kamsteeg, Frans H. 1998. *Prophetic Pentecostalism in Chile: A Case Study on Religion and Development Policy*. Studies in Evangelicalism 15. Lanham, Md.: Scarecrow Press.
Keil, Carl F. 1884. *Manual of Historico-Critical Introduction to the Canonical Scriptures of the Old Testament*. Translated by George C. M. Douglas. Edinburgh: T&T Clark.
———. 1975 [1853]. *Minor Prophets*. Vol. 10 of *Commentary on the Old Testament*. Repr. Eerdmans: Grand Rapids.
Kenny, Anthony. 1986. *A Stylometric Study of the New Testament*. Oxford: Clarendon.

Kent, Roland G. 1953. *Old Persian: Grammar, Texts, Lexicon.* AOS 33. 2d ed. New Haven: American Oriental Society.

Kessler, John. 2002. *The Book of Haggai: Prophecy and Society in Early Persian Yehud.* VTSup 91. Leiden: Brill.

Keyes, Charles F. 2002. Weber and Anthropology. *Annual Review of Anthropology* 31:233–55.

Kimchi, David. 1837. *Rabbi David Kimchi's Commentary on the Prophecies of Zechariah.* Translated and annotated by A. McCaul. London: James Duncan.

Kipling, Rudyard. 1968. *Barrack-Room Ballads I.* Pages 437–498 in *The Best of Kipling.* Garden City, N.Y.: Nelson Doubleday.

Kirkpatrick, A. F. 1915. *The Doctrine of the Prophets.* London: Macmillan.

Klausner, Joseph. 1955. *The Messianic Idea in Israel.* Translated by W. F. Stinespring. New York: Macmillan.

Kline, Meredith G. 2001. *Glory in our Midst: A Biblical-Theological Reading of Zechariah's Night Visions.* Overland Park, Kans.: Two-Age Press.

Köbben, J. F. 1960. Prophetic Movements as an Expression of Social Protest. *International Archives of Ethnography* 49: 117–64.

Koehler, Ludwig, and Walter Baumgartner, eds. 1994–2000. *A Hebrew and Aramaic Lexicon of the Old Testament.* 4th ed. 4 vols. Leiden: Brill.

Kraeling, Emil G. H. 1924. The Historical Situation in Zech 9:1–10. *American Journal of Semitic Languages and Literature* 41:24–33.

Kraus, H-J. 1986. *Theology of the Psalms.* Minneapolis, Minn.: Augsburg.

"Kru." *Encyclopedia Britannica.* Cited August 4, 2003. Online: http://search.eb.com/eb/ article?eu=47366.

Kselman, J. 1985. The Social World of the Israelite Prophets: A Review Article. *RelSRev* 11:120–29.

Lacocque, André. 1981. *Zacharie 9–14.* Pages 127–216 in *Aggée, Zacharie, Malachie.* Vol. 11c of *Commentaire de L'ancien Testament.* By Samuel Amsler, André Lacocque and René Vuilleumier. Neuchatel: Delachaux et Niestlé.

Lamarche, Paul. 1961. *Zacharie IX–XIV: Structure Littéraire at Messianisme.* Paris: Librairie Lecoffre.

Lambek, Michael. 2002. *A Reader in the Anthropology of Religion.* Oxford: Blackwell.

Lang, Bernhard. 1983. *Monotheism and the Prophetic Minority: An Essay in Biblical History and Sociology.* The Social World of Biblical Antiquity 1. Edited by J. W. Flanagan. Sheffield, England: Almond Press.

———. 1984. Max Weber und Israels Propheten. *ZRGG* 36:156–65.

Lanternari, Vittorio. 1965. *The Religions of the Oppressed.* New York: Mentor Books.

Lari, S. Mujtaba Musawa. 1990. The Prophet of Islam: A Biographical Outline. *Al-Tawhid: A Quarterly Journal of Islamic Thought and Culture* 8:73–94.

Larkin, Katrina J. A. 1994. *The Eschatology of Second Zechariah: A Study of the Formation of a Mantological Wisdom Anthology.* CBET 6. Kampen: Pharos.

———. 2001. Zechariah. Pages 610–15 in *The Oxford Bible Commentary.* Oxford: Oxford University Press.

Leithart, Peter J. 1995. Death and Transfiguration of the Holy City: The Literary Structure of Zechariah 9–14. Biblical Horizon Occasional Paper 21. Niceville, Fla.: Biblical Horizons.
Leupold, H. C. 1971. *Exposition of Zechariah*. N.p.:Wartburg Press. 1956. Repr. Grand Rapids: Baker.
Levenson, Jon. 1988. *Creation and the Persistence of Evil*. San Francisco: Harper & Row.
Lewis, Ioan M. 1971. *Ecstatic Religion*. Baltimore: Penguin.
———. 1989. *Ecstatic Religion: A Study of Shamanism and Spirit Possession*. 2d ed. London: Routledge.
Lindblom, J. 1962. *Prophecy in Ancient Israel*. Philadelphia: Fortress.
Lindenberger, James M. 1994. *Ancient Aramaic and Hebrew Letters*. SBLWAW 4. Atlanta: Scholars Press.
Linton, Ralph. 1972. Nativistic Movements. Pages 497–503 in *Reader in Comparative Religion: An Anthropological Approach*. 3d ed. Edited by W. A. Lessa and E. Z. Vogt. New York: Harper & Row. 1943. Repr. *American Anthropologist* 45:230–40.
Lipinski, E. 1970. Recherches sur le Livre de Zacharie. *VT* 20:25–55.
Livingston, James C. 1993. *Anatomy of the Sacred: An Introduction to Religion*. 2d ed. New York: Macmillan.
Long, Theodore E. 1986. Prophecy, Charisma, and Politics: Reinterpreting the Weberian Thesis. Pages 3–17 in *Prophetic Religions and Politics*. Edited by Jeffrey K. Hadden and Anson Shupe. Vol. 1 of *Religion and the Political Order*. 3 vols. New York: Paragon.
———. 1988. A Theory of Prophetic Religion and Politics. Pages 3–16 in *The Politics of Religion and Social Change*. Edited by Jeffrey K. Hadden and Anson Shupe. Vol. 2 of *Religion and the Political Order*. New York: Paragon.
Love, Mark Cameron. 1999. *The Evasive Text: Zechariah 1–8 and the Frustrated Reader*. JSOTSup 296. Sheffield: Sheffield Academic Press.
Luckenbill, Daniel D. 1924. *The Annals of Sennacherib*. OIP 2. Chicago: University of Chicago Press.
The Lumpa Uprising: Newspaper Reports, Monday 27th July to Monday 10th August 1964. Cited March 20, 2003. Online: http://www.nzramplus.com?Site%20 Resources/Lumpa/lumpa/html.
Malamat, Abraham. 1950–51. The Historical Setting of Two Biblical Prophecies on the Nations. *IEJ* 1:149–59.
———. 1973. Tribal Societies: Biblical Genealogies and African Lineage Systems. *Archives Européennes de Sociologie* 14:126–36.
Mannheim, Karl. 1936. *Ideology and Utopia: An Introduction to the Sociology of Knowledge*. New York: Harcourt, Brace.
Martin, Marie-Louise. 1975. *Kimbangu: An African Prophet and His Church*. Translated by D. M. Moore. Foreword by Bryan R. Wilson. Oxford: Basil Blackwell.
Mason, Rex. 1976. The Relation of Zech 9–14 to Proto-Zechariah. *ZAW* 88:227–39.
———. 1977. The Purpose of the "Editorial Framework" of the Book of Haggai. *VT* 27:413–21.

Mason, Rex. 1982a. The Prophets of the Restoration. Pages 137–54 in *Israel's Prophetic Tradition: Essays in Honour of Peter R. Ackroyd*. Edited by Richard Coggins, Anthony Phillips and Michael Knibb. Cambridge: Cambridge University Press.

———. 1982b. Some Examples of Inner Biblical Exegesis in Zech. 9–14. *Studia Evangelica* 7:343–54.

———. 1984. Some Echoes of Preaching in the Second Temple: Tradition Elements in Zechariah 1–8. *ZAW* 96:221–35.

———. 1990. *Preaching the Tradition: Homily and Hermeneutics after the Exile*. Cambridge: Cambridge University Press.

———. 2003. The Use of Earlier Biblical Material in Zechariah 9–14: A Study in Inner Biblical Exegesis. Pages 2–208 in *Bringing out the Treasure: Inner Biblical Allusion in Zechariah 9–14*. Edited by Mark J. Boda and Michael H. Floyd. JSOTSup 370. London: Sheffield Academic Press.

May, Herbert G. 1968. "This People" and "This Nation" in Haggai. *VT*. 18: 190–97.

Mayes, A. D. H. 1989. *The Old Testament in Sociological Perspective*. London: Marshall Pickering.

Mbiti, John S. 1970. *African Religions and Philosophy*. Garden City, N.Y.: Doubleday.

McComiskey, Thomas E. 1998. Zechariah. Pages 1003–1244 in *Zephaniah, Haggai, Zechariah, Malachi*. Vol. 3 of *The Minor Prophets*. Edited by Thomas E. McComiskey. Grand Rapids: Baker.

McEvenue, Sean. 1981. The Political Structure in Judah from Cyrus to Nehemiah. *CBQ*. 43:353–64.

McKane, William. 1986. *Jeremiah 1–25*. Vol. 1. International Critical Commentary. Edinburgh: T&T Clark.

Merrill, Eugene H. 1994. *An Exegetical Commentary: Haggai, Zechariah, Malachi*. Chicago: Moody.

Meyers, Carol L. and Eric M. Meyers. 1987. *Haggai, Zechariah 1–8*. AB 25B. Edited by David Noel Freedman. Garden City, N.Y.: Doubleday.

———. 1992. Zechariah 1–8. Pages 1061–65 in vol. 6 of *The Anchor Bible Dictionary*. Edited by David Noel Freedman. New York: Doubleday.

———. 1993. *Zechariah 9–14*. AB 25C. Edited by David Noel Freedman. New York: Doubleday.

———. 1995. The Future Fortunes of the House of David: The Evidence of Second Zechariah. Pages 207–22 in *Fortunate the Eyes that See: Essays in Honor of David Noel Freedman in Celebration of his Seventieth Birthday*. Edited by Astrid B. Beck, et al. Grand Rapids: Eerdmans.

Meyers, Eric M. 1983. The Use of *Tora* in Haggai 2:11 and the Role of the Prophet in the Restoration Community. Pages 69–76 in *The Word of the Lord Shall Go Forth: Essays in Honor of David Noel Freedman in Celebration of his Sixtieth Birthday*. Edited by Carol L. Meyers and M. O'Connor. Winona Lake, Ind.: Eisenbrauns.

———. 1987. The Persian Period and the Judean Restoration: From Zerubbabel to Nehemiah. Pages 509–22 in *Ancient Israelite Religion: Essays in Honor of Frank Moore Cross*. Edited by Patrick D. Miller, Paul D. Hanson and S. Dean McBride. Philadelphia: Fortress.

Mickler, Michael L. 1986. Charismatic Leadership Trajectories: A Comparative Study of Marcus Garvey and Sun Myung Moon. Pages 35–51 in *Prophetic Religions and Politics*. Edited by Jeffrey K. Hadden and Anson Shupe. Vol. 1 of *Religion and the Political Order*. New York: Paragon.

Miller, Patrick, D. 2000. *The Religion of Ancient Israel*. Library of Ancient Israel. Louisville, Ky.: Westminster John Knox.

Milosz, Czeslaw. 1955. *The Captive Mind*. New York: Vintage.

Miranda-Garcia, Antonio, and Javier Calle-Martin. 2005. The Validity of Lemma-based Lexical Richness in Authorship Attribution: A Proposal for the Old English Gospels. *ICAME Journal* 29:115–30.

Mitchell, Hinckley G. 1912. A Commentary on Haggai and Zechariah. Pages 1–362 in *A Critical and Exegetical Commentary on Haggai, Zechariah, Malachi and Jonah*. By Hinckley G. Mitchell, John Merlin Powis Smith and Julius A. Bewer. ICC. Edinburgh: T&T Clark.

Mkhize, Thabo. 2000. The Shembe Way. *The Sunday Times*, November 19, 2000. Cited April 26, 2004. Online: http://www.suntimes.co.za/2000/11/19/lifestyle/travel/travel01.htm.

Mol, Hans. 1976. *Identity and the Sacred: A Sketch for a New Social-Scientific Theory of Religion*. Oxford: Basil Blackwell.

Moore, Thomas V. 1856. *The Prophets of the Restoration: Haggai, Zechariah and Malachi*. New York: Robert Carter.

Morgenstern, Julius. 1956. Jerusalem–485 B.C. *HUCA* 27:101–79.

———. 1957. Jerusalem–485 B.C. (Continued). *HUCA* 28:15–47.

Morris, Donald R. 1965. *The Washing of the Spears: A History of the Rise of the Zulu Nation under Shaka and Its Fall in the Zulu War of 1879*. New York: Simon and Schuster.

Moseman, R. David. 2000. Reading the Two Zechariahs as One. *RevExp* 97:487–98.

Motyer, J. Alec. 1998. Haggai. Pages 963–1002 in vol. 3 of *The Minor Prophets: An Exegetical and Expository Commentary*. Edited by Thomas E. McComiskey. Grand Rapids: Baker.

Mowinckel, Sigmund. 1923. *Psalmenstudien III: Kultprophetie und prophetische Psalmen*. Kristiana: Jacob Dybwad.

M'Timkulu, D. 1977. Some Aspects of Zulu Religion. Pages 13–30 in *African Religions*. Edited by Newell S. Booth. New York: NOK Publishers.

Muilenberg, James. 1965. The "Office" of Prophet in Ancient Israel. Pages 74–97 in *The Bible in Modern Scholarship*. Edited by J. P. Hyatt. New York: Abingdon Press.

Mulenga, Maidstone. 2003. Alice Lenshina Mulenga: Founder of the Lumpa Church. Cited March 20, 2003. Online: http://www.geocities.com/maiddie/lenshina.html.

Musambachme, M. C. Review of At Ibenburg, *"All Good Men": The Development of the Lubwa Mission, Chinsali, Zambia, 1905–1967*. *International Journal of African Historical Studies* 31:185–87.

Nasr, Seyyed Hosein. 1966. *Ideals and Realities of Islam*. London: Unwin and Allen.

Niebuhr, H. Richard. 1957 [1929]. *The Social Sources of Denominationalism*. New York: Meridian Books.

Nogalski, James D. 1993a. *Literary Precursors to the Book of the Twelve*. BZAW 217. Berlin: Walter de Gruyter.
———. 1993b. *Redactional Processes in the Book of the Twelve*. BZAW 218. Berlin: Walter de Gruyter.
———. 2000. Joel as "Literary Anchor" for the Book of the Twelve. Pages 91–109 in *Reading and Hearing the Book of the Twelve*. Edited by James D. Nogalski and Marvin A. Sweeney. SBL Symposium Series 15. Atlanta: Society of Biblical Literature.
———. 2003. Zechariah 13:7–9 as a Transitional Text: An Appreciation and Re-evaluation of the Work of Rex Mason. Pages 292-304 in *Bringing Out the Treasure: Inner Biblical Allusion in Zechariah 9-14*. Edited by Mark J. Boda and Michael H. Floyd, with a major contribution by Rex Mason. JSOTSup 370. London: Sheffield Academic Press.
Nogalski, James D. and Marvin A Sweeney, eds. 2000. *Reading and Hearing the Book of the Twelve*. SBL Symposium Series 15. Atlanta: Society of Biblical Literature.
North, F. S. 1956. Critical Analysis of the Book of Haggai. ZAW 68:25–46.
North, Robert. 1992. Postexilic Judean Officials. Pages 86–90 in vol. 5 of *The Anchor Bible Dictionary*. Edited by David Noel Freedman. New York: Doubleday.
Noss, John B. 1974. *Man's Religions*. 5th ed. New York: Macmillan.
Noth, Martin. 1967. Office and Vocation in the Old Testament. Pages 229–249 in *The Laws in the Pentateuch and Other Studies*. Philadelphia: Fortress.
———. 1987. *The Chronicler's History*. Translated with an introduction by H. G. M. Williamson. JSOTSup 50. Sheffield: JSOT Press. Translation of *Uberlieferungsgeschichtliche Studien I*. Halle, 1943.
Nxamalo, C. The Shembe Story. No pages. Cited 2/7/05. Online: http://www.acs.ucalgary.ca/~nurelweb/books/shembe/s-index.html.
O'Brien, Julia M. 1990. *Priest and Levite in Malachi*. SBLDS 121. Atlanta: Scholars Press.
O'Connor, M. 1980. *Hebrew Verse Structure*. Winona Lake, Ind.: Eisenbrauns.
Oden, Thomas C. 1990. *After Modernity . . . What? Agenda for Theology*. Grand Rapids: Academie.
O'Leary, Stephen D. 1994. *Arguing the Apocalypse: A Theory of Millennial Rhetoric*. New York: Oxford University Press.
Olmstead, A. T. 1948. *History of the Persian Empire*. Chicago: University of Chicago Press.
Oosthuizen, Gerhardus C. 1992. *The Healer-Prophet in Afro-Christian Churches*. Studies in Christian Mission 3. Leiden: E.J. Brill.
Oppenheim, A. Leo. 1977. *Ancient Mesopotamia: Portrait of a Dead Civilization*. Rev. ed. completed by Erica Reiner. Chicago: University of Chicago Press.
Otto, E. 1982. M. Webers Religionssoziologie des antiken Judentums. ZAW 94: 187–203.
Otzen, Benedikt. 1964. *Studien über Deuterosacharja*. Copenhagen: Prostant Apud Munksgaard.

Overholt, Thomas W. 1982. Prophecy: The Problem of Cross-Cultural Comparison. *Anthropological Perspectives on the Old Testament*. Edited by Robert C. Culley and Thomas W. Overholt. *Semeia* 21:55-78.
———. 1984. Thoughts on the Use of Charisma in Old Testament Studies. Pages 287-303 in *In the Shelter of Elyon: Essays on Ancient Palestinian Life and Literature in Honor of G.W. Ahlström*. Edited by W. Boyd Barrick and John R. Spencer. JSOTSup 31. Sheffield: JSOT Press.
———. 1986. *Prophecy in Cross-Cultural Perspective*. Atlanta: Scholars Press.
———. 1989. *Channels of Prophecy: The Social Dynamics of Prophetic Activity*. Minneapolis: Fortress.
———. 1996. *Cultural Anthropology and the Old Testament*. Minneapolis: Augsburg Fortress.
Parker, R. A. and W. H. Dubberstein. 1942. *Babylonian Chronology 626 B.C.-A.D. 45*. Ancient Oriental Civilization 24. Chicago: University of Chicago Press.
Parsons, Talcott. 1947. Introduction. Pages 3-86 in *Max Weber, The Theory of Social and Economic Organization*. Edited by Talcott Parsons. Translated by A. M. Henderson and Talcott Parsons. New York: Oxford University Press.
———. 1965. Max Weber 1864-1964. *ASR* 30: 171-75.
Perowne, John J. S. 1875. Zechariah. Pages 3598-3610 in vol. 3 of *Dr. William Smith's Bible Dictionary*. New York: Hurd and Houghton.
Person, Raymond F. 1993. *Second Zechariah and the Deuteronomic School*. JSOTSup 167. Sheffield: JSOT Press.
Petersen, David L. 1979. Max Weber and the Sociological Study of Ancient Israel. Pages 117-49 in *Religious Change and Continuity*. Edited by H. Johnson. San Francisco: Jossey-Bass.
———. 1981. The Roles of Israel's Prophets. JSOTSup 17. Sheffield: JSOT Press.
———. 1984. *Haggai and Zechariah 1-8: A Commentary*. OTL. Philadelphia: Westminster.
———. 1988. Zechariah. Pages 747-52 in *Harper's Bible Commentary*. Edited by James Luther Mays. San Francisco: HarperCollins.
———. 1995. *Zechariah 9-14 and Malachi: A Commentary*. OTL. Philadelphia: Westminster Press.
———. 2002. *The Prophetic Literature: An Introduction*. Louisville: Westminster John Knox.
Petersen, David L., ed. 1987. *Prophecy in Israel: Search for an Identity*. IRT 10. Philadelphia: Fortress.
Pierce, Ronald W. 1984a. Literary Connectors and a Haggai/Zechariah/Malachi Corpus. *JETS* 27:277-89.
———. 1984b. A Thematic Development of the Haggai/Zechariah/Malachi Corpus. *JETS* 27:401-11.
Pleins, J. David. 2001. *Social Visions of the Hebrew Bible: A Theological Introduction*. Louisville: Westminster John Knox.
Plöger, Otto. 1968. *Theocracy and Eschatology*. Translated by S. Rudman. Oxford: Basil Blackwell.
Polley, M. E. 1989. *Amos and the Davidic Empire*. New York: Oxford University Press.

Polzin, Robert. 1976. *Late Biblical Hebrew: Toward an Historical Typology of Biblical Hebrew Prose*. Harvard Semitic Monograph 12. Missoula, MT: Scholars Press.
Porten, Bezalel and Jonas C. Greenfield. 1974. *Jews of Elephantine and Arameans of Syene*. Jerusalem: Academon.
Portnoy, Stephen L. and David L. Petersen. 1984. Biblical Texts and Statistical Analysis: Zechariah and Beyond. *JBL* 103:11–21.
Pritchard, James B. 1969. *Ancient Near Eastern Texts Relating to the Old Testament*. 3d ed. Princeton: Princeton University Press.
Pusey, E. B. 1892. *The Minor Prophets with a Commentary*. Vol. 2. New York: Funk and Wagnalls.
Rad, Gerhard von. 1962. *The Theology of Israel's Historical Traditions*. Vol. 1 of *Old Testament Theology*. Translated by D. M. G. Stalker. New York: Harper & Row.
———. 1966 [1934]. The Levitical Sermon in I and II Chronicles. Pages 267–80 in *The Problem of the Hexateuch and Other Essays*. New York: McGraw-Hill.
Radday, Yehoshua T. and Dieter Wickmann. 1975. The Unity of Zechariah Examined in the Light of Statistical Linguistics. *ZAW* 87:30–55.
Raphaël, F. 1971. Max Weber et le judaisme antique. *Archives européenes de sociologie* 11:297–336.
Ray, Benjamin C. 2000. *African Religions: Symbol, Ritual and Community*. 2d ed. Upper Saddle River, N.J.: Prentice Hall.
Redditt, Paul L. 1993. The Two Shepherds in Zechariah 11:4–17. *CBQ* 55:676–86.
———. 1994. Nehemiah's First Mission and the Date of Zechariah 9–14. *CBQ* 56:664–78.
———. 1995. *Haggai, Zechariah, Malachi*. The New Century Bible Commentary. Grand Rapids: Eerdmans.
———. 1996. Zechariah 9–14, Malachi, and the Redaction of the Book of the Twelve. Pages 245–68 in *Forming Prophetic Literature: Essays on Isaiah and the Twelve in Honor of John D. W. Watts*. Edited by James W. Watts and Paul R. House. JSOTSup 235. Sheffield: Sheffield Academic Press.
Redditt, Paul L. and Aaron Schart, eds. 2003. *Thematic Threads in the Book of the Twelve*. BZAW 325. Berlin: Walter de Gruyter.
Reid, S. B. 1985. The End of Prophecy in the Light of Contemporary Social Theory: A Draft. Pages 515–23 in *SBL Seminar Papers 1985*. Edited by Kent H. Richards. Atlanta: Scholars Press.
Rendsburg, Gary. 1980. Late Biblical Hebrew and the Date of "P." *JNES* 12:65–80.
———. 2002. Some False Leads in the Identification of Late Biblical Hebrew Texts: The Cases of Genesis 24 and 1 Samuel 2:27–36. *JBL* 121:23–46.
Rendtorff, Rolf. 1991. *The Old Testament: An Introduction*. Philadelphia: Fortress.
———. 1998. *The Covenant Formula: An Exegetical and Theological Investigation*. Translated by Margaret Kohl. OTS. Edinburgh: T&T Clark.
Reventlow, Henning Graf. 1993. *Die Propheten Haggai, Sacharja und Maleachi*. ATD 25,2. Göttingen: Vanderhoek & Ruprecht.
Rippen, Andrew. 1990. *The Formative Period*. Vol. 1 of *Muslims: Their Religious Belief and Practices*. London: Routledge.

Roberts, Andrew D. 1970. The Lumpa Church of Alice Lenshina. Pages 513–68 in *Protest and Power in Black Africa*. Edited by Robert I. Rotberg and Ali A. Mazrui. New York: Oxford University Press.

Robinson, George L. 1895–96. The Prophecies of Zechariah with Special Reference to the Origin and Date of Chapters 9–14. *AJSL* 12:1–92.

———. 1965. *The Twelve Minor Prophets*. Harper and Brothers. 1926. Repr. Grand Rapids: Baker.

Rodd, Cyril S. 1981. On Applying Sociological Theory to Biblical Studies. *JSOT* 19:103–05.

Rodinson, Maxime. 1957. The Life of Muhammad and the Sociological Problem of the Beginnings of Islam. *Diogenes* [English Edition] 20:28–51.

———. 1980 [1961]. *Muhammad*. New York: Pantheon.

Rogers, Robert W. 1912. *Cunieform Parallels to the Old Testament*. New York: Eaton and Mains.

Rooker, Mark F. 1994. Diachronic Analysis and the Features of Late Biblical Hebrew. *BBR* 4:135–44.

Rose, Wolter H. 2000. *Zemah and Zerubbabel: Messianic Expectation in the Early Postexilic Period*. JSOTSup 304. Sheffield: Sheffield Academic Press.

———. 2003. Messianic Expectations in the Early Postexilic Period. Pages 168–85 in *Yahwism After the Exile: Perspectives on Israelite Religion in the Persian Era*. Edited by Rainer Albertz and Bob Becking. Studies in Theology and Religion 5. Assen: Royal Van Gorcum.

Rosenbaum, Stanley N. 1990. *Amos of Israel: A New Interpretation*. Macon, Ga.: Mercer University Press.

Rudman, Joseph. 1998. The State of Authorship Attribution Studies: Some Problems and Solutions. *Computers and the Humanities*. 31:351–65.

Rudolph, Wilhelm. 1976. *Haggai–Sacharja 1–8–Sacharja 9–14–Maleachi*. KAT. Gütersloh: Gerd Mohn.

Ruether, Rosemary Radford. 1990. Prophetic Tradition and the Liberation of Women: Promise and Betrayal. *JTSA* 73:24–33.

Saebø, Magne. 1998. On the Relationship between "Messianism" and "Eschatology" in the Old Testament: An Attempt at a Terminological and Factual Clarification. Pages 197–231 in *On the Way to Canon: Creative Tradition History in the Old Testament*. By Magne Saebø. JSOTSup 191. Sheffield: Sheffield Academic Press.

Sauer, Georg. 1967. Serubbabel in der Sicht Haggais und Sacharjas. Pages 199–207 in *Das Ferne und Nahe Wort* (Leonhard Rost Festschrift). Edited by Fritz Maass. BZAW 105. Berlin: Alfred Töpelmann.

Schmidt, Werner H. 1995. *Old Testament Introduction*. 2d ed. Translated by Matthew J. O'Connell. Louisville: Westminster John Knox.

Schneider, Dale Allan. 1979. "The Unity of the Book of the Twelve." Ph.D. diss. Yale University.

Schwartz, Regina. 1990. *The Book and the Text: The Bible and Literary Theory*. Oxford: Blackwell.

Scolnic, Benjamin E. 1999. *Chronology and Papponymy: A List of High Priests of the Persian Period*. South Florida Studies in the History of Judaism 206. Atlanta: Scholars Press.

Sealey, Raphael. 1976. *A History of the Greek City States ca. 700–338 B.C.* Berkeley: University of California Press.
Segal, Robert A. 2003. Clifford Geertz's Interpretive Approach to Religion. Pages 17–34 in *Selected Readings in the Anthropology of Religion: Theoretical and Methodological Essays*. Contributions to the Study of Anthroplogy 9. Edited by Stephen D. Glazier and Charles A. Flowerday. Westport, Conn.: Praeger.
Seitz, Christopher R. 1985. The Crisis of Interpretation Regarding the Meaning and Purpose of the Exile: A Redactional Study of Jeremiah 21–43. *VT* 35: 78–97.
———. 1989. *Theology in Conflict: Reactions to the Exile in the Book of Jeremiah*. BZAW 176. Berlin: Walter de Gruyter.
Shils, Edward. 1961. Center and Periphery. Pages 117–31 in *The Logic of Personal Knowledge: Essays Presented to Michael Polanyi*. London: Routledge and Kegan Paul.
———. 1965. Charisma, Order and Status. *ASR* 30: 199–213.
Smith, Daniel L. 1989. *The Religion of the Landless: The Social Context of the Babylonian Exile*. Bloomington: Meyer-Stone Books.
Smith, Donald C. 1987. *Passive Obedience and Prophetic Protest: Social Criticism in the Scottish Church 1830–1945*. New York: Peter Lang.
Smith, George Adam. 1928 [1898]. *The Book of the Twelve Prophets*. Two volumes. Rev. ed. New York: Harper and Brothers.
Smith, Morton. 1971. *Palestinian Parties and Politics that Shaped the Old Testament*. New York: Columbia University Press.
Smith, Ralph L. 1984. *Micah-Malachi*. WBC 32. Waco, Tex.: Word.
Soggin, J. Alberto. 1976. *Introduction to the Old Testament*. Rev. ed. OTL. Philadelphia: Westminster.
Spuler, B. 1960. *The Age of the Caliphs*. Translated by F. R. C. Bagley. Part I of *The Muslim World: A Historical Survey*. Leiden: E. J. Brill.
Stade, Bernhard. 1881. Deuterozacharja: eine kritische Studie. *ZAW* 1:1–96.
———. 1882a. Deuterozacharja: eine kritische Studie. *ZAW* 2:157–72.
———. 1882b. Deuterozacharja: eine kritische Studie. *ZAW* 2:275–309.
Stark, Rodney. 1985. Church and Sect. Pages 139–49 in *The Sacred in a Secular Age: Toward Revision in the Social Scientific Study of Religion*. Edited by Phillip E. Hammond. Berkeley: University of California Press.
Stark, Rodney and William S. Bainbridge. 1985. *The Future of Religion: Secularization, Revival and Cult Formation*. Berkeley: University of California Press.
———. 1996. *A Theory of Religion*. New Brunswick: Rutgers University Press.
Steck, Odil Hannes. 2000. *The Prophetic Books and their Theological Witness*. St. Louis: Chalice.
Stern, Ephraim. 1982. *Material Culture of the Land of the Bible in the Persian Period 538–332 B.C.* Warminster: Aris & Phillips.
———. 2001. *Archaeology of the Land of the Bible*. Vol. 2. New York: Doubleday.
Steyn, Anna F. and Colin M. Rip. 1974. The Changing Urban Bantu Family. Pages 61–87 in *Selected Studies in Marriage and the Family*. 4th ed. Edited by Robert F. Winch and Graham B. Spanier. New York: Holt, Rinehart and Winston.

Stuhlmueller, Carroll. 1988. *Rebuilding with Hope: A Commentary on the Books of Haggai and Zechariah.* International Theological Commentary. Grand Rapids: Eerdmans.
Sundkler, Bengt G. M. 1961. *Bantu Prophets in South Africa.* 2d ed. International African Institute. London: Oxford University Press.
———. 1987. Shembe, Isaiah. Pages 239–40 in vol. 13 of *The Encyclopedia of Religion.* Edited by Mircea Eliade. New York: Macmillan.
Sweeney, Marvin A. 2000. *The Twelve Prophets.* 2 vols. Berit Olam: Studies in Hebrew Narrative and Poetry. Collegeville, Minn.: Liturgical Press.
———. 2003. The Place and Function of Joel in the Book of the Twelve. Pages 133–54 in *Thematic Threads in the Book of the Twelve.* BZAW 325. Berlin: Walter de Gruyter.
Taylor, John V. and Dorothea A. Lehmann. 1961. *Christians of the Copperbelt: The Growth of the Church in Northern Rhodesia.* World Mission Studies. London: SCM.
Tcherikover, Victor. 1972. The Political Background. Pages 5–32 in *The Hellenistic Age.* Vol. 6 of *The World History of the Jewish People.* Edited by Abraham Schalit. New Brunswick: Rutgers University Press.
Terrien, Samuel. 2003. *The Psalms: Strophic Structure and Theological Commentary.* Eerdmans Critical Commentary. Grand Rapids: Eerdmans.
Theodore of Mopsuestia. 2004. *Commentary on the Twelve Prophets.* Translated by Robert C. Hill. Fathers of the Church 108. Washington, D. C.: Catholic University of America Press.
Thomas, George B. 1977. Kimbanguism: Authentically African, Authentically Christian. Pages 275–96 in *African Religions.* Edited by Newell S. Booth, Jr. New York: NOK Publishers International.
Thucydides. *History of the Peloponnesian War.* 1954. Translated by Rex Warner. Hammondsworth, UK: Penguin.
Tidiman, Brian. 1996. *Le Livre de Zacharie. Commentaire Évangélique de la Bible.* Cherbourg: Édifac.
Tollington, Janet E. 1993. *Tradition and Innovation in Haggai and Zechariah 1–8.* JSOTSup 150. Sheffield: JSOT Press.
Troeltsch, Ernst. 1968. *The Social Teaching of the Christian Churches.* 2 vols. Translated by Olive Wyon. Introduction by H. Richard Niebuhr. New York: Harper and Row.
Tucker, Gene. 1977. Prophetic Superscriptions and the Growth of a Canon. Pages 56–70 in *Canon and Authority: Essays in Old Testament Religion and Theology.* Edited by George W. Coats and Burke O. Long. Philadelphia: Fortress.
Turner, Bryan S. 1974. *Weber and Islam: A Critical Study.* London: Routledge and Kegan Paul.
Turner, Harold W. 1967. A Typology for Modern African Religious Movements. *Journal of Religion in Africa* I:1–34.
Van Binsbergen, Wim M. J. 1981. *Religious Change in Zambia: Exploratory Studies.* Monographs from the African Studies Centre. London: Kegan Paul.
Van Hoonacker, A. 1902. Les chapîtres ix–xiv du livre Zecharie. *RB* 11:161–83; 347–78.

VanderKam, James C. 2004. *From Joshua to Caiaphas: High Priests after the Exile.* Minneapolis: Fortress.
VanGemeren, Willem A., ed. 1997. *New International Dictionary of Old Testament Theology and Exegesis.* 5 vols. Grand Rapids: Zondervan.
Vaux, Roland de. 1961. *Ancient Israel.* 2 vols. New York: McGraw-Hill.
Verhoef, Pieter A. 1987. *The Books of Haggai and Malachi.* NICOT. Grand Rapids: Eerdmans.
Vilakazi, Absolom, with Bongani Mthethwa and Mthembeni Mpanza. 1986. *Shembe: The Revitalization of African Society.* Johannesburg: Skotaville Publishers.
Wach, Joachim. 1962 [1944]. *Sociology of Religion.* Chicago: Phoenix/University of Chicago Press.
Walker, Sheila S. 1983. *The Religious Revolution in the Ivory Coast: The Prophet Harris and the Harrist Church.* Studies in Religion. Chapel Hill: University of North Carolina Press.
———. 1987. Harris, William Wade. Pages 199–201 in vol. 6 of *Encyclopedia of Religion.* Edited by Mircea Eliade. 16 vols. New York: Macmillan.
Wallace, Anthony F. C. 1969a. Revitalization Movements. Pages 30–52 in *Studies in Social Movements: A Social Psychological Perspective.* Edited by Barry McLaughlin. New York: Free Press. 1956. Repr. *American Anthropologist* 58:264–81.
———. 1969b. *The Death and Rebirth of the Seneca.* New York: Vintage Books.
Waltke, Bruce K. and M. O'Connor. 1990. *Introduction to Biblical Hebrew Syntax.* Winona Lake, Ind.: Eisenbrauns.
Warraq, Ibn, ed. 2000. *The Quest for the Historical Muhammad.* Amherst, N.Y.: Prometheus Books.
Waterman, Leroy. 1954. The Camouflaged Purge of Three Messianic Conspirators. *JNES* 13:73–78.
Watt, W. Montgomery. 1961. *Muhammad: Prophet and Statesman.* Oxford: Oxford University Press.
Watts, James W. and Paul R. House. 1996. *Forming Prophetic Literature: Essays on Isaiah and the Twelve in Honor of John D. W. Watts.* JSOTSup 235. Sheffield: Sheffield Academic Press.
Watts, John D. W. 1987. *Isaiah 33–66.* WBC 25. Waco, Tex.: Word.
Webb. Barry. 2003. *The Message of Zechariah: Your Kingdom Come.* The Bible Speaks Today: Old Testament Series. Downers Grove, Ill.: InterVarsity Press.
Weber, Max. 1952 [1921]. *Ancient Judaism.* Edited and translated by H. H. Gerth and D. Martindale. Glencoe, Ill.: Free Press.
———. 1963. *The Sociology of Religion.* Translated by E. Fischoff. Boston: Beacon Press.
———. 1968. *Max Weber on Charisma and Institution Building: Selected Papers.* Edited and introduction by S. N. Eisenstadt. Chicago: University of Chicago Press.
———. 1978 [1921]. *Economy and Society: An Outline of Interpretive Sociology.* Edited by Guenther Roth and C. Wittich. Berkeley: University of California Press.

Weinberg, Joel P. 1992. *The Citizen-Temple-Community*. Translated by Daniel L. Christopher-Smith. JSOTSup 151. Sheffield: Sheffield Academic Press.
Weis, Richard D. 1992. Oracle. Pages 28–29 in vol. 5 of *The Anchor Bible Dictionary*. Edited by David Noel Freedman. 6 vols. New York: Doubleday.
Wellhausen, Julius. 1898. *Die Kleinen Propheten Übersetzt und Erklärt*. Berlin: Georg Reimer.
———. 1903. Zechariah, Book of. Pages 5390–5395 in vol. 4 of *Encyclopaedia Biblica*. Edited by T. Cheyne. New York: Macmillan.
———. 1983. *Prolegomena to the History of Israel*. Gloucester, Mass.: Peter Smith. Reprint of *Prolegomena to the History of Israel*. Translated by J. S. Black and A. Menzies. Preface by W. Robertson Smith. Edinburgh: Adam and Charles Black. Translation of *Prolegomena zur Geschichte Israels*. 2d ed. Berlin: G. Reimer. 1883.
Westermann, Claus. 1967. *Basic Forms of Prophetic Speech*. Translated by Hugh Clayton White. Philadelphia: Westminster.
Widengren, Geo. 1977. The Persian Period. Pages 489–538 in *Israelite and Judean History*. Edited by John H. Hayes and J. Maxwell Miller. London: SCM.
Williams, J. 1969. The Social Location of Israelite Prophecy. *JAAR* 37: 153–65.
Williams, Tyler F. 1997. Accordance Software for Biblical Studies 2.1. *Chorus: Exploring New Media in the Arts and Humanities*. (June): 1–4. Cited July 11, 2006. http://www-writing.berkeley.edu/chorus/bible/reviews/accordance/accordance_4 .html.
Williamson, H. G. M. 1982. *1 and 2 Chronicles*. New Century Bible Commentary. Grand Rapids: Eerdmans.
———. 1985. *Ezra–Nehemiah*. Vol. 16 of Word Biblical Commentary. Waco, Tex.: Word.
———. 1992. Persian Administration. Pages 81–86 in vol. 5 of *The Anchor Bible Dictionary*. Edited by David Noel Freedman. 6 vols. New York: Doubleday.
———. 1999. Exile and After: Historical Study. Pages 236–65 in *The Face of Old Testament Studies: A Survey of Contemporary Approaches*. Edited by David W. Baker and Bill T. Arnold. Grand Rapids: Baker Academic.
Wilson, Bryan R. 1973. *Magic and the Millennium: A Sociological Study of Religious Movements of Protest Among Tribal and Third-World Peoples*. New York: Harper and Row.
———. 1975a. Foreword to *Kimbangu: An African Prophet and His Church*, by Marie-Louise Martin. Translated by D. M. Moore. Oxford: Basil Blackwell.
———. 1975b. *The Noble Savages: The Primitive Origins of Charisma and its Contemporary Survival*. Berkeley: University of California Press.
Wilson, Robert R. 1973. Form-critical Investigation of the Prophetic Literature: The Present Situation. *SBLSP* 12:100–21.
———. 1979. Prophecy and Ecstasy: A Reexamination. *JBL* 98:321–27.
———. 1980. *Prophecy and Society in Ancient Israel*. Philadelphia: Fortress.
———. 1984. *Sociological Approaches to the Old Testament*. GBS. Philadelphia: Fortress.
Winter, J. Alan. 1977. *Continuities in the Sociology of Religion: Creed, Congregation and Community*. New York: Harper & Row.

Wiseman, D. J. 1956. *Chronicles of the Chaldaean Kings: (626–566 B.C.) in the British Museum*. London: Trustees of the British Museum.
———. 1979. Babylonia. Pages 391–402 in vol. 1 of *The International Standard Bible Encyclopedia*. Four vols. Edited by Geoffrey W. Bromiley. Grand Rapids: Eerdmans.
Wolff, Hans Walter. 1988. *Haggai: A Commentary*. Translated by Margaret Kohl. Minneapolis: Augsburg.
Wolters, Al. 1995. Review of Carol L. and Eric M. Meyers, *Zechariah 9–14, A New Translation with Introduction and Commentary*. *JBL* 114:504–07.
———. 1999. Semantic Borrowing and Inner-Greek Corruption in LXX Zechariah 11:8. *JBL* 118:685–90.
Wood, Richard A. 1991. The Use and Significance of Models for Historical Reconstruction. Presented at the annual national meeting of the SBL, Kansas City, Kans. November 25.
Worsley, Peter. 1968. *The Trumpet Shall Sound: A Study of "Cargo" Cults in Melanesia*. 2d ed. New York: Schocken.
Wright, Charles H. H. 1980. *Zechariah and His Prophecies, Considered in Relation to Modern Criticism*. Minneapolis: Klock & Klock. Repr. of London: Hodder & Stroughton, 1879.
Wright, J. Stafford. 1965. Zechariah, Book of. Pages 1355–57 in *The New Bible Dictionary*. Edited by J. D. Douglas. Grand Rapids: Eerdmans.
Yamauchi, Edwin M. 1990. *Persia and the Bible*. Grand Rapids: Baker.
Yinger, J. Milton. 1967 [1963]. Religion and Social Change: Functions and Dysfunctions of Sects and Cults among the Disprivileged. Pages 482–95 in *The Sociology of Religion: An Anthology*. Edited by R. D. Knudten. New York: Appleton-Century-Crofts.
———. 1970. *The Scientific Study of Religion*. New York: Macmillan.
Young, Edward J. 1949. *Introduction to the Old Testament*. London: Tyndale.
Young, Ian. 2003. *Biblical Hebrew: Studies in Chronology and Typology*. Sheffield: Sheffield Academic Press.
Zeitlin, Irving. 1984. *Ancient Judaism: Biblical Criticism from Max Weber to the Present*. New York: Basil Blackwell.
Zimmerli, Walther. 1979. *Ezekiel 1*. Hermeneia. Philadelphia: Fortress.
———. 1983. *Ezekiel 2*. Hermeneia. Philadelphia: Fortress.

ANCIENT AND MEDIEVAL SOURCES

Genesis
8–9   198
8:22   224
10   173
10:10   142
11:2   142
15:18   169

Exodus
10   261
14:20   133
15:1   212
19:6   158
28:3   135
28:11   132
28:36   259
39:30   259
40:38   133

Leviticus
5:20–26   140
16   136
19:12   247
27:16–17   187

Numbers
14   210

Deuteronomy
4:35–39   228 n. 66
28:28–29   212
32:43   182, 243

Judges
20:2   191 n. 31

1 Samuel
5:12   168 n. 11
13:19   132
14:38   191 n. 31

2 Samuel
8   168–69
8:3–12 167
8:12   169
12:13   246
16:5   205
24:10   146

1 Kings
6:1   100 n. 37, 112 n. 55
6:37–38   100 n. 37, 112 n. 55
8:2   100 n. 37, 112 n. 55
8:60   228 n. 66
14:25   100 n. 37, 112 n. 55
20:13–22   14
22:17   187

2 Kings
6:17   133
9:26   235 n. 68
12:12   132
23:11   143
25:1   103 n. 44
25:3   103 n. 44
25:8   100 n. 37, 112 n. 55

1 Chronicles
1   173
3:18   84
3:19   85, 205, 220

2 Chronicles
3:2   100 n. 37, 112 n. 55
15:10   100 n. 37, 112 n. 55
16:7–10 270
16:9   269
20   261
29:3   100 n. 37, 112 n. 55
29:17   100 n. 37, 112 n. 55
36:21   110

Ezra

1:8	84
1:11	84
2:2	84
2:33	86
2:64–65	86
3:1	100 n. 37, 112 n. 55
3:2	84
3:8	100 n. 37, 112 n. 55
4:4	151 n. 41
4:7–23	203
4:17–23	83 n. 4
4:24	100 n. 37, 112 n. 55
5:1	92
5:3	84–85
5:6	84–85
5:7–17	88
5:13	191
5:14	84
6:6	84
6:11	141
6:13	84
6:14	92, 133, 153–54
6:14–15	179
6:15	100 n. 37, 112 n. 55
6:22	191
6:32	233
7:12–24	180 n. 19

Nehemiah

1:3	203
5:14–15	202
6:10–14	200
6:11	149 n. 38
6:14	149 n. 38
7:5	86 n. 11
11:1	86 n. 11
12:4	92
12:10–11	204
12:21	178
12:26	204

Job

1–2	134

Psalms

18:22	135 n. 19
42:7	155 n. 1
72	172
76:5	115 n. 1
109:6	134

Proverbs

21:4	141 n. 28

Isaiah

4:2	135
4:3	239, 260 n. 94
6:1	94
6:10	147
6:13	218
7:1	94
7:18	192 n. 32
8:2	231 n. 67
11:1	135–36
11:11	142, 192 n. 32
11:16	192 n. 32
13–23	167
13:2–14:23	235 n. 68
13:20	245
14:2	243
14:9	193
14:24	236
14:28–32	235
14:29–32	235 n. 68
15:1–16:12	235 n. 68
17:1–11	235 n. 68
19:1–25	235 n. 68
19:23–25	192 and n. 32
19:25	236
20:1	94
20:4	192 n. 32
21:1–10	235 n. 68
21:11–12	235 n. 68
21:12–17	235 n. 68
22:1–14	235 n. 68
23:4	236
23:1–18	235 n. 68
24	198
27:13	192 n. 32
30:6–7	235 n. 68

Ancient and Medieval Sources Index

36:1	94	25:22	169
37:22	172	25:34–38	196 n. 35
38:1	94	27:1	110 n. 52
39:1	94	27:1–7	109
39:1	94	27:3	169
40:2	173	27:7	110
44:3	214	27:15	249 n. 87
44:24–45:7	178	28:1	96–97, 103 n. 44
50:8	192 n. 32	28:17	96–97, 103 n. 44
52:2	244	29:9	249 n. 87
53	214	29:10	109, 131
53:2	135	29:21	249 n. 87
53:6	218	29:23	249 n. 87
60:4	147	32:1	95–96
66:1–2	130 n. 16	32:2	244
66:6	130 n. 16	33:15	136
66:19	173	34:1	95
		36:1	96
Jeremiah		36:9	96–97, 103 n. 44
1:1–3	96 n. 30	36:22	103 n. 44
1:2	96	36:23	97
1:3	95–97, 103 n. 44	36:32	149
2:18	192 n. 32	39:1	96–97, 103 n. 44
2:36	192 n. 32	39:2	96–98, 101, 103 n. 44
14:1–22	188 n. 26	39:9	239
14:14	249 n. 87	44:7	239
17:6	245	45:1	96
17:25	245	46–51	167
17:26	260	46:2	96
22:20–23	194	47:4	169
22:23	260	50:13	245
22:24	91	50:39	245
23:1	199	51:59	96
23:1–4	197	51:64	97
23:5	136	52:4	96–97
23:18–22	135	52:5	96, 98
23:25	249 n. 87	52:6	96–98
24:1	95	52:12	95–97
25:1	95–96, 109, 179	52:12–13	97
25:1–3	96	52:28	95–96, 98
25:1–14	95	52:29	95–96, 98
25:5	260	52:30	95–96, 98
25:11	109, 131	52:31	95–97, 102
25:11–12	109		
25:12	223		

Lamentations
2:14	161 n. 2
5:6	192 n. 32

Ezekiel
1:1	98, 99 n. 34
1:2	99 n. 34
2:10	140
5:2–4	218
5:13	143
7:27	151 n. 41
8:1	99 n. 34
12:11–16	235 n. 68
13:16–22	198
20:1	99 n. 34
22	188
24:1	99 n. 34
25–32	167
26:1	99 n. 34
26:29	245
27	180
27:12–25	180 n. 21
27:13	173
27:19	173
29:1	99 n. 34
29:11	245
29:17	99 n. 34
30:20	99 n. 34
31:1	99 n. 34
32:1	99 n. 34
32:17	99 n. 34
33:21	98
34	197
34:8	187
35:7	245
36:25–26	215
36:35	245
37	197
38:6	143 n. 30
38:15	143 n. 30
39:2	143 n. 30
40:1	98, 100 n. 35
47:16–17	169 n. 12
48:1	169 n. 12

Daniel
1:1	100 n. 38, 142
2:1	100 n. 38
7	132
7:1	100 n. 38
8:1	100 n. 38
9:1	100 n. 38
9:2	109 n. 51
10:1	100 n. 38

Hosea
2:1	218
2:23	266
2:25	218, 266
7:1	247
7:11	192 n. 32
9:3	192 n. 32
9:16	252
11:5	192 n. 32
11:11	192
12:1	192 n. 32
14:10	252

Joel
2:23	115 n. 2
2:27	228 n. 66
3:4	169
4	181

Amos
1–2	167
1:2	261
4:9	252
9:5–6	252
9:11–12	252
9:13	261

Jonah
2:4	245

Micah
2:11	247
4:1–5	261
4:10	244
4:13	244
6:12	247

Ancient and Medieval Sources Index

7:12	192 n. 32	**Zechariah**	
7:19	245	1:1	91–93, 126–27, 148
		1:1–6	126–27, 148
Nahum		1:1–6:8	125
1:2–3:19	235 n. 68	1:2	128
3:4	244	1:2–5	128
3:7	245	1:2–6	233, 236, 260–62
		1:3	129, 148, 153
Habakkuk		1:4	129
1:2–2:20	235 n. 68	1:4–5	149
2:8	249 n. 85	1:6	129, 239
2:18	247	1:7	93, 110, 126–27, 148
		1:7–17	110
Zephaniah		1:7–6:8	126, 236, 262
1:1	94 n. 26	1:7–6:15	127, 129–30, 147, 262
2:9	239	1:8	190, 213, 245
3:14	244	1:8–11	255
3:14–18	186	1:8–17	131
3:14–20	172, 231	1:8–6:15	188 n. 27
3:19–20	186 n. 25	1:10	131
		1:11	131
Haggai		1:12	110, 124 n. 12, 131, 247
1:1	81, 85, 93, 127	1:13	131
1:2	88	1:17	131, 245, 252
1:2–4	85	1:18	130
1:2–11	88	2:1	130
1:12	85, 88	2:1–4	132, 143
1:13	88	2:1–13	185
1:14	85	2:2	132, 192
1:15	81	2:4–17	185
1:15–2:1	93	2:5	130, 133
2:1	81	2:5–17	133
2:2	85	2:8	92, 133, 245
2:2–9	88	2:10	133, 143, 244
2:4	87, 151 n. 41	2:11–13	133
2:10	81, 93, 127	2:12	134, 246, 247, 250
2:11	89 n. 16	2:13	244, 247
2:11–19	88–89	2:14	172, 244, 257
2:14	82 n. 2	2:15	244, 266
2:20	81, 93, 127	2:16	182
2:21	91	3:1	134
2:21–23	88	3:1–10	125–26, 134, 137, 139, 144
2:23	85	3:3	258
		3:4	246
		3:6–10	138

Zechariah, continued

3:8	136
3:8–9	252
3:9	125, 134–35, 139, 199, 226, 246, 258–59
4:1–14	130, 136–37
4:2	137 n. 21
4:4	137
4:6	137, 147, 255, 259
4:6–10	137–39, 144
4:7	135 n. 19, 138 n. 25, 244, 259
4:8	92, 112
4:9	144, 154, 244, 269
4:10	134, 135 n. 19, 136 n. 20, 199, 246, 269
4:11	247
4:12	225
4:14	143
5:1	130, 240
5:1–4	130, 139–40, 152
5:1–11	130
5:1–6:22	153
5:3	265
5:4	135 n. 19, 267
5:5	130
5:5–11	130, 141
5:6	141, 246
5:8	135 n. 19, 136 n. 20
5:10	142
5:11	166
6:1	130, 240
6:1–8	142
6:6	143, 247
6:7	244
6:8	166, 245
6:9	92, 112
6:9–15	125–26, 144–46, 148, 253
6:10	253 n. 88
6:11	125, 144–45, 247
6:11–13	144
6:12	144
6:12–13	146
6:13	144–46, 252
6:14	144, 147, 247, 262
6:15	148, 149, 153, 244, 250
7:1	93, 101, 111, 124, 126–27, 148–49, 235 n. 69
7:1–3	150, 267
7:1–8:23	126–27, 148
7:1–14:21	125
7:2	149–50
7:3	110, 152 n. 42, 150, 200, 250, 254
7:4	92, 112
7:4–5	150
7:4–8:23	233
7:5	111–12, 246
7:5–8:23	261
7:7	245, 247, 260
7:8–10	150
7:8–12	150
7:9–10	260
7:12	141, 260
7:12–14	150
7:13	239, 250
7:13–14	150
7:14	245
8:1–3	150
8:2–8	150
8:3	239
8:4–6	150
8:6	134, 246
8:7–8	150
8:8	150, 266
8:9	92, 149 n. 38, 152 n. 42, 244, 254
8:9–12	92
8:9–13	111, 150
8:10	244, 247
8:11	141
8:12	266
8:13	151, 244
8:14	239
8:14–15	150
8:14–19	111
8:15	111, 239
8:16	244
8:16–17	150, 152
8:17	244
8:18	92, 113
8:18–19	150, 266

Ancient and Medieval Sources Index   311

8:18–23	125	10:3–12	163, 187–93, 270
8:19	111	10:4	190, 193, 263
8:20–23	149–50, 239, 259–60, 265, 267	10:6	192 n. 32, 207, 218, 247
8:20–23	226	10:10	192, 207
8:21	149	10:10–11	119, 191, 232–33
8:22	149	10:11	191, 192 n. 32, 193, 245, 252
9:1	127, 161, 163, 166–68, 245–46	10:12	192 n. 32
9:1–2	169	11:1	194, 201, 236, 244
9:1–6	167	11:1–3	125, 157, 161, 163, 185, 193–97, 201, 219, 229, 263, 271, 280
9:1–8	155, 161, 163–70, 172, 192, 226, 232–33, 270	11:1–13	195 n. 35
9:1–10	120	11:1–17	125, 184
9:1–17	156, 184, 209, 225 n. 63	11:1–13:6	119
9:1–11:17	127, 235 n. 68	11:3–16	236
9:3	169	11:4	126
9:4	209	11:4–14	217
9:5	245, 252	11:4–17	4, 120, 125, 157, 161, 163, 185, 194–97, 200–5, 209, 214, 218–19, 226, 229–30, 263, 278–80
9:5–6	169		
9:6	164		
9:7	207, 226, 246, 252, 259		
9:8	134, 166, 199, 246, 244–45	11:5	201
9:9	172, 207, 209, 223, 257	11:6	200, 244
9:9–10	161, 163, 173, 262–63, 270	11:7	200, 239, 252
		11:8	121, 155, 198, 232
9:9–17	170–72, 182	11:9	198, 244, 252
9:11	172, 191, 251	11:10	200, 217
9:11–12	173	11:11	199
9:11–13	182	11:12	246–47
9:11–17	161, 163, 181, 190, 270	11:12–13	118
9:11–11:3	120	11:12–14	209
9:13	119, 172–74, 178, 181, 232–33, 252	11:13	235, 254
		11:14	235
9:14	247	11:14–16	233
9:15	135 n. 19	11:15	125, 199
9:16	135 n. 19, 207, 243, 247	11:15–16	157
9:17	172	11:15–17	202
10:1–2	161, 163, 186–88, 193, 270	11:16	162, 199, 201
10:1–3	4	11:17	125, 161–63, 185, 196 n. 42, 197–98, 216–18, 246, 270
10:1–12	156–57, 184, 186, 185, 188		
		12:1	127, 161–63, 208, 240
10:2	188, 200, 229, 245	12:1–9	221
10:3	192 n. 32, 193, 229	12:1–1	184, 207–8

Zechariah, continued
12:1–13:1	157
12:1–13:6	120, 157, 162–63, 209, 211, 216, 219–20, 222–23, 225, 229, 234
12:1–14:21	127, 235 n. 68
12:2	162, 208
12:2–13:6	208
12:3	135 n. 19
12:4	134, 246, 252
12:6	162, 245, 247
12:7	162
12:7–8	263
12:8	215, 255
12:9	213, 244, 244
12:1	155, 214–15, 213, 217, 221, 246, 252, 259
12:10–14	213, 221
12:10–13:6	215
12:11	214
12:12	205, 246
12:13	205
12:14	162, 215
13:1	162, 214–15, 258, 263
13:1–6	208, 215
13:1–9	184
13:2	162, 213
13:2–3	215
13:2–6	157, 200, 215, 219
13:3	247, 267
13:4	162
13:4–6	215
13:5	213
13:6	162, 213, 236
13:7	213, 217–18, 263
13:7–9	4, 120, 157, 161–63, 208–9, 216–19, 230
13:7–14:1	119
13:8–9	223
13:9	218, 266
13:12	246
14:1	162, 208, 240, 247
14:1–21	120, 157, 162–63, 184, 207–9, 218, 221–22, 225, 228, 230, 234
14:2	222, 246
14:3	244
14:4	247
14:5	223
14:6	162
14:6–8	265
14:8	252, 266
14:9	225, 236
14:10	247, 245, 254
14:11	225, 245, 265
14:12	162
14:12–21	226
14:12–25	163
14:13	244
14:16–18	239
14:16–19	260
14:16–21	149, 259, 265
14:20	226, 260, 266
14:20–21	228, 235, 254
14:21	229, 254

Malachi
1:2–3:24	235 n. 68
2:11	142 n. 29
3:5	247
3:22–24	276

Matthew
27:9–10	118

John
9:16	13 n. 6
19:37	214

1 John
2:16	141 n. 28

Revelation
1:7	214

1 Esdras
5:1–6	85
7:5	180 n. 20

1QS
IX, 11	147 n. 45

Ancient and Medieval Sources Index

Abarbanel	115	Josephus	
		A.J. 11.7.1	203
'Avot			
2:5	151 n. 41	Kimchi, David	116 n. 3
Didymus the Blind	116 n. 3	Theodore of Mopsuestia	82 n. 2, 116 n. 3
Herodotus	174–75, 181, 205		
		Thucydides	176
Jerome	115, 116 n. 3, 155		

MODERN AUTHORS

Aberle, David 51 n. 16
Abrams, Philip 7 n. 3
Ackroyd, Peter 81 n. 1, 82 n. 2, 109, 112 n. 57, 116 n. 3, 121, 144–45, 235
Adams, James L. 75 n. 40
Aelred, Cody 115 n. 3, 173
Aharoni, Yohanan, 169
Ahlström, Gösta W. 14 n. 7
Albertz, Rainer 83 n. 3, 229
Albright, William F. 101 n. 40, 232
Alter, Robert 34 n. 9
Amsler, Samuel 82 n. 2, 115 n. 3
Andersen, Francis I. 183
Andersson, Efraim 43, 45
Armstrong, Karen 58
Avi-Yonah, Michael 169

Bainbridge, William S. 36, 47 n. 5
Baker, David W. 29 n. 1
Baldwin, Joyce G. 82 n. 2, 115 n. 3, 121, 123, 232
Barnes, D. F. 17 n. 10
Baron, David 115 n. 3, 123, 232
Barratt, Brian 68 n. 37
Barrett, David 47, 57
Baumgartner, W. 171 n. 13
Bedford, Peter R. 82 n. 2, 116 n. 3, 117 n. 3
Bellah, Robert 33 n. 6
Bendix, R. 9 n. 5
Ben Zvi, Ehud 122
Berger, Peter L. 7 n. 3, 18 n. 11, 19
Berquist, Jon L. 29 n. 1, 82 n. 2, 116 n. 3, 117 n. 3, 131, 138 n. 24, 145 n. 32
Berlin, Adele 183
Betlyon, John W. 90, 117 n. 3
Beuken, W. A. M. 81 n. 1, 82 n. 2, 94 n. 25, 101, 109, 116 n. 3, 121
Beyer, Bryan 117 n. 3, 138

Bickerman, Elias 103 n. 44, 105 n. 47
Blenkinsopp, Joseph 8 n. 3, 12, 22 n. 14, 25, 28 n. 1, 82 n. 2, 116 n. 3, 117 n. 3, 152 n. 42, 180 n. 20
Bloomhardt, Paul F. 82 n. 2, 90
Boda, Mark J. 87 n. 13, 110 n. 53, 91 n. 20, 117 n. 3, 132 n. 17, 137 n. 22, 139 n. 26, 256 n. 91
Bond, George 33 n. 6, 66, 72–73
Bormann, Ernest G. 35
Briant, Pierre 85 n. 10, 117 n. 3, 177, 179, 268
Brueggemann, Walter 29, 37–38, 78, 79, 88, 256
Buthelezi, M. 55, 58 n. 25
Butterworth, Mike 116 n. 3, 149, 151, 160

Calvin, John 82 n. 2, 116 n. 3
Can, Fazli 240, 272
Carroll, Robert P. 128 n. 14
Carter, Charles E. 8 n. 3, 29 n. 1, 83 n. 2, 86, 117 n. 3
Chary, T. 82 n. 2, 116 n. 3
Childs, Brevard S. 115, 122, 131 n. 16, 160, 265, 267
Chisholm, Robert B. 82 n. 2, 117 n. 3, 149
Clark, David J. 148 n. 36, 151 n. 40
Clarke, David L. 27
Cody, Aelred 173–74, 181
Coggins, Richard J. 82 n. 2, 116 n. 3, 234–35
Collins, Jeff 240
Collins, John J. 159–60
Conrad, Edgar 34 n. 9, 115 n. 3, 124, 128 n. 14, 132 n. 17,
Cook, J. M. 175, 177, 268
Cook, Stephen L. 116 n. 3, 126 n. 13, 146, 159, 211, 220, 234
Coote, Robert 27, 31–32

Cross, Frank M. 204
Cutter, Charles H. 47 n. 4

Davenport, T. R. H. 50 n. 14
Davies, Philip R. 117 n. 3
Davies, W. D. 117 n. 3
Davis, Ellen F. 99, 101
Dearman, J. Andrew 29 n. 1
Delcor, M. 116 n. 3, 123
De Vries, Simon J. 269
Donovan, James M. 7 n. 1
Dubberstein, W. H. 93 n. 21, 103
Dube, J. L. 50 n. 15

Eckardt, R. 239, 242
Eichrodt, Walther 20, 21 n. 12
Eisenstadt, S. N. 3, 8 n. 3, 12–13, 15, 123 n. 11
Eissfeldt, Otto 96 n. 31
Ellis, Richard S. 139
Emmerson, Grace 31
Emmet, Dorothy 3, 8 n. 3, 15
Eshkenazi, Tamara 117 n. 3
Ewald, H. G. A. 22, 162, 218

Farganis, James 26
Fasholé-Luke, E. 47 n. 3
Fernandez, James 36, 38
Ferriero, Alberto 82 n. 2
Finkelstein, Louis 117 n. 3
Floyd, Michael H. 1, 3, 79, 82 n. 2, 115 n. 3, 116 n. 3, 118 n. 4, 124–25, 160, 164, 185, 212 n. 50, 222, 225 n. 63, 231, 235 n. 69, 256 n. 91, 277
Forbes, A. D. 183
Freedman, David N. 94 n. 23, 102 n. 41, 183–84, 273
Freedy, K. S. 102 n. 40
Friebel, Kevin G. 144 n. 31, 197 n. 43
Fried, Lisbeth S. 117 n. 3

Geertz, Clifford 43
Gellner, Ernest 58

Gerth, H. H. 8 n. 3
Gesenius, Wilhelm 119
Gevirtz, Stanley 268 n. 102
Ginsberg, C.D. 162
Githieya, Francis K. 47 n. 3
Glassner, Jean-Jacques 102 n. 41, 104 n. 45, 105 n. 47, 107 n. 49
Glazier-McDonald, Beth 236 n. 70
Gordon, Robert P. 29 n. 1
Gottwald, Norman 28 n. 1, 41 n. 11, 118
Gould, Stephen Jay 9 n. 4
Gowan, Donald E. 91 n. 19, 116 n. 3, 211, 219, 227, 254
Grabbe, Lester 20, 29 n. 1
Grayson, A. K. 102, 104 n. 45, 108 n. 50
Greenfield, Jonas C. 181 n. 23
Grunneweg, A. 19

Hadden, Jeffery K. 17, 36
Haldar, A. 19
Halligan, John M. 117 n. 3
Hallo, William W. 104–5
Hanson, Paul D. 1–2, 28 n. 1, 82 n. 2, 87 n. 12, 88, 115, 116 n. 3, 118 n. 4, 122, 129, 131, 136, 156–60, 162 n. 5, 166, 174, 185, 190, 192, 197, 209–10, 214 n. 52, 217 n. 55, 218, 219, 228, 256, 267–68, 272, 277–79
Harrelson, Walter 116 n. 3, 226 n. 64
Harrison, R. K. 123, 232, 242, 253 n. 89, 258, 267 n. 100
Hayes, John H. 27 n. 3, 31 n. 3, 174
Hengstenberg, Ernst 115 n. 3, 119, 123, 231, 255 n. 90, 261
Heschel, Abraham 21 n. 13
Hexham, Irving 50 n. 15
Hill, Andrew E. 94 n. 23, 116 n. 3, 123–24, 183, 192, 236 n. 70, 239, 256, 268, 270, 272, 275–76, 277
Hoehner, Harold W. 242 n. 75
Hoglund, Kenneth G. 176, 178, 268

Holladay, William L. 96 n. 31, 110 n. 52, 132, 221 n. 60, 239
Holmes, David I. 241, 272
Hölscher, G. 22
House, Paul R. 122
Hugenberger, George P. 142 n. 29
Hurvitz, Avi 268 n. 102
Hutton, Rodney R. 8 n. 3, 12, 29 n. 1

Ipenburg, At 64 n. 34

Jepsen, A. 21 n. 12
Johnson, A. R. 19
Johnson, Walton 33 n. 6, 63
Jones, Douglas R. 82 n. 2, 115 n. 3, 116 n. 3, 120
Jules-Rosette, Bennetta 36, 38

Kamsteeg, Frans H. 3 n. 1, 29
Keil, C. F. 82 n. 2, 115 n. 3, 119–20, 123, 231
Kenny, Anthony 242 n. 75
Kent, Roland G. 85 n. 10
Kessler, John 81 n. 1, 82 n. 2, 86, 94 n. 25, 101 n. 39
Keyes, Charles F. 8 n. 3, 14
Kipling, Rudyard 49
Kirkpatrick, A. F. 121
Klausner, Joseph 121, 123, 232
Kline, Meredith G. 116 n. 3, 123, 124–25, 130, 135, 137 n. 22, 162 n. 5, 197, 235 n. 69, 255 n. 90
Koehler, Ludwig 171 n. 13
Kraeling, Emil G. H. 116 n. 3
Kraus, H.-J. 14 n. 7
Kselman, J. 30–31

Lacocque, André 115 n. 3, 214 n. 53, 222, 273
Lamarche, Paul 115 n. 3, 121, 155
Lang, Bernhard 8 n. 3, 17 n. 9, 28 n. 1, 76 n. 41
Larkin, Katrina 116 n. 3, 160–61, 209, 234, 261, 262
Lehmann, Dorothea 62, 65 n. 35, 66, 68–69

Leupold, H. C. 115 n. 3, 232
Lewis, Ioan M. 21 n. 13, 38
Lindblom, J. 21 n. 13
Lindenberger, James 181 n. 23
Linton, Ralph 36, 48, 51 n. 16
Lipinski, E. 116 n. 3
Livingston, James C. 36, 45, 61 n. 29
Long, Theodore E. 3, 8 n. 3, 15–20, 25, 32–33, 37, 76, 278
Love, Mark C. 34 n. 9, 115
Luckenbill, Daniel 102 n. 41, 104 n. 45

Malamat, Abraham 41 n. 11, 116 n. 3
Mandell, Sara 174
Mannheim, Karl 159
Martin, Marie-Louise 43, 46
Mason, Rex 2, 81 n. 1, 82 n. 2, 94 n. 24, 100 n. 36, 101, 109, 116 n. 3, 122–23, 256–59, 260–65, 267
May, Herbert G. 82 n. 2, 89 n. 17
Mayes, A. D. H. 8 n. 3, 29 n. 1
Mbiti, John S. 67 n. 36
McComiskey, T. 115 n. 3, 124 n. 12, 215
McEvenue, Sean 85 n. 9, 117 n. 3
McKane, William 96 n. 31
Merrill, Eugene H. 82 n. 2, 115 n. 3, 123, 139, 143, 232, 273
Meyers, Carol L. 1, 3, 8 n. 3, 29 n. 1, 81, 82 n. 2, 85 n. 9, 87 n. 12, 90–91, 101, 110 n. 54, 112, 113 n. 58, 115 n. 3, 116 n. 3, 117 n. 3, 118 n. 4, 119 n. 6, 121–24, 129, 132n. 17, 137 n. 21, 138 n. 25, 144–45, 147–48, 161 n. 4, 183–84, 190, 196 n. 42, 201, 204, 214, 220, 224–25, 261, 264, 268–70, 272
Meyers, Eric M. 1, 3, 81, 82 n. 2, 85 n. 9, 87 n. 12, 90–91, 101, 110 n. 54, 112, 113 n. 58, 115 n. 3, 116 n. 3, 117 n. 3, 118 n. 4, 119 n. 6, 121–24, 129, 132n. 17, 137 n. 21, 138 n. 25, 144–45, 147–48,

Modern Authors Index

161 n. 4, 183–84, 190, 196 n. 42, 201–2, 204, 214, 220, 224–25, 261, 264, 268–70, 272
Mickler, Michael L. 38, 63 n. 32
Mikelson, Thomas 75 n. 40
Miller, Patrick D. 8 n. 3, 12
Mills, C. Wright 8 n. 3
Milosz, Czeslaw 155
Mitchell, Hinckley G. 82 n. 2, 115 n. 3, 118 n. 4, 120, 123, 135, 140 n. 27, 193 n. 34, 196 n. 41, 214, 218, 223, 231 n. 67, 235–40, 242, 252, 254, 261 n. 96
Mol, Hans 33 n. 6
Moore, Thomas V. 82 n. 2, 115 n. 3
Morgenstern, Julius 205 n. 49
Morris, Donald R. 49–50, 54
Moseman, R. David 117 n. 3
Motyer, J. Alec 82 n. 2
Mowinckel, Sigmund 19
Mthethwa, Bogani 54 n. 21, 55 n. 22
M'Timkulu, D. 49 n. 13, 50 n. 15, 56 n. 24, 57
Muilenberg, James 22 n. 14
Mulenga, Maidstone 64
Musambachme, M. 64 n. 34

Nasr, Seyyed Hossein 61, 77
Niebuhr, H. Richard 36, 47 n. 5
Nogalski, James D. 122, 123, 173–74, 181, 218 n. 58, 261
North, F. S. 82 n. 2
North, Robert 117 n. 3
Noth, Martin 20, 269

O'Brien, Julia M. 142 n. 29
O'Connor, Michael Patrick 172 n. 14, 196 n. 42
Oden, Thomas C. 32–33
O'Leary, Stephen D. 234, 274
Olmstead, A. T. 85, 89 n. 17, 90, 117 n. 3, 268
Oosthuizen, G. C. 48 n. 10, 50 n. 15, 52 n. 18
Oppenheim, A. Leo 105 n. 47

Otzen, Benedict 116 n. 3, 120–21, 174
Overholt, Thomas W. 14 n. 7, 15, 27, 28 n. 1, 40 n. 10, 51 n. 16

Parker, R. A. 93 n. 21, 102, 103
Parsons, Talcott 8 n. 3, 10
Patton, Jon M. 272
Perowne, John J. S. 116 n. 3, 119, 231, 268 n. 101
Person, Raymond F. 116 n. 3, 225 n. 62
Petersen, David L. 1, 3, 7 12–14, 20–22, 28 n. 1, 81, 82 n. 2, 115 n. 3, 116 n. 3, 121–24, 132 n. 17, 135, 137, 138 n. 25, 155, 160, 167, 172 n. 15, 182, 195 n. 39, 197, 201, 211, 222, 224, 234, 256 n. 91, 271–72
Pierce, Ronald W. 5, 116 n. 3, 122
Pleins, J. David 29 n. 1, 88 n. 14
Plöger, Otto 156
Polley, M. E. 31 n. 3
Polzin, Robert 268–70
Porten, Bezalel 181 n. 23
Portnoy, Stephen L. 271–72
Pritchard, James B. 105
Pusey, E. B. 82 n. 2, 115 n. 3, 120, 231, 252

Rad, Gerhard von 2, 14–15, 21, 257
Radday, Yehuda T. 241, 270–72
Raphaël, F. 8 n. 3
Ray, Benjamin C. 43
Redditt, Paul L. 82 n. 2, 115 n. 3, 116 n. 3, 121, 122, 144, 144–45, 155, 161, 197 n. 44, 198, 273, 276
Redditt, Paul L. 122
Redford, Donald B. 102 n. 40
Rendsberg, Gary 268 n. 102
Rendtorff, Rolf 261, 265, 266 n. 99
Reventlow, Henning 82 n. 2, 92, 115 n. 3, 228 n. 65, 272
Rip, Colin M. 49 n. 12
Rippen, Andrew 59

Roberts, Andrew D.   64 n. 33, 65, 67
Robinson, George L.   116 n. 3, 118 n.
    4, 120, 123, 231, 240–42, 244 n.
    77, 245, 252–53, 261
Rodd, C. S.   26–27
Rodinson, Maxime   58
Rogers, Robert W.   102 n. 41
Rooker, Mark F.   268 n. 102
Rose, Wolter 116 n. 3, 130 n. 15,
    136, 137 n. 22, 146
Rosenbaum, S. N.   31, 32 n. 5
Rudman, Joseph   241, 272
Rudolph, Wilhelm   82 n. 2, 115 n. 3
Ruether, Rosemary Radford   29

Saebø, Magne   91 n. 19
Sauer, Georg   82 n. 2, 116 n. 3
Schart, Aaron   122
Schneider, D. A.   122
Schwartz, Regina   34 n. 9
Scolnic, Benjamin E.   204 n. 46
Sealey, Raphael   177
Seitz, Christopher R.   95 n. 28
Shils, Edward   3, 12–13, 15
Shupe, Anson   17
Smith, Daniel L. 29 n. 1, 48 n. 10, 82
    n. 2, 89 n. 17
Smith, Donald C.   29
Smith, George Adam 82 n. 2, 115 n. 3
Smith, Morton   87 n. 12
Smith, Ralph L. 82 n. 2, 115 n. 3,
    273
Soggin, J. Alberto   117–18, 256
Stade, Bernhard 116 n. 3, 119, 120,
    123, 173–74, 177, 178, 181, 191
Stark, Rodney   36, 47 n. 5
Stern, Ephraim   85 n. 9, 117 n. 3
Steyn, A. F.   49 n. 12
Stuhlmueller, Carroll 82 n. 2, 115 n.
    3, 139, 254–55, 273
Sundkler, Bengt 36, 48, 50 n. 15, 52
    n. 19, 54 n. 21, 55–57
Sweeney, Marvin A. 32 n. 5, 82 n. 2,
    89 n. 15, 91 n. 18, 116 n. 3, 122,
    124–25, 132 n. 17, 193, 200, 217

n. 55, 222, 235 n. 69, 261, 272,
    278

Taylor, John V. 62, 65 n. 35, 66,
    68–69
Terrien, Samuel   252
Thomas, George B.   43
Tidiman, Brian   115 n. 3, 123, 232
Tollington, Janet E. 82 n. 2, 116 n. 3
Troeltsch, Ernst   36, 47 n. 5, 159
Tucker, Gene   275
Turner, Bryan S.   59
Turner, Harold W.   36, 47 n. 3

Van Binsbergen, W.   72
Van Hoonacker, A.   123, 232
VanderKam, James 84 n. 7, 117 n. 3,
    204 n. 46
VanGemeren, Willem A.   195 n. 38
Vaux, Roland de   40, 109
Verhoef, Pieter A.   82 n. 2
Vilakazi, Absolom 47 n. 7, 50, 51 n.
    17, 54, 56 n. 24

Wach, Joachim   36, 45
Walker, Sheila S.   33 n. 6
Wallace, Anthony F. C. 36, 45, 47 n.
    6, 48, 74 n. 39, 75
Waltke, Bruce K. 172 n. 14, 196 n.
    42
Warraq, Ibn   59
Waterman, Leroy 82 n. 2, 90, 116 n.
    3, 145
Watt, W. M.   58–60
Watts, James W.   122
Watts, John D. W.   90
Webb, Barry 116 n. 3, 123, 124,
    232, 235 n. 69
Weber, Max 2–3, 7–20, 25–26,
    36–37, 43, 76, 159
Weinberg, Joel P.   86
Weis, Richard   164, 185
Wellhausen, Julius 1–3, 22, 34, 82 n.
    2, 117, 116 n. 3, 119, 144, 146,
    263
Westermann, Claus   24, 28, 166

Widengren, Geo 83 n. 3
Wickmann, Dieter 241, 270–72
Williams, J. 19
Williamson, H. G. M. 84 n. 6, 86, 117 n. 3, 180 n. 18, 221 n. 59, 269
Wilson, Bryan R. 9, 36, 43, 45, 47, 50 n. 15, 51 n. 16, 57, 61, 66–67, 74, 210
Wilson, Robert R. 3, 12, 15, 21 n. 13, 22 n. 14, 28–31, 38, 51 n. 16, 88, 122
Winter, J. Alan 33 n. 6
Wiseman, D. J. 102 n. 42, 104 n. 45
Wolff, Hans Walter 82 n. 2, 89 n. 17, 93 n. 22

Wolters, Al 118 n. 4
Wood, Richard 26–27
Worsley, Peter 51 n. 16
Wright, C. H. H. 115 n. 3, 119, 120, 123
Wright, J. Stafford 123, 231–32, 242, 253 n. 89, 258 n. 93, 267 n. 100

Yamauchi, Edwin M. 85 n. 10
Yinger, J. Milton 51 n. 16
Young, Edward J. 123, 232
Young, Ian 268 n. 102
Younger, K. Lawson 104 n. 45, 105

Zimmerli, Walther 99, 180 n. 21

SUBJECT INDEX

Africa 4, 25, 33 n. 6, 37, 40–45, 47–54, 49 n. 11, 50 n. 15, 52 n. 18 and 19, 53 n. 20, 57, 60, 62 and n. 30, 64–78, 67 n. 36, 181, 256, 272
African Indigenous Church (AIC) 47–48, 52, 54
   See also Zion type AIC
Alexander the Great 117 n. 3, 119–20, 167, 173, 232, 268
Alt, Albrecht 117 n. 3
amaNazaretha 47–58, 77–78
Amos, the prophet 2, 30–32, 39, 60, 275
anthology 104, 161, 163, 211, 261
apocalyptic 29 n. 1, 109 n. 51, 115–17, 120, 122, 126, 156–60, 173, 209–10, 220, 227–29, 234, 267–68, 274 and n. 103
   proto-apocalyptic 126, 228
   middle apocalyptic 157
apocalyptic eschatology
   See eschatology
Artaxerxes I, King 83 and n. 4, 141, 154, 177, 180 and n. 19, 202–3, 273
Ashur/Assyria 105 and n. 48, 107, 119–21, 132, 167, 174, 191–94, 233
Athens/Athenians 175–77
authority 3, 7–16, 37, 39, 51 n. 16, 68–70, 72, 75–77
   bureaucratic 9, 11–12, 14 n. 7, 21
   central 3, 31 n. 4, 39, 57, 63, 77, 89, 92, 113, 130, 139, 170, 182, 188, 220, 254, 278–79
   central authority prophet
   See prophet
   charismatic *See* charisma
   legal 8
   traditional 8–9, 11, 13, 70, 75

authorship
   attribution of 129, 232, 240–43, 272, 275–76
   multiple 1, 3, 33, 120, 123, 231, 234–40
   unitary 1, 115 n. 3, 116 n. 3, 119–20, 123, 231–32, 235, 241, 250, 252, 265, 270, 272, 274, 279

Babylon/Babylonian Empire 83–85, 87, 95, 97–99, 102 n. 40, 42, 102–10, 112, 117, 121, 127–28, 131–34, 141–44, 152 n. 42, 174, 179, 191, 193, 203, 222–23,
Babylonian calendar 102–4, 109
Babylonian Chronicle 103–8
   Neo-Babylonian Chronicles 102–4, 108–9, 112, 234
Babylonian exile 83–4, 95, 96 n. 33, 98–99, 101, n. 40, 109–11, 116, 128–29, 131, 133–34, 143–44, 147, 149–51, 156, 182, 190, 192, 207, 219, 222, 228–30, 258, 265
   See also golah-community
Behistun Inscription 85, 131, 179
Bemba 43, 64–66, 68–70, 74–76
Berechiah 92, 231 n. 67, 275, 279
Bertholdt, L. 119
Book of the Twelve 2, 4–5, 35, 93, 122, 149, 186, 231, 238, 241–47, 261, 266, 275–76, 279

Cambyses, King 90, 121, 175
Carpov, J. C. 118
charisma 3, 7–22, 29 n. 1, 56, 76, 78, 88, 278
   and institution 3, 9–12, 14, 16–17, 19, 29, 37, 40, 46–48, 77, 278–79

Subject Index

as a revolutionary force 1, 9–12, 16, 18, 35, 75–76, 88, 141, 278
See also responses, supernaturalist
charismatic authority 3, 7–9, 11–13, 16, 18, 21
charismatic leadership 9–17, 20, 27, 38
routinization of 10–12, 16–17
chiasm 121, 149–150
Childs, Brevard S. 265–67
Christology 115 n. 3, 146
Zulu 57
Chronicler, the 2, 101, 110, 156, 158, 268–70
Chronistic milieu 82 n. 2, 101, 103, 109, 121
cleansing 214–15, 258–59, 263–64, 267
colon, cola 217, 252–53,
pentacola 252–53
colonialism/neocolonialism 37, 41, 44, 46 n. 2, 48 n. 9, 51 n. 16, 53, 62–64, 67–71, 78
postcolonial 37, 41, 48 n. 9, 69
Congo, Democratic Republic of (Zaire) 43–47, 63–64, 73, 77, 273, 277
conversionist response
See responses, supernaturalist
Corrodi, H. 118, 119 n. 6
covenant formula 151–52, 162, 218, 260 n. 95, 265, 266 n. 99, 267
criminalization 63 and n. 32
criticism
canonical 122
form 28, 124, 271
historical 33–35, 118
literary 271
prophetic 29, 130 n. 16, 153, 202
social 1, 29
textual 145, 246
See also lectio difficilior
crown 117 n. 3, 125–26, 144–48, 172, 182, 207, 247, 249, 253, 262

Cyrus, King 83, 116 n. 3, 117 n. 3, 121, 133, 154, 174, 178–80, 191, 193, 233

Damascus 165–70, 169 n. 12, 245, 258
Darius I, King 93, 112, 121, 125–27, 131, 133, 140, 149, 153–54, 175–76, 178–80, 191, 199, 205, 233–34
date formula 92–104, 106, 109, 110 nn. 52 and 54, 112, 127, 148, 179, 234–35, 235 n. 69, 243
David(ic), King, 38, 91 and n. 18, 131, 135
Davidides, house of David 84–85, 91 and n. 18, 130, 135–37, 138 n. 25, 145–48, 163, 178, 190–91, 193, 203, 205, 207, 214–15, 217, 219–21, 227, 263–65, 279–80
deprivation theory 50, 51 n. 16, 53, 159–60, 211
Deuteronomic/Deuteronomist 14, 21 n. 12, 100 n. 37
Deuteronomistic History 168 n. 10
Deuteronomic redaction 100 n. 37, 116 n. 3, 225 n. 62
Deuteronomic tradition 14
Deutero-Zechariah 1, 23, 27, 39, 41, 94 n. 23, 116 n. 3, 117 n. 3, 119, 120, 234, 241 n. 72, 254, 256, 258 n. 92, 259–62, 264, 266–67, 270–73, 277
Hellenistic dating of 116 n. 3, 119–20, 123, 125, 166–67, 173, 191–92, 193 n. 34, 233, 268
dislegomena 182, 241–42, 247
divine warrior
hymn 156–57, 159–60
motif 158–59, 223, 255

Egypt 30, 82 n. 2, 90, 102 n. 40, 109, 119–20, 167, 169, 174–79, 190–93, 204–5, 232–33
Eichorn, J. G. 119

Ekuphakameni 54–55, 57–58, 77
Elnathan 85, 203–5, 221, 255, 264
eschatology 82 n. 2, 90–92, 101,
    109 n. 51, 110–13, 116 n. 3, 126,
    145, 147, 149, 152–53, 155–60,
    162–64, 169 and n. 12, 181, 191,
    217–30
  apocalyptic 156, 209–12,
    227–28, 234
  eschatological battle 157, 164,
    217 n. 55, 221, 229, 263
  eschatological "hymnbook" 258
    n. 92
  eschatological narrative 162–63,
    207–8, 211, 218, 221–22, 237,
    258–59,
exile *See* Babylonian Exile
exilic era 40, 83, 101, 246
Ezra, priest 2, 84, 131, 133, 141,
    178, 180, 268,
establishment 14, 17, 25
  anti-establishment 12, 25
  Judean 31, 153, 279

Feast of Tabernacles 116, 149, 158,
    226 and n. 64, 228, 239, 253,
    260, 267
flock 163, 171, 182, 187, 195–201,
    214, 216–18, 229, 253, 255, 280
  "doomed to slaughter" 157, 195,
    197, 207, 218, 263
  See also sheep
Flügge, B. G. 118

golah-community 87, 131, 142, 270
  See also non-*golah* 87, 142
Greece/Greeks 159, 171, 173–78,
    180–82, 233, 253, 256, 268 and
    n. 101
  See also Yavan
Guiard, P. 271

Hadrach 165, 167–69, 192, 208, 233
Haggai the prophet 1, 3, 21 n. 12,
    81, 82 n. 2, 83, 87–92, 101,
    111–13, 128, 130 n. 16, 137 n.
    22, 138, 149, 152–54, 210, 220,
    233, 275, 277, 279
Haggai/Zechariah/Malachi corpus
    4–5, 35, 116 n. 3, 122
Hammond, Henry 118
Hananiah, prophet 97
Hananiah, son of Zerubbabel 205,
    220–21
  See also Meshullam
Hanson, Paul D. 1–2, 88, 115–17,
    122, 129, 130 n. 16, 131, 136,
    138, 148, 156–60, 166, 173–74,
    185, 190, 192, 209–10, 219, 228,
    256, 267–68, 272, 277–79
hapax legomenon 167, 182, 241–43
  See also dislegomenon
Harrist churches 62 n. 30
Harris, William Wade 62 n. 30
healer/healing 44, 45 n. 1, 48 n. 10,
    50 n. 15, 51–52, 67,
Hellenistic
  era 121, 123, 125, 173
  kingdoms 167, 193 n. 34, 233
Herodotus, historian 174–75, 181
    and n. 24, 205
hierocracy/hierocrats 129, 148,
    156–58, 209, 214, 219
  See also visionaries
Hill, Andrew E. 123, 183, 239, 268,
    270, 275–76
hinneh-clauses 236–37, 252
historical criticism *See* criticism
historical linguistics *See* linguistics
hope 111, 126, 128, 145, 182,
    209–10, 252, 279–80
hymn/hymnody
  Kimbanguist 44
  Lumpa 64–65, 67, 73
  Shembite 54, 56
  western hymnody 67, 73,
  See also divine warrior hymn
Hystanes (Ushtannu) 85

Iddo, chief priest 92, 204, 277
implosion, social 71–72, 74, 76, 78,
    233, 273

inclusio 149, 153, 166, 172, 227, 260, 266
institution *See* charisma and institution
institutionalization 17, 29, 37, 46–47, 77
Isandhlwana, Battle of 50
Islam 10–11, 32, 39, 43, 58–61, 74, 77, 277

Jehoiachim, King 85, 98, 99, 102, 194
Jehoiakim, King 94, 97, 101 n. 40, 102 n. 40, 103 n. 44, 109, 121, 194
Jeremiah, prophet 2, 39, 60, 94–110, 118, 131, 173, 228, 260,
 seventy-year prediction of 95, 97, 109–12, 179
Jerome 115–16, 121, 155
Jerusalem 3, 21 n. 12, 30–32, 48 and n. 10, 81, 82 n. 2, 83, 86 and n. 11, 92–100, 103, 110–11, 113, 119, 125–26, 130–34, 144, 147, 149, 152–54, 156–59, 162, 164, 166, 170–71, 173, 177, 181, 192–94, 197, 200, 203, 205, 207, 211–13, 215, 221–30, 235, 245, 251, 253, 255, 257–60, 262–65, 280
Jesus Christ 13 n. 6, 39, 44–45, 53, 65, 214
Joiakim, high priest 178, 204–5, 255, 264
Joshua, high priest 3, 84, 92, 130, 133–39, 141, 145–48, 153, 178–79, 204–5, 210, 253, 259, 262, 264, 279
Josiah, King 94 and n. 26, 109, 118, 214
judgment-salvation oracles 157, 163–64, 172, 188

Kaunda, Kenneth 69, 71–72, 77
Kidder, Richard 118

Kimbangu, Simon 43–46
Kimbanguism 43–47, 77, 273, 277
Köster, F. D. 118

leaders, leadership
 African tribal leaders 45, 48 n. 10, 55–57, 62–3, 66, 68
 prophets as leaders 9–17, 20–21, 28 n. 1, 38
 Yehud's leaders 83–85, 92, 101, 130, 142, 148, 156–57, 163, 179, 188, 191, 193–94, 200–3, 212–15, 219, 225 n. 63, 226, 229, 254–55, 262–65, 277–80
 as sign of new age 262–65
 See also charismatic leadership
Lebanon 125, 161, 190, 194, 201, 229, 253, 258, 263, 279
 See also Palace of the Lebanon Forest
lectio difficilior 195 n. 39, 213, 221 n. 59, 252
 See also criticism, textual
Lenshina, Alice, prophetess 43, 62 n. 30, 64–78, 159, 233, 274–77
lexical studies 235–42, 254, 267, 271
 density 237, 240–43, 246–48, 250
 linguistics 235, 240, 254, 274, 277
 historical 36, 94, 116, 123, 183, 202, 232, 256, 268–70, 277
 statistical 270–72
Long, Theodore E. 8 n. 3, 15–19, 25, 32, 37, 76, 278
Lumpa Church 62, 64, 66–78, 159, 233, 273–74, 277

Maccabees 89 n. 15, 117 n. 3, 121, 123, 214 and n. 52
 Maccabean date for Zech 9–14 121, 123, 214 and n. 52
Malachi, prophet 268–69, 275–76, 278

mal'ak Yahweh 131, 134, 143, 189 n. 27, 213, 215, 222, 255
Malawi/Nyasaland 43, 62–64, 77, 273
marginalization 4, 21 n. 13, 30 and n. 2, 32, 38–39, 47–48, 55, 58, 61–63, 74, 76–77, 89, 117, 128–29, 170, 202, 209–11, 228, 230, 233–34, 264, 278
Mason, Rex 2, 81 n. 1, 82 n. 2, 94 n. 24, 100 n. 36, 101, 103, 109, 116 n. 3, 122–23, 140, 149, 256–65, 267 and n. 100
massa', genre 124–25, 127, 161 and n. 2, 162, 164, 166, 182, 185, 200, 202, 206–8, 218, 221, 229, 236 and n. 70, 253–54, 258, 275–76, 279
matrix, social *See* social matrix
Mecca 58–62, 74, 77–78, 128, 153, 233, 273
Mede, Joseph 118
Medina/Yatrib 60 n. 26, 62, 74, 78, 233, 273
menorah 130, 136–37
Meshullam, son of Zerubbabel 205, 220–21 *See also* Hananiah
messiah 90, 121, 135 and n. 19, 138, 147 and n. 35, 190, 211, 214, 260 n. 95, 262–65
African 45
messianic conspiracy theory 82 n. 2, 86, 90, 138 n. 24, 145, 214
millennialism 62–63, 71, 116 n. 3, 159, 220, 234, 274
millennial groups 116 n. 3, 234
Mitchell, Hinckley G. 120, 123, 235–40, 242, 254
model, sociological
See under sociology
monotheism 225, 228
montage 211–21, 222
Moses 15, 30, 53, 121, 187, 240
Muhammad 10–11, 43, 58–62, 74, 77–8, 128, 153, 210, 233, 273, 277

Mwana Lesa *See* Nyirenda, Tomo

Nathan, house of 205, 215
nativistic movement 45, 47–8, 51, 53–4, 56, 63, 73, 77
Nebuchadnezzar, King 95, 96 n. 33, 97–98, 102 n. 42, 103 n. 44, 108–9, 169, 179
Neco, Pharaoh 169, 214
Nehemiah, governor 84, 85 n. 9, 86 n. 11, 117 n. 3, 131, 133, 177–78, 200–4,
Neo-Babylonian Chronicles
See under Babylonian Chronicle
New Testament 146, 242
Newcombe, William 118
night visions
See vision/vision report
Nogalski, James D. 122–23, 173–74, 181, 218 n. 58, 256 n. 91, 262
Nyasaland *See* Malawi
Nyirenda, Tomo, the *Mwana Lesa* 62–63, 67, 273

oracle 90–91, 95, 109–10, 126, 128–29, 131, 134, 137, 144, 147, 153, 158, 161, 163–64, 166, 169, 172, 179, 182, 185–90, 194, 208, 216–17, 263 n. 97
oracular prose *See* prose
orthodoxy, orthodoxies 32–33

Palace of the Lebanon Forest 194, 201
participles 236–40
patronym 87, 91–92
Persia/Persian Empire 41, 85, 88, 90–91, 117 n. 3, 121, 131, 133, 143, 174–81 268 and n. 101
Persian–Greek conflict 174–78, 232, 256, 268 and n. 101
Persian loyalty 178–81
Persian period 3, 5, 7, 19, 25, 29 n. 1, 41, 81, 83 n. 2, 85–86, 94, 113, 116 n. 3, 121–25, 169, 174, 178, 181–82, 192, 200, 202–4,

Subject Index

232, 256, 267–68, 268 n. 101, 273, 277, 279
Petersen, David L. 1, 3, 12–14, 20–22, 30, 122–24, 155, 160, 167, 182–83, 211, 222, 271–72
Philistia/Philistines 165–70, 192, 194, 207, 226, 252, 259
pierced/stabbed one 213–15, 217–19, 221, 230, 246, 251, 263
poetry 125, 155–56, 161, 173, 182–84, 187, 192, 197, 209, 217, 234, 252, 271
postexilic era 15, 140, 156, 209, 215, 225, 230, 267, 270
 See also Persian period; restoration era
postexilic prophets
 See under prophets
preaching 25, 44, 62, 66, 83, 87, 111, 153, 236, 239, 260, 262, 274
 Levitical 2
 temple 2, 116 n. 3, 149
pronouns, personal 112, 196 n. 42, 197, 201, 214, 217–18, 224, 240, 250–52, 257
prophets
 African 40
 call experience of 7, 44, 52 and n. 18, 56, 65, 77, 133,
 central authority 3, 31 n.4, 39, 57, 63, 77, 89, 92, 130, 170, 182, 220
 definition of 9, 18–20
 former/earlier 110, 129, 135, 149–50, 152–53, 164, 185, 195, 260–61, 265
 peripheral 31
  See also marginalization
 postexilic 3, 29 n. 1, 35, 36, 93, 116 n. 3, 184, 268
 reform/reformist 17, 22, 30–32, 38, 40, 88–89, 278
  See also responses, supernaturalist, reformist

prophetic tradition 2, 22 n. 14, 152
prose 81–82, 125, 156, 158, 161–62, 164, 180 n. 21, 181 n. 22, 183, 185, 186 n. 25, 192, 197, 208, 221, 234, 268, 270–71
 oracular prose 161 n. 4, 183, 197
 prose particles 164–65, 170, 183–87, 189. 192–93, 208
 prose particle density (PPD) 164–65, 170, 183–86, 189, 192–93, 195–96, 208, 216–17, 221–22
Ptolemy/Ptolemaic Empire 104, 119–20, 191–92, 193 n. 34

Rad, Gerhard von 2, 12, 14, 228, 257
Realpolitik 90, 209
redaction
 Deuteronomistic 100 n. 37, 116 n. 3
 history 5, 81, 121–23
 of Amos, book of 31–32
 of the Book of the Twelve 231, 261, 275–76
 of Haggai–Zech 1–8, book of 81, 92, 101, 121, 276
 of Jeremiah, book of 9 n. 28
 of Zechariah, book of 4, 28, 111, 116 n. 3, 121–23, 126 and n. 13, 137, 144, 151, 231, 247, 267, 275–76, 279
 redactional unity 4–5, 122, 231, 247, 267
reformist response *See under* responses, supernaturalist
religion 3–4, 7–9, 11, 15–23, 25, 28 n. 1, 29, 31–33, 36–41, 43, 45–46, 48–52, 55, 57–59, 61–64, 70–71, 74–77, 84, 88, 116 n. 3, 117 n. 3, 133, 139, 141, 158, 200–1, 205, 209–10, 215, 219, 256, 263, 265, 268, 274, 279
 African 4, 25, 40–41, 43–58, 62–79, 277

definition of 7
prophetic 4, 7, 15–20, 23, 25, 32, 36–37, 39–41, 256, 274, 279
religious movements 4, 7, 36–41, 45, 51
religious typology *See under* sociological typology
responses, supernaturalist 37, 45 n. 1, 61 and nn. 28–29, 74, 220, 274
conversionist 61 and n. 28, 210
reformist 45 n. 2, 61 and n. 29, 74, 88–89, 210
revolutionist 61 n. 29, 74, 210
thaumaturgical 45 and n. 1, 67, 73–75, 210, 274
restoration/restoration era 82 n. 2, 84, 110, 113, 116 n. 3, 126–27, 130, 134, 137, 139, 148, 153, 156, 173, 178, 186, 193, 220, 222, 232, 255, 262, 270
Judean monarchy, restoration of 102 n. 40, 145, 147, 163, 214,
See also temple restoration
restorationist ideology 170, 186, 209
revitalization movement 45–48, 50 n. 15, 51, 63, 74–77
revolutionist response *See under* responses, supernaturalist
rhetoric 35–36, 88, 144 n. 31, 149, 152–53, 172, 209, 215, 238, 240 n. 72, 254, 262, 277–78
rhetorical vision/rhetorical trajectory 35, 234, 255, 274 and nn. 103–4,

salvation-judgment oracle
See judgment-salvation oracle
SBL
See Society of Biblical Literature
Schlosser, Katesa 57
Seleucids/Seleucid Empire 102 n. 42, 119–21, 191, 193
Shaka, Zulu king 49, 50 n. 14, 54
sheep 187, 197, 199–200, 218, 236
See also flock

sheep-merchants 163, 195–97, 204–5, 219, 226, 229, 236, 244, 263
Shelomith, daughter of Zerubbabel 85, 203–4, 220–21, 255, 264,
Shembe, Isaiah 43, 47–58, 77, 274
shepherd 157, 178, 182, 187–90, 192–201, 204, 207–9, 214–19, 229–30, 233, 243, 246, 255, 263
good shepherd 201, 217–18, 263
Shepherd Allegory
See shepherd sign-enactment narrative
shepherd sign-enactment narrative 4, 116 n. 3, 120–21, 125–26, 157, 161–63, 195–206, 217, 229, 233, 253, 263, 278–80
Sheshbazzar 84–85, 141, 203
Shimei, house of 205, 215
Sidon 165, 167, 169, 181, 236
sign-enactment report
See shepherd sign-enactment narrative
social center 12–13, 17, 19–20, 31–32, 37–39, 47–48, 58, 63, 73, 77, 88–89, 220, 233, 273, 278
social location 3–5, 7–23, 25–41, 43, 57, 77–78, 82–83, 113, 130, 148, 153, 156, 159, 164, 182, 194, 197, 201–2, 209–11, 219–20, 228–30, 233–34, 273–74, 279
social location trajectory 4, 23, 25, 28, 31–32, 36–38, 47, 58, 63, 75–76, 89, 202, 255–56, 258, 264–65, 279
social location trajectory analysis 25, 38, 41, 43, 78–79, 113, 267, 273–75
social matrix 1–5, 23, 25, 28, 43, 79, 124, 231, 275, 277
social periphery 4, 37–38, 48, 76, 233, 278
social role 3–4, 8, 16–17, 19–20, 22, 28 n. 1, 30, 75, 220
Society of Biblical Literature 122

sociology/sociological 2–4, 7–23, 25–29, 32–34, 36–38, 40–41, 43, 45, 47–48, 50, 55, 61, 63 n. 32, 73, 76, 78–79, 81, 82 n.2, 113, 122, 156, 158, 229, 232–34, 278–79
  model, sociological 4, 8, 20–22, 25–28, 36, 38, 45 n. 2, 57, 75, 113, 210
  typology, sociological 4, 23, 26–28, 36–38, 45 n. 1, 47 n. 5, 52 n. 18, 61, 63, 73, 78, 278
  Weberian 3, 7–8, 13, 15–21
sociologists 18 n. 11, 19, 26, 32, 40, 45, 47, 50, 61, 76, 78, 278
Sparta/Spartans 174, 176–77
Stade, Bernhard 166 n. 3, 119–20, 123, 173–74, 177–78, 181, 191, 195 n. 37, 231, 261, 279
Suffering Servant 90, 214–15, 217 and n. 55
Sweeney, Marvin A. 32 n. 5, 91 n. 18, 121–22, 124–25, 193, 200, 261, 272, 278

Tattanai 84–85
temple
  Babylonian 103, 106, 107 and n. 49, 108
  Ezekiel's 99–100, 169 n. 12
  Jerusalem 15, 21 n. 12, 28, 89 n. 15, 112, 121, 126, 134, 136–37, 158, 166, 194, 197, 199, 200, 204, 227–29, 234–35, 254, 261 n. 96, 164, 277, 279
  temple menorah *See* menorah
  restoration of Jerusalem temple 3, 8, 82 n. 2, 83 and n. 4, 88–93, 100 n. 37, 101, 111–12, 116 n. 3, 117 n. 3, 121, 123, 127–28, 130 and n. 16, 138–39, 141–44, 146–47, 152–54, 157, 170, 178, 180 and nn. 19–20, 234–35, 240, 253, 255, 257, 262, 269

thaumaturgical response *See under* responses, supernaturalist
theodicy 210, 220
tradent 1–5, 23, 28, 31, 35, 38, 39, 41, 48, 78, 92, 100, 103, 124, 130, 164, 170, 184–86, 192, 197, 214–15, 219–21, 225 n. 62, 226, 228 n. 65, 233, 256, 258 n. 92, 260, 263–64, 275–76, 279
tradition history 36, 38, 116 n. 3, 121–22, 256, 265, 271
tradition maintenance 32, 33 and n. 6, 35, 279
tribe, tribal
  African 25, 40–41, 44–45, 48–49, 64, 66, 71, 75–78,
  Arabian 59–60
  Bemba 43, 64–70, 73–76
  Israelite 40, 41 and n. 11, 84 n. 6, 165, 190
  Nyasa 62–63
  Zambian 75–76
  Zulu 52, 54, 56–58
Trito-Zechariah 157, 159, 162, 271
typology, sociological
  See under sociology
Tyre 165, 167, 169–70, 180–81, 209

United National Independence Party (UNIP, Zambia) 69–72, 74–75, 77–78, 159
universalism 259–60, 265
Ushtannu, *See* Hystanes

Vatke, J. H. W. 119
vision/vision report 51–52, 92, 99–100, 110, 126 n. 13, 129–48, 169 n. 12, 234, 237, 240, 245–46, 253, 257–59, 262
visionaries 156–58, 209, 217, 219, 275
  See also hierocrats
vox populi 153

Wansbrough, John 58
Weber, Max 2-3, 7-23, 25-6, 36-7, 43, 76, 159
  Ancient Judaism 7, 13
  Economy and Society 7
  See also charisma
Wellhausen, Julius 2, 3, 22, 34 and n. 8, 119-20, 144-46
Wette, W. M. L. de 34, 119
Whiston, William 118
witch, witchcraft 62-63, 67-69, 73-74, 77,

Xerxes, King 176-77, 181, 205

Yavan/sons of Yavan 119, 173, 174 n. 16, 178, 180-82, 232-33, 253, 257
  See also Greece/Greeks
Yehud 23, 28-29, 82 n. 2, 83-87, 90-92, 110, 117 n. 3, 124, 127-28, 130-34, 137, 141-42, 144-45, 147, 153, 157, 166, 174, 178-79, 181, 188, 194, 201-3, 205, 207, 212-13, 225 n. 62, 226, 229, 252, 255, 258, 261, 278-80
  geographic size of 86-87
  governors of 3, 84-86, 88, 91-92, 117 n. 3, 130, 133, 137-39, 144, 202-5, 210, 221, 229, 254, 279
  population of 86-87
yod-campaginis 196 n. 42

Zaire *See* Congo, Democratic Republic of
Zambia 43, 64, 69, 72-78, 273

Zechariah, prophet 3, 23, 81-84, 86, 88, 91-92, 101, 110-13, 123-25, 128-39, 144-45, 147-49, 152 n. 42, 153-54, 160, 170, 178, 182, 185, 192, 200, 202, 204-5, 210, 219-21, 225 n. 62, 228, 230-34, 241 n. 72, 254-55, 261-62, 264, 269, 271, 272, 274-75, 277-80
  tradent group 1, 3, 124-25, 185, 221, 230, 233, 225, 230, 257, 261, 264, 279
Zedekiah, King 94, 96, 103 n. 44, 110 n. 52, 121, 173, 223
Zemah, the 116 n. 3, 130 and n. 15, 135-36, 145-48, 191, 211, 219, 227, 252, 262
Zerubbabel, governor 3, 82 n. 2, 84-86, 90-92, 116 n. 2, 117 n. 2, 130, 133, 135-39, 141, 144-46, 148, 153-54, 179, 203, 205, 210, 214-15, 220, 221 and n. 59, 255, 262, 264, 269, 279
Zion (Jerusalem) 92, 127-33, 138, 149, 152, 171-74, 178, 182, 186, 207, 209, 211, 219, 223, 225, 227-28, 251, 253-54, 257-58, 260 and n. 94, 262, 264-65
  Lumpa Zion (Kasomo/Sioni) 68 and n. 37, 72, 75
  Zion tradition 130, 131 and n. 16, 182, 212, 228, 230, 257-58
  Zionist type of African Indigenous Church (AIC) 48 and n. 10, 50 n. 15, 52 n. 18, 56-57
  Zulu Zion (Ekuphakameni) 54-55, 57-58, 77
Zulu 43, 47-58, 77, 273
  tradition 52, 57